The Dissolution of Monasteries

The Dissolution of Monasteries
The Case of Denmark
in a Regional Perspective

Edited by
Per Seesko
Louise Nyholm Kallestrup
Lars Bisgaard

University Press of Southern Denmark 2019

University of Southern Denmark
Studies in History and Social Sciences vol. 580

© The authors and University Press of Southern Denmark 2019
Printed by Tarm Bogtryk A/S
Typesetting and cover by Dorthe Møller, Unisats Aps
Cover Photo: The Tombstone of Abbess Margrethe Urne of Maribo Abbey, died 1582. Drawing
by Søren Abildgaard, 1765. *Photo: The National Museum of Denmark*
ISBN 978-87-408-3211-2

The Dissolution of Monasteries is published with support from:
Den Hielmstierne-Rosencroneske Stiftelse
Ingeniør N.M. Knudsens Fond
Jens Nørregaard og Hal Kochs mindefond
Publikationsudvalget ved Det Humanistiske Fakultet, University of Southern Denmark

University Press of Southern Denmark
55 Campusvej
DK-5230 Odense M
www.universitypress.dk

Distribution in the United States and Canada:
Independent Publishers Group
814 N. Franklin Street
Chicago, IL 60610
USA
www.ipgbook.com

Distribution in the United Kingdom:
Gazelle
White Cross Mills
Hightown
Lancaster
LA1 4 XS
U.K.
www.gazellebookservices.co.uk

Contents

Preface

This volume is dedicated to Tore Nyberg, who passed away in spring 2018. Nyberg was a renowned scholar on the Brigittine Order and St Birgitta. His own dissertation was on the Brigittine Order and St Birgitta, and his extended network throughout Europe brought several experts on monasticism to Odense. Over the years Nyberg often suggested that the annual November symposiums organized by the Centre for Medieval and Renaissance Studies at the University of Southern Denmark should explore a monastic order, theme or period.

The idea was also pushed forward by the 500th anniversary of the Reformation in 2017. The jubilee spurred on a great interest in the effects of the Reformation on Danish society. Although the anniversary was commemorating the proclamation of Luther's theses in 1517, the perspective was already broadened during the preparations for the jubilee. Events celebrated not only Luther as a person but also his influence on the Reformation, the course of events, and not least how it affected members of and structures in society. In a Danish context, however, the Reformation in 1536 played a much more prominent role than the year 1517. This was the year the Danish king pronounced the kingdom to be reformed, and it penetrates the works published as part of the jubilee. The present volume is no exception, although when the conference took place in 2014 it was difficult to predict this would become the recurring theme.

This volume should be regarded as the contribution from Centre for Medieval and Renaissance Studies at University of Southern Denmark to mark the anniversary of *Luther 500*.

This edited volume would not have been published without the generous contributions from *Den Hielmstierne-Rosencroneske Stiftelse*, *Jens Nørregaard og Hal Kochs mindefond*, *Ingeniør N.M. Knudsens Fond*, *Publikationsudvalget ved Det Humanistiske Fakultet* and the Dean of the Faculty of Humanities at the University of Southern Denmark. Prof. Brian Patrick McGuire has kindly read and commented on all of the articles. We are sincerely grateful and wish to use this opportunity to thank them all.

Odense March 2019

Per Seesko   Louise Nyholm Kallestrup   Lars Bisgaard

Introduction

Lars Bisgaard

The year of the Reformation, 1536, is of great importance in Danish history. A long political strife for the throne was settled. Although a lasting solution was postponed for another seven years until peace was reached with the Emperor, Charles V, the outline of a permanent new constitutional arrangement seemed clear. King Christian III, former duke of the duchies of Schleswig and Holstein, had triumphed. Unchallenged he could form and reform the kingdom he had won, in accordance with his wishes. The bishops were all charged with treason and imprisoned. Their seats in the Council of the Realm, recognized for generations, were taken from them and given to members of the nobility. Thus the leading members of the old church were held responsible for the long political unrest, not least the violent Count's Feud (*Grevens Fejde*) that had taken place from 1534-36. In other words, the introduction of an Evangelical Lutheran Church was an inseparable part of the solution to end dynastic strife. In tactical terms this manoeuvre was a masterpiece.

The dynastic conflict had begun in 1523 when the lawfully elected King Christian II was deposed and fled to the Netherlands. In the following years he posed a constant threat. His departure meant the breakup of the Kalmar Union among Denmark, Sweden and Norway. The Swedes had revolted in 1521 against Christian's violent attempt to bring them back into a union that had become increasingly unpopular, and in Norway magnates saw the opportunity to expand their power after his flight. The Danish rebellion against King Christian that followed was centered in Jutland, with the support of the duchies. In the end, Christian's uncle, Duke Frederik, usurped power which he was able to keep until his death in 1533.

At a crucial Parliament (*Herredag*) that year, the Council refused to elect any of his sons as his successor, one being too young, the other too Protestant, complicated by the fact that the Norwegian delegation simply had stayed away.[1] The election was postponed for another year, but instead, intervention came from abroad. The Hanseatic League, in agreement with the Danish cities of Malmö and Copenhagen, sent in mercenaries led by Count Christopher of Oldenburg to advocate for the return of King Christian II. Other European princely candidates soon joined. Not long afterwards, disruption among noblemen, peasants and townsmen followed, according to their differing interests. The long-feared civil war was a reality. Except for some freeholders in Jutland, the victorious Duke Christian cleverly exonerated his new subjects of any charges, except for the bishops. This amnesty helped to secure the success of the Reformation. Resisting Evangelical Lutheranism would inevitably lead to a reopening of the conflict. The attitude is reflected in statements repeatedly found in documents from the central administration from the second half of the sixteenth century. They stipulated that church matters were all resolved in the reign of Christian III and so it was unnecessary to dwell on them any longer.[2] The *Kirkeordinansen* (*Ordinatio Ecclesiastica*, the Church Ordinance) dating from 1537/39, with some amendments from 1542, could not be changed.[3]

Neglected monasteries in research

A distinct scholarly tradition in Denmark has long prevailed for separating the study of ecclesiastical affairs from other social matters. It is as if the Lutheran idea that religion ought not to interfere with secular matters and vice versa had an effect on the scientific mindset early on, preventing the establishment of a comprehensive view. The exact development of this tradition is yet to be studied.

Among the professional historians of the late nineteenth century, this tradition was commonly accepted. The influential historian Erik Arup (1876-1951) was unusual in spending time reflecting on the matter. He defended the separation from a practical point of view. Historians were not educated in religious ideas, he pointed out, and properly they ought to leave the field

---

1 The best introduction to the crucial Parliament is still Arnold Heise's article in *Historisk Tidsskrift* (1872). Regarding Norway, Ladewig Petersen made some adjustments in 1972.

2 Frederik II wrote in 1585 to the professors at the University of Copenhagen and commanded them to stick to "den Læreform og de Kirkeskikke, som var i Brug i min højlovelige Faders Tid" (the theology and rituals that were in use during my praiseworthy Father's reign). Kornerup (1959), p. 153.

3 *Kirkeordinansen 1537/39* (1989).

to church historians.[4] He extended his defense of the distinction by focusing on ongoing specialization within the humanities, which in his eyes brought forth a useful division of the surviving source material. For Arup division of labour was at stake, nothing more.[5] The growth of cultural history along with the internationalization of the discipline have, however, recently brought about an integration of church history into traditional lay history.

One can hardly blame Danish church historians for neglecting the fate of the monasteries. These were after all on the losing side in the conflict and opposed to the victorious Lutheran ideas. In the eyes of the church historians, the practical dispositions for the new Church were of much greater importance. Historians could have filled out the gap, but apart from some interest in the establishment of crown fiefs of the old monastic land and a discussion on improvements or not in the care of sick people,[6] they respectfully left the end of monasticism to the indifferent church historians. Historians took much greater interest in lamenting how Holstein's influence in Danish royal circles prevented the incorporation of the duchy of Schleswig, or regretting the exclusion of all other groups but noblemen in government subsequent to the victory of Christian III. Monastic history after 1536 was simply forgotten. Monasteries and religious houses had taken part in the course of events leading up to the Reformation, but fair to say, their role in political debate was inferior. Nor were there any spectacular events during their abolition which might create interest. As a rule, they were allowed to continue until the last nun or monk had passed away. In religious terms, however, the monastic vocation was fiercely discussed during the years of unrest in the 1520s and 1530s. This was especially true of the mendicants. In some towns their buildings were violently taken away from them and in the towns of Ystad and Malmö in Scania brethren were injured. This sad chapter has often been neglected in historical overviews.

Studying the monasteries is complicated by the fact that developments took place quite differently depending on which part of the realm is examined. To the south, the duchies were at first at the forefront in terms of removing the monasteries, but in the end they formed their own conservative policy on monasteries; Gotland to the east became a refuge for Swedish Catholics in the 1520s and, although some hesitation and caution were expressed during

---

4   Arup 1932; Ingesman (1992).
5   It is a simple fact that historians have primarily edited large series with central political and juridical documents, whereas church historians have published editions with Church laws or the works of central ecclesiastic figures.
6   Dahlerup (1979), Selch Jensen (2008).

the reign of Christian III (r. 1536-59), his son Frederik II (r. 1559-88) intervened and turned the island into an eighth Danish bishopric and subject to the Church Ordinance.[7] To the north, the Reformation in Norway had dramatic consequences. Strangely, the towns of the country had seen almost no reformation activity before 1536, so in this sense the Norwegians were unaffected. Politically, however, the Nidaros archbishop had entered the Count's Feud supporting the return of King Christian II, who on a princely level was supported by the Catholic emperor Charles V, his brother-in-law. This engagement turned out to be a major mistake and the winning sovereign, Christian III, let the whole of Norway pay for the archbishop's disloyalty. In the former union between Norway and Denmark, each country had their own Council of the Realm, but now the Norwegian one was dissolved. To sum up, the debate about the monasteries and religious houses and their dissolution in this wider geographical context has hitherto not been studied as a whole.

The most neglected aspect of the history of the monasteries, however, has been their long afterlife following 1536. To a broader audience it still comes as a great surprise that they were not dissolved immediately. In fact, monasteries were only slowly abolished, not only in Denmark but also in the region as a whole, a story to be unfolded later in the volume. The untold history of the monasteries in the sixteenth century may more precisely be imputed to the joint understanding in historiography of the dramatic events in 1536 as a notorious break. As a consequence, interest in aspects of continuity has generally suffered.[8] For this reason the present volume focuses on how monasteries in the sixteenth century were looked upon, treated and in the end dissolved, not only in Denmark but also in the duchies, Norway and in neighbouring regions of Sweden and Northern Germany.

The early years

During the Middle Ages we know of 138 monastic foundations in Denmark. At the time of the Reformation 116 of these still existed.[9] Recently the number has been compared with England's more than a 1,000 cloisters, convents and religious houses, but if one takes into consideration the earlier establishment

---

7   Denmark had eight dioceses, but one of them was the duchy of Schleswig, and from 1241 and onwards the area was separated from the kingdom. Therefore Gotland is here numbered as the eighth.
8   For an international audience two general introductions exist: Grell (1995), Larsson (2010). Neither focuses on the monastic theme.
9   Krongaard Kristensen (2013), p. 18.

of a Christian culture and the considerably larger geographical area of England, their density is more or less the same. Compared to Norway and Sweden, which had 31 and 51 monasteries respectively, the Danish numbers are substantially higher. In a recent paper the Danish archaeologist Krongaard Kristensen juxtaposes the numbers with German neighbouring states and stresses an important difference. The numerical numbers may not differ significantly, but if the time of establishment is taken into account, considerably more monasteries and religious houses were founded in Denmark than in Northern Germany during the Later Middle Ages, most prominently in Danish towns.[10]

What might be at play is a later and different kind of urbanization in Denmark compared to Northern Germany. Here, a number of larger towns along the coast of the Baltic had been established in the thirteenth and fourteenth centuries which in the fifteenth century attracted immigration and kept lesser settlements from turning into towns. In a wider perspective, these Hanseatic cities also influenced Danish towns, which all remained small. In order to survive, the Danish towns formed a very stable alliance with the king who not only repeatedly confirmed their rights to produce and trade but also in 1422 gave general laws for market towns (*købstæder*). In any case, Danish towns also expanded and harbored a local devotional life. The presence of German merchants and craftsmen, well accustomed to rich, religious opportunities in their hometowns, might even have furthered institutional growth with more convents in Danish market towns.[11]

In a Reformation context this is an important result. It has often been stated that Reformation debate in Denmark, as also in Germany, was chiefly an urban phenomenon.[12] As was the case in Germany. On the other hand, a similar religious debate is hard to grasp in Sweden, where preachers more often figured as advisers for the king, and certainly in Norway where traces of Evangelical activity is scarce, almost non-existent. In other words, a similar range of religious possibilities seem to have existed in German and Danish towns. To give an example one may point to the special Northern German "*kalande*" which was well known in the Danish towns, too.[13]

Another question is how and when a more critical attitude towards monasteries developed among the reformers. This is examined in the contribution by Euan Cameron. Focusing on Luther, the important years were

---

10   Krongaard Kristensen (2019 forthcoming)
11   Poulsen & Krongaard Kristensen (2015).
12   Lausten (2011a).
13   Bisgaard (2007).

1520-21. His preliminary and undated theses on the monastic vow formed the basis on his treatise *De Votis Monasticis* (Judgment on Monastic Vows), published in 1521. Luther argued that vows of poverty, obedience and chastity were all temporary and provisional and hard to combine with the premise of faith and Christian freedom. Remarkably, he also viewed vows in a historical perspective. In the early Church, monasteries and convents had begun as places of education where young people could undergo ascetic discipline to prepare themselves for pastoral ministry. Prior to this, Erasmus had put forward a similar historical reflection on St Jerome's monastic years in the fourth century which, he stressed, should be conceived as something other than contemporary monasticism.

Luther especially disliked the mendicant interpretation of the vow. Their houses often competed with parish churches to attract donations and their zeal to produce good works prevented the inner contemplation leading to faith that Luther preferred. To these reservations, his personal disdain was added as events progressed. The papal commissioner for the sale of indulgences in Germany, Fr Johann Tetzel, had been a Dominican and several among Luther's later inquisitors were brought from the same order. When the row was stirred up in the 1520s, mendicants came into the front line all over Northern Europe. This development is examined more thoroughly by Johnny Grandjean Gøgsig Jakobsen in his contribution on the specific role of the Dominicans.

In a Danish context, Dominicans have not been given the same attention as Franciscans. The main reason is that we are much better informed on the greyfriars' activities in the Reformation dispute. Later in the sixteenth century, a chronicle was written on their expulsion from their buildings and houses, providing valuable data from thirteen Danish towns (*De Expulsione Fratrum Minorum*). The chronicle was probably intended to form a juridical plea of some kind if a lawsuit ever should occur.[14] In comparison, information on the Dominican friars is much more fragmentary. The best way to interpret it is to contextualize with what happened in the neighbouring countries. This is exactly Jakobsen's approach. For the first time, someone is capable of providing an overview on the Dominican's role in a Scandinavian context and this is most welcome. Similar to the German experience, Jakobsen stresses the importance of the activity of the friars as inquisitors and learned adherents of the old faith. Hence they were offered the difficult task of representing the old Church at the Parliament, held in Copenhagen in 1530, which most scholars agree was prepared to bring about a general reformation, al-

---

14   Heilesen (1967).

though in the end it did not. In the present volume, archaeologist Morten Larsen takes a closer look at the Franciscans, who were also the topic of his dissertation.[15] In his survey of the Franciscans' and their building complexes in the whole of the sixteenth century, he has some interesting remarks concerning the early years. He opposes the view formulated in the Franciscans' chronicle that their expulsion had been well planned by a responsible king. Instead, Larsen insists that their banishment was the result of a long-existing discontent among merchants and other townsmen with the friars' growing wealth. He points to the fact that in some towns, like Kalundborg, the friars left voluntarily, a feature also found in the duchies, where the nuns in Schleswig did the same in 1529 (see Auge). Another of Larsen's arguments is that the friaries after 1536 were reused for such different purposes that a coherent master plan could not have existed. Larsen acknowledges that King Frederik might have complied with townsmen and opposed the mendicants in order to strengthen his volatile popularity.

In a wider perspective, Euan Cameron is inclined to point to the interests of the secular rulers as an important trigger in the coming of the Reformation. Secular rulers should not be understood as only princes, because magistracies often had a clear interest in tightening the rules for religious houses according to their command. Cameron accepts Luther's theological arguments as an initial advantage and the printing press as the new medium to spread his ideas quickly, but he denies that the abolition of the monasteries was purely a result of theological rethinking. Luther might have laid out some principles for the reforming of convents and monasteries in the Saxon town of Leisnig (1523), but during the Peasants' War in 1525 and in the major North German towns the fate of the monastic houses was out of his control and subject to other solutions.

Considering Jakobsen's evidence from the early confrontations in Wismar, Bremen and Hamburg in 1522, the conclusion seems to be that the clashes were still based on a general feeling of discontent with part of the old Church, and Luther's treatise on monastic vows, only formulated the year before, could hardly have been a trigger. The response of the magistracies also varied considerably. Some supported the Evangelical preachers directly, others tried to win time, and yet others remained loyal to the old faith. On a general level, however, magistracies all had an interest in making monastic institutions accept their regulations and involvement. The precise circumstances in the Danish towns are hard to grasp as we lack information, but in

---

15   Larsen (2015).

larger cities like Copenhagen and Malmö they seem to be the decisive factor (*Ratsreformation*).[16]

For the Parliament held in Copenhagen 1530 a Protestant confession was formulated. It contained two articles on the monasteries[17]:

Tredie oc tiunde artickell (23rd article)
Om Closter leffnitt oc mwncke løffthe tro oc sige wi att thet kan icke befestiss aff then hellige scrifft, men theriss leffnitt oc selffdictede gudz tienneste oc Ceremonier, orkesløshedt oc theriss meste handell er modt gud oc scrifften.

On monastic life and monks' vows, we believe and say that Holy Writ does not confirm them, but their lives and self-made services and rituals and idleness and most of their activities are against God and Scripture.

xxiiii artickell (24th article)
Muncke løffte er oc mod Christen fryhedt, oc løgnactige, ware the end ellerss gode for werden, tha ere the dog gud vbehagelige i thet the ere effter menniskens bud, oc ingen tieniste er gudt tacknemmelig vdhen thet er effter hanss befalning.

A monk's vow is also against Christian Freedom and mendacious, and even if they were good for the world, they are nonetheless unbecoming for God because they are ordered by men and no service makes God thankful unless it is according to his command.

German princes had during the late medieval period gradually been able to establish a kind of territorial church in which their influence matched or even surpassed that of the pope. To give an example, one could point to Saxony and Brandenburg where sovereigns had made special agreements with Rome in order to appoint their own candidates as bishops or prelates in chapters. The Danish dynasty, the House of Oldenburg (1448-), was inspired by this policy and, from Christian I's visit to Rome in 1474 onwards the king became an even more dominant figure in ecclesiastical appointments.[18] The policy was strengthened during the reign of King John (*Hans*) who convinced or forced

---

16   Grell (1993).
17   Andersen (1954), p. 22
18   The pope permitted Christian I to appoint the two most important prelates in each of the chapters in the whole of Scandinavia, Finland and Iceland. Ingesman & Pedersen (2012), 712ff. It has long been recognized that a Danish territorial church was on its way from the days of Valdemar IV (r. 1340-1375).

the monasteries to pay for the maintenance of the army (*borgeleje*), a duty the bishops had long recognized. It is to be remembered that the Oldenburgs had longstanding and strong relationships with Northern Germany, maintained by successive marriages; Christian I (r. 1448-81) married Dorothea of Brandenburg and King John (r. 1481-1513) Christine of Saxony. The dukes of Schleswig and Holstein followed a similar tradition, merely on a lower social level.

The persistent integration of the Church into the affairs of the Crown is offered a new perspective by the valuable study by Grethe Jacobsen. She examines the introduction of secular guardians (*forstandere*) at convents and monasteries. The first guardian is mentioned in the 1490s and rapidly their numbers grew in the following decades. Jacobsen interprets the development as a kind of early crown fiefs, given to noble men and women from the magnate group, which made the later transfer of the monastic institutions to royal authority during the Reformation smoother. After 1536, the monasteries turned into real crown fiefs, administered by the same aristocratic top circle (see below).

A regional approach

In a wider perspective, Northern Europe mainly experienced Lutheran Reformations and in the long run, despite the critical Thirty Year's War in the seventeenth century, they turned out to be successful. One reason for the outcome is the tradition for strong kingdoms in the region.[19] On the other hand, one may argue that kingdoms were also strengthened by Lutheran ideas. Sweden's rise to power in the seventeenth century might be one example. A number of anthologies have been published focusing on the internal comparison between the Nordic countries, but so far Northern Germany and the Baltic have only to a minor degree been included. It is a pity for at least three reasons: Wittenberg was a center for Reformation ideas and these were spread directly by visiting students or indirectly through the Hanseatic cities. Secondly, the Kalmar Union's leading force, the Oldenburg House, was politically strongly influenced by Mecklenburg, Brandenburg and Saxony. And thirdly, rural production had similar geographical conditions in at least Denmark and Northern Germany and was in both places dominated by the aristocracy.

The first Lutheran Reformation in the region took place in 1525 in the

---

19   Grell (1994).

inner Baltic. It was part of an odd political arrangement which tore down the Teutonic Order only to let the same geographical area emerge as Ducal Prussia (*Herzogliches Preußen*). The last Grand Master, Albert of Branden-burg-Ansbach, adopted the Lutheran faith and in agreement with Poland he was elected duke and his land renamed. It might be a coincidence that a very special state with a strong monastic heritage was the first place to see a Lutheran inspired reform, but the setting fitted ideally.

The first Reformation in Scandinavia was soon to follow. In the duchies of Schleswig and Holstein, Junker Christian (the later King Christian III) had attended the Diet in Worms and heard Luther defend his position and was impressed by his performance. His private tutor was Wolfgang von Utenhof, a former student in Wittenberg and a convinced Lutheran, and he probably played a decisive role in Christian's formative years.[20] In the years 1526-28 Christian imposed a reformation in the fief he held himself (Haderslev and Tørning Len), with the help of Johannes Bugenhagen and other theologians from Wittenberg. The Swedes soon followed suit. At the Diet in Västerås in 1527, King Gustav Erikson Vasa (r. 1523-61) demanded of the Estates that they help him financially, especially the Church and the monastic orders, none of which were allowed to take part in the crucial decisions that would form their fate. The king's wish was granted and a Reformation followed, more or less through the backdoor. For the time being, the king strengthened his position but in the long run, a controversy on the exact nature of the Swedish confession had just begun, lasting until 1593 when a strict Lutheran confession was accepted.

In the present volume, Martin Berntson examines the role of the monasteries in the Swedish Reformation. He opposes an older interpretation of the Diet in Västerås in which a certain well prepared plan for the fate of the monasteries was decisive. Unforeseen events, peasant riots supporting monastic Christianity, and different sovereigns' religious engagements all played a role. Specifically, early agreements were reached between the king and several of the monasteries concerning provision of the nuns and, according to Berntson, these explain why the last of the nunneries, the large Brigittine monastery in Vadstena, was allowed to continue as late as 1595.[21]

The Swedish and Danish Reformations have often been opposed and seen as two different types of reformations. However, focusing exclusively on the monastic theme, some similarities are indeed made clear. In both countries

---

20 Lausten (2011b), p. 91.
21 Berntsons dissertation from 2003 is the authoritative work to consult.

the mendicant orders formed a vulnerable group. The last reported house in Sweden was the Franciscan one in Krokek (1544), situated on the western side of Vättern, but the majority of the mendicants were driven out in the late 1520s and early 1530s, exactly in the same years as mendicants were evicted in Denmark. The theological arguments were by all means the same, as Luther had strongly opposed their special vows (see Cameron). Most monasteries in the countryside were also turned into crown fiefs in Sweden, similar to the lines Grethe Jacobsen has drawn for Denmark.

Some differences are also to be noted: Firstly, part of the arrangement at the Diet in Västerås was to return the aristocracy landed property donated to monasteries after 1454, as a kind of bait to the noble families to win their needed support. Such an offer was never made to noblemen in Denmark. After the passing of the Church Ordinance, several noble families argued that since services were no longer held in the old manner, property once given to maintain chantries should now be returned. Still, the Crown argued that donated property should stay in the hands of the Church and be transferred to new tasks derived from the Gospel, like schools, hospitals and almshouses. Although never thoroughly examined, the editor who published the extensive law suits from 1537-39 has later argued that the king's wish to keep the land for ecclesiastical purposes were most often followed and laid down in the sentences.[22] Secondly, female convents were, except for one, not accepted in Denmark, as we will shortly hear.

The more surprising it is to learn that four female convents eventually survived in the duchies of Schleswig and Holstein. Their Church Ordinance dating from 1542 stipulated, like its Danish predecessor from 1537/1539, that nuns should be free to be released from their vows, but if they chose to remain loyal to them, they could stay as long as they attended Lutheran services. A nunnery would not be dissolved before the last nun had died. The interesting case is studied by Oliver Auge and he concludes that pressure from the strong nobility in Schleswig and Holstein prevented dissolution and that nunneries in Itzehoe, Preetz, Uetersen and Schleswig were instead turned into Lutheran women's convents. The exact date of this decision is unclear, but it seens reasonable that it was made in the 1560s. Berntson also asks whether noble pressure could account for the prolonged survival of the Swedish nunneries, but rejects the idea, because no argument supporting it is mentioned in the sources.

---

22 *Det kongelige Rettertings Domme og Rigens Forfølgninger fra Christian III's Tid* (1959-1969); Dahlerup (1987).

For the other monastic institutions, the dissolution in the duchies fell in two waves. The first occurred in the later part of Frederik I's rule and did away with most of the mendicant houses: In other words, the same procedure as we have met in Sweden and the Kingdom of Denmark. The second happened in the 1560s, apparently in close collaboration with Frederik II of Denmark. The last monastic institution was dissolved in 1582. Although the Danish king was sovereign of the duchies and could have interfered, he turned a blind eye to the continuation of nunneries. Only at the end of the seventeenth century were Lutheran women's convents introduced in Denmark.[23]

In a comparative perspective, Norway represents a unique experience. The case is examined by Øystein Ekroll. Apparently, the country was not affected by Evangelical preaching in the 1520s. Not even Bergen, commonly agreed to be the largest city in Scandinavia, saw major disturbances, although strong connections to Lübeck existed. The consequence was that mendicant houses, unlike in the neighboring countries, continued more or less uninfluenced. In other words, their demise was deferred and a final reformation became more severe for the Norwegian monasteries, in which urban and rural institutions were affected at the same time.

In many ways, Norway was in a vacuum in the 1520s and 1530s. The Kalmar Union was seriously shaken when the Swedes chose their own king in 1523. The new Danish sovereign, Frederik I, was not elected in Norway, and both Sweden and Denmark tried to establish allegiances with the most influential magnates in the country. Apart from the archbishop, Norwegian bishops were not able to support monastic institutions sufficiently and the guardian system for monasteries that had been introduced under King John now spread rapidly, as skillfully shown by Ekroll. In the end, Norway experienced two waves of attacks against the monasteries, just as her neighbouring countries, but they differed crucially in nature: the first one was inspired by the internal struggle for power and saw magnates acting like guardians to get hold of monastic property; the second was mainly an urban affair taking place in the first generation after Christian III took control and introduced the Reformation in 1536. Some truth may still be found in the description of Norway in the 1520s given by the Danish friar Poul Helgesen when he called it a *desperatorum asylum*, a refuge for desperate men.[24] He was probably hinting that quite a few monastic persons had fled from Sweden and Denmark in the hope that Norway might secure their traditional way of life.

---

23   The first was founded in Roskilde in 1699. See Holstein (2015), p. 442.
24   'Chronicon Skibyense' (1937), p. 122.

The individual orders

What is often neglected in descriptions of the Danish Reformation is the looting done by citizens during the years of unrest in the 1520s and early 1530s. A remarkable letter survives from 1528 from the small town of Stege.[25] It is a report sent to the lord of the castle explaining how townspeople had looted the altars in the town church in order to get hold of what they considered theirs in so far as they had donated gold and silver to the holy vessels. Similar things must have happened to monasteries, and in Svend Clausen's contribution on the church furniture in monasteries (see below) some valuable examples have been collected. From Norway, Ekroll offers some cases, although mostly from the Post-Reformation period. Quite instructive is the situation in Visby on Gotland. In the later Middle Ages, the city had several monasteries and churches, but after the Reformation had taken place, complaints were sent to the Danish king with the extraordinary piece of information that no funds now existed to support more than two Evangelical preachers.[26] In his elegant survey on the Cistercian monasteries Brian Patrick McGuire states that the richest of the abbeys, the one in Sorø on Zealand, had lost approximately 1/6 of its income during the years of unrest. In the following years, until the abbey was transformed into a knightly academy in 1586, twice as much was lost, but this time mainly as a result of the exchange of property between the king and nobles. No extensive study on looting and manipulation of monastic property, however, has so far been carried out, but it is most needed. So far, the king's exploitation of the unrest has attracted all the attention.[27]

The story of Sorø is also illuminating when it comes to another aspect, namely what has often been called "the harsh Danish Reformation". The abbot of the rich institution, Henrik Tornekrans, had a seat in the Council of the Realm before the Reformation and, even though he most probably opposed the election of the Protestant Duke Christian at the parliament in 1533, abbots were not arrested and jailed, like bishops were, in 1536, and Tornekrans could keep his seat in the Council. By the irony of fate, he thus formally sanctioned the Evangelical Lutheran Church Ordinance in 1537. He also stayed in control of the property of the abbey and his position as spokesman for all the Cistercian abbeys in Denmark was not affected. Seen in this light, the historian Troels Dahlerup has described the Danish Reformation as founded on

---

25 MS Copenhagen, Rigsarkivet, Privatarkiver før 1660, *Anders Berntsen til Søholm Bille. Breve m.m. paa Papir 1500-1563.*

26 Lausten (1987), pp. 378ff.

27 Rørdam (1867-1868).

rights; no one in the Church was to lose any of the rights connected to their office. Hence abbots, monks, nuns, parish priests and so forth could remain in office until they died as long as they did not publicly speak against the new confession.[28] The exception was the bishops, which highlights the political dimension of their imprisonment. Grethe Jacobsen might well be right in pointing at the old control system with secular guardians as a precondition for this largesse on monasteries.

During the second half of the sixteenth century, the crown fiefs tended to grow in size, reducing on the one side the actual numbers of guardians and on the other transferring their rights to the holder of the crown fief. For the individual monasteries, the consequence was that their buildings became of less importance which touched upon their very existence. By the second half of the sixteenth century, most of their inhabitants had died off, and the role of monasteries as centres of learning was surpassed by the University of Copenhagen or cathedral chapters, both being placed in more fashionable city environments. This development meant a change among those who were the supporters of monasteries. In 1536, the king had been their protagonist because he needed as much support as he could get, and the aristocracy was their enemy, as they unceasingly tried to regain control of previously donated land. Now, a generation later, the roles had shifted. The king wished to rationalize and raise money and the nobility wished to secure the survival of minor crown fiefs which nobles would administer, or to protect the existence of nunneries for their unmarried daughters. Seen in this light, King Frederik II's often proclaimed statement that all ecclesiastical matters had been solved during the reign of his father Christian III was clearly political.

In Auge's contribution on the duchies of Schleswig and Holstein, he stresses that the 1560s were the crucial years for the fate of the monasteries and he assigns a decisive role to Frederik II. At the same time, in the Kingdom of Denmark, the debate on nunneries was at its peak, not least concerning the two Brigittine houses in Maribo and Mariager. Frederik was not inclined to follow the aristocracy who wished to let them continue. As he was in the beginning of what became a seven-year-long war with Sweden (1563-70) and the support of the magnates was much needed, he probably gave way and had only one of them dissolved. After the war, in 1572, the nunnery in Maribo was given a new ordinance. The case is studied thoroughly by Rübner Jørgensen. His contribution is most valuable because so little is known of the fate of the individual Danish monasteries in general, and Maribo probably delivers

---

28   Dahlerup (1987).

some of the best surviving records. Here, prof. McGuire's complaint, that the voice of the individual monk and nun is hardly heard after the Reformation, is for a moment answered.

The case of the monastery in Antvorskov, belonging to the order of St John of Jerusalem, has in recent years caused some controversy. In a major study by Erik Reitzel-Nielsen, the argument was set forth that the order never really was dissolved but instead preserved as a kind of dormant military order.[29] Berntson has strongly opposed the view and, in this volume, he is supported by Janus Møller Jensen. He stresses that the last prior was elected in 1580 and in 1582 the monastery was certainly dissolved and turned into a castle. Two years later, it was forbidden to call it Antvorskov Monastery. Its correct name was now Antvorskov Castle. Frederik II died at his castle in 1588. However, Møller Jensen has revealed a new interest in the purpose that drove the Hospitallers. It is found in letters dated to the end of the sixteenth century and the beginning of the seventeenth. Møller Jensen argues that this development materialized in the establishment of the royal order of chivalry of the Armed Arm by Christian IV.

Remaining buildings, books and furniture

Few of the monasteries in the countryside have survived. Apparently, some were demolished already in the sixteenth century. The exact dates are not known, but at least six in Jutland and three in Scania were dissolved before 1550.[30] In a royal letter from 1561, monasteries were called useless houses (*unyttige huse*).[31] The expression concerned the Cistercian abbey Øm in Jutland. The monastery had been secularized a year earlier, but since the crown fief was rather small the decision was taken to let bricks and other building materials become part of the rebuilding of a royal castle in the neighbourhood.[32] Another common procedure was to sell monasteries to loyal men of the Crown, usually understood as a special favour. In the second half of the sixteenth century, this became a well-established tradition, but in Christian III's reign it only occurred three times.[33] The first was Holme, a Cistercian abbey on Funen. The monastery and its land were sold to a member of the Hardenberg

---

29 Reitzel-Nielsen (1984).
30 Krongaard Kristensen (2013), p. 439.
31 *Kancelliets Brevbøger*, 1561-1565, p. 77 (6th October).
32 Gregersen & Selch Jensen (2003), pp. 201-204.
33 Krongaard Christensen (2013), p. 439.

family, which had provided support for the king in The Count's Feud. This took place in 1541. Ten years later, however, the abbey was reestablished and brought back under the Crown. This was due to some heavy complaints against a quarrelsome widow, who among other things had sold furniture from the church to be used for secular purposes. Thus a retable with the iconography of the 10,000 knights was supposedly turned into a dining table for a local pastor.[34] The charge may have been a convenient one, but it shows that concern and respect for the religious aspect of monastic life still functioned politically in the 1550s.

Another aspect of the Holme case is studied by Per Seesko. His topic is dissolutions and their impact on local parish organization. Monasteries established early on in the countryside often had the duty of pastoral care for some of the parish churches situated on their land. Holme was founded in the 1170s and at least three local churches were serviced by priests from the monastery. In 1555, after the return of Holme as a crown fief, Christian III laid out an ambitious plan for the Danish parish organization in order to secure a more equal dispersion of rich and poor parishes. The plan stipulated that Holme's large Cistercian church was to replace two local churches, which had formerly been under monastic pastoral care. Another nearby parish church, Krarup, was to serve as a chapel-of-ease, served by the new pastor at the abbey church, though a promissory clause was that this transfer should not come into force before the present pastor there had passed away. Fortunately for the parishioners, their pastor lived on for years and, upon his death, the parishioners managed to have a new priest appointed. In spite of the efforts of the new noble owners of the monastery, the Rantzau family, he too could not be removed from his office without compensation, and half a century after the royal decree of 1555, Krarup still managed to hold on to its independence. This case and several others are examined by Seesko in the first attempt for a long time to study the matter. In other cases too, where rural monastery churches were meant to replace older parish churches, parishioners did not see these acts as gifts, but as a burden, and argued that they could not possibly maintain such a huge church.

Concerning the fate of the religious houses in towns, we are better informed. In the early years, before the Reformation, when the showdown with the Franciscans was at its most hectic, their churches were often transformed into regular parish churches. We know less about what happened to the rest

---

34 Bisgaard (2006), p. 35. Frederik II resold the estate to another magnate family, the Rantzaus, within a few years.

of their buildings, which had increased extensively in the fifteenth century. After 1536, a more varied use of the buildings became common. Some were turned into schools, others into almshouses, yet others became town halls. The case of Nykøbing Falster, a small town on one of the islands south of Zealand, is indicative. Each wing was given a new purpose, and school, town hall and parish church now came to exist side by side in the old friary.[35] In his contribution, Morten Larsen stresses that some friaries also came into the hands of aristocratic families and points to the case of Copenhagen, where the friary was conveniently sold to one of the leading aristocratic families, the Ulfeldts, in 1545. We do not have the same exact knowledge concerning the Dominicans, the Black Friars, but there is reason to believe that the reuse of their buildings followed the same lines.

In the study by Rasmus Agertoft, special attention is paid to the importance of medieval funerals in the monasteries. The argument is that their very existence could determine whether a monastic church would survive or not. The best example originates from Odense. Back in 1512, the Council of the Realm had accepted that King John and his spouse Christine could be buried in the Greyfriars' Church here. Their sepulchral monument was one of the largest established in the whole of the Danish Middle Ages. In 1536, it saved the monastery from being demolished and the seemingly well-functioning city church of St Alban was sacrificed instead, as the city could not maintain all of its medieval churches.

The old aristocratic funeral monuments in monastery churches were of less importance. Nonetheless, Agertoft is able to show that quite a few of these survived, if not in situ, then by being relocated to parish churches close to the manor houses of the descendants. The process saw two developments: In the first part of the sixteenth century, a practical attitude seem to have been predominant, but as crown fiefs were laid down and monasteries sold, more ambitious plans evolved. Agertoft has collected several cases from the second half of the century and he stresses the importance of kinship in this second development. His study is valuable, because it brings attention to other themes than propaganda, which for too long has dominated Danish art history.

Several pieces of church furniture from monasteries have survived. Often, it has been described in individual institutional histories of which it was part, but seldom, if ever, has a study been dedicated to it alone. Svend Clausen has the courage to enter the vast field. Some interesting observations are found

---

35   Krongaard Kristensen (2013), p. 438.

in his article. First and foremost, it concerns his preliminary result that mon-astery churches, except for mendicant churches, only rarely seem to have been demolished in the sixteenth century (for some instances, see above). Secondly, the king seems to have been a prime mover concerning the reuse of monastic church furniture. In the second half of the sixteenth century, aid to improve poor parish churches began to be systematized. From the same time, we have the first list of genuine inventories on church books and furniture.[36] They stem from the islands of Falster and Lolland, which functioned as a kind of dower for the queen mother. Later, during the reign of Christian IV (1588-1648), the system had evolved so that his bailiffs could redistribute in favour of churches in need of furniture or to help finance the purchase of new pulpits. The Crown's share of the tithe was often involved.[37]

The stronger administrative grip on redistribution and relocation, howev-er, does not seem to have put a strong emphasis on purging certain Catholic remains (for books, see below). The bishop and his provosts were in com-mand here. The visitations done by the Funen bishop, Jacob Madsen, in the years 1588-1604 featured some recommendations that certain iconographic motifs ought to be removed, but in the overall perspective, old church furni-ture could remain.[38] Seen in this light, the king's redistribution mainly had the practical purpose of helping out. Clausen gives some interesting examples of extraordinary survivals: a medieval cabinet for St Samson's relics still existed in Halsted Benedictine church in the 1700s, three medieval altar pieces in the Antonine church in Præstø in 1800, on the whole side altars remained, etc. If this volume had included a contribution on Norwegian churches, strong Catholic iconographic motifs would have been documented.[39]

The scribe in his scriptorium is a strong icon of medieval monasticism and manuscripts seem to encompass the essence of a lost spirituality. Disap-pointingly, only few of these have survived, as our last contribution by Bir-gitte Langkilde on monastic books shows. This is even more striking, when compared to the large amount of church furniture. Langkilde is probably the most knowledgeable scholar when it comes to monastic books in Denmark.[40] She has examined the books and manuscripts that are either mentioned in studied material or actually surviving in libraries, and she reaches an esti-mate of 564 altogether. This is disturbingly few. 378 of these come from one

---

36 MS Copenhagen, Rigsarkivet, *Enkedronning Sofies brevmateriale.*
37 Slottved (1984), Rask (1991).
38 *Jacob Madsens visitatsbog* (1995).
39 Von Aachen (1996).
40 Langkilde (2005).

monastery alone, the rich Cistercian house of Øm in Jutland, because an inventory has miraculously survived.

It is always risky to make an estimate, but to illustrate an approximate loss one has to be daring. Two entries from the records are important. The first is an inventory from 1537 made in the Premonstratensian monastery of Børglum, situated in the north of Jutland. Here, 150 volumes are registered, unfortunately without titles. The monastery ran a diocese and we do not know whether the books of the monastery were separated from the books of the bishop, but there is reason to believe they were. If so, the numbers might be seen as typical for a library of a middle-sized monastery. The entries are at least more realistic than is the case with the rich foundation in Øm. Given the existence of 116 monastic institutions at the eve of the Reformation, we can make a cautious guess of 17,400 manuscripts and books. With a corpus of 562 books in our records, we have merely a few percent and less than one percent has survived (132).

Whether or not this estimate is reliable and ought to be slightly higher or smaller is in this context less important. The conclusion is quite clear: monastic books must have been destroyed on purpose. The establishment of a book list from the 1570s is certainly a hint in that direction; the ruthless behaviour ordered by Christian IV of letting old manuscripts function as torches at a royal banquet is another.[41]

Concluding remarks

In Sweden, Berntson has made extensive studies on the fate of monasteries in the wake of the Reformation. In the duchies a major project on the theme has been running its course for several years. We are happy to bring some of it results. Solid institutional histories have been written on the basis of the scarce number of Norwegian monasteries. This is also the case in Denmark. Krongaard Khristensen's publications are the most prominent recent example. So far, however, no general analysis of monastic history and the Reformation has been published in Denmark. For this reason, this introduction has grown so much in size. It is our hope that this anthology will stimulate further research.

---

41   Nielsen (1937), p. 164; Blom (1869) pp. 93-95; 'Adskillige Optegnelser af Etatsraad Langebeks Papirer' (1793), p. 187.

Manuscript Sources

MS Copenhagen, Rigsarkivet, Privatarkiver før 1660, *Anders Berntsen til Søholm Bille. Breve m.m. paa Papir 1500-1563*.

MS Copenhagen, Rigsarkivet, *Enkedronning Sofies brevmateriale*.

Bibliography

von Achen, Henrik, *Norwegian Medieval Altar Frontals in Bergen Museum* (Bergen, 1996).

'Adskillige Optegnelser af Etatsraad Langebeks Papirer', in *Nye samlinger til den danske Historie*, vol. 2, ed. P. F. Suhm (Copenhagen, 1793), pp. 183-192.

Andersen, Niels Knud, *Confessio haffniensis Den københavnske bekendelse af 1530* (København 1954)

Arup, Erik, *Danmarks Historie* (Copenhagen, 1932).

Berntson, Martin, *Klostren och reformationen. Upplösningen av kloster och konvent i Sverige 1523-1596* (Skellefteå, 2003).

Bisgaard, Lars, 'Adelige kvinder og livet på Arreskov i renæssancen', *Fynske Årbøger* 2006, pp. 31-46.

Bisgaard, Lars, 'Det middelalderlige kalente – et bindeled mellem kirke og folk', in *Konge, Kirke og Samfund. De to øvrighedsmagter i dansk senmiddelalder*, Agnes Arnórsdóttir, Per Ingesman, Bjørn Poulsen (eds.) (Aarhus, 2007), pp. 443-470.

Bisgaard, Lars & Tore Nyberg (eds.), *Tidlige klostre i Norden* (Odense, 2006).

Bisgaard, Lars, Sigga Engsbro, Kurt Villads Jensen & Tore Nyberg (eds.), *Monastic Culture. The Long Thirteenth Century. Essays in Honour of Brian Patrick McGuire* (Odense, 2014).

Blom, Otto, 'Middelalderlig Literaturs Skæbne', *For Ide og Virkelighed. Et Tidsskrift* 1869, pp. 93-95.

'Chronicon Skibyense', in *Skrifter af Paulus Helie*, vol. 6, Marius Kristensen & Hans Ræder (eds.) (Copenhagen, 1937), pp. 51-149.

Dahlerup, Troels, 'Den danske reformation i dens samfundsmæssige sammenhæng', *Acta Jutlandica* LXII:23 Teologisk Serie 14 (Aarhus 1987), pp. 65-79.

Dahlerup, Troels, 'Den sociale forsorg og reformationen i Danmark', *Historie Jyske Samlinger*, 1979, pp. 194-207.

'de Expulsione Fratrum Minorum', in: *Scriptores Minores historiae Danicæ medii ævi*, M.Cl. Gertz (ed.) (Copenhagen, 1917-1922).

Det kongelige Rettertings Domme og Rigens Forfølgninger fra Christian III's Tid, vol. I-II, Troels Dahlerup (ed.) (Copenhagen, 1959-1969).

Gregersen, Bo & Carsten Selch Jensen, *Øm Kloster. Kapitler af et middelalderligt cistercienserabbedis historie* (Odense, 2003).

Grell, Ole Peter, 'The Emergence of Two Cities: The Reformation in Malmø and Copenhagen', in *The Danish Reformation against its International Background*, Leif Grane og Kai Hørby (eds.) (Copenhagen, 1993), pp. 129-145.

Grell, Ole Peter, 'Introduction', in *The Scandinavian Reformation. From evangelical movement to institutionalization of reform*, ed. Ole Peter Grell (Cambridge, 1995), pp. 1-11.

Heilesen, Henning, 'Indledning', in *Krøniken om Graabrødrenes fordrivelse fra deres klostre i Danmark* (Copenhagen, 1967), pp. 7-21.

Heise, Arnold , 'Herredagen i Kjøbenhavn 1533', *Historisk Tidsskrift*, vol. 3, IV ser., 1872-1873, pp. 222-517.

Holstein, Henrik & Poul, "Forsørgelse og statussymbol," in *Adel. Den danske adel efter 1849*, Lars Bisgaard & Mogens Kragsig Jensen (eds.) (Copenhagen, 2015), pp. 438-459.

Ingesman, Per, 'Radikalisme og religion i dansk middelalderforskning. En fagtraditions magt i historiografisk lys', *Foenix* vol. 16, 2, 1992, pp. 45-62.

Ingesman, Per & Nils Arne Pedersen (eds.), *Kirkens historie*, vol. I (Copenhagen, 2012).

Jacob Madsens visitatsbog = Biskop Jacob Madsens visitatsbog 1588-1604, Jens Rasmussen & Anne Riising (eds.) (Odense, 1995).

Kancelliets Brevbøger = Kancelliets Brevbøger vedrørende Danmarks indre Forhold. I Uddrag, C.F Bricka et al. (eds.), 1551-1660 (Copenhagen, 1885-2005).

Kirkeordinansen 1537/39; det danske Udkast til Kirkeordinansen (1537). Ordinatio Ecclesiastica Regnorum Daniae et Norwegiae et Ducatuum Sleswcensis Holtsatiae etc (1537). Den danske kirkeordinans (1539), Martin Schwarz Lausten (ed.) (Copenhagen, 1989).

Kornerup, Bjørn, 'Det lærde tidsrum 1536-1670', in *Den danske Kirkes historie*, vol. IV, Hal Koch & Bjørnerup (eds.) (Copenhagen, 1959), pp. 11-379.

Krongaard Kristensen, Hans, *Klostre i det middelalderlige Danmark* (Aarhus, 2013).

Krongaard Kristensen, Hans, 'Afviklingen af de middelalderlige klostre i Danmark og Nordtyskland', *KUML* 2019 (forthcoming).

Ladewig Petersen, Erling, 'Omkring herredagsmødet i København 1533', *Kirkehistoriske Samlinger* 1972, pp. 24-57.

Langkilde, Birgitte, *Libri monasterium Danicorum mediae aetatis – index ad tempus compositus* (Danske middealderklostres bøger – en foreløbig registrant) (Aarhus, 2005).

Larsen, Morten, *Klosterkultur mellem ideal og realitet. Arkæologiske studier af Danmarks middelalderlige Tiggerklostre* (unpubl. PhD thesis, Aarhus University, 2015).

Larson, James L., *Reforming the North. The Kingdoms and Churches of Scandinavia, 1520-1545* (Cambridge, 2010).

Lausten, Martin Schwarz, *Biskop Peder Palladius og kirken (1537-1560)* (Copenhagen, 1987).

Lausten, Martin Schwarz, *Reformationen i Danmark* (Copenhagen, 2011a).

Lausten, Martin Schwarz, *Johann Bugenhagen. Luthersk reformator i Tyskland og Danmark* (Copenhagen, 2011b).

Nielsen, Lauritz, *Danmarks Middelalderlige Haandskrifter* (Copenhagen, 1937).

Poulsen, Bjørn & Hans Krongaard Kristensen, *Danmarks byer i middelalderen* (Aarhus, 2015).

Rask, Sven, 'Tiende', in *Dansk kulturhistorisk Opslagsværk*, vol. II, Erik Alstrup & Poul Erik Olsen (eds.) (Højbjerg, 1991) pp. 886-888.

Reitzel-Nielsen, Erik, *Johanniterordenens historie med særligt henblik på de nordiske lande*, vol. 1 (Copenhagen, 1984).

Rørdam, Holger Fr., 'Om Beskatningen af Kirkerne og Plyndringen af deres Klenodier i Kong Frederik I's Tid', *Nye kirkehistoriske Samlinger*, vol. 4, 1867-1868, pp. 26-45.

Selch Jensen, Carsten, 'Fattigdom og fattigforsørgelse i middelalder og tidlig moderne tid', *Nyt fra historien* 57, 1 (2008), pp. 65-75.

Slottved, Ejvind, 'Studier over kongetienden efter 1536', in *Tradition og Kritik. Festskrift til Svend Ellehøj*, Grethe Christensen et al. (eds.) (Copenhagen, 1984), pp. 121-147.

Reforming Monasticism in Reformation History and Practice

Euan Cameron

For many years historians of the Reformation told the story of monasticism in sixteenth-century Protestantism as a narrative of theological critique and institutional destruction. The monastic life contradicted the basic theological premises of the Reformation. Its communities either abandoned their way of life because they embraced the new ideas, or resisted them and became opponents or victims. Either way, the monastic order was doomed from the first decades of the Reformation. One of the landmarks in the reforming process in the towns and cities of Europe was the closing down of monastic houses. Yet in the last few decades the story has come to be told in a more nuanced and complex way. First, there was a disjunction between the reformers' disapproval of the monastic ideal in itself, and the policies which they advocated to deal with the houses and communities that existed in their own day. Monasticism was not just a theological issue: it was a social and ethical challenge. Real people needed to be cared for. Secondly, the reformers had no actual institutional control (as opposed to influence) over what happened to religious property. Secular rulers could and did step in more aggressively than theologians might ever have wished.

Monastic communities responded to the reformers' challenges in different ways. Some brothers and sisters escaped from their houses with loudly proclaimed relief. Others (especially female religious) either feared the consequences of being thrust on to a society that was unready for secularized single people, or passionately believed in their vocations and fought as hard as they were able to stay in their communities in some form or another. Those pressures provoked, for those monastic communities that wished to remain, the search for a third way between the continuance of their former medieval pattern of life on one hand and complete abolition on the other. The history of many monasteries in Germany and Scandinavia is a history of gradual transformation rather than tempestuous abolition. Finally, any account of the fate of monasticism in the Reformation needs to take account of the obvious fact that, several centuries later, the impulse to live in the monastic way regained considerable popularity and respect in parts of the Anglican and the Lutheran traditions.

This paper will explore two aspects of the Reformation response to the monastic order. First, it will consider that response on the plane of the intellect. The reformers analysed the monastic ideal on both theological and historical levels. Their theological analysis depended on historical research and historical claims. The reformers knew well that in the earlier, putatively holier and purer ages, of the Church, some form of monastic life was already practised. They therefore needed to demonstrate that the monasticism of late antiquity was somehow not contaminated by those theologically and ethically repugnant elements that they denounced in modern monasticism. The theologians of the Reformation 're-formed' monasticism in their historical imagination before they set about reforming it in actual life. They read the history of the Christian past selectively and programmatically, so as to demonstrate to their own satisfaction what a godly Christian community of common life ought to be like. Then, insofar as their political circumstances allowed, they advocated for a re-fashioning of the *actual* communities of religious people that still survived, in accordance with this historical-theological model.

The theological arguments against monasticism

It would be easy to assume that the theological arguments against the monastic life arose as axiomatic deductions from the theology of justification by grace without works. Surely the monastic, ascetic style of life presented the pre-eminent instance of a 'work' done to earn salvation, and moreover provoked many of Martin Luther's spiritual toils and travails? So it was; however, the precise configuration of the arguments affected how the monastics were treated. Luther began exploring his critique of monastic vows in the 'theses' on vows that he probably wrote in 1521, possibly as a set of notes to himself.[1]

---

1   Luther, *Werke*, WA 8, pp. 330-5: 'Themata de votis (1521) … An liceat perpetuum vovere votum'.

These theses were prepared in the light of Luther's extraordinarily productive years of writing in 1520-21, and reflect many of the concerns of those years. Luther began these theses with the principle of Gospel liberty, very much as he had done in *On Christian Freedom* a few months earlier. Gospel freedom could use all kinds of things but was not tied to any of them. Vows could not rightly conflict with Christian freedom: so one must have the right to keep them or not as circumstances required. 'Marriage is good, virginity is better, but the freedom of faith is best of all.'[2] What was necessary (freedom) was not to be violated for the sake of something that was unnecessary. Christians vowed themselves to Christian freedom in baptism; so a subsequent vow could not invalidate that first one. Monastic saints such as St Bernard kept their vows because they spontaneously wished to live the religious life; moved by the spirit of God, they lived under a vow but without a vow.[3] Essentially, what mattered was the free choice to live a holy life, not that it was thought to be constrained by a vow. Even if the saints lived well under a vow, that fact should not inspire all to follow them.

As others would comment later, Luther observed that there was an inconsistency in vows of poverty and obedience, insofar as monastics who were raised to bishoprics or other positions of eminence had to exercise authority, rather than be subject to it, despite their earlier vow. Their vows of obedience must therefore be temporary and revocable.[4] After proving that the vows of poverty and obedience were in truth temporary and provisional, Luther went on to argue the same about the vow of chastity. Monasteries were, in truth, 'paedagogia' for the formation of Christian youth, since it was healthy to learn under bodily discipline for a time.[5] Concluding the theses, Luther made a slightly intricate argument that the validity of a vow must depend on the continuance of faith in the one who made it. If one lost one's faith, the vow became worthless: only a vow made in faith was valid and binding. (Parenthetically, Luther distinguished between spiritual and worldly liberty. The freedom of the Gospel did not exempt one from obligations undertaken in worldly affairs, for instance through marriage or debts owed in money.) Perpetual vows were a human invention, not ordained or advised in scripture. The Law of Moses provided some examples of vows as a prefiguring of

2 'Bonum coniugium, melior virginitas, sed optima fidei libertas'. Thesis 21, p. 330.
3 Theses 21, 24-7, WA 8, p. 331: 'Sanctus Bernhardus et quicunque sancti religiosi vota sua libere servaverunt. … Nihil enim contra libertatem, sed solum pro libertate potuerunt. Imo sequitur, nullum eorum servasse suum votum. Non enim votum quia votum, sed quia placitum sponte servaverunt. Acti enim spiritu dei sub voto sine voto vivebant.'
4 Theses 66-74, WA 8, p. 332. Luther went on to discuss possible objections on this point at greater length. Note also the development of this point in WA 8, p. 648; LW 44, p. 367.
5 Theses 97-100, WA 8, p. 333.

baptism: but these were all related to temporal goods, and said nothing about chastity.

The slightly rushed and clipped quality of the *Theses on Vows* conceals just how rigorously Luther was thinking about these matters while he had so many other concerns on his mind. Around the same time, he was developing these arguments in a much fuller and more discursive way in what became his *Judgment on Monastic Vows*.[6] In that treatise Luther also incorporated historical convictions about the origins of monasticism which he had already proposed earlier, in *To the Christian Nobility*. Luther's arguments about monastic vows would – whether by parallel development or borrowing it is very difficult to say – be largely followed within the Reformation mainstream even by those theologians in Switzerland who disagreed with him so strongly on other topics.

Luther's *Judgment on Monastic Vows* laid the chief emphasis on the theological issue of faith, as one might have expected. Those who had faith lived in a Spirit-filled way and had no need of vows; those who did not have faith and took vows pledged themselves to something meaningless and impossible. Secondly and just as importantly, vows could only be taken by a faithful person in such a way as to confirm a way of life that such a person had chosen freely for their own convenience, and without any claim to spiritual superiority or to earn a reward from God. Luther imagined the only way in which a vow might be made so as to be consistent with this principle, and so phrased it as to be (perhaps) deliberately unrealistic, at least in the early sixteenth century:

> Further, a man taking his vows in a Christian and godly way would of necessity think thus in the presence of God, "Look, O God, I vow to thee this kind of life, not because I think this is a way to attain righteousness and salvation or to make satisfaction for my sins. Such an attitude might turn away thy mercy from me. This would cause harm to my Lord Christ, since it would be to deny his merits and profane his blood, and to hold thy Son as a reproach. To him alone belongs the glory of being the Lamb of God who takes away the sin of the world. He washes and justifies all with his blood. I will not so blasphemously reject thy grace. My expectations and hopes I shall set in him alone, never at all trusting in myself or in any other creature, to say nothing of trusting in my vows and good works. I do this because I must live in the flesh and cannot be idle. I take this way of life upon

---

6   Martin Luther's *Judgment on Monastic Vows* is edited in WA 8, pp. 564-572 (introduction), pp. 573–669 (text); English translation in LW 44, pp. 243-249 (introduction); pp. 251-400 (text).

myself for the sake of disciplining my body to the service of my neighbour and meditating upon thy word. I do this just as another man may take up farming or a trade—every man a job—without any thought of merits or justification. Justification exists first and foremost in faith. It will always be the most important and will always reign supreme, etc."[7]

Indeed – as Luther went on to say – only someone who was given a special gift of grace could honestly make a vow in such a spirit. A truly Christian vow could only be made by someone who was already elect.[8] Moreover, the performance of a vow also depended on the gift of special grace, so to make a vow was often to promise something that it was not in the power of the person making the vow to offer. As Luther remarked about promising to live in chastity:

> In vowing chastity what does the monk vow but something which is not and cannot be in his hands, since chastity is a gift from God alone, which a man can accept, but never proffer. He is mocking God, therefore, when he takes such a vow. It is no different from vowing to become a bishop or an apostle, a prince or a king, since he knows perfectly well that none of these things lies within the power of the man making the vow, but rather within the will and authority of another who has the power to confer such appointment.[9]

The whole theological emphasis, for Luther, must lie on the fact that the grace to be redeemed and to live a (partially) sanctified life is a gift promised in the Gospel. Consequently, anything invented by human ingenuity to attain that gift or (still worse) to substitute for it was a blasphemy.

Luther's metahistorical arguments

Some of the arguments that Luther used against the sixteenth-century understanding of religious vows combined theological and historical perspectives, in an at times striking anticipation of elements of later historicism. For Luther, faith was eternal, but its expressions in time and culture were not. The same faith might inspire God's people to different actions at different times:

---

7   WA 8, p. 604; LW 44, pp. 294-295.
8   WA 8, p. 610; LW 44, p. 304.
9   WA 8, p. 658; LW vol. 44, pp. 383-384.

'All saints live by the same Spirit and by the same faith, and are guided and governed by the same Spirit and the same faith, but they all do different external works. For God does not work through them at the same time, in the same place, in the same work, or in the sight of the same people. He moves at different times, in different places, in different works, and in different people, but he always rules them by the same Spirit and in the same faith … And each one is compelled by the work, place, time, persons, and circumstances, previously unknown to him, to follow God as he rules and guides him.'[10]

Consequently, those who simply sought to imitate the lives of the saints while not understanding their faith would go astray: they might even find themselves imitating the mistakes of the saints rather than following their principles. In this context, Luther made much of the statement allegedly made by St Bernard near the end of his life, that his whole life of energetic monastic self-discipline had been a waste. 'For that reason he abandoned his own righteousness and betook himself to Christ, declaring that his own righteousness was wasted.'[11]

As things had turned out, the spiritual goals promised in monastic vows no longer achieved their objectives even on their own terms. At considerable length Luther argued that the poverty, chastity and obedience vowed by monastics no longer meant what those words were supposed to mean at all. Poverty as actually experienced by monastics was an illusion, 'Our monks … take vows to a general abundance which is liberally meted out to them. ... They enter their orders not to live in want but in plenty. They are moved to do so because they know that there are full granaries in the monasteries which afford enough from generation to generation'.[12] The obedience practiced by monastics fell far short of the obedience owed by every Christian to another: as Luther had argued in *On Christian Freedom*, the Christian was both perfectly free and the servant of all.[13] Monastics, in contrast, vowed to obey only their superiors according to the rule.[14] Finally, their vow of chastity was meaningless since for many it was insupportable in their inner dispositions.[15]

---

10 WA 8, p. 588; LW 44, p. 269.
11 WA 8, p. 601; LW 44, p. 290.
12 WA 8, p. 642; LW 44, pp. 357-358.
13 WA 7, pp. 21, 49; LW 31, p. 344.
14 WA 8, pp. 645-646; LW 44, pp. 362-363.
15 WA 8, pp. 651-654; LW 44, pp. 371-375.

The historical argument: modern monasticism is not like ancient monasticism

Yet the fundamental argument that Luther made, to which he returned again and again, was even more essentially historical. Luther argued that, quite simply, early monasticism was not like contemporary monasticism: the modern version was a corrupt and degraded form. This argument would suffuse all his writing on the subject; moreover, it would disseminate itself throughout the Reformation movement. A constructive re-fashioning of what monasticism had been in the past determined how the reformers proposed to reform monastic institutions in their own times. In essence, Luther and the other reformers argued that monastic communities had begun as places of education. They were intended to serve as retreats, as places where the young (especially) would undergo the restraints of ascetic discipline to prepare themselves for the rigours of pastoral ministry in dangerous and difficult times. Two consequences followed. First, the restraints of monastic life were only temporary: monastics undertook them for the duration of their stays in the community, and not for life. Second, the rationale for monastic discipline was pragmatic: it was like the training of soldiers for combat. There was no assumption that monastic life represented *per se* a higher form of Christian life than the ordinary. Finally, the monasteries did not claim exemption from the discipline of their bishops, and indeed formed part of the common life of the Christian church in their region.

As early as the address *To the Christian Nobility of the German Nation* Luther was quite sure of this fundamental point that monasteries were established as places of education. 'In those days [*the early church*] convents and monasteries were all open to everyone to stay in them as long as he pleased. What else were the convents and monasteries but Christian schools where Scripture and the Christian life were taught, and where people were trained to rule and to preach? … And in truth all monasteries and convents ought to be so free that God is served freely and not under compulsion. Later on, however, they became tied up with vows and became an eternal prison.'[16] As part of his prescriptions for wholesale reform of German society, he argued for more (real) schooling: 'Would to God that every town had a girls' school as well, where the girls would be taught the gospel for an hour every day either in German or in Latin. Schools indeed! Monasteries and nunneries began long ago with that end in view, and it was a praiseworthy and Christian

16   WA 6, pp. 439-440; LW 44, p. 174.

purpose, as we learn from the story of St. Agnes and of other saints. Those were the days of holy virgins and martyrs when all was well with Christendom. But today these monasteries and nunneries have come to nothing but praying and singing.'[17]

Luther developed this argument at greater length in *On Monastic Vows*. The vow was 'not altogether ridiculous' if it was taken for a limited time and for a specific purpose. Vows were taken for a limited period by those who wished to study with those who were more learned in the faith. Christian schools for boys and girls grew from this practice, and some developed into monasteries. It was only with the degradation of the custom in later years that lifelong vows were used to ensnare recruits who were no longer taught.[18] Luther returned to this same point later: 'All vows are a matter of free choice. … In God's sight the manner in which to take vows is nothing but what we described earlier, "I vow the rule for the time being and at the discretion of the prior." And monasteries would then have the character God intended them to have and nothing else. They would simply be Christian schools for youth, designed to establish ardent young people in the faith by means of a godly upbringing, till they reached the years of maturity.'[19] Luther converted his historical reading of monasticism into a normative principle. He concluded that 'monastic obedience is an elementary and infantile obedience; it is instituted for a limited duration for the instruction of the young. It is not otherwise acceptable to God or otherwise permissible, unless you want to create an impious, sacrilegious obedience.'[20]

The question arose of how monasticism had changed from this simple, educational exercise into the massive institution of permanent vows that it had subsequently become. Here Luther presupposed – as others would also do – that religious practices tended to suffer from progressive overelaboration and corruption over the course of time. He developed this argument most fully in a later polemical work, *On Councils and the Churches*, which he published in 1539 in the wake of the summons to the abortive Council of Mantua. It was a failure of the early church councils that they took no notice of the spread of monasticism and allowed it to grow unchecked. By the time of the Council of Constantinople, Eutyches, Luther observed, was an 'archimandrite', meaning the ruler of an enclosure or compound – showing how monasteries had

---

17   WA 6, p. 461; LW 44, p. 206. Compare also Luther's address *To the Councilmen of All Cities in Germany That They Establish and Maintain Christian Schools*, in WA 15, p. 47, and LW 45, p. 371, which makes the same point.
18   WA 8, pp. 614-615; LW 44, p. 312-313.
19   WA 8, p. 641; LW 44, p. 355.
20   WA 8, p. 649; LW 44, pp. 368-369.

grown by that time. The mistaken growth proved stronger than the original stock. 'Just as happens in a garden, where the weeds grow much higher than the true fruit-bearing shoots, so it also happens in the garden of the church: these new saints, who sprout and grow out from the side and yet want to be Christians, nourished by the sap of the tree, grow far better than the true old saints of the Christian faith and life.' In the Middle Ages the number of houses and the range of orders proliferated so that 'one could well say it rained and snowed monks'.[21]

And not just Luther

Some of Luther's arguments from the early years of the Reformation remained as his own idiosyncratic views or insights. His perspective on the origins and proper use of the monastic way of life did not. On the contrary, nearly every major reformer, including many in Switzerland, adopted or rediscovered the same argument. It was not at all surprising that Johann Carion's *Chronicle* as revised by Philipp Melanchthon adopted the same view: monasteries had arisen as places of refuge in the times of persecution; they 'at that time had not yet been completely transformed from their first and most ancient custom of [being] schools'. Indeed, their educational function prompted donors to enrich them with gifts.[22]

However, arguments remarkably similar to Luther's were also deployed in reformed Switzerland, despite the differences in emphasis from Luther that can be detected in other parts of humanist-reformed historiography.[23] Joachim Vadian, the humanist physician and many-times *Bürgermeister* of St Gallen, addressed the issue of monasticism at many points scattered through his works. In his *Epitome* of biblical historical geography, published first in 1534, and later in his extensive *Chronicle of the Abbots of St. Gallen*, Vadian deployed arguments so similar to those of Luther that it is well-nigh impossible to suppose that he had not been influenced by the Saxon reformer. First, Vadian was as convinced as Luther that monasteries had originally started out as training schools for ministry. 'Then, as this pattern of life grew, and pupils were attracted to it, monasteries were founded everywhere, that is, schools for the conducting of the ancient pattern of education: just as the mind was to be exercised by the reading and the learning of the Scriptures,

---

21   WA 50, pp. 610-611; LW 41, pp. 125-127.
22   [Carion] (1572), pp. 418, 436.
23   Cameron (2012), pp. 27-51.

so the body was to be exercised in turn by regular physical work'.[24] [Basil of Caesarea] 'is also said to have founded monasteries, that is schools, where the cares of the world were cast aside and there was space to attend to learning, manners, modesty and continence, for a purer worship of God and service of one's neighbor. For that was what monasteries were at that time.'[25] Again, in the *Chronicle of the Abbots*:

> 'One can understand clearly from the description of Jerome and from the books of Basil that these gatherings of the ancients were nothing other than schools, in which, with exercises and accustomed good work, for instance with mortification of the body, watching, fasting, that is, abstaining from food, one learned moderation and tolerance, and to avoid idleness, and to conduct oneself in a diligent shared life, to forsake worldly cares and troubles, and through daily learning, reading and studying to devote oneself uniquely to the service of God …[26]

Consequently, the monasteries of the primitive Church lacked strict, complex rules and were run simply and according to charity and reason. No-one was compelled to stay any longer than they wished; indeed, the whole object was to send monks back into the world to serve the Church.[27]

In three chapters of the *Chronicle of the Abbots*, Vadian echoed Luther's critique to the effect that monastic vows as taken in his own time ('the "new monkery"') failed to achieve their objectives. In the fourth chapter he argued that the abundance of rules and regulations in the monastic order were self-defeating. Celibacy was a gift from God that could not be claimed by mere human effort, so marriage should be available to all those who needed it.[28] In the fifth he argued that the vow of poverty was constantly contaminated by the sin of simony, especially when money was demanded for the monks' prayers.[29] In the sixth chapter Vadian demonstrated that monks did not show obedience towards the broader Church, because of the tissue of exemptions claimed by the monasteries: in fact, monastics were schismatics because of their retreat from the rest of the community. True Christian service was to be exercised in community, not separate from it.[30] In other words

---

24 Vadian (1534), pp. 187-188.
25 Ibid., p. 433.
26 Vadian (1875-1879), vol. 1, p. 14.
27 Vadian (1875-1879), vol. 1, p. 5; Vadian (1534), pp. 187-188.
28 Vadian (1875-1879), vol. 1, pp. 16-20.
29 Ibid., pp. 20-26.
30 Ibid., pp. 26-33.

– and very much as Luther had argued – modern monasticism had betrayed its own roots, such that it took vows but failed to perform them in the spirit in which they were originally devised.

Rather interestingly, Vadian's close friend Heinrich Bullinger of Zürich, in his *On the Origin of Error*, took a slightly different view of the early history of monasteries. He perceived the primitive monasteries as not only 'schools of discipline and piety' where the higher intellectual disciplines were taught, but also 'hostels for the poor' where alms were dispensed to those in need. They produced leaders for the Church and grew in reputation. That good reputation encouraged wealthy donors to endow them with greater wealth. The consequences were fatal:

> 'Who would not approve these holy institutions? Who would not praise the piety of those who brought their resources to support something both holy and most useful to the Church? But what followed? Religion begat wealth, and the daughter devoured the mother, that is, wealth drove out piety and introduced luxury. With piety neglected, a way was open for error; error in turn filled everywhere with superstition; superstition then suppressed good letters, and in their place implanted barbarism.'[31]

Bullinger's argument, on this issue and other aspects of his theologized church history, was that many of the worst things about the contemporary Church arose because a good idea, or something devised with a good intention, tended to deteriorate over time. The flaws in the Church were products of human fallibility, but they were not apparent at once. History and the gradual decay of human institutions explained why the Reformation was so necessary.

The continuing influence of Luther's arguments may be seen in a somewhat tedious and repetitive controversy over the celibacy of clergy that broke out around 1550 between the expatriate Italian reformer Piermartire Vermigli and the English conservative theologian Richard Smyth. Vermigli, recently installed as Regius Professor of Divinity at Oxford, delivered a series of lectures on the First Letter to the Corinthians where he attacked clerical celibacy. Richard Smyth (who had been dismissed from Oxford to make room for Vermigli) fled abroad, and from Louvain issued works denouncing Vermigli's arguments. Vermigli was eventually persuaded to issue rebuttals of Smyth's arguments in 1559, though he declined repeated invitations from the Elizabe-

---

31   Bullinger (1568) fo. 26ʳ. Compare Carion (1572), pp. 417-422.

than bishops to return to England.[32] Vermigli made many arguments similar to those of Luther, for instance that when a monk was raised to the rank of bishop the monastic rule was at once dispensed with: so why could that not happen in the case of intolerable celibacy?[33] With formidable erudition in patristic and later sources, Vermigli argued that it was absurd that almost every vow could be dispensed with at need, except apparently for the vow of celibacy.

Where did the historical argument come from?

Such a clear-cut and widely shared image of primitive monasticism had to have come from somewhere. Luther was not over-generous in citing his sources; and the haste with which he was pouring out tracts in 1520-21 probably prevented him from checking widely in his sources, let alone documenting them. The only source that Luther repeatedly referred to was the *Life of St Agnes* by Ambrose, which referred briefly to Agnes attending school before the crisis that would lead to her martyrdom. The text made no suggestion that this was a monastic school, so Luther's citing of this source amounted more to a proof-text for an idea already formed, rather than anything more formative.[34] Joachim Vadian was a little more helpful to his readers. He cited Basil of Caesarea's letter to Gregory of Nazianzus on the solitary life, a letter that had been recently translated by Francesco Filelfo.[35] Basil's letter once again proved only of limited help. What it did demonstrate was that the attraction of the solitary life lay in the escape from material and familial cares in order to study better, rather than in any supposed 'special virtue' inherent in living by a vow. A life of quiet stability without distractions and vexations was the best way to prepare for one's sanctification.[36]

However, Vadian almost certainly betrayed the real source of the reformed view when he cited a much more recent source, Erasmus's *Life of Jerome*, writ-

---

32 See Oxford Dictionary of National Biography, article 'Vermigli, Pietro Martire' at http://www.ox-forddnb.com/view/article/28225?docPos=1 ; Smyth (1550); Vermigli (1559).

33 Vermigli (1559), p. 343 [actually 243 but mis-paginated in the 1559 edition]; note that Vermigli expresses approval of Luther's views on p. 345 [245].

34 Luther cites the story of St Agnes in LW 44, pp. 174, 206, 312; the reference to Agnes being desired by the prefect of Rome "as she came from school" is found in her life in Jacobus de Voragine (1900), vol. 2, pp. 245-252.

35 Vadian (1534), pp. 433-435; Basil's 'Epistola de vita solitaria', translated by Francesco Filelfo, appeared in several miscellaneous collections of texts e.g. Calco (1503); also Poliziano (1508).

36 Basil of Caesarea, Letter II, in *Basil: Letters and Select Works*, in Schaff (1956), vol. 8, pp. 110-112.

ten to accompany the edition of Jerome's writings that Erasmus completed in 1516.[37] In a crucial passage, Erasmus wrote that Jerome chose, after careful consideration, to become a monk. However, Erasmus insisted that the monasticism of Jerome's time was nothing like the monasticism of his own age. Monks in those early years were not bound to strict rules. They would choose when to worship and how. They would wear sober but not special clothing. Above all, they were allowed to leave whenever they wished, and there was no punishment for leaving the house except for potential harm to one's reputation.[38] Erasmus in turn cited as evidence several writings of Jerome which he claimed supported this portrait of fourth-century monasticism: the life of Hilarion, the letters to Rusticus and Paulinus, or the letter entitled 'Hear, daughter' where Jerome described the threefold pattern of monks in Egypt.[39]

Erasmus wrote, of course, as a disillusioned and disappointed monk himself. He had entered a monastery in the expectation that it would support his studies and provide the emotional and physical security that he needed; but the life did not suit him as well as he had hoped. He left relatively soon afterwards, taking up the life of a travelling scholar and ultimately living by the proceeds of his publications. In much later life he would obtain formal dispensation from his vows as an Augustinian, long after he had definitively rejected the manner of life that those vows represented.[40] His description of monasticism in the time of Jerome suggests wish-fulfilment. If only the monasteries of the late fifteenth century had been like those of the fourth century, he would not have had the problems that he did. The nearest equivalent to Erasmus's vision of ideal monasticism in his own time was François Rabelais's fantasy of the Abbey of Thélème (not an example that was cited by any of the reformers!).[41]

The reformed image of monasticism blended what were at least arguable historical insights with a certain amount of self-referential selection of the evidence. It was justifiable to argue that early monasticism lacked the rigid forms and rules that were characteristic of the later Middle Ages. The early advocates of monasticism, such as Basil, did indeed recommend this manner of life because of its spiritual utility and convenience, rather than because any

---

37 Erasmus (1516).

38 Erasmus, (1517), sigs. b2^r-b2^v.

39 Jerome, *Works*, in Schaff (1956), vol. 6, pp. 22-41 (the letter to Eustochium which begins 'hear, daughter') esp. sects. 34-36 on pp. 37-38; 96-102 (Letter to Paulinus); 244-252 (letter to Rusticus); 303-315 (Life of Hilarion).

40 On Erasmus's experiences of monastic life see Halkin (1993) pp. 5-11; Schoeck (1990), pp. 84-131.

41 Rabelais (1906), Book 1, Chapters 52-7, in vol. 1, pp. 121-131.

special virtue or merit was supposed to reside in the vow itself. Most obviously, the reformers were right to say that many monasteries served as places of culture and education (though perhaps less so in claiming that they were *only* places of education). Indeed, the role of monasteries as conservators of culture and literature not only persisted through late antiquity, but proved essential for the transmission of classical culture through the early Middle Ages. The monastic schools of the early-to-high Middle Ages (about which the reformers tended to say rather less) were fundamental to Christian learning until the rise of the universities in the twelfth and early thirteenth centuries.

However, the reformed view of ancient monasticism entailed a good deal of tendentious selection and omission. The reformers touched very lightly – if at all – on the reputation of the early monastics for spectacular holiness through ascetic self-discipline. They either did not grasp, or concealed, the fact that the introduction of monastic rules such as that of Benedict was intended at least in part to restrain the proneness of over-zealous monks for excessive self-mortification. Moreover, while the reformers acknowledged that the early apostles performed miracles, their theology of the miraculous – based on the assumption that miracles ceased relatively soon after the establishment of the Church – prevented them from recognizing the many miraculous feats attributed to the monastic saints of the fourth or fifth centuries.[42] Finally, the reformers would have had difficulty with the notion that the monastic life entailed a constant and unrelenting spiritual struggle with evil spirits. Even though there was nothing inconsistent with Protestant theology about belief in demons, the attribution of sacral power against demons to holy individuals was seen as problematic. One of relatively few Lutheran scholastics to address this topic, Lucas Osiander the elder in his monumental history of the Church, the *Annals*, addressed the stories of the temptations of St Antony with withering scepticism:

> '[Antony] was often tempted and troubled by demons: if we believe the account of him who wrote the life of Antony … If Antony had not chosen this superstitious way of life, of living in the desert, but had lived among other Christians, he would undoubtedly have been free from such vexations of Satan (if indeed they are not feigned). Therefore this ought not to be praised, that he exposed himself to many temptations and dangers by the solitary life. … Even if I do not doubt that this Antony the hermit obtained eternal salvation because of Christ,

---

42 Cameron (2010), pp. 206-208; Walker (2015), pp. 373-385. Generally, the reformers did not try to identify a particular date at which miracles ceased.

in whom he believed ... all the same we must distinguish between the superstitious works that he invented for himself (by which God is worshipped vainly) and those which he did following the commandments of God ... which God approves and rewards'.[43]

To a later-generation Protestant scholastic like Osiander, the Church was definitely and deeply corrupt by the time of Gregory the Great and after: miracle stories were spread abroad which were either false or the result of the impostures and delusions of demons.[44] The stories of heroic monastic virtue partook of that same deeply deceptive and/or deluded culture.

The reformers' historical view of monasticism was, then, ambivalent and divided, and profoundly shaped by their theological concerns. By reconstructing a historical image of early monasticism as a rational lifestyle based on education and discipline in preparation for ministry, they justified one form of monastic vocation but not others. On the other hand, every Protestant critic, following humanist critics such as Erasmus, believed that the monastic order had undergone severe degradation and decline in the Middle Ages. Those who claimed to be monastics in the sixteenth century were perpetuating the errors and mistakes of their founders, not their principles and ideals.

What happened to monasteries in the Reformation?

Monastic houses by the early sixteenth century were, of course, not just places of communal life and discipline. By the later Middle Ages, many if not most had become dominated by monks or friars who were also ordained priests and who served their patrons among the laity by saying multiple masses for the souls of the departed. While they competed in this market with colleges of secular priests, the monastics remained in the eyes of the reformers contaminated by a blasphemous form of works-worship.[45] Many monasteries, even quite modest ones, funded their activities through the exhibition of relics and the indulgences granted to those who visited and gazed upon such

---

43   Osiander (1592-1604), Cent. 4, pp. 99-103.
44   Osiander (1592-1604), Cent. 6, pp. 3-4.
45   In pre-Reformation Strasbourg, the Carmelites were able to stave off a general tendency for laypeople to give less to the monastic orders, by offering cut-price masses for the benefit of the poor. See Rapp (1974), pp. 397–404.

relics.[46] There was, in short, ample theological justification for taking a hard line with the monasteries, and some reformed communities did so. The more moderate and merciful alternative was to allow the communities to continue to exist either without new recruits, or on condition of radical changes in the way that they operated. Given the historical image of ancient monasteries as schools, one of the most popular changes required of monasteries was that they should convert into schools, colleges or seminaries of some kind.

Martin Luther, possibly distinguishing himself from the more radical and iconoclastic zealots in Wittenberg and elsewhere, adopted a pragmatic, progressive approach to dealing with actual monks and nuns and real monasteries from very early on. In the draft ordinance for the Common Chest of the Saxon town of Leisnig (1523) Luther proposed strategies for dealing with the monasteries. Those situated in rural areas such as the Cistercians (which could not help with community worship) should never have come into existence; the best tactic was to allow them to dwindle away by allowing voluntary departures and forbidding further new admissions. Those monastics who could not face going out into the world should be allowed to finish their lives in the cloister. With some compassion, Luther observed that those who mistakenly entered the religious life had learned no other trade to support themselves. All these reforms were to be carried out through the authority of the civil power and without reference to the Pope or the bishops. [47]

One of the *Articles of Schmalkalden* of 1537 addressed the reform of chapters and monasteries in a similar way but with a more formal procedure. Foundations and monasteries formerly established to educate men and women should be returned to that use, to bring up pastors for the churches, administrators for the community as a whole, and well-educated women to work in the domestic sphere. However, their former purpose of offering 'blasphemous services invented by men', forms of worship not commanded by God nor useful to the community was not to be continued; if any insisted on continuing in such practices and would not convert themselves to schools, they should be demolished or abandoned.[48]

This was Luther's recommended strategy to deal with the religious hous-

---

46   As an example, on 14 May 1519 a group of Cardinals issued an indulgence to the Dominican nuns of Unterlinden, Colmar, in Alsace, for the benefit of those who visited the monastery on 11 October of each year, when an image of the Virgin Mary 'said to resemble those painted by St Luke' was exhibited. The letter of indulgence survives in the Burke Library at Union Theological Seminary, New York, as UTS Ms. 67.

47   Luther, *Preface to the Ordinance for a Common Chest at Leisnig*, in WA 12, pp. 12-13; LW vol. 45, pp. 170-172.

48   *Book of Concord* (2000), p. 306.

es; and as is discussed elsewhere in this volume, many Lutheran regions, especially in Scandinavia, made serious attempts to follow it. In Europe as a whole, policies varied considerably. Secular rulers did not always follow Luther's injunction to give the remaining inmates at least as generous a provision as in the past, 'so that men may realize that this is not a case of greed opposing clerical possessions, but of Christian faith opposing monasticism'.[49] Many rulers were more than content to oppose – and seize – clerical possessions. The most spectacular case of royal acquisitiveness occurred in England. The moves taken by Henry VIII's government against monasteries were marked by an astonishing combination of duplicity and lack of evident principle. A somewhat spurious investigation of the alleged immorality of the monastic houses in 1535 led to parliamentary legislation in 1536 to abolish all houses below an annual income of £200 (on the supposed basis that smaller houses were more likely to be decadent). Houses were allowed to buy themselves out of this provision, and many did so. Notwithstanding that lifeline, in the following four years the king's officials demanded the surrender and the effective abolition of all the remaining houses: the last was gone by the end of 1540. Monks were pensioned modestly, nuns poorly, friars not at all.[50] It was extremely dangerous to resist the royal policy: some of the most committed English monastics, such as the Observant Franciscans and the Carthusians, fell foul of royal vindictiveness and many were brutally punished.[51] However, some evidence from England suggests that some communities tried to preserve a form of existence in the face of dissolution. Abbess Katharine Bulkeley of Godstow in Oxfordshire tried to argue to Thomas Cromwell that her house was not engaged in any offensively conservative religious practices. The nuns of St Mary's Winchester tried to live communally outside their former cloister, and appear to have continued this common life until 1551.[52]

In England, this massive campaign of expropriation and conversion of lands to secular use was justified without any explicit theological rationale. Indeed, defining such a rationale would have been difficult while the king's court was bitterly divided between conservatives who could not declare allegiance to the Pope, and evangelicals who dared not mention the reformers. Nor was the English regime's concern for education particularly impressive where monastic foundations were concerned. The explicitly Protestant

---

49   Luther, *Preface to the Ordinance for a Common Chest at Leisnig*, in WA 12, p. 13; LW vol. 45, pp. 171-172.
50   For a recent review of the English story, see Bernard (2011).
51   See Elton (1977), pp. 187-193.
52   On Katharine Bulkeley, see Erler (2013), pp. 67-72; on the Winchester nuns, see ibid., pp. 74-78.

government of the young King Edward VI in the 1540s came close to abolishing even those colleges of secular clergy that had been founded explicitly to support schools, such as Eton and Winchester, on the grounds that they had (like so many other foundations of their kind) been established for the 'superstitious' purpose of saying memorial masses – and the endowments could therefore be confiscated to the Crown's coffers.[53]

In much more consistently reformed Scotland, the process was quite different. Catholic worship was quite suddenly and apparently unexpectedly abolished on the establishment of reformed Protestantism in 1560. At that point, the Scottish parliament left the old Church in possession of most of its former endowments under a curious provision known as the "thirds of benefices", but legally disabled it from providing religious services. Since much of the estates of the old monasteries had been leased away as 'feus' in the decades before the Reformation, much of the monastic order was effectively converted into secular estates by voluntary action before 1560. The abbey churches fell into gradual disrepair as the members of the communities melted away or died off. In the debatable border lands with England where many important houses were located, chronic lawlessness contributed to monastic decline. Some of the more conveniently situated monastic churches were adapted to parish use (as for instance in Dunfermline or Melrose) while others crumbled and were plundered for building materials.[54] Scotland had three universities by the Reformation (and would soon acquire a fourth) and a relatively well-established system of public schools, so the pressure to use monastic resources for education was not strong.

In the Holy Roman Empire and the Swiss confederation the fate of the monastic houses was considerably more complicated: the complex mosaic of territories held by different princes, prince-bishops and cities complicated jurisdictions; many of the larger abbeys, moreover, were in their own right free lordships of the empire, not subject to any intermediate ruler below the Emperor. In practice, secular rulers whose lands were situated very close to or enfolding the estates of a religious house would often try to take possession and, if reformed, to dissolve or transform it. The ruinous effects of the Edict of Restitution in 1629, which threatened to expropriate from the Lutheran princes religious estates secularized since 1555, show how far this process had gone. However, the historic abbey of St Gallen in eastern Switzerland re-

---

53   For an old (and highly polemical) description of the plundering of collegiate endowments at this period, see Leach (1896). The medieval colleges of education were in the main allowed to survive.
54   On the Scottish dissolutions, see e.g. Wormald (1981), pp. 96-98; Ryrie (2006), pp. 78-79. On the 'thirds of benefices', see Kirk (1995).

sisted pressure from the reformed town of the same name until 1798: clearly proximity did not count for everything.

Some of the stronger Lutheran princes were willing and able to institute reforms which approximated to the ideals of Luther and his colleagues. In Württemberg under Duke Christoph and his successors, some level of genuine effort was made to adapt the monasteries for the purposes of education. This initiative led to the establishment of Lutheran *Klosterschulen*. These were in effect boarding schools in the countryside, where talented graduates of the town schools were sent to be trained for the ministry. 13 schools (though by 1599 reduced to 5) were supported by the endowments of suppressed monasteries and located in their former buildings. These institutions validated the reformers' historical view of monasticism (though in being rural and remote they contradicted Luther's early advice, which was to abolish the houses situated away from centres of population). A temporary, time-limited version of quasi-monastic discipline was instituted for the pupils and students. The chief teacher was called the 'abbot'; the students were called 'novices'; and the instruction was shaped around the hours (though several of the traditional canonical services were replaced with classes). The next stage in clergy training, the Tübingen *Stift*, had this same quasi-monastic character. The 'monastic' instruction programme was intended only to be temporary, in good Lutheran manner, and was to prepare the student for parish ministry. It has been observed, however, that education in this hothouse environment may have given Lutheran pastors in Württemberg a cadre mentality which could potentially distance them from their congregations once they went into the parish.[55]

Although Württemberg presents the most systematic example of the application of monastic foundations to educational purposes, similar efforts were made in Saxony and elsewhere.[56] Amelungsborn, a Cistercian house in Lower Saxony, adopted the Augsburg Confession under Abbot Andreas Steinhauer in 1568, who founded a monastic school on the site. The title of Abbot survived changes in the school's location until the restoration of the monastic community in the 20th century.[57] At Loccum, the Cistercian house was reformed in 1600 and subsequently became a seminary for preachers of the *Landeskirche* of Hannover. The head of the seminary retains the title

---

55 Tolley (1995), pp. 24-43.
56 For a general review of the complex pattern of change and (in some cases) partial survival in German monasteries, see Chadwick (2001), pp. 162-175.
57 For Amelungsborn, see http://www.kloster-amelungsborn.de/

of 'Abbot'.[58] Similarly, a professor in the Göttingen theological faculty has the honorary title of 'Abbot' of Bursfelde.[59] Among the women's houses, the canoness house of Quedlinburg was turned into a school for both boys and girls.[60] Since the liturgical movement and the revival of sympathetic interest in monasticism in many of the churches of the Reformation, many former religious communities have found new existence as retreat centres or other forms of spiritual communities. In Germany these are recognized as the 'Heirs of the Cistercians' in their digital identity.[61]

It has long been recognized that communities of women religious were more likely to try to cling on to their vocation than male communities. One reason was that the natural option open to men, of becoming pastors in churches, was not accessible to women until centuries later. One of the most celebrated defenders of female monasticism in the Reformation era, Caritas Pirckheimer of Nuremberg, was able to achieve some precious years' continued existence for her house, not least because her connection with the city patriciate through her brother Willibald gave her vital influence.[62] The desire of religious women to continue to live in common could form part of a determined rejection of the Reformation; or it could be negotiated through a readiness to make the theological and liturgical concessions that the civil authorities demanded in order to survive. In other words, the monastic impulse could be to some degree detached from commitment to Catholicism itself. The female houses of Braunschweig-Lüneburg and especially those of the Lüneburg Heath, which fell under the jurisdiction of various branches of the Welf dynasty, present an exceptional instance of this phenomenon. Some of them passionately desired to stay as female communities and resisted the Reformation. Rather than being driven out, they were converted, under the patronage of Elisabeth of Braunschweig-Lüneburg-Calenberg from the 1540s onwards into Lutheran communities of noblewomen. As such they served a social purpose which female religious houses had long served. They provided places for unmarried daughters or widows of the nobility to live without the dynastic pressure of marriage or the cost of a dowry. In this form the houses of the Lüneburg Heath, especially Barsinghausen, Bassum, Ebstorf, Isenhagen, Lüne, Marienwerder, Medingen, Obernkirchen, Walsrode, Wen-

---

58 For Loccum, see http://www.kloster-loccum.de/
59 At the time of writing, this position of "abbot" is held by the Luther scholar Dr. Thomas Kaufmann.
60 For Bursfelde, see http://www.kloster-bursfelde.de/ and http://www.uni-goettingen.de/de/56194.html
61 http://www.evangelische-zisterzienser-erben.de/
62 On Caritas, see [Pirckheimer] (2006); Krabbel (1982).

nigsen, Wienhausen and Wülfinghausen, survived beyond the Reformation. Ultimately they were reorganized by the house of Hanover in 1818 under the governmental office known as the *Klosterkammer*, which still exists.[63]

Conclusion

A certain sense of paradox accompanies the history of monasticism in the Reformation. On one hand, the reformers were implacably hostile to many of the theological principles which in their eyes accompanied a monastic vocation. Monks and nuns, it was supposed, were better Christians than the rest, leading lives of a higher degree of Christian purity.[64] Those who adopted an ascetic lifestyle, who mortified their lower natures for the sake of the Gospel, maybe thought that by their abstinence they could place God under some kind of obligation to reward them. Most serious in the reformers' eyes was the whole tissue of rules and ideas behind the religious vow: both because of its spurious sanctity, and because it was administered so inconsistently, some aspects of the vow apparently regarded as more dispensable than others.

On the other hand, the reformers do not appear to have disapproved in principle of all forms of religious life lived in common. Provided that communal life was adopted without any pretensions to higher spiritual status or merit; provided that it was not entangled with supposedly perpetual vows; and provided that it was not established to perpetuate repugnant forms of worship or spiritual practice, the reformers could in principle allow it to continue. Here the reformers' insights based on history proved crucial. By a selective reading of church history, filtered through the wishful thinking of humanists like Erasmus, the Lutheran reformers imagined a primitive monasticism that gave spiritual benefits without the theological costs. They believed that in the ancient monastic records, and especially in the correspondence of the fathers, they had found a kind of monasticism without rules, without rigid vows, without claims to higher sanctity: a pragmatic lifestyle suited to the training, discipline and formation of those destined for pastoral ministry and the government of the Church. In conjuring up this image the reformers used

---

63   For the Hannover *Klosterkammer* and its constituent houses, see http://www.klosterkammer.de/html/
     start.html and the linked pages.
64   The constructive exegeses that reinterpret Scripture to praise virginity in patristic and medieval com-
     mentaries are too many to cite. As just one example, the reference in Matthew 13:8 to the good seed
     that 'brought forth fruit, some an hundredfold, some sixtyfold, some thirtyfold', was taken as a refer-
     ence to those living as monastics, those living as celibate laity and the married, respectively.

their sources highly selectively. They minimized the ascetic heroism of the desert fathers. They paid little attention to the miraculous feats of resistance to demonic temptation that bulked so large in the early accounts of the first monks and hermits. Their image was selective but had its own inner logic. So, it was perfectly consistent with their vision that the reformers allowed a transformed monastic lifestyle to continue, especially where schools could be established within the cloisters. Such a transformation will have seemed not like a deformation of monasticism but a restoration of the monastic order to its ancient roots – a 'reformation' in the true sense in which the word was understood in the sixteenth century.

Bibliography

Bernard, G. W., 'The Dissolution of the Monasteries' in *History* 96 (October 2011) Issue 324, pp. 390–409.

The Book of Concord: the Confessions of the Evangelical Lutheran Church, trans. Charles Arand ... [et al.], ed. Robert Kolb and Timothy J. Wengert (Minneapolis, 2000).

Bullinger, Heinrich, *De Origine Erroris Libri Duo* (Zürich, 1568).

Calco, Tristano (ed.), *Index operum quæ in hoc uolumine continentur: Censorini de die natali liber…* (Milan, 1503).

Cameron, Euan, *Enchanted Europe: Superstition, Reason and Religion 1250-1750* (Oxford, 2010).

Cameron, Euan, 'Primitivism, Patristics and Polemic in Protestant Visions of Early Christianity' in *Sacred History: Uses of the Christian Past in the Renaissance World*, eds. Katherine van Liere, Simon Ditchfield and Howard Louthan (Oxford, 2012), pp. 27-51.

[Carion, Johannes], ed. Philipp Melanchthon and Caspar Peucer, *Chronicon Carionis expositum et auctum multis et veteribus et recentibus historiis ... ab exordio mundi usque ad Carolum Quintum imperatorem ...* (Wittenberg, 1572).

Chadwick, Owen, *The Early Reformation on the Continent* (Oxford and New York, 2001).

Elton, G. R., *Reform and Reformation: England 1509-1558* (London, 1977).

Erasmus, Desiderius, *Eximii doctoris Hieronymi Stridonensis vita, ex ipsius potissimum literis contexta* (Cologne, 1517).

Erler, Mary C., *Reading and Writing during the Dissolution: monks, friars, and nuns 1530-1558* (Cambridge and New York, 2013).

Halkin, Léon-E., *Erasmus: A Critical Biography*, trans. John Tonkin (Oxford, 1993).

Jacobus de Voragine, *The Golden Legend, or, Lives of the Saints*, trans. William Caxton and ed. Frederick Startridge Ellis, 7 vols. (London, 1900).

Jerome, St., *Omnium operum Divi Eusebii Hieronymi Stridonensis*, ed. Desiderius Erasmus, 9 vols. (Basel, 1516).

Kirk, James (ed.), *The Books of Assumption of the Thirds of Benefices: Scottish ecclesiastical rentals at the Reformation* (Oxford, 1995).

Krabbel, Gerta, *Caritas Pirckheimer: ein Lebensbild aus der Zeit der Reformation*, 5th edn. (Münster, 1982).

Leach, A. F., *English Schools at the Reformation 1546-8* (Westminster, 1896).

Luther, Martin, *M. Luther, Werke: Kritische Gesamtausgabe*, 58 vols. plus indexes [many vols. subdivided] (Weimar, 1883-1948). Abbreviated as *WA*.

Luther, Martin, *Luther's Works*, American edition, ed. Jaroslav Pelikan and H. T. Lehmann, 55 vols. (St. Louis, MO and Philadelphia, PA, 1955-86). Abbreviated as *LW*.

LW = Luther, Martin, *Luther's Works*, American edition, ed. Jaroslav Pelikan and H. T. Lehmann, 55 vols. (St. Louis, MO and Philadelphia, PA, 1955-86).

Osiander, Lucas [the Elder], *Epitomes Historiae Ecclesiasticae, Centuriae* I.-XVI., 10 vols. (Tübingen, 1592-1604).

[Pirckheimer, Caritas], *Caritas Pirckheimer: a journal of the Reformation years, 1524-1528*, ed. and trans. Paul A. MacKenzie (Cambridge, 2006).

Poliziano, Angelo (ed.), *Subnotata hic continentur: Magni Athanasij in psalmos opusculum …* (Strasbourg, 1508).

Rabelais, François, *Les Cinq livres de F. Rabelais*, 2 vols. (Paris, 1906).

Rapp, F., *Réformes et réformation à Strasbourg: église et société dans le diocèse de Strasbourg (1450–1525)* (Paris, 1974).

Ryrie, Alec, *The Origins of the Scottish Reformation* (Manchester, 2006).

Schaff, P. et al. (eds.), *A Select Library of the Nicene and Post-Nicene Fathers*, 2nd series (Grand Rapids, MI, 1956). Available online at http://www.ccel.org/ccel/schaff/npnf206 .

Schoeck, R. J., *Erasmus of Europe: The Making of a Humanist 1467-1500* (Edinburgh, 1990).

Smyth, Richard, *De coelibatu sacerdotum liber vnus. Eiusdem de votis monasticis liber alter* (Louvain, 1550).

Smyth, Richard, *Defensio sacri Episcoporu[m] & sacerdotum caelibatus, contra impias & indoctas Petri Martyris Vermelij nugas, & calumnias* (Paris, 1550).

Tolley, Bruce, *Pastors and Parishioners in Württemberg during the late Reformation, 1581-1621* (Stanford, Calif., 1995).

Vadian, Joachim, *Epitome Trium Terrae Partium, Asiae, Africae et Europae compendiarum locorum descriptionem continens, praecipue autem quorum in Actis Lucas, passim autem Evangelistae et Apostoli meminere …* (Zürich, 1534).

Vadian, Joachim, *Chronik der Aebte des Klosters St Gallen*, in *Deutsche historische Schriften: Joachim v. Watt (Vadian)*, ed. Ernst Götzinger, 3 vols. (St Gallen, 1875-1879), vol. 1.

Vermigli, Pietro Martire, *Defensio D. Petri Martyris Vermilii Florentini Diuinarum Literarum In Schola Tigurina professoris, ad Riccardi Smythaei Angli, olim Theologiae professoris Oxoniensis duos libellos de Caelibatu sacerdotum, & Votis monasticis* (Basel, 1559).

WA = Luther, Martin, *M. Luther, Werke: Kritische Gesamtausgabe*, 58 vols. plus indexes [many vols. subdivided] (Weimar, 1883-1948).

Walker, D. P., 'The Cessation of Miracles', in Helen Parish (ed.) *Superstition and Magic in Early Modern Europe: A Reader* (London and New York, 2015), pp. 373-385.

Wormald, Jenny, *Court, Kirk and Community : Scotland 1470-1625* (London, 1981).

The
Early
Years

Monasteries and Convents as Crown Fiefs, 1500-1600

– Especially for (Noble) Women?

Grethe Jacobsen

One of the more mundane issues that arose with the introduction of the Danish Reformation was that of administering the properties and buildings of monasteries and convents, which were secularized after becoming crown property in 1536. This issue was solved by incorporating these properties into the crown fief system (*lensadministration*), which was an instrument for administering crown lands. This system developed during the later Middle Ages. Crown property was divided into a varying number of crown fiefs of different sizes. Some, which by later historians have been defined as "major crown fiefs", included a county (*herred*) as well as a royal castle or fortress, while smaller crown fiefs, later defined as "minor crown fiefs", could be anything from a few farms to several villages and manors. The holder of a crown fief administered the property and collected ordinary and extraordinary taxes, fees and services imposed on the subjects of the Crown. In addition, the holder maintained law and order, in particular by keeping an eye on how the local courts functioned. Holders of major crown fiefs also had the obligation to provide equipped troops in case of war or attacks on the kingdom.

Several ways were possible for becoming the holder of a crown fief: one could receive the crown fief as surety for loans to the Crown, as a reward for services to the crown and as a regular office. Conditions for holding a crown fief took three major forms: by account (*på regnskab*), by fees (*på afgift*) and by service (*på tjeneste*). A holder of a crown fief by account received a fixed wage for administering the crown fief and in return surrendered all income received to the royal treasury, subtracting all documented expenses.

A holder of the crown fief by fees paid an annual fixed sum to the Crown and could keep all income of the crown fief but in return had to pay all expenses incurred in administering the fief. A holder of the crown fief by service was obliged to muster armed soldiers in case of war as well as entertain the king and his officials whenever they resided in the area, but could otherwise manage the crown fief as if it were private property.

This administrative system also became a central institution in the secular exercise of power in fifteenth- and sixteenth-century Denmark. Controlling who obtained the position as holder of a crown fief and the ratio of the three types of conditions for holding a crown fief was a decisive factor in exercising power during late medieval and Reformation era, and thus sought after by both of the secular powers of the period, king and aristocracy. In 1449, the aristocracy, through the Council of the Realm (*rigsråd*), had been strong enough to dictate the rules for the distribution of crown fiefs in the coronation charter of the new king, Christian I, namely that no crown fief should be occupied without the consent of the Council of the Realm. This procedure became the rule for the succeeding kings including the Reformation era kings.

As with all power relations, the balance of power was never at a standstill for any length of time, yet overall, the aristocracy was the stronger party vis-à-vis the king until the early seventeenth century, that is, before and after the Danish Reformation in 1536. Concurrently, the Danish nobility became a closed class, which meant that no newcomers in principle were to be admitted to the group and enjoy their privileges. I will henceforth use the term, 'nobility' and 'nobles'.

It was, however, not all members of the nobility, who enjoyed all the benefits of the crown fief system. A small group of families, those making up the magnate group (*højadel*), in reality exercised the power that control over the system of crown fief offered because they occupied the seats in the Council of the Realm. This group was composed of women as well as men, and noble women could also share in the benefits of the group, including holding crown fiefs. Both men and women appear as holders of crown fiefs, including those created after 1536 from the lands, the buildings and the services, formerly owned and claimed by monasteries and convents.[1] However, as in all patriar-

---

1   General works about the crown fief system: W. Christensen (1903/1974), p. 196-286; H. Christensen (1983); Erslev (1879/1970). Erslev (1879) is an (almost) complete list of crown fiefs and their holders from about 1500 to 1596. Unless otherwise noted, the following information about crown fiefs, including monastic institutions, is found in Erslev (1879).

chal societies, there was a "glass ceiling": women could not become members of the Council of the Realm.

Before the Reformation, monastic institutions were in principle part of the Church, convents were under the authority of the local bishop and monasteries under that of the leaders of their order whose authority included control of monastic property. From the late fifteenth century on, we find secular guardians (*forstandere*) of convents and monasteries, appointed by the bishop. One of the earliest is Anders Ebbesen Ulfeldt, who is mentioned as guardian of Dalum, a Benedictine convent situated near Odense, between 1495 and 1500, probably appointed by the bishop.[2] At one point after that year, he was removed from the office by King John (*Hans*) who appointed another guardian.[3] At this time, we also find a guardian by royal appointment. Sometime between 1497 and 1513 the king appointed Søren Norby guardian of the Benedictine convent Börringe in Scania[4] and he retained the office until 1518. Apparently, this was not a singular case. After the death of King John, the Council of the Realm complained that he had appointed secular guardians of convents against the liberties of the Church and the bishops.[5]

In his coronation charter of 1513, King Christian II, John's son and successor, had to promise not to violate the rights of the chapters and monastic institutions by imposing guardians against their will.[6] In spite of this promise, we find several secular guardians of convents, including one noblewoman, Mette Ivarsdatter Dyre, who in 1515 became guardian of the St Agnes convent in Roskilde, a convent for Dominican nuns. In this position, she succeeded a nobleman, Mads Eriksen Bølle, who had been appointed to the position in 1508 by the bishop of Roskilde and who had earlier served as an episcopal fief holder and apparently done a good job. His task had been to bring order into the administration of the convent and especially to increase its income, to which end he ordered a cadaster and an account be created which is still extant.[7]

The appointment of Mette Dyre was political, and not a devaluation of Mads Bølle's administration. Mette Dyre was a Danish noblewoman who through three successive marriages became heavily involved in the turbulent politics of the final decades of the Kalmar Union. Her first two husbands

---

2   *Repertorium. Ser. secunda*, nr. 7854 (12 March 1495), 8409 (17 June 1497), 8746 (2 February 1499), 8879 (31 August 1499), 9169 (1 October 1500), 13070 (undated).
3   Erslev 1879, p. 152.
4   *Repertorium. Ser. secunda*, nr. 12613. (undated).
5   Christensen (1903/1974), p. 278.
6   *Den danske Rigslovgivning 1513-1523*, p. 23 § 5.
7   *Roskilde Sankt Agnete klosters jordebøger*, pp. 32-36: klosteradministrationen.

were Norwegian noblemen, who were both members of the Norwegian Council of the Realm. Her second husband was an opponent of King John and joined forces with the Swedish opposition who wanted a Swedish king as head of the Kalmar Union. In 1502, Mette's husband was murdered in Oslo during negotiations with King John's representative and Mette fled to Sweden, where she joined the opposition party, led by Svante Nilsson (Sture) who in 1504 became regent of Sweden. He and Mette married shortly after. Svante died in 1511. His son from a previous marriage, Sten Sture (the Younger), was appointed regent of Sweden by the Swedish council of the Realm in 1512 after lobbying ruthlessly. During this process, Sten Sture also claimed all the lands that Mette had received as a dower from Svante and in 1515 forced her to accept a cash payment in return for handing over the deeds to the properties. Mette returned to Denmark, ostensibly to collect the documents. Her old adversary, King John, had died in February 1513, and Mette made peace with his successor, King Christian II. Mette's opposition to Sten Sture suited King Christian's plans for installing himself as head of the Kalmar Union. He gave Mette the office as secular guardian of the wealthy convent.[8] He apparently had the approval of the bishop of Roskilde, Lave Urne, who was a supporter of the king and who spent a great deal of the second decade of the sixteenth century travelling as his representative.

The appointment of Mette Dyre as secular guardian of the convent may reveal that monastic institutions were increasingly considered part of the royal economy to be used as payment for services to the king, as a favour or as surety for loans just as the regular crown fiefs. Mette's economic experience no doubt helped her keep the guardianship of the convent for another ten years, well into the reign of King Frederik I. As wife of Svante Nilsson (Sture), she had in fact been in charge of the income from the Finnish crown fiefs.[9]

Shortly before Mette Dyre was given the guardianship of a convent, a doctor Bartram was awarded an annual wage in cash and Dutch cloth (apparently from the royal coffers and supplies) "until such time that my Lord gives him charters so that he can receive the sum and the cloth from one of his Lord's towns".[10] However, three years later (in 1517), the doctor and his wife were awarded the Cistercian convent of Slangerup as a crown fief for life in return for his services to the king.[11] They may have kept it until 1523,

---

8   Olesen (2000-01); Gillingstam; Mette Dyre is not listed in Erslev 1879.
9   Utterström (1968), p. 229 (letter of 19 September 1507).
10   "indtiil swo lenge myn herre bebreffuer oc forwiiser hannom swodanne pendinge oc klede vdi noger hans nades kiøbstedher vdi syn liiffs thiidt" (*Nye samlinger*, vol. 2-1, p. 113-114)
11   *Nye samlinger*, vol. 2-1, p.153-54

when another holder, a nobleman, is mentioned. After his death in 1529, the sculptor and architect Martin Bussert and his wife received the convent as crown fief, which they kept until 1553 when she, as the longest living of the spouses, died. In this case, both King Christian and his successor considered the convent property and a means to pay for services to the Crown.

It is no accident that the first institutions with secular guardians appointed by the king were convents. The role of the guardian was to take care of the property belonging to the institution with everything involved: collecting taxes, foodstuff and livestock, trading the surplus, going to courts to defend property and have acquisition of property legally confirmed. This role could easily be fulfilled by the abbot or prior of a monastery, whereas the abbess of a convent was restricted by the demands of enclosure, which made it more difficult for her to participate in the daily business outside the convent. Looking at the chronological list of monastic institutions, for whom the king appointed secular guardians before 1532, we do not find a monastery before 1527, when Kristoffer Huitfeldt obtained the guardianship of the Dominican Our Lady monastery in Ribe, and two years later Mogens Krabbe became the guardian of the Premonstratensian monastery of Tommerup (*Tommarp*) in Scania. Mogens Krabbe is listed as master (*magister*) and secretary, so perhaps he was a member of the clergy. The next two secular guardians of monasteries, Hans Emmiksen (Essenbæk) and Anders Bille (Dalby) were supposedly elected by the monks to be their guardians, which may or may not be true but at least indicates a formal recognition of the monks' rights. We find no notice that the same was true for the convents, for whom a guardian was appointed.

TABLE I: Secular guardians of monasteries and convents before 1533

			Secular guardians of monasteries and convents before 1533			
	Name	Family name	Convent/ Monastery	From	To	Type
1	Anders Ebbesen	Ulfeldt	Dalum	1495	1500-	convent
2	Mads Eriksen	Bølle	Roskilde St Agnes	1507	1515	convent
3	Severin	Arildsen	Gavnø	1515	1519	convent
4	Mette Ivers-datter	Dyre	Roskilde St Agnes	1515	1527	convent
5	Dr. Bartram		Slangerup	1517	1523?	convent
6	Hans	Mikkelsen	Börringe	1518	1523	convent
7	Niels	Lykke	Gavnø	1519	1523	convent

8	Axel	Brahe	Börringe	1523	1551	convent
9	Mogens	Gøye	Gavnø	1523	1544	convent
10	Otto	Brockenhus	Slangerup	1523	1529	convent
11	Anders Ebbesen	Galt	Roskilde St Agnes	1527	1529	convent
12	Erik	Krabbe	Aalborg Our Lady	1527	1530	convent
13	Kristoffer	Huitfeldt	Ribe Our Lady	1527	1537	monastery
14	Niels	Friis	Sebber	1528	1537	convent
15	Mogens	Krabbe	Tommarp	1529	1532	monastery
16	Pernille	Gøye	Roskilde St Agnes	1529	1539	convent
17	Martin	Bussert	Slangerup	1529	1550	convent
18	Johan	Friis	Dalum	1529	1570	convent
19	Hans	Emmiksen	Essenbæk	1529	153?	monastery
20	Klaus	Gjordsen	Ring	1529	1532	convent
21	Anders	Bille	Dalby	1530	1535	monastery
22	Anne	Rud	Roskilde Our Lady	1530	1533	convent
23	Esge	Bille	Roskilde Our Lady	1530	1552	convent
24	Hans	Pogwisch	Grinderslev	1531	1542	monastery
25	Anders	Gyldenstierne	Hundslund	1531	1537	monastery
26	Kristiern	Skram	Gudum	1531	??	convent
27	Claus	Sested	Ribe St John's	1531	1547	monastery
28	Jørgen	Koch	Tommerup	1532	1533	monastery
29	Mogens	Gøye	Ring	1532	1544	convent
30	Ove	Bille	Voer	1532	1536	monastery
31	Jesper	Daa	Aalborg Our Lady	1532	??	convent

Uncertain beginning date						
1	Niels	Hak	Börringe	15??	15??	convent
2	Søren	Norby	Börringe	15??	1518	convent
3	Henrik	Krummedige	Roskilde Our Lady	15??	1530	convent
4	Hans	Rostrup	Alling	15??	1535	monastery
5	Tønne Tønnesen	Viffert	Roskilde St Clare	152?	1536	convent
6	Sofie	Gøye	Tvilum	??	1537	monastery
7	Mogens	Kaas	Stubber	15??	1538	convent

Secular guardians of monasteries and convents appointed by the king (and in a few cases the bishop)

Returning to the St Agnes convent, we find that Mette was succeeded by other nobles, all appointed by the king. The first was Anders Ebbesen Galt, who held it as crown fief for two years (1527-29); then his widow Pernille Gøye was the crown fief holder from 1529 to 1539, when her second husband, Børge Trolle, took over the convent and its lands as a royal crown fief which he held for thirty-two years until his death in 1571. By that time, the convent had ceased to exist as such and the two remaining nuns had been pensioned off. After 1571, the property was divided, some farms and lands were sold, others added to the crown fiefs of Copenhagen Castle, Roskildegaard and Kalundborg Castle.

The story of the transition of St Agnes' convent from a monastic institution to crown fief appears to be typical of several convents and monasteries. In principle, this process should have begun in 1536 when church lands became crown property. In practice, we see a more fluid transition beginning with King John appointing secular guardians and continuing under his successors, Christian II and Frederik I. This development also implies that already before the Reformation the king and the nobility had come to look at the property of the monasteries and especially the convents in a very secular manner. I am not implying that this never occurred during the Middle Ages. What I would like to suggest is that monastic property was increasingly considered part of the system of crown fief administration. TABLE I reveals an accelerating number of secular guardians, first of convents, then also of monasteries in the 1520s and early 1530s but not a steady acceleration. During the reign of Christian II, five convents received guardians during the years 1515-18. After Christian was deposed in early 1523, his uncle, Frederik I, became king. On June 22, 1523, Mogens Gøye was appointed guardian for life of Gavnø convent, in a charter given "in our camp outside of Copenhagen" that is before the city had surrendered to the king.[12] In August 1523, Otto Brockenhuus, was appointed guardian of "the convent of his Majesty and the Crown, Slangerup, for life".[13] Brockenhuus' title is not given but this sounds like appointment to a crown fief. In 1524, on August 31, Axel Brahe, received a "fief holding charter" (*forleningsbrev*) for Börringe convent, according to the register,[14] treating this position as equivalent to a secular crown fief holder. In 1527, the king granted three noblemen charters to two convents and one

---

12 *Kong Frederiks den Førstes danske registranter*, s. 9: 'Kr. Magenns Gøye fik livsbrev på Gabnøe Kloster …Vor Feltlejr for Køpnehaffn'
13 *Kong Frederiks den Førstes danske registranter*, s. 16: 'Otte Braachenhws fik livsbrev paa Kgl. Majestæts og Kronens Kloster Slangerup'
14 *Kong Frederiks den Førstes danske registranter*, s. 51: 'Hr Axell Brae fik Forleningsbrev paa Byrdinge Kloster'

monastery, while in 1528, the king confirmed that a cantor, Niels Friis, received Sebber convent as episcopal fief holding from the bishop of Viborg.[15]

What we can see from these examples is that, at least from 1523, the king and the Council of the Realm controlled the office of secular guardian of convents and from 1527 also of monasteries, making the transition of monastic institutions from church lands to crown lands a steady development rather than an abrupt event beginning in 1536. This rather smooth transition may in part be explained by developments within the nobility and the social profiles of the leaders of the Danish Church during the late Middle Ages. The Danish nobility split into a smaller group of magnate families who dominated the Council of the Realm, controlling the distribution of crown fiefs, and a larger group of families, whose men were often clients of a major secular or ecclesiastical lord. This split continued throughout the sixteenth century. Men from the magnate families also held almost all of the episcopal seats during the decades prior to the Reformation, so the men who controlled crown as well as episcopal fiefs came from the same families.

Christian III began systematically to issue charters of crown fief holdings to monastic institutions in 1535, before he was victorious in the civil war of 1533-36 and before the official introduction of the Lutheran Church, but some of those holders were the current abbot, prior or abbess.

TABLE II: *Crown fief holders of monastic institutions, 1535-36*

	Name	Family name	Monastery/Convent	From	To
1	Jens	Brahe	Bäckaskog	1535	1535
2	(Abbot) Peder		Bäckaskog	1535	1537
3	(Dean) Henrik	Jensen	Dalby	1535	1540
4	Jep Tordsen	Falk	Helne Kirke (All Saints')	1535	1535
5	(Abbot) Kristian		Helne Kirke (All Saints')	1535	1558
6	Arvid Jensen	Ulfstand	Herrevad	1535	1535
7	(The Abbot)		Herrevad	1535	1565
8	Birger (Børge)	Ulfstand	Tommarp	1535	1540
9	Kristoffer	Huitfeldt	Öved	1535	1536
10	Tage Ottesen	Thott	Aas	1535	1562
11	Johan	Høcken	Alling	1535	1562

---

15 *Kong Frederik den Førstes danske Registranter*, s. 152: 'Mester Niels Friis, Cantor i Viborg, fik Stadfæstelse på et brev af hr. Iyrgenn Friis, Biskop i Viborg, hvorved denne under og tilsiger Mester Niels Sybergh Kloster at nyde i hans livstid i fri forlening af Bisperne i Viborg.'

12	(The Abbots)		Vitskøl	1535	1563
13	Jep Tordsen	Falk	Bosjö	1536	1536
14	Verner	Parsberg	Öved	1536	1537
15	The Prior		Antvorskov	1536	1580
16	(The Abbots)		Esrum	1536	1560
17	(The Abbots)		Ringsted	1536	1592
18	Kirstine (Christense)	Ulfstand	Roskilde St Clare	1536	1544
19	(The Abbots)		Sorø	1536	1586
20	(The Abbot)		Haldsted	1536	1538
21	The Abbesses		Maribo	1536	1621
22	Erik	Krummedige	Odense St John's	1536	1541
23	(The Abbots)		Øm	1536	1560
24	(The Abbot)		Voer	1536	1538
25	The Prior		Børglum	1536	1540
26	The Prior		Dueholm	1536	1538

Charters issued by Christian III to crown fief holders 1535-36 (no charters issued/extant 1533-34)

In 1536, the country officially became Lutheran and in 1539 a church ordinance was issued which also determined the fate of the monastic institutions and their members. Those monks and nuns who wanted to leave their convent or monastery were free to do so, but if they stayed, they had to remain obedient to the abbot or abbess. They also had to cease wearing the outward signs of Catholic monks and nuns, such as tonsure and scapular, and, of course, adhere to the new tenets.[16]

The educational activities of the monastic institutions also came to an end – but again, gradually. The function of monasteries as educational centres for noble boys ceased shortly after the Reformation, whereas the convents continued for a longer period,[17] ostensibly with teachers and pupils of the Lutheran faith. However, we find glimpses of Catholicism remaining. In a Latin funeral oration held for Else Laxmand (1543-75), we are told that she was educated at Bosjö convent (in Scania) but – the author emphasizes – for the sake of learning, not for acquiring a taste for convent life. He also adds that Else Laxmand as an adult referred to the nuns as gluttonous, lecherous,

---

16   *Kirkeordinansen 1537/39*, p. 236-238
17   Andersen (1971), p. 28.

superstitious and popish, which information, of course, also serves to emphasize that Else was a good Protestant.[18] Indirectly, the information also reveals that, in the 1540s and early 1550s at least, the nuns of Bosjö convent had not completely accepted Lutheran tenets. The royal crown fief holder from 1537 to 1552 was Torben Bille, who until 1536 had been archbishop-elect of Lund. Maribo convent also continued as an institution for unmarried noble women, but does not appear to have continued its educational function. Few children entered the convent to receive education, maybe because frequent internal strife between the abbesses and the sisters and among the sisters throughout the later sixteenth century gave Maribo a bad reputation.[19] In one case, that of Karine Knudsdatter Gyldenstierne (1542-96), we find a direct connection between convent education and crown fief holding. In her funeral sermon, we are told that she was placed in school in Ø convent which her parents held as a crown fief. There, a nun taught her to read, write, sew and do embroidery.[20]

Why could this transfer of control of property and the power emanating from this control happen already before the civil war and the Reformation? One simple answer is that no real change in the circle of powerful people in fact occurred. While the bishops and the archbishop were no longer members of the Council of the Realm after 1536, their secular relatives remained – and some of the bishops appear after the Reformation as secular crown fief holders. Torben Bille (d. 1552), the previous archbishop-elect of Lund, mentioned above, is one example. Another is Knud Henriksen Gyldenstierne (c. 1490-1560). He received a master's degree and aimed for an ecclesiastical career, but worked first as a secretary in the chancellery of Christian II. In 1520, he received Ring convent as an episcopal fief holding and the same year was appointed dean at Viborg Cathedral. In 1529, he was appointed bishop of Odense and thus became a member of the Council of the Realm. As bishop, he supported the evangelical preachers. In 1531-32, he appointed Jørgen Sadolin, one of the leading Danish reformers, as co-bishop in charge of teaching the Augsburg Confession to parish priests. In 1536, Knud Gyldenstierne lost his crown fiefs and was briefly jailed together with the other bishops. After his release, he married and settled down as a major landowner and a crown fief holder. From 1542-59, he held Ø convent, partly as surety for a loan to the Crown, in 1556 he received another crown fief as surety for a loan and in 1557 Vestervig monastery as crown fief on account. Knud Gyldenstierne died in

---

18 Machabæus (1577), A 4 recto-verso.
19 Andersen (1971) p. 30.
20 Nilssøn (1596) p. 91.

1568, and his wife took over as crown fief holder of Vestervig monastery until she died in 1578, and then their son held it for 3 years. So both as a member of the clergy before the Reformation and as a secular lord after the Reformation, Knud Gyldenstierne held crown fiefs, including monastic institutions.

TABLE III: Number of charters issued 1500-1596
Charters issued to crown fief holders during the sixteenth century by decade

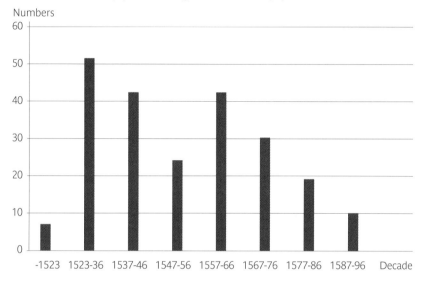

As can be seen from TABLE III, the number of charters issued concerning monastic institutions as crown fiefs has three peaks. The first one occurs during the 13 years that cover the reign of Frederik I (1523-33) and the civil war (1533-36). 51 charters are known, of which 25 were issued between 1523 and 1532, and 26 during the brief period 1535-36. The second peak occurs during the first decade after the Reformation (42 charters registered 1537-46) and the third peak occurs during the third decade after the reformation (also 42 charters 1557-66). The last peak can be explained by two factors: the death of male crown fief holders during the Nordic Seven Years War (1563-70) and the death from more natural causes or retirement by the first generation of post-Reformation crown fief holders.

Subsequently, the number of appointments to crown fiefs created from former monastic institutions drops rather dramatically during the last three decades of the sixteenth century (30, 19, 10). This change is closely connected to the development within the crown fief system. During the second half of the sixteenth century, the king sought to gain greater control of the crown fief administration by reducing the number of crown fiefs and by turning them into ones held by account. He did so together with the magnates within the nobility, in particular those belonging to families represented in the Council of the Realm. They were the ones to get the major crown fiefs into which the smaller were merged, while the middle and lower nobility, who had benefitted from the many small crown and (before 1536) episcopal fiefs, lost this source of income.

With two exceptions, no monastic institution became a major crown fief, probably because they were not strategically located for military and administrative purposes, so no fortification or castle grew out of a former monastic site, or because they did not have enough property to become a major crown fief. The two exceptions were Sorø Abbey (Cistercians) and the monastery of Antvorskov (Order of St John). Sorø continued until 1586 under abbots, who received charters of crown fief holdings and were thus incorporated into the crown fief system. In 1586, Sorø became a school for noble and non-noble boys. The monastery of Antvorskov continued with priors as crown fief holders until 1580 when an outside crown fief holder took over. One of his duties was to provide the prior and the remaining three monks as well as twelve pupils (*disciple*) with food, clothing and housing. In 1586, Antvorskov was proclaimed a castle and received some of the property belonging to Sorø Abbey. King Frederik II died here in 1588.

The other monastic institutions experienced a steady whittling away of their properties: some properties were added to the holdings of major crown fiefs; others were pawned to wealthy noblemen and women, while still other properties were sold, primarily to noblemen and women. With the transfer or sale of property followed the buildings as well as farms and the taxes and services imposed on the peasants living on the farms.

A few cases will illustrate this: Esrum monastery, the former prominent Cistercian abbey, remained under the abbots until 1560. Then the last monks were transferred to Sorø Abbey and Esrum's buildings and property became a farm (*ladegård*) under the newly erected Frederiksborg Castle, whose bricks partly came from the torn-down buildings of the monastery. Before that, however, several farms had been pawned to nobles and merchants in return for cash. The remaining property of St Agnes' convent in Roskilde was, as mentioned, divided between two major crown fiefs, Roskildegaard and Kalundborg in 1571. In 1553, fifty-four of the peasants of Slangerup convent were told henceforth to pay taxes and give services to Copenhagen Castle. Halsted monastery on Lolland ceased as a crown fief in 1578 and became part of Ravnsborg, a major crown fief. Jacob Hardenberg held Holme monastery (now Brahetrolleborg) on Fyn as a crown fief until 1542, when he bought it. In 1551, his widow sold it back to the Crown, not entirely of her own free will,[21] and it remained a crown fief until 1558, when the widowed Queen Dorothea took over and used it as surety for a loan. In 1566, Henrik Rantzau held it for two years and then purchased it – and it has remained in private hands since then. St John's priory in Horsens was a crown fief until 1575, when the widow of the last holder, Karen Gyldenstierne, was appointed crown fief holder, succeeding her husband, Holger Rosenkrantz. Shortly after, she was allowed to purchase it, which she did. Prior to that final deed, twelve farms, belonging to the monastery, had been pawned between 1551 and 1558. The final example is Tvis monastery, also a Cistercian abbey, in the diocese of Ribe, which the abbot kept for a year until 1537. Then the former bishop of Ribe, Olaf Munk, received it for life as crown fief and purchased it in 1547.

The large majority of crown fief holders were noble, which is true also for those holding former monastic institutions. During the sixteenth century, 210 charters granting a crown fief of a monastic institution were issued to noblemen and women, while eight were issued to non-noble persons. Not included in these numbers are the charters issued to (often unnamed) abbots, abbesses, priors and deans, where it is impossible to determine whether the person in question was noble or not.

Of the eight non-nobles mentioned, five were given monastic institutions before 1536, but only two kept theirs after that year. The sculptor and architect, Martin Bussert, and his wife, Bodil, received Slangerup convent as crown fief for life in 1529, as mentioned above, and he kept it until he died in 1550 while Bodil held it until her death in 1553. Bodil's father, Hans Mikkelsen, was one of the staunch supporters of Christian II and he had received Börringe convent in 1518 but lost it in 1523. Another supporter of Christian II was the mayor of Malmö, Jørgen Kock, who received Tommarp monastery in 1532-33, during the civil war. After the Reformation, two other non-nobles are mentioned as holding former monastic institutions as crown fief: Kristoffer Hansen had Holme monastery 1539-41 and Kristoffer Trundsen had Æbelholt monastery from 1544 to 1560 when the monastery and its property became a farm under Frederiksborg Castle.

---

21   Bisgaard (2006), pp. 34-36.

Looking at the noble persons who became crown fief holders of monastic institutions and especially their family backgrounds, we find that the 210 crown fiefs were held by 171 individuals coming from 83 families. The distribution, however, is not even, as TABLE IV shows. More than half of the families (=51 %) held only one crown fief; and if we add those with two or three fiefs each, we have already covered sixty-four families (=78 %) who together held less than half of the monastic crown fiefs (45 %). In contrast, eighteen families (=22%), each holding between four and fourteen crown fiefs, occupied more than half (55 %) of the monastic crown fiefs. The top eight families, who make up 9.6 % of the families, occupied one-third of the crown fiefs (33.8 %)

TABLE IV: Number of noble families with crown fief holdings

			% of all families	total	% of all holdings
1 holding	43	families	51,8%	43	20.5%
2 holdings	14	families	16.9%	28	13.3%
3 holdings	8	families	9.6%	24	11.4%
4 holdings	6	families	7.2%	24	11.4%
5 holdings	4	families	4.8%	20	9.5%
6 holdings	1	family	1.2%	6	2.9%
7 holdings	3	families	3.6%	21	10.0%
8 holdings	1	family	1.2%	8	3.8%
10 holdings	1	family	1.2%	10	4.8%
12 holdings	1	family	1.2%	12	5.7%
14 holdings	1	family	1.2%	14	6.7%
	83		100%	210	100,0%

The names of the most prominent families will be well known to Danish historians of the period.

TABEL V: Names of families holding four or more crown fiefs

	Families	# of fiefs
1	Gyldenstierne	14
2	Bille	12
3	Ulfstand	10
4	Friis	8
5	Gøye	7

6	Lykke	7
7	Oxe	7
8	Brahe	6
9	Huitfeldt	5
10	Kaas	5
11	Sehested	5
12	Ulfeldt	5
13	Krabbe	4
14	Munk	4
15	Rantzau	4
16	Rud	4
17	Skeel	4
18	Sparre	4

Members of these families sat on the Council of Realm, with one exception: Sparre, and held both major and minor crown fiefs. I do not yet have exact numbers for families and individuals holding major and minor crown fiefs, but in surveying the list of all crown fiefs during the sixteenth century, I find that these names dominate the pages. So, like the major and minor crown fiefs, the monastic institutions as crown fiefs remained a benefit almost exclusively for the high nobility.

Turning to the question raised in the title: Were monastic institutions especially for women? Several women have been mentioned in the above discussion and a cursory glance at the lists of crown fief holders would seem to indicate this situation. If, however, we count the names listed for all crown fiefs, we find – as TABLE VI shows – that the share of female crown fief holders is almost the same for minor crown fiefs as for monastic institutions.

TABLE VI: Percentage of female crown fief holders c. 1500-1600

	Men	Women	Total	Women as % of total
Major crown fiefs	746	89	835	11%
Minor crown fiefs	779	164	943	17%
Monastic institutions	182	35	217	16%

The share is almost double that for major fiefs, so noble women seem to have gained relatively more by monastic institutions becoming minor crown fiefs, as these were more likely to be given to women from the magnate families. Most of the female crown fief holders were widows who took over the crown fief after their husbands had died. Some widows only kept the crown fief until the accounts had been approved by the chancellor, others held it for a year and still others for several years, in one case for thirty-nine years.[22] We also find women receiving crown fiefs in their own right, either as surety for loans or in return for favours paid the king. One may argue that the abbesses lost out at the Reformation, when it came to controlling property, while their secular sisters gained. Whether it was an even loss or gain remains to be seen.

Conclusion

Incorporating the properties of monastic institutions into the crown fief system after the Reformation may well be described as "business as usual". It was a process that began before 1536 and allowed for monasteries and convents to be considered – not only as spiritual places – but also as crown property, which the king could use as surety for loans, to raise cash and to distribute favours under the watchful eyes of the Council of the Realm and the chancellor. It was desirable for a nobleman or woman to get a crown fief made up of former monastic property, not because of its history, but because of the economic and social benefits this brought the crown fief holder.

One example of this development is found in a letter of April 1530 from Anne Rud to her daughter, Sofie Krummedige, in which Anne describes the death of her husband and Sofie's father, Henrik Krummedige, in March of that year. She then relates how she is lining up support so she can keep the crown fiefs that she and her husband had received for life. Those included the (Cistercian) Convent of Our Lady in Roskilde but she does not specify the property. Later in the letter, she discusses the possibilities that she sees for Sofie and her husband, Eske Bille, for obtaining further crown fiefs (Eske Bille had Bergen Castle in Norway at the time). Anne informs them that no crown fiefs seem to be available except perhaps monasteries, but even they seem to have been occupied, as she has heard that Anders Bille had just been given Dalby monastery and Mogens Krabbe Tommarp monastery.[23]

Looking at this process of incorporation, we may well ask: Does it tell us anything about the Reformation in Denmark? Does it not confirm the view-

---

22 Numbers calculated from Erslev (1879).

23 "… jnghñ fforlæningh leff(ss?)ett vden herreklostre ock tigge klosthre dogh hør jegh at dij er alle fforlenth dogh er her jngen indførdt vthñ dalby kloster thz haffu her anders bille ock Tomerup klosther thz haffuer vist morthñ Krabbe". MS Copenhagen, Rigsarkivet. Privatarkiver: Krummedige, Henrik og hustru Anne Jørgensdatter Rud. Anne Rud brev April 1530. Transcribed by Birgitte Jørkov

point of older historians that Danish nobles – with few exceptions – were a bunch of land-grabbing, power-hungry people to whom religion did not matter and who therefore could turn Protestant when they saw an economic profit? This explanation is, of course, too simple. We should take into consideration that many more members of the nobility than has traditionally been believed might have been positive towards Lutheran ideas. They would have had ample opportunity to hear or even read about criticism of the Church and to become acquainted with reform activities within the Church. One should also consider the many reform movements of the fifteenth century, which had involved both royalty and nobility. Consequently, many more noblemen and women than the few usually mentioned (Mogens Gøye and Knud Gyldenstierne) would have been ready for the message of the evangelical preachers, which included criticism of monastic life.[24] In addition, as I have demonstrated, the process in fact began before the Reformation with the installation of secular guardians of convent and monasteries by the king.

This development also provides an answer to a pertinent question: Why did the families of the Catholic bishops so completely accept that some of their male relatives were deposed as bishops, excluded from the Council of the Realm and jailed? Looking at the persons who held crown fiefs consisting of monastic property after the Reformation, it is obvious that these families retained control over crown property. They no longer did so through those male relatives who were bishops and archbishops, but through those male and female relatives who knew how to take advantage of the opportunities that arose to become part of the crown fief administration. Thereby, they assured that control of this administration and of crown lands remained within the magnate group. Those who in the end had to pay for this development were members of the less powerful and often economically insecure families from the lower nobility who lost their former opportunities for gaining an income by holding one or more of the smaller crown or episcopal fiefs.

24 I have argued this in more detail in Jacobsen (2008)

Manuscript source

MS Copenhagen, Rigsarkivet, Privatarkiver: Krummedige, Henrik og hustru Anne Jørgensdatter Rud, *Anne Rud brev April 1530*.

Bibliography

Andersen, Birte, *Adelig opfostring. Adelsbørns opdragelse i Danmark 1536-1660* (Copenhagen, 1971).

Bisgaard, Lars, 'Adelige kvinder og livet på Arreskov i renæssancen', *Fynske Årbøger* (2006), pp. 31-46.

Christensen, Harry, *Len og magt i Danmark 1439-1481: De danske slotslens besiddelsesforhold analyseret til belysning af magtrelationerne mellem kongemagt og adel. Med særlig fokus på opgøret i slutningen af 1460'erne* (Aarhus, 1983).

Christensen, William, *Dansk Statsforvaltning i det 15. Aarhundrede* (Copenhagen, 1903; reprint 1974).

Den danske rigslovgivning 1513-1523, ed. Aage Andersen (Copenhagen, 1991).

Erslev, Kr. *Danmarks Len og Lensmænd i det sextende Aarhundrede (1515-1596)* (Copenhagen, 1879).

Erslev, Kr. *Konge og Lensmand i det sextende Aarhundrede* (Copenhagen 1879; reprint 1970).

Gillingstam, Hans, 'Mette Iversdotter', in *Svenskt biografiskt lexikon*, vol. 25 (1985-87), p. 434; online: http://sok.riksarkivet.se/SBL/Presentation.aspx?id=9294 (accessed May 11 2015).

Jacobsen, Grethe, "Med Gud befalendes' – det guddommelige i adelens breve fra reformationstiden', in *Kirkehistorier: Festskrift til Martin Schwarz Lausten i anledning af 70 års fødselsdagen den 6. juli 2008*, eds. Carsten Selch Jensen and Lauge O. Nielsen (Copenhagen, 2008), pp. 175-188.

Kirkeordinansen 1537/39, ed. Martin Schwarz Lausten (Copenhagen, 1989).

Kong Frederik den Førstes danske Registranter, ed. Kr. Erslev and W. (Copenhagen, 1879).

Machabæus (Mac Alpine), Christian, *Epistolae dvae de Vita et obitv nobilis matrone dominæ Elisæ magnifici d: Hilarii Grvbbe de Lystrop, Regni Danici Cancellarii etc.: Coniugis charissimæ. Parentationis et officii cavsa scriptæ Anno Domini M.D. LXXVII* (Copenhagen, 1577).

Nilssøn, Jens, *En Predicken / som i Erlige Velbyrdige Fru Karine Gyldenstierns Liigs Begraffuelse blef forhandlit i Oslo Domkircke i Norge / Quasimodo geniti, Søndag / som vaar den 18. Aprilis, Aar etc. M.D.XCVI* (Copenhagen, 1596).

Nye samlinger til den danske Historie, vol. 2, ed. P. F. Suhm (Copenhagen, 1793).

Olesen, Jens E., 'Dyre, Mette Iversdatter', *Dansk Kvindebiografisk Leksikon*, vol. 1 (Copenhagen 2000-2001), p. 412.

Repertorium diplomaticum regni Danici mediaevalis. Series secunda, ed. William Christensen (Copenhagen, 1928-1939).

Roskilde Sankt Agnete klosters jordebøger og regnskaber 1508-1515, ed. Thelma Jexlev (Copenhagen, 2001).

Utterström, Gudrun, *Fem skrivare. Metta Ivarsdotters brev till Svante Nilsson. Studier i senmedeltida svenskt brevspråk* (Stockholm, 1968).

The Dominicans and the Reformation in Northern Europe

Johnny Grandjean Gøgsig Jakobsen

When Fr Hans Nielsen[1] was elected prior provincial for the thirty-two con-vents of the Dominican province of Dacia at a provincial chapter held in Næstved in the late summer of 1519 – within a month exactly 300 years after the first admission of Scandinavian friars into the order – he most probably had no expectation whatsoever that he was to become the last of his kind. Eighteen years later, Roman Catholicism had been officially replaced by Lu-theran Evangelism in all of Scandinavia, and the Dominican Order was no longer allowed to operate in the province. An interesting question, at least for present-day scholarship, is whether he may have had any premonition of what was coming? Was the Lutheran Reformation and the abrupt termination of mendicant monasticism in most parts of Northern Europe a more-or-less given end-point for a development begun long before? This view has certain-ly dominated Protestant history-writing in Scandinavia since the nineteenth century and to some extent long into the twentieth, describing late medieval monasticism as one long disciplinary decline, leading to growing fatigue in the rest of society with the greedy, morally depraved and hypocritical monks and friars. More recent scholarship has, however, questioned this view and found no signs of monastic decline or unpopularity in the early sixteenth century, at least until Evangelical preachers launched a campaign against the papal church in general and the mendicant friars in particular. Several stud-

---

1   *Fr* is in this article used as abbreviated honorific for the Latin title *Frater*, the standard prefix used in medieval texts for men of the regular clergy, here always used on mendicant clergy, corresponding to *Friar* in English and *broder* in Danish. *Dr* is used in its common meaning *Doctor*, although in this article always referring to doctors of theology.

ies from around Northern Europe seem to show continuing mendicant popularity. In Yorkshire, for instance, no discernible evidence can be found for any decline in testators' endowments to mendicant orders, even in the last years before the Reformation. For the city of York itself, the proportion of citizens making bequests to the four York convents actually rose, to over 40%, during the period 1531-38, the last years that such gifts were legally possible.[2] In Elbląg, where the citizens turned Protestant in 1525 and thus prohibited the Dominican friars from any further preaching, there were no indications of criticism when the priory church burned down twenty-one years earlier. At that time, monetary donations poured in from all social layers of the town and adjacent villages with such an abundance that a new church was consecrated in 1514 – in which the friars held two annual masses in honour of their many local benefactors.[3] Likewise, hardly any wills preserved from pre-Reformation Lund fail to include endowments for the local mendicant convents.[4]

In spite of having studied Dominican history in medieval Scandinavia for more than ten years now, I still have not come to any decisive conclusion to the question of monastic decline, as evidence of both diminishing and continuing popularity can be observed from the sources. The number of known burials of lay persons in the Dominican priories of Dacia is, for instance, remarkably stable within the period 1450-1529, with one to four burials recorded for each decade, and, if anything, numbers grew slightly in the later part of the period with three to four burials per decade in 1500-29 (see Figure 1). Neither does the number of recorded mass foundations with the Dominicans appear to drop before 1520, with its highest peak (of twelve) occuring as late as in 1510-19. For all recorded donations in general, the number actually appears to grow significantly from around 1480 to 1509, falling back to 'pre-1490'-levels in 1510-19 and reaching its lowest point after 1520.

---

2   Dobson (1984), p. 116.
3   Carstenn (1937), pp. 305 and 309.
4   Blomqvist (1944), p. 114.

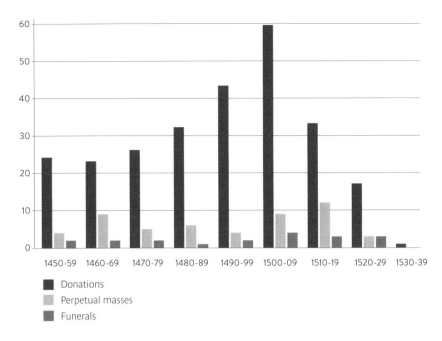

Numbers of donations, foundations of masses and burials of lay persons recorded for the Dominican Order in the province of Dacia as distributed in decades from 1450 to the time of the Lutheran Reformation. Data collected by the author.

On the other hand, if there was no latent dissatisfaction with the mendicants at all in at least some groups within lay society, it is astonishing that so relatively few reformed preachers were able to raise such a profound anger against them almost overnight in what seems to be wide circles of burghers and craftsmen, as evidenced by numerous accounts in one Northern European city after the other. Rather than recording a straightforward decline of the friars' appeal to the rest of society, a closer study of the Dacian sources may suggest a change in the social mix of those among whom the friars found their best friends. Whereas the Dominican Order of the thirteenth century was strongly supported by royalty, the higher ranks of nobility and secular clergy, lower nobility and bourgeoisie gradually grew in importance for the order throughout the fourteenth and fifteenth centuries. But from the late fifteenth century onwards, it could appear as if Dominican support within urban society was predominantly restricted to the leading patriciate families and the secular prelates of the Church. The main financial and political allies of the friars were by then found outside the town walls in the rural countryside: in manors of the higher nobility, vicarages and peasant farms.[5]

One reason for this apparent decline in mendicant popularity among large groups of urban burghers by the beginning of the sixteenth century may be that they were caught in the increasing social tensions between patriciate elite and urban middle classes, where the former by large remained loyal to Catholicism and the friars, while the latter found support in the new belief. In Lübeck, for instance, the Lutheran Reformation coincided with a change of power, when a new burgher committee succeeded in deposing and exiling the old patriciate city council.[6] One should, however, not fall into the pit of writing off the entire Protestant Reformation as a merely social revolution, as several close studies do indeed point to religious motives as responsible for bourgeois attacks on the mendicants.[7] An additional reason may to some extent have been caused by a change in the Dominican Order itself – which was, rather paradoxically, implemented to produce the exact opposite effect. From the 1460s, the Dominican Order went through an internal reform movement, which gradually involved still more convents throughout Northern Europe, especially in the Low Countries and along the Baltic coast cities of Germany and Livonia. The reforms were meant to secure a more disciplined monastic way of life in various aspects, partly to comply with an internal wish from one side of the order, partly to make the convents more popular and acceptable to the rest of society; indeed, had it not been for a distinct pressure from especially princely rulers and city magistrates, only a few Dominican convents had probably ever been reformed.[8] The reforms do seem at first to have increased Dominican popularity in local lay society, but in the long term, they may have had the completely opposite effect. One important issue for the reformers was to abolish the existing social hierarchy within the convents, which since the fourteenth century had increasingly benefitted those friars who had wealthy family relations outside the order with a number of special privileges. Many friars of local, influential families were now being transferred to distant houses to prevent any disciplinary abuse, and the reformed convents henceforth rapidly lost attraction in terms of recruitment and donations from such families. Thus, the internal reform movement of the Dominican Order appears to have led to a growing alienation and indifferent

---

5   These observations are drawn from my still unpublished studies of the social relations of the Dominicans in medieval Scandinavia and Tallinn.
6   Dixon (2002), pp. 104 and 111-112.
7   Foggie (2003), p. 235.
8   Jakobsen (forthcoming).

attitude between convent and local society, as the convent was no longer to the same extent considered to be manned with 'local boys' and certainly no longer enjoyed the same protection from the families that formerly held the best positions in the convent. This development meant that at the arrival of the Lutheran Reformation around 1520, many reformed Dominican convents were living the most disciplined monastic life seen in the order for centuries, but nevertheless they were extremely vulnerable to outside criticism, as they no longer had local interests to support them.[9] Certainly, it is striking to note for the entire Baltic Sea region that especially the Dominican convents that had been reformed within the preceding fifty years were the first to fall when Lutheran preachers raised their voices against them in the 1520s.

However, regardless of how townspeople, peasants, nobility, city magistrates and secular clergy felt about local mendicant convents, the decisive factor for whether they would survive Protestant criticism was eventually in the hands of one person: the princely ruler. As long as the local king, duke or margrave truly supported Catholicism and mendicant monasticism, the convents could endure Protestant turmoil, even if it meant temporary exile. When such princely support was lost, however, final dissolution was just a question of time. Unfortunately for the mendicant orders of Northern Europe, almost all princely rulers of the region eventually converted to Protestantism.[10] Their reasons for doing so seem to have included personal religious devotion as well as political and economic concerns, and probably often a combination of these factors.

Dominican inquisition and attacks against Lutheran heresy

Throughout late medieval Europe, the Dominicans saw themselves as the chief defenders of Catholicism and the true interpretation of God's word as articulated by leading theologians in Rome and Paris, who themselves were often Dominicans. This view was to a large part shared by society in general,

---

9   Springer (1999), pp. 35, 41 and 335; Jakobsen (forthcoming).
10 The first one to shift was the Duke of Prussia (1525), followed by the Duke of Schleswig (1525-26), the King of Sweden (1525-27), the Duke of Pomerania (1531-34), the Margrave of Brandenburg (1535), the King of Denmark (1533-36), the King of England (1536-39) and the Duke of Mecklenburg (1547). Only the Habsburg emperors (who ruled the Netherlands) and the kings of Poland remained Catholic, but while the former lost the Northern Netherlands to Calvinism in the 1570s, the latter had to allow equality between the two Christian beliefs in 1573.

both within the ecclesiastical institutions of the Roman Church and in lay communities.[11] Laypeople and secular clergy alike listened to the sermons of the Dominicans, the bulk of literature on all aspects of theology was written by Dominicans, and most (in)famously in this respect was the leading Dominican role in the inquisition against heresy. Since 1231, leading Dominican friars were officially installed as papal inquisitors all around Europe to counter heretical thoughts and the people expressing them, basically to prevent this 'cancer of the soul' from spreading and endangering the salvation of God's people. This anti-heretical alertness can be detected far outside the nominal inquisitors of the order, and seems to have been deeply anchored in the very core of most Dominican friars' *raison d'être*.[12] The Dominican Friars Preachers, inquisitors and non-inquisitors alike, recurrently challenged all who spoke or wrote in ways they found to be in opposition to orthodox Roman Catholic theology. It did not matter whether their opponents were clerical or lay, or even within their own order. Thus, when Erasmus of Rotterdam from around 1500 launched his humanist criticism against various abuses within the Church, it was a local Dutch Dominican, Father Laurentius, who zealously opposed him.[13]

When the apostate Augustinian, Dr Martin Luther, put up his theses in Wittenberg in 1517, he was, in the eyes of the Dominicans, just another confused heretic. It was therefore only natural for the Order of Preachers to take up the Lutheran challenge, as it had done with all the others. It was, in fact, also a Dominican friar, who in one sense started the Lutheran Reformation: Fr Johann Tetzel, who in 1516 was appointed chief papal commissioner for the sale of indulgences in Germany in favour of the rebuilding of St Peter's Basilica in Rome. It was, indeed, not least the clearly material connection between heavenly salvation and cash payments to the Church, manifested in the legendary sales slogan of Johann Tetzel, *"As soon as the coin in the coffer rings, the soul from Purgatory springs!"*, that provoked Martin Luther in 1517 to nail his 95 theses to the church door in Wittenberg – or, perhaps rather, posted them to the archbishop of Mainz. The archbishop then sent the theses on to Rome, where they were checked for heresy by yet another Dominican, Fr Silvestro Mazzoleni, whose report to the Pope paved the way for the summons of Luther to the Imperial Diet in Augsburg in 1518, where a third Dominican, Cardinal Thomas Vio de Cajetan, acted as inquisitor and chief

---

11 Jakobsen (2013).
12 Ames (2009), pp. 6-8.
13 Brada (1982), p. 39.

theological opponent to Luther. Of course, from the Catholic point of view, all done in vain.

As Luther's ideas started to spread to all layers of society in Northern Germany from the early 1520s, Friars Preachers stood ready to oppose them – led by the Dominican inquisitors. The chief papal inquisitor of Northern Germany at this time was Fr Joachim Rathstein, who had a busy schedule disputing the growing number of reform preachers in his inquisitorial precinct, in which he was assisted by still more of his fellow friars.[14] On what seems to have been their own initiative, lectors, priors, doctors and other experienced preachers of the individual Dominican convents replied whenever Lutheran preachers entered the local scene and introduced their reforming views. Often, the Dominicans were joined by their local Franciscan colleagues in doing so. Also on a national scale, one of the most persistent enemies of Protestantism in Germany was indeed a Franciscan, Fr Nikolaus Ferber (or Herborn), who after being expelled from his convent in Marburg continued fighting for Catholicism from the University of Cologne, and even was invited by the Danish bishops to take part as a kind of 'key note lecturer' for the Catholic side at the Parliament held in Copenhagen in 1530.[15] However, many Franciscan convents around Northern Germany also became known as apostate breeding grounds for reformed preachers, such as the ones in Rostock and Hamburg, and often Dominican preachers faced former, now apostate, Franciscan colleagues in the disputes.[16] This was for instance the case in Wismar, where the new belief was introduced in 1522 by an apostate Franciscan, Heinrich Nevers, who was immediately met by a quite zealous Catholic opposition from the local Dominican Fr Matthäus Vorstermann and the secular parish priest Dr Johann Knudsen.[17] Elsewhere, the two mendicant orders fought side by side, as in Bremen, where the reformer Heinrich von Zutphen, an apostate Augustinian Hermit, was from 1522 countered by the local leading Dominicans and Franciscans jointly. Their opposition, however, only took place from the pulpits of their respective priory churches. When Zutphen in 1523 challenged his opponents to meet him face to face in a dispute before the city council, the friars had to decline, since their orders explicitly prohibited them to engage publicly in theological disputes with

---

14 Ulpts (1995), pp. 367-368.
15 Gallén (1960), p. 200. By the Danish Lutherans, he was mockingly referred to as Nikolaus 'Stagefyr'. It has, however, recently been questioned whether this *Niels Stagefyr* is at all to be identified with Dr Nicolaus Ferber de Herborn OFM. Jørgensen (2017).
16 Hauschildt (1982), p. 188.
17 Kleiminger (1938), pp. 119-121.

their inferiors. As poor as this excuse must have seemed to others, it was actually perfectly in accordance with Dominican regulations, but it was clearly seen by the rest of society as a cowardly retreat, and the city council used it at the time to prohibit the friars from all preaching hereafter.[18] In other cities, the city council at first sided with the bishops and friars against the reformers, such as in Lübeck, where the councillors in 1524 tried to counter the Evangelicals by sponsoring masses in the city churches, enjoining the clergy to pray for the protection of the city against war, bad weather and the threat of heresy. As a more tangible measure, the city also allowed the Dominican inquisitor to expel one of the most intransigent troublemakers from the city.[19] Indeed, in several places, the Lutherans were at first successfully checked by the old well-established instrument of the inquisition. When the Lutheran preacher Johann Widenbrügge, an apostate Premonstratensian canon from Stade, came to Hamburg in 1522 by invitation from local Evangelicals, he was immediately brought to questioning before the chief theologian of the cathedral chapter, Johann Engelin. When the Hamburg Dominicans subsequently set up an inquisitorial trial against him, Widenbrügge decided to leave the city immediately after his arrival.[20] Less fortunate, or foreseeing, was the above-mentioned Heinrich von Zutphen, who left his safehaven of Bremen in late 1524 to comply with an invitation from Evangelical circles in Meldorf, Dithmarschen. At his arrival, the local Dominican prior tried to stop him from preaching, but as he failed to do so, he instead sent for one of the order's tougher agents, Fr Willehad Solzhusen, who came from Hamburg to Meldorf. Heinrich von Zutphen was arrested, brought before an inquisitorial trial, which in the name of the archbishop found him guilty of "preaching against Mary, the mother of God, and Christian faith", for which the sentence was death, after which he was handed over to the local bailiff for immediate execution – all of it implemented within a few days, before any assistance could arrive from Bremen.[21] But even the Dominicans in Hamburg eventually needed fraternal assistance from outside the city, when the Evangelicals in 1523 found themselves a new chief agitator in Stephan Kempe, a former Franciscan friar from the notorious house in Rostock. The local Dominicans formed a united front with the secular clergy, the city council and the archbishop of Bremen against Kempe, declaring him a heretic, but he nevertheless managed to stay clear of the inquisition and continuously gained still

18   Löhr (1930), p. 51*.
19   Hauschildt (1982), p. 204.
20   Hauschildt (1982), p. 187.
21   Freytag (1977), p. 174; Hansen (1999), pp. 578-579.

more supporters for his cause. In 1525, Mayor Salzborch called in a famous Dominican preacher from Lübeck, Fr Augustin van Getelen, to help "save the common people" from the heresy, and eventually the Dominican priory of St John became the last Catholic stronghold in Hamburg, even naming the most conservative Catholic community of the city as '*Johannislüde*', before the cause was lost in Hamburg in 1529.[22] In Rostock, the reform-minded Franciscans and their Lutheran allies were for long countered by a strong alliance between the patriciate families of the city council, the collegiate canons and the Dominicans – the latter especially represented by Inquisitor Joachim Rathstein and the local prior, Dr Cornelius van Sneek. When an outside reformer, Joachim Schlüter, first approached Rostock in 1525-26, he had to flee the city in haste, and when he later returned, an attempt was made on his life at the Franciscan guesthouse.[23]

From Germany, Lutheranism rapidly spread from the mid-1520s to all other regions of Northern Europe. In those countries, where a Dominican-led papal inquisition already existed, such as in Livonia, Poland and the Low Countries, these inquisitors became the obvious centre of Catholic and Dominican counter-measures against the Evangelicals. The bishops of Utrecht regularly assigned local Dominican friars as inquisitors of the diocese, for which especially the convents in Groningen and Zwolle appear to have been rich on possible candidates.[24] Also Dominican friars without a nominal function within the inquisition took it upon themselves to defend the cause. Thus, it was a Dominican, Fr Simon Grunau of the convent in Elbląg, who in a chronicle attacked the Prussian Bishop Georg of Samland for having given an Evangelical sermon at Christmas in the cathedral of Königsberg in 1523.[25] Lutheranism reached Livonia very early, in 1519-20, and here, too, local Dominicans soon became the main defenders of traditional religion.[26] Friars Preachers of the Dominican convent in Tallinn, without any formal appointment as inquisitors, are said to have preached regularly against Evangelical preachers, causing grave annoyance for the latter, by stating that their teaching was 'erroneous, deranged, heretical and condemnable'. This opposition took place both from the church pulpit and in the private homes of burghers, but when the Lutheran preachers came to the priory to debate with the friars and prove their theological points, the Dominicans excused themselves by stating that they were not allowed to

---

22 Hauschildt (1982), pp. 188-189 and 194.
23 Ulpts (1995), pp. 367-368.
24 Löhr (1930), p. 50*; Brada (1982), pp. 39-40; Brada (1983), pp. 44-45 and 56.
25 Zimmermann (1981), p. 261.
26 Hansen (1885), p. 131.

engage in such debates with inferiors. Just as in Bremen, this response only inspired the city council in April 1524 to prohibit the friars from preaching altogether, although here with the additional condition that they were no longer allowed to preach at all in Estonian, a language evidently not mastered by the Lutherans. Preaching in German was still permitted, but henceforth only the pure word of God.[27] One of the main contestants in the dispute appears to have been Fr Thomas Recken, who had studied theology at the Dominican *studium generale* in Paris, and now held daily sermons on the true meaning of the Scriptures in the priory church – until he was arrested when the convent was dissolved by the city council in 1525.[28]

Although no Dominican friar was ever appointed papal inquisitor in the British Isles or in Scandinavia, zealous Friars Preachers here as well soon took the forefront in the Catholic counterattack against the Evangelicals. When Archbishop James Beaton of St Andrews set up inquisition-like tribunals to deal with Lutheran heresy in Scotland, he naturally included Dominican friars to assist him in the trials. The most famous case is probably the one against Patrick Hamilton in 1528, where the Dominican prior in St Andrews, Fr Alexander Campbell, led the accusations that eventually brought Hamilton to the stake. According to a later Protestant writ, Fr Campbell subsequently felt so conscience-stricken for his part in the martyr's unjust death that he himself died from guilt a few days later.[29] Another famous trial of the Scottish Reformation was the one against Adam Wallace in 1550, which took place outside the Dominican church in Glasgow, up against the chancel wall. When Wallace had been convicted for heresy and sentenced to death, he was given two Dominican friars to whom he could confess before his execution, but as he only used the opportunity to engage in a theological discussion with them, they despondently walked away without being able to save his lost soul.[30] Further south, English Dominicans were involved with the so-called "Pilgrimage of Grace", a procession organized in Yorkshire in 1536 against King Henry VIII and his disruption of the Church. A hymn for the movement, which seems to have grown quite popular, was written by Fr John Pickering, prior of the Dominican convent in York and one of the most intransigent opponents of Thomas Cromwell, for which he was executed at Tyburn in London in 1537.[31] A new and nominal inquisition with Dominican

---

27 DOPD 1524 9/4; DOPD 1527 20/4.
28 Löhr (1930), p. 43*.
29 Foggie (2003), pp. 38-39 and 41.
30 Foggie (2003), pp. 123-125.
31 Dobson (1984), p. 120.

participation was, in fact, established against the Protestants in England in the 1550s, but on neither papal nor episcopal initiative. It was an institution organized by Queen Mary Tudor, whose notorious *Marian Persecutions*, led by Archbishop Reginald Pole of Canterbury, were clearly inspired by the Spanish Inquisition (and, indeed, with Spanish-Dominican participation), and appear more as a religious vendetta and modern age-political purge than as an inquisition in the medieval sense.

As already stated, there were no Dominican inquisitors installed in Scandinavia to oppose the Lutheran heresy when it arrived here from the mid-1520s. There had, in fact, been papal inquisitors appointed for Scandinavia throughout the fifteenth century, but all of these were Franciscan, and the last known one died in 1496. It has even been suggested that it may have been the absence of a successor in the inquisitorial office that eased the way for Lutheran reformers in Scandinavia.[32] However, as shown above, the Evangelical faith had already prevailed throughout the North-German Hanseatic cities at the time when it gained a foothold in Scandinavia, in spite of wholehearted resistance in these cities from the full Dominican inquisitorial programme. Moreover, the lack of papal inquisitors did not mean that inquisition as such was not a possible means for the Catholic Church in Scandinavia, since inquisitions against heresy could be instigated by every bishop concerned. It does, in fact, look as if Archbishop Åge Sparre of Lund in 1528 tried to set up an inquisitorial trial against the Lutherans in Malmö, albeit in vain.[33] The problem was that although the inquisition was a measure nominally controlled by the bishops, it was completely toothless and useless if not backed by the secular swords. These were in Scandinavia held by the kings, Frederik of Denmark-Norway and Gustav Vasa of Sweden, by this time both openly amicable towards Evangelical reformers, who in Denmark had enjoyed official royal protection since 1527. It was not until King Frederik had died in 1533 that the archbishop of Lund, Torben Bille, himself dared to call on the secular sword, together with Lord Tyge Krabbe of the Danish Council of the Realm, against the Lutheran heretics of his archdiocese. When the cathedral chapter of Lund in August 1533 deposed and expelled three Evangelical preachers from Helsingborg, Landskrona and Trelleborg, their alleged 'sowing of depraved heresy' was among the reasons for the sentence given in a later justification, and although the term 'inquisition' is not noted anywhere in connection with their trial and condemnation, the whole case certainly

---

32   Bandlien & Knutsen (2008), p. 450.
33   Græbe (1970), p. 34.

bears the mark of an inquisition, not least because the canons subsequently stated that the priests should consider themselves lucky not to have been burned at the stake.[34] If the process is to be seen as an episcopal inquisition, it is interesting to note that a Franciscan friar had been invited by the canons to speak against the Evangelicals at Lund Cathedral – possibly, as suggested by Rørdam, Guardian Niels Pedersen of the convent in Svendborg, who appears to have been especially hated by the Lutherans in Malmö, and was nicknamed 'The Grey Wolf of Svendborg' by the reformed writer Peder Laurentsen.[35]

As elsewhere in Europe, even without an inquisition, the Dominican Order in Scandinavia was still capable of countering what it saw as heresy. Already in 1523, Bishop Hans Brask of Linköping praised Fr Nils Hvit, prior of the Friars Preachers in Kalmar, for his and his convent's continued resistance to Lutheranism, not least as promulgated by Luther's Swedish disciple, Master Olaus Petri of Strängnäs, King Gustav Vasa's Evangelical councillor.[36] The bishop of Linköping also elsewhere found Dominican arguments against the Lutherans, as when Hans Brask quoted Thomas Aquinas on a number of issues in his public disputes with Olaus Petri, such as the Holy Virgin and the saints, the value of sermons given in the church, how to differentiate between God's will and the thoughts of the priest – and the clergy's right to beg.[37] Although we have no further explicit evidence showing that Swedish reformers were encountered by Dominican preachers, the aggressive Evangelical stance against the mendicants certainly suggests that they were seen – at least potentially – as important opponents.[38] The king was soon convinced of the political danger in letting friars tour the country as they pleased. Several Dominican friars were accused of stirring up social riots in Dalarna and elsewhere against the new king, who among other things was accused by the peasants of heresy, and for this reason Fr Nils Karlsson of Västerås was arrested and executed after riots in 1525.[39] King Gustav especially mistrusted mendicant friars of non-Swedish origin, for which reason the Norwegian-born vicar provincial of the Dominicans in Dacia, Fr Robert Jonsen, along with a group of his brethren was expelled from Sweden in 1525; had they not left the kingdom by midsummer, the king "would find a different kind of mercy for

34 Peder Laurentsen, *Expostulatio*, pp. Cii-Ciii; Fabricius (1936), p. 183.
35 Peder Laurentsen, *Vnderuisning om Preste Embede*, pp. Ki-Kii; Rørdam (1868), p. xxxiii.
36 DOPD 1523 4/7.
37 DOPD 1523 Apr-Jun.
38 Lindroth (1975), p. 238; Berntson (2003), pp. 91-93.
39 DOPD 1525 7-8/4 and 1525 14/6; Berntson (2003), pp. 90-91 and 112-113.

them".[40] Some Swedish Dominicans, on the other hand, were in favour with the king. When King Gustav Vasa of Sweden in 1525 enjoined his archbishop, Johannes Magnus of Uppsala, to initiate a translation of the New Testament into Swedish for the benefit of the people, the responsibility for translating the various sections of the Testament was divided between the leading ecclesiastical institutions of Sweden. The vicar general of the Friars Preachers in Sweden, Fr Martin Skytte, and his fellow brethren were thus told to translate the Epistle to Titus and the Letter to the Hebrews.[41] The archbishop himself was soon taken out of the project, which instead was left to Olaus Petri and other learned Evangelicals. It is uncertain to what extent the 'Dominican chapters' were produced and incorporated in the actual publication of the New Testament, which appeared already in 1526.[42] Fr Martin Skytte, who was put in charge of the project, certainly had a very pragmatic attitude towards Lutheranism and remained in high esteem with King Gustav, who in 1528 made him bishop of Turku.

Within the Danish realm, the ideas of Luther first entered the duchy of Schleswig, where reformed preachers acted from 1525 onwards. When an especially zealous advocate of the new belief, the former Augustinian Reinhold Westerholt, took over the task in the city of Schleswig in 1529, he immediately entered into harsh disputes with leading local friars of both mendicant orders – which led to the expulsion of both convents the very same year.[43] According to one source, a similar fate had been visited upon the Dominican friars in Haderslev, the Evangelical centre of the duchy, already in January 1527, but other sources suggest a Dominican presence in Haderslev for several years to come.[44] Further north and east, in the kingdom of Denmark, the new faith progressed more gradually. The Catholic front against the reformers here was led by the bishops, not least by Ove Bille of Aarhus, and whereas the most well-known monastic voice on the Catholic side came from the humanist Carmelite, Fr Poul Helgesen of Elsinore, scholarship has traditionally completely written off any significant Dominican involvement in events in Denmark, as in Scandinavia as a whole.[45] On closer scrutiny, however, this claim does not appear entirely just. A perhaps somewhat odd source for this is the Danish tale of *Peder Smed og Asser Bonde* ('Peter the Smith and Asser the

---

40   DOPD 1525 30/5.
41   DOPD 1525 11/6.
42   Bergman (1995), pp. 86-87.
43   Heilesen (1962), p. 42.
44   DOPD 1527 6/1; DOPD 1528 25/4; DOPD 1534 24/6.
45   E.g. Gallén (1960), p. 200; Lausten (2004), p. 117.

Farmer'), an anti-Catholic writ from around 1530, which is a problematic text in many ways as it is both propagandistic, clearly fictitious and also a Danish version based on an older German original. All these factors nevertheless do not remove its relevance to Dominican involvement in the religious dispute of the Reformation.[46] The scene of the tale is an inn in Skive in northern Jutland, where the surprisingly well-informed and eloquent blacksmith Peder meets a simple farmer from Salling, called Asser, as well as a local parish priest and a monk. The first thing to note is the fact that the monk is not just any monk, but a Dominican Blackfriar, by the name of Fr Kurt. It is not stated from which convent Fr Kurt was supposed to come, but a Dominican frequenting an inn in Skive would most likely have originated from Viborg – which at this time was also the hotspot of Danish Evangelism. The fictitious Fr Kurt is, however, not the only Dacian Blackfriar in the tale. When Peder Smed wants to stress that even the highest Danish clergy cannot produce any true wonders, he lists three specific regular clergymen immediately after the anonymous group of secular prelates: the provincial of the Blackfriars; Lector Poul in Elsinore; and Master Søren Jakobsen. Lector Poul is of course the Carmelite professor Poul Helgesen, while Søren Jakobsen refers to an uncompromising anti-Lutheran Franciscan friar from Halmstad, who literally died in combat for his Catholic faith when the convent in Ystad was taken by a Protestant mob in 1532. But prior to both of these well-known Danish personalities and opponents of the Lutheran Reformation, the author places the Dominican prior provincial. He gives no name, but it is known from other sources: Dr Hans Nielsen, mentioned in the beginning of this paper. He was a doctor of theology and lector at the convent in Lund, before he was elected head of the Dominican province of Dacia in 1519. One could, of course, argue that the author only wanted to include people from all three mendicant orders in the list (which contains no further regular clergy), but from other sources we know that the Dominican prior provincial in fact took active part in Counter-Reformation disputations around this time. The Dacian-Dominican provincial's involvement in the intense and often harshly-worded theological dispute in Denmark around 1530 is known indirectly through a writ by the Malmö reformist, Peder Laurentsen, an apostate Carmelite friar and lector at the University of Copenhagen. In 1529, he was made lector at a new Evangelical school in Malmö, and it was from here he wrote *Malmøbogen* ('The Book of Malmö'), a treatise evaluating the implementation of Lutheran reformation in Malmö. The book launched several writs in response from

46   Jakobsen (2008), pp. 18-19.

Catholic opponents, most famously in 1530 with *Mod Malmøbogen* ('Against the Book of Malmö') by the Carmelite Fr Poul Helgesen. A contemporary – and unfortunately now lost – response was according to Peder Laurentsen himself authored by "the false monk and illiterate doctor, Fr Hans Nielsen, *prevaricatorum provincialis*" as it was deliberately distorted, 'provincial of prevaricators' (i.e. 'those who evade the truth').[47]

Protestant attacks on Dominicans

Dominican participation in official and unofficial inquisitions around Northern Europe led to several expulsions, arrests and executions of Protestant reformers, but eventually, it was the Dominican hardliners themselves, who suffered the main risk of losing life and limb, not to speak of their civic privileges and worldly possessions. Although the mendicants of Bremen in 1523 had been prohibited from preaching by the city council, the leading Dominican friars continued to do so, eventually leading to their formal expulsion from the city in 1524.[48] In 1524-25, the Dominican lector in Stralsund, Fr Heinrich Westfal, had to endure corporal punishment for his criticism against the reformer Ketelhodt; one of his brethren was stabbed after a sermon; and a third Stralsund friar, who had preached in favour of the Pope and the sale of indulgences, would have been burned at the stake by an angry mob, along with pictures of saints, had not the city council intervened.[49] Gradually, one city council after the other around the Baltic Sea turned towards Lutheranism – and against local mendicant convents. In 1531, the council of Rostock prohibited all regular clergy from wearing their habits outside the monasteries, and friars were not allowed to give public sermons.[50] In neighbouring Wismar, townspeople entered the Dominican church during a Christmas sermon, shouting obscenities against the preacher, Lector Matthäus Vorstermann, who was particularly hated among the Lutherans, and then started singing in an ungodly manner, so that all the friars had to leave the choir. The following Christmas, public riots in Wismar grew even more dangerous, as hostile citizens this time not only cast angry words against the friars in the choir during service, but also stones, snowballs and blocks of ice. The con-

---

47   DOPD 1530.
48   Löhr (1930), p. 51*.
49   Löhr (1930), p. 50*.
50   Ulpts (1995), pp. 370-371.

frontation developed into complete mayhem, with pillaging and destruction, while friars and Catholic visitors ran terrified around the priory church. At this time, the duke of Mecklenburg was still favourable towards the friars, but even the threat of ducal anger could not keep the Lutherans at bay.[51]

As the tide began to turn decisively against the Catholic side all over Northern Europe, the General Chapter of the Dominican Order began to introduce means to protect its friars, for instance by admonishing them not to provoke the Lutherans unnecessarily with aggressive sermons and disputes. Instead, they were to be mild and pragmatic, and thus make the public see who was truly right. But since this change of strategy was perhaps problematic for many a zealous Dominican preacher, another response was simply to transfer compulsorily the most radical friars from on-going hotspots to less tense locations. This was obviously the case for the Dutch Dr Willem de Buren, a former prior of the convents in Schleswig and Haderslev, who as lector and an exceptionally eager debater at the convent in Hamburg had made himself so many enemies among the Lutherans that Dominican leadership in 1527-28 decided to deport him back home to Holland; both for his own safety and for that of his fellow brethren.[52] A similar growing Dominican understanding for the necessity of a measured response is seen in the acts of the provincial chapter of Germania inferioris (i.e. the Netherlands) in 1531, where the friars were again urged by their own superiors to be careful and thoughtful regarding their words against the Lutherans.[53]

Some convents apparently found this admonition more difficult to comply with than others. When Protestant ideas began to gain ground in the city council of Ypres around the mid-sixteenth century, the local Dominican prior on several occasions denied both magistrate and townspeople access to the priory precinct, even when they came for completely peaceful and customary reasons, because of the heretical nature of the trespassers. This unyielding policy turned out less profitable in the long term, as militant Calvinists in 1566 seriously ravaged the Dominican priory along with other Catholic churches in the city – after having forced the friars to serve them food and beer.[54] Such Protestant attacks on Dominican priories had been still more common practise since April 1524, when it happened to the friars in Riga, followed by the Dominican houses in Stralsund, Gdańsk, Tallinn and Tartu in 1525 – every time causing severe damage to buildings and their interi-

51 Kleiminger (1938), pp. 119-121 and 126-134; Ulpts (1995), pp. 370-371.
52 Wolfs (1964), p. 89 note 355.
53 Brada (1983), p. 44.
54 De Pue (1982), pp. 48-49 and 53-54.

ors, and often physical abuse to the friars, if not also casualties.[55] Some of these assaults could take a more sophisticated and spectacular form, as when Protestant thugs in 1543 broke into the priory in Perth. Among the goods confiscated by force, they took the soup pot of the friars, which subsequently was carried through the streets of Perth as a trophy of the Protestant victory. This can be seen as a mock procession, where the usual relics borne by the Dominicans were replaced by the one object that the friars, at least according to the reformers, worshipped more than anything.[56] And when the nobility of the northern-most parts of the Netherlands carried out an iconoclastic attack on all Catholic churches of the region in 1566, the Dominican priory church in Winsum was also ravaged, allegedly while noble women sat themselves by the church organ and accompanied the bizarre event with joyful music.[57]

Actual attacks by Lutherans are not explicitly recorded on any of the Dominican priories in Scandinavia, but may to some extent be indicated by the sources for the convents in Haderslev, Schleswig and Viborg.[58] As several such assaults allegedly took place against the Danish Franciscans, according to the order's own 'Chronicle of Expulsion', their Dominican colleagues are likely to have received similar treatment – or at least lived in fear of it.[59] In 1527, the Dominican prior provincial of Dacia, Dr Hans Nielsen, obtained a letter of protection for his brethren in Denmark from King Frederik of Denmark-Norway, which was aimed not least of all at the king's own officials.[60] This guarantee was apparently also needed, as a Dominican friar on his way from Vejle to Viborg allegedly was attacked the same year on the road by two royal henchmen who stabbed the poor friar to death.[61]

King Frederik's protection of mendicant convents appears to have been quite superficial. On more than one occasion, he promised that mendicant churches and monastic buildings were to be handed over to the local town magistrates when the last friars had left. In this way, he provided an incentive for the townspeople to make this happen sooner rather than later. During the second half of the reign of King Frederik, i.e. 1527-33, 29 (out of initially 48) mendicant convents in Denmark were dissolved; not least the Franciscans were already in this early period severely reduced (from 25 to 7), while

---

55 Löhr (1930), p. 50*; Walther-Wittenheim (1938), pp. 126-127 and 130; Rebane (2001), p. 59.
56 Foggie (2003), p. 166.
57 Brada (1982), pp. 40-41.
58 DOPD 1527 6/1 (Haderslev); Radtke (1974), p. 50 (Schleswig); DOPD 1532 (Viborg).
59 Especially in Malmö (1530), Halmstad (1531) and Ystad (1532), and to some extent in Viborg (1529-30). *Cronica expulsionis*, passim.
60 DOPD 1527 28/8.
61 DOPD 1527.

half of the Dominican and Carmelite houses still existed in 1533, especially on Zealand and in Scania. The most obvious political ally for the mendicant friars during the Reformation was the rest of the Catholic clergy, but it is generally difficult to spot any combined forces. The noble prelates of the well-off abbeys in Scandinavia are practically invisible in the extant sources of the Reformation in both religious and political terms, aside from their narrow interests in their own estates and positions. The main Catholic defense was taken by the bishops, some more whole-heartedly than others, but there is little evidence of episcopal support when individual friars, convents and orders were under attack. At the beginning of the interregnum after King Frederik's death in 1533, the Council of the Realm led by the Danish bishops did proclaim a 'back-to-normal'-policy, where all possessions, items and privileges taken by force from monastic orders should be handed back, but as they had no material power to back their injunctions, nothing, of course, happened. Not even the mendicant orders as a whole were able to form a united front in Denmark, as the *de facto* chief theologian on the Catholic side, the Carmelite Poul Helgesen, a humanist himself, expressed much criticism against the two old mendicant orders.[62] These two, the Dominicans and the Franciscans, do, however, appear to have joined forces to produce a collective defence treatise for future mendicant existence in Denmark. The author chosen to put it all together was the Roskilde Franciscan, Peder Olsen, whose numerous preserved chronicles are well-known and an apparently quite trustworthy collection of sources for Danish medieval history. But what has been less appreciated by scholarship is how surprisingly well-informed this Franciscan friar of the early sixteenth century is about Danish Dominican history in the eastern part of the kingdom going back to the early thirteenth century, not preserved from any other known sources. His information in fact suggests that he had access to Dominican chronicles which were later lost. Their purpose was to justify the existence and privileges of the two orders, possibly to be presented at a national diet in 1534.[63] The main support with any real power that the friars had to lean on in Denmark and the rest of Northern Europe seems to have been the Catholic families among the high nobility – usually the very same families that were connected to the friars through altars, family burial places and perpetual masses. In Tallinn, for instance, it was the rural nobility of the surrounding provinces Harjumaa and Virumaa

---

62 Poul Helgesen, *Mod Malmøbogen*, pp. 59-60 and 222-234.
63 Rasmussen (1976), p. 35; Vellev (1993), pp. 53 and 58. The diet, however, never took place due to the outbreak of war.

that stood up for the local Dominicans after their expulsion in 1525;[64] in Rostock, the House of Bülow defended the friars against the city council so they could keep their valuables, which the Bülows claimed had been given mainly by them;[65] and one nobleman in the Northern Netherlands, who also happened to be a military commander, conscripted a guard of twelve soldiers to protect the Dominican convent in Winsum from further Protestant attacks.[66] In Denmark, close ties to leading noble families are recorded just prior to or during the years of Reformation for the Dominican convents in Haderslev (Rantzau), Viborg (Gyldenstierne and Bielke), Odense (Urne), Næstved (Bille), Åhus (Brahe) and Halmstad (Krummedige and Ulfstand), but it is not known whether they provided any protective measures for the friars. Eventually, also noble families took back the landed possessions and valuables that they had been donating to the friars for generations. This behaviour may have been seen as a welcome opportunity by some family members to enrich and free themselves from obligations set by their ancestors. Many families, however, seem to have done so not out of discontent with the friars, but to secure what they saw as rightfully theirs before it was confiscated by the king, town magistrates and the plundering mob.[67]

From the late 1520s, the Dominican Order in Northern Europe suffered severely from the effects of the 'Lutheran pest', as it was commonly referred to in the order's documents. From being the aggressive leaders of the Roman Church against anything non-Catholic – the *Domini canes* or 'Hounds of the Lord', as the Dominicans liked to portray themselves – Friars Preachers all around Northern Europe had to take a still more defensive line, being forced to endure public ridicule in satire propaganda, verbal and physical assaults both outside their priories and within, growing restrictions on their right to preach and collect alms, and eventually withdrawal of their fundamental right to be in their priories at all. As still more friars began to reconsider their call, and either fled to convents in more hospitable surroundings or decided to leave religious life altogether, it became increasingly difficult to maintain convent life in the 'infested areas' according to order regulations. According to the provincial acts of 1528, only few Dominican houses in the province of Saxonia by then had sufficient manpower to continue the full conventual programme.[68] Something similar is likely to have been the case for the remaining

---

64 E.g. DOPD 1525 26/3; DOPD 1526 Mar; DOPD 1527 15/3.
65 Ulpts (1995), pp. 370-371.
66 Brada (1982), p. 42.
67 Knudsen (1849-52), p. 368.
68 Löhr (1930), p. 40*.

houses in Dacia, even if some friars from the earliest abandoned houses (in Jutland and Sweden) gradually concentrated in the longest-lasting ones (in Finland, Norway, Scania and the Danish Isles). Even where they were not made to leave by force, financial erosion and an almost complete end to new recruitment inevitably led all mendicant convents in Lutheran-dominated areas to dissolution.

Dissolution of Dominican convents

As with other events of the Lutheran Reformation, final dissolution of Dominican convents in Northern Europe first took place along the German and Livonian coasts of the Baltic Sea. The first convent to close seems to have been the one in Riga in 1524, followed by those in Narva (1524), Tallinn (1525) Tartu (1525) and Stralsund (1525).[69] In Tallinn, the Dominican closure was dictated by the city council, whose representatives forced their way into the priory on 12 January 1525. The friars were enjoined to give up the habit of their order and renounce Catholicism, or to leave the priory and the city immediately. The officials also demanded all valuable items and written privileges to be handed over, but since the convent leaders had anticipated what was coming, these valuables and documents had previously been hidden with friends outside the priory. When the city councillors became aware of this situation, the prior, subprior and procurator of the convent were detained for several weeks under arrest, but apparently without revealing the whereabouts of the desired effects.[70] A similar fate subsequently was visited upon the Dominican convents in Bremen (1528), Hamburg (1529), Lübeck (1530), Rostock (1534) and Greifswald (1534-35).[71] Whereas the friars were to leave immediately (or convert to Lutheranism) in Livonia, Stralsund, Hamburg and Lübeck, a more lenient approach was implemented elsewhere. In Bremen, the Dominican friars were allowed to stay if they abstained from begging, preaching and performing Catholic ceremonies. Under these conditions, some of them continued in the semblance of a convent, selling priory valuables for their livelihood, until 1534, when the remaining seven friars donated the priory to the magistrate in return for board and lodging for the rest

---

69 Walther-Wittenheim (1938), pp. 125-126 (Narva) and 126-129 (Tallinn); Rebane (2001), p. 59 (Tartu); Löhr (1930), p. 50* (Stralsund).
70 DOPD 1525 12/1; Walther-Wittenheim (1938), p. 129.
71 Löhr (1930), p. 51* (Bremen); Hauschildt (1982), p. 197 (Hamburg); Löhr (1930), pp. 53-54* (Lübeck); Ulpts (1995), pp. 372-373 (Rostock); Löhr (1930), p. 61* (Greifswald).

of their lives.[72] Likewise in Rostock, Dominican friars were permitted to stay on as pensioners in one of the priory buildings, while the old refectory was turned into a Latin school. The convent members in their retirement actually upheld some sort of pseudo-monastic life, with continued election of priors and disciplinary regulations, from 1534 to 1556.[73] A different development took place in Elbląg and Meldorf, where the official introduction of Lutheran Evangelism in reality put a stop to Dominican life in 1525 and 1532-33 respectively, but the convents were not formally dissolved until the last friars in the early 1540s gave up their existence as members of the Dominican Order.[74]

Although mendicant presence in Sweden was not officially prohibited until the end of the sixteenth century, severe restrictions were introduced against the friars by King Gustav Vasa at a national diet in 1527. The event took place in Blackfriars Priory in Västerås, after which the mendicants were no longer allowed to function outside their priories for more than ten weeks a year. Although this decision may not seem excessively harsh, it completely undermined the friars' financial basis, and so practically all mendicant convents disappeared within the following year.[75] The Dominican convents in Västerås, Stockholm, Strängnäs, Skänninge and Sigtuna were all dissolved in 1528-29, followed by the ones in Lödöse and Kalmar in the early 1530s, Turku in 1537, and Skara and Vyborg by 1540-41 at the latest.[76] Thus, Dominican disapperance in Sweden seems mainly to have derived from financial pressure caused by limiting their ability to preach and collect alms in the countryside through *terminario*.[77] This development varied by region, as all houses had vanished from Svealand and Östergötland by 1529, whereas the friars apparently found better opportunities for survival in Västergötland and Finland.[78]

In Denmark, the dissolution of mendicant convents appears rather to be the result of religious motives than was the case in Sweden and Norway, although economic and political interests undoubtedly were at play here as well. The first Dominican convents to be closed were, not surprisingly, the two situated in the duchy of Schleswig, where Duke Christian – the later

72 Löhr (1930), p. 51*.
73 Ulpts (1995), pp. 372-373.
74 Carstenn (1937), pp. 309 and 313-314 (Elbląg); Löhr (1930), 58*, Seeman (2011), p. 95 (Meldorf).
75 DOPD 1527 25-27/6; Berntson (2003), pp. 94-96 and 114-115.
76 Berntson (2003), passim.
77 On the importance of Dominican *terminario* in Scandinavia, see Jakobsen (2015).
78 In Gotland, which at this time formally belonged to the Danish realm, the Dominican convent and priory in Visby seems to have been destroyed during a military attack by Lübeck troops on 13 May 1525, which may have killed several of the friars; after this, the convent is not mentioned again in the sources. Lindström (1895), pp. 276-277.

King Christian III – had converted to Lutheranism in 1525-26. Thus, there was no ducal protection to back Dominican and Franciscan friars, when they were faced with increasing Lutheran criticism in the following years, and the convents in Haderslev and Schleswig were, as earlier mentioned, dissolved in 1527 and 1529 respectively. The two main centres of Lutheran Evangelism within the actual kingdom of Denmark were Viborg and Malmö, which both held Dominican communities, although the latter was only a subordinate house to the convent in Lund. In Viborg, the Lutheran party led by Hans Tausen began in 1528 to gradually take over the Franciscan church, while a royal captain of Protestant views, Jens Hvass, made his headquarters in the town's Dominican priory from early 1529 until 1532.[79] Furthermore, in February 1529, both mendicant churches were given to the burghers of Viborg as parish churches,[80] and while Tausen delivered his sermons in Greyfriars Church, his assistant Jørgen Sadolin preached in Blackfriars. Apparently, this development took place while the friars were still living there. While the Friars Minor by 1530 had suffered enough and left for exile on Zealand, we do not know for how long the Friars Preachers endured, but probably until about the same time.[81] In Malmö, the Franciscans were expelled in 1530,[82] and most likely, their Dominican colleagues left around this time as well.[83] Soon after followed Dominican convent dissolutions in Vejle (1529-30), Aarhus (1529-30) and Halmstad (1531).[84] Then came a temporary period of stabilisation, and of the remaining nine Dominican convents in Denmark, only one is known to have been closed during the War of Reformation ('Grevens Fejde') from 1534 to 1536. While the troops of Count Christopher of Oldenburg and Duke Christian of Schleswig were fighting in 1534-35 for control of Zealand, the Friars Preachers in Holbæk apparently realized that no matter which side emerged victorious, Dominican prospects in the small town were dim. In two extant letters from the beginning of 1535, when the military outcome was still uncertain, Prior Hans Pedersen and his convent handed over the entire priory to the town magistrate to be used and kept for the benefit of poor and sick people. The convent appears to have been driven to

---

79 DOPD 1529 20/3; Köcher (1929), pp. 20-21.
80 DOPD 1529 23/2.
81 Severinsen (1932), pp. 352-355.
82 Lindbæk (1914), pp. 211-215.
83 DOPD 1530 12/2.
84 The exact date of dissolution is not recorded for any of these, but the years suggested here are qualified guesses based on the last recorded instances of still active convents and the first indications showing that the friars had gone.

this decision not because of religious opposition but for economic reasons: "*It should be known that we have not done this out of will or pleasure, but out of grave sorrow and sadness, pressure and need, and overwhelmingly great poverty and destitution, which make it impossible for us to keep [the priory] any longer, as many people will know…*".[85]

In 1536, King Christian III finally won all of Denmark, and on 30 October issued the so-called 'Copenhagen Recess',[86] in which Catholicism was abolished in favour of Lutheran Evangelism. Begging performed by healthy people was prohibited. Then followed the Church Ordinance of 2 September 1537, explicitly prohibiting mendicant monasticism altogether in Denmark from that time onwards,[87] It was at this point that the last eight Dominican convents in Ribe, Odense, Næstved, Roskilde, Elsinore, Helsingborg, Åhus and Lund were dissolved – and, in effect, along with them the Dominican province of Dacia as such.[88] As one of his last official acts as Dominican prior provincial, Dr Hans Nielsen in September 1537 handed over to the royal chancellery the few remaining chalices and valuable vestments from the priory churches in Roskilde, Helsingborg and Lund.[89]

The Dominican prior provincial's prominent position within the Catholic Church in Denmark and its recognition among his Lutheran opponents is finally also seen in the treatment that Dr Hans Nielsen was given by King Christian III in the aftermath of the Reformation. When the king in November 1536 called upon twenty-nine of the leading theologians and canonists of the country to help Johann Bugenhagen produce a new Lutheran-Evangelical church ordinance for Denmark and Norway, planned to take place in Odense on 6 January 1537, most of the invited scholars were, of course, Lutherans, but a small group of Catholics was also included – and among them, as the only representative of the regular clergy, Dr Hans, "provincial of all Dominicans".[90] The planned council in Odense was apparently replaced by another held in Haderslev later in January, and while the draft ordinance to come from this meeting was signed by the Catholic canons secular – although according to a later statement against their free will – the Dominican prior provincial had apparently declined to take part.[91] Hans Nielsen was nevertheless recognized

---

85   DOPD 1534-35; DOPD 1535 24/2.
86   DOPD 1536 30/10.
87   DOPD 1537 2/9.
88   Again, the sources offer no exact dates on the individual convent dissolutions, and particularly those in Næstved and Elsinore may in fact have happened earlier.
89   DOPD 1537 Sep.
90   DOPD 1536 11/11.
91   *Kirkeordinansen 1537/39*, p. 68; Engelstoft (1860-62), p. 378; Rørdam (1867-68), p. 25; Lausten (1989), pp. 14-18.

enough by the reformed King Christian III to be appointed caretaker of a hospital in Åhus in October 1537 and even to become an Evangelical parish priest in the nearby village of Rynkeby.[92]

Like the Dacian prior provincial, some Dominican friars found themselves a new role in post-Reformation society as parish vicars within the Protestant Church. Others decided to stay in the habit of the order and left for other provinces, where Catholicism and mendicant life was still a possibility. Numerous English friars are known to have gone to Scotland, after King Henry VIII put a stop to English monasticism in 1539-40,[93] and when the turn later came to Scotland in 1559-60, many Scottish friars left for Flanders. So did, of course, numerous Dominican friars from the northern Low Countries, when this region decisively turned Protestant in the 1580-90s.[94] In Germany, friars who wanted to maintain their Dominican vocation could do so in the southern regions of the empire or in Poland. To what extent Friars Preachers from the province of Dacia continued a Dominican life elsewhere in Europe after the Scandinavian dissolutions from 1527 to 1537 is unknown. Whereas several Danish Franciscan friars are known to have gone abroad,[95] not one single friar from the Dacian-Dominican province is recorded in other provinces after the Reformation. The friars had, of course, also the possibility of choosing a whole new career outside the Church altogether, depending on family relations and personal talents. When the Dominican convent in Neuruppin, Germany, was dissolved in 1552, some of its friars gained great recognition in their civil afterlife as beer-brewers.[96]

Conclusion

The conclusion of this article may at first sight appear to be that the entire Lutheran Reformation was a Dominican affair. It was a Dominican who provoked Martin Luther to start the process. It was Dominicans who declared him to be a heretic, and Dominicans who eagerly fought all his followers around Northern Europe – albeit eventually in vain. Of course, I do not intend to make the Dominicans the centre of all that happened. There were many other important stakeholders in the Reformation as well, and the entire

---

92   Rørdam (1867-68), pp. 25-26.
93   Foggie (2003), p. 40.
94   Bakker (1988), pp. 52, 60-61 and 72.
95   Lindbæk (1914), pp. 89-93.
96   Kleiminger (1938), p. 118.

course of events may indeed have been more or less the same, and led to the same outcome, without the involvement of the Dominican Order. My central conclusion is merely that the Dominican Order very much *was* involved. It was simply impossible for its friars *not* to take part. It was the Dominican *raison d'être* for every priestly ordained friar not only to preach according to the papally approved interpretation of God's word and will, but also to zealously oppose anyone who had misunderstood this message. It was paramount to oppose any fools who tried to convince others of their heretical misbeliefs. From a Dominican point of view, heresy was like a cancer constantly seeking to erupt in the different 'body parts' of Christianity, and since the friars according to the order's own self-concept were the prime 'doctors of the soul', it was their basic responsibility to treat the cancer with all means available to prevent it from ruining the entire body of the Church – and thereby endanger the salvation of all souls. For the Dominican Order, Dr Martin Luther at first was considered to be just one more outbreak of this well-known disease, but soon the 'Lutheran pest' appeared to be too contagious for the friars to cure. Why Lutheran Evangelism gained so widespread popularity in sixteenth-century North-European society is a question beyond the scope of this study, but it may have caught the mendicant orders at a time when they were vulnerable to the counter-offensive that Evangelical preachers launched against them. Especially relevant is the fact that the Dominicans became trapped in an on-going social friction between a rising urban bourgeoisie and the old patriciate elite. At the same time, the mendicant convents had through a preceding internal reform movement alienated themselves from local power structures. First and foremost, however, mendicant chances of survival in Northern Europe were inevitably linked to the religious direction chosen by the local lay sovereign. As long as the princely ruler remained Catholic, the friars had every chance of enduring the Lutheran challenge, but if the prince, too, turned to Protestantism, there were no prospects of survival.

All around the North-European Continent, the Dominican Order long before Luther's arrival held a central position in the defense against heresy: the inquisition. But as this article has shown, not only the formally appointed Dominican inquisitors, but also numerous others of their brethren – be they priors provincial, priors, lectors or rank-and-file friars – took it upon themselves to oppose Evangelical preachers and publications. Also in the British Isles and in Scandinavia, where no Dominican friar was ever appointed papal inquisitor, Dominicans inevitably were drawn into the centre of the theological-pastoral dispute, causing numerous casualties on both sides. Even in

Denmark, where scholarship has traditionally pointed to the Carmelite Dr Poul Helgesen as the sole theological capacity on the Catholic side, along with a group of conservative bishops and canons mainly worried about their personal privileges and income, I have tried to show how Dominicans and Franciscans from the very beginning and until the end of the Reformation did exactly the same as their brethren elsewhere in Northern Europe: they indefatigably tried to stop Lutheranism. The Evangelical preachers clearly saw Dominican and Franciscan friars as their main and most dangerous opponents, and therefore devoted a great deal of attention to undermining the friars' authority, credibility and popularity – with great success. Still, only one of these Dominican personalities opposed to the Protestant Reformation in Denmark is known by name: Fr Hans Nielsen, doctor of theology and head of the Dominican province of Dacia. As it seems, he simultaneously tried to prevent Lutheran Evangelism from spreading in Denmark, and to protect as much as possible the convents and friars of his order. Since Lutheran Evangelism was officially introduced as the only legal religion in Denmark from 1536, and the Dominican Order was prohibited from existence in Denmark in the following year, it is easy to conclude that he failed on all accounts. But it should be recognized that both he and, it seems, numerous of his fellow brethren tried their very best, which is apparent both from the hostility directed against them by their contemporary opponents (and later Lutheran historiography) and by the esteem, positive and negative, with which not least Dr Hans Nielsen was treated by his opponents. In the end, he too had to accept that the day was lost for both Catholicism and Dominican monasticism in Denmark. He had to hand over the keys and the last valuable items of the remaining houses of his order to King Christian III. At this point, I find it noteworthy that he was called by the king to take part in writing the new Evangelical Church Ordinance, as the sole representative of Danish regular clergy, but all the same declined to do so, while still accepting an offer to become a simple vicar in the Scanian parish of Rynkeby. To me, this response suggests fighting spirit, sense of responsibility, pride, humility and pragmatism. Not the worst characteristics for a leader of an influential institution.

Bibliography

Ames, Christine Caldwell, *Righteous persecution - Inquisition, Dominicans, and Christianity in the Middle Ages* (Philadelphia, 2009).

Bakker, Folkert Jan, *Bedelorden en begijnen in de stad Groningen tot 1594* (Groningen, 1988).

Bandlien, Bjørn & Gunnar W. Knutsen, 'Kjetterinkvisitorer i Norge', *Historisk Tidsskrift* (Norway) (2008:3), pp. 433-450.

Bergman, Gösta, *En kortfattad svensk språkhistoria*, 5th print (Stockholm, 1995 (1968)).

Berntson, Martin, *Klostren och reformationen - Upplösningen av kloster och konvent i Sverige 1523-1596* (Göteborg, 2003).

Blomqvist, Ragnar, 'Danmarks första dominikanerkloster i Svartbrödraklostret i Lund', *Kulturen* 1943 (publ. 1944), pp. 107-149.

Brada, Willibrordus Menno, *Dominicanen in Winsum* (Leusden, 1982).

Brada, Willibrordus Menno, *Dominicanen in Utrecht: »na de preek van 1579«* (Leusden, 1983).

Carstenn, Edward, *Geschichte der Hansestadt Elbing* (Elbląg, 1937).

Cronica seu breuis processus in causa expulsionis fratrum minoritarum de suis cenobiis prouincie Danice, et primo prefaco est (1533-34). MS Copenhagen, The Royal Library, NKS 276 8°; Barth. K. pp. 539-565. Ed. H. Knudsen, *Kirkehistoriske Samlinger* 1:1 (1849-52), pp. 325-419; ed. M.Cl. Gertz, in *Scriptores minores historiæ Danicæ* II (Copenhagen, 1920), pp. 325-367; trans. H. Heilesen, *Krøniken om Graabrødrenes fordrivelse fra deres klostre i Danmark* (Copenhagen, 1967).

De Pue, Piet, *Geschiedenis van het oud Dominikanenklooster te Ieper (1263-1797)* (Leuven, 1982).

Dixon, C. Scott, *The Reformation in Germany* (Oxford, 2002).

Dobson, Barrie, 'Mendicant ideal and practice in late medieval York', in *Archaeological papers from York presented to M.W. Barley*, eds. P.V. Addyman & V.E. Black (York, 1984), pp. 109-122.

DOPD = *Diplomatarium OP Dacie online*, ed. J.G.G. Jakobsen (Centre for Dominican Studies of Dacia, 2005-), http://www.jggj.dk/DOPD.htm (accessed June 30 2015).[97]

Engelstoft, C.T. 'Kirke-Ordinantsens Historie' (VI), *Kirkehistoriske Samlinger* 2:2 (1860-62), pp. 369-442.

Fabricius, L.P., *Danmarks Kirkehistorie* 2 (Copenhagen, 1936).

Foggie, Janet P., *Renaissance religion in urban Scotland: the Dominican order, 1450-1560* (Leiden, 2003).

Freytag, Erwin, 'Die Klöster als Zentren kirchlichen Lebens', in *Schleswig-Holsteinische Kirchengeschichte* 1, ed. P. Meinhold (Neumünster, 1977), pp. 147-202.

Gallén, Jarl, 'Reformationen i Norden – brytning eller kontinuitet. Några synpunkter', *Lumen – Katolsk teologisk tidsskrift* 10 (1960), pp. 196-208.

Græbe, Karen Just, 'Tiggerklostrenes nedlæggelse i Frederik I's tid' (unpublished MA-thesis, University of Copenhagen, 1970).

Hansen, Gotthard von, *Die Kirchen und ehemaligen Klöster Revals*, 3rd edn. (Tallinn, 1885).

Hansen, Reimer, 'Die Klöster des Landes Dithmarschen - Einrichtungen für das Heil und zum Schutz der spätmittelalterlichen Bauernrepublik', in *Vita Religiosa im Mittelalter - Festschrift für Kaspar Elm zum 70. Geburtstag*, eds. F.J. Felten & N. Jaspert (Berlin, 1999), pp. 563-579.

---

97 Most source instances regarding Dominicans in the province of Dacia, referred to in this article, are published online at the DOPD; see there for references to earlier publications.

Hauschildt, Wolf-Dieter, 'Die Reformation in Hamburg, Lübeck und Eutin', in *Schleswig-Holsteinische Kirchengeschichte* 3, ed. W. Göbel (Neumünster, 1982), pp. 185-226.

Heilesen, Henning, 'De sønderjyske gråbrødreklostres undergang - Et blad af reformationens historie i Sønderjylland', *Sønderjyske årbøger* (1962), pp. 40-50.

Jakobsen, Johnny Grandjean Gøgsig, 'Prædikebrødrenes samfundsrolle i middelalderens Danmark' (unpublished PhD-dissertation, University of Southern Denmark, 2008); available for download at http://www.jggj.dk/phd-afhandling.pdf (accessed June 30 2015).

Jakobsen, Johnny Grandjean Gøgsig, "What Jesus means is…' – The Dominican Order as theological authority for laity and clergy in medieval Northern Europe', in *Authorities in the Middle Ages. Influence, Legitimacy, and Power in Medieval Society*, eds. S. Kangas, M. Korpiola & T. Ainonen (Berlin, 2013), pp. 123-144.

Jakobsen, Johnny Grandjean Gøgsig, '»Them friars dash about« - Mendicant *terminario* in medieval Scandinavia', in *Travels and mobilities in the Middle Ages - From the Atlantic to the Black Sea*, eds. M. O'Doherty & F. Schmieder (Turnhout, 2015), pp. 3-29.

Jakobsen, Johnny Grandjean Gøgsig, 'Dominican Observance to Poverty - Ideals and Practice of a Mendicant Reform Movement in Late Medieval Northern Europe', in *Poverty, Society and the Sacred*, eds. C. Mews & A. Welch (Oxford & New York, (forthcoming)).

Jørgensen, Kaare Rübner, 'Biskoppernes ægyptiske jordemødre - De tyske teologer på herredagen i København 1530', in *Kirkehistoriske Samlinger* 2017, pp. 7-43.

Kirkeordinansen 1537/39, ed. Martin Schwarz Lausten (Copenhagen, 1989).

Kleiminger, Rudolf, *Das Schwarze Kloster in Seestadt Wismar. Ein Beitrag zur Kultur- und Baugeschichte der norddeutschen Dominikanerklöster im Mittelalter* (München, 1938).

Knudsen, H., 'En gammel Krönike om Graabrødrenes Udjagelse af deres Klostre i Danmark', *Kirkehistoriske Samlinger* 1:1 (1849-52), pp. 325-419.

Köcher, A., *Viborg Søndre Sogns Kirkes Historie* (Viborg, 1929).

Lausten, Martin Schwarz, *Danmarks kirkehistorie*, 3rd edn. (Copenhagen, 2004).

Lindbæk, Johannes, *De danske Franciskanerklostre* (Copenhagen, 1914).

Lindroth, Sten, *Svensk lärdomshistoria*, vol. 1 (Stockholm, 1975).

Lindström, Gustaf, 'Dominikanerna eller Prædicatores i S:t Nicolai kloster i Wisby', in *Anteckningar om Gotlands medeltid* vol. 2, ed. G. Lindström (Stockholm, 1895), pp. 261-298.

Löhr, Gabriel M., 'Die Kapitel der Provinz Saxonia im Zeitalter der Kirchenspaltung 1513-1540 (Einleitung)', *Quellen und Forschungen zur Geschichte des Dominikanerordens in Deutschland* 26 (1930), pp. 1*-79*.

Peder Laurentsen, *En sand oc ret cristen Vnderuisning om Preste Embede och om deriss Leffnit, Gifftermaal, oc ret Kyskhed. Desligest om Kloster-folckis Løfte och Frihed etc.* (Malmö, 1533), The Royal Library, Copenhagen, Hielmst. 233 4° (LN 128).

Peder Laurentsen, *Expostulatio ad Canonicos Lundenses* (Malmö, 1533), The Royal Library, Copenhagen, Hielmst. 570 824° (LN 125 8° copy 1).

Peder Smed og Asser Bonde (Viborg, c.1530), ed. J.F. Fenger, *Kirkehistoriske Samlinger* 1:2 (1853-56), pp. 327-382; ed. S. Grundtvig, *Peder Smed - et dansk Rim fra Reformationstiden* (Copenhagen, 1880); ed. S. Mogensen, *Peder Smed og Adser Bonde - efter trykket 1559* (Copenhagen, 1936).

Poul Helgesen, *Mod Malmøbogen* (Copenhagen, 1530), ed. M. Kristensen, in *Skrifter af Paulus Helie* 3 (Copenhagen, 1933), pp. 57-284.

Radtke, Christian, 'Untersuchungen zur Lokalisierung und zur Gründungsgeschicte des Schleswiger Dominikanerklosters', *Beiträge zur Schleswiger Stadtgeschichte* 19 (1974), pp. 49-63.

Rasmussen, Jørgen Nybo, *Broder Peder Olsen som de danske franciskaneres historieskriver* (Copenhagen, 1976).

Rebane, Siiri, 'Geschichte des Dominikanerklosters in Tartu (Dorpat)', in *Estnische Kirchengechichte im vorigen Jahrtausend*, ed. R. Altnurme (Kiel, 2001), pp. 55-60.

Rørdam, Holger Fr., 'Den sidste Dominikanerprovincial i Danmark, Dr. Hans Nielsen', *Kirkehistoriske Samlinger* 2:4 (1867-68), pp. 20-26.

Rørdam, Holger Fr., *Malmøbogen af Peder Laurenssen* (Copenhagen, 1968).

Seeman, Georg, 'Die Reformation - Auflösung der alten kirchlichen Ordnung', in *Glauben - Wissen - Leben. Klöster in Schleswig-Holstein*, eds. J. Ahler, O. Auge & K. Hillebrand (Kiel, 2011), pp. 95-102.

Severinsen, P., *Viborg Domkirke med Stad og Stift i 800 Aar* (Copenhagen, 1932).

Springer, Klaus-Bernward, *Die deutschen Dominikaner in Widerstand und Anpassung während der Reformationszeit* (Berlin, 1999).

Ulpts, Ingo, *Die Bettelorden in Mecklenburg - Ein Beitrag zur Geschichte der Franziskaner, Klarissen, Dominikaner und Augustiner-Eremitten im Mittelalter* (Werl, 1995).

Vellev, Jens, 'Viborg Gråbrødreklosters første år og Peder Olsens to notater', *hikuin* 20 (1993), pp. 53-64.

Walther-Wittenheim, Gertrud von, *Die Dominikaner in Livland - Die natio Livoniae* (Rome, 1938).

Wolfs, S.P., *Acta capitulorum provinciae Germaniae Inferioris Ordinis Fratrum Praedicatorum ab anno MDXV usque ad annum MDLIX* (Den Haag, 1964).

Zimmermann, Albert, *Albert der Grosse: seine Zeit, sein Werk, seine Wirkung* (Berlin & New York, 1981).

Continuity or Change?

The Danish Franciscans and the Lutheran Reformation

Morten Larsen

Introduction

In the coronation charter of Frederik I from 1523, the king vowed to defend the Church against heretical Lutheranism.[1] Despite the king's devout promise, he did nothing to prevent the townsmen from driving the friars out of their houses when the Lutheran preachers began in 1528 in Viborg. A decade later, the last of the twenty-nine houses of the Franciscan Order in the Danish realm was closed.[2]

Thus, the dissolution of the Franciscan friaries and the decision concerning the disposal of their buildings in most cases happened prior to the actual Lutheran Reformation in Denmark. In some cases the buildings were demolished within a few years of the Reformation, while in others it took a long time. In yet other cases, the buildings remained standing, serving other functions to society.

In this paper I intend to discern what role the king, the nobility and the patricians and other townspeople played in the dissolution of the Danish Franciscan friaries and to investigate on the basis of archaeological and historical sources what happened to the physical remains of the Franciscan friaries.

---

1 *Samling af danske Kongers Haandfæstninger* (1856-58) [1974], p. 67.
2 Larson (2010), pp. 219-220; Krongaard Kristensen (2013), pp. 433-434.

The material sources – the Franciscan friaries of Denmark

A total of twenty-nine Franciscan houses are known from the Danish Middle Ages, consisting of twenty-six male institutions and three nunneries. The majority of Franciscan convents were established during the course of the thirteenth century, for which reason the order became an integral part of the urban community in late medieval Denmark. The order's popularity increased during the fifteenth century, where several new convents were founded and by the time of the Reformation, the order was among the largest monastic organisations in the country.

Today, only a few Franciscan friaries are partly preserved. In Horsens, Nykøbing Falster and Ystad, in present-day Sweden, the churches are preserved and still in use as parish churches. Remains of friary buildings are preserved in Viborg, Schleswig, Flensburg, Odense, Ystad, Nykøbing Falster and Copenhagen. With regards to the remainder, they were either torn down in the years immediately after the Reformation or demolished, especially during the eighteenth and nineteenth centuries.[3]

Despite the poor condition of preservation, most friaries are well-known from the archaeological record. During the past century, excavations have taken place within the precincts of most of the Danish friaries, often unearthing a large and complex archaeological material.[4]

The archaeology of Reformation

In the field of medieval and historical archaeology, the emphasis on the period *after* the Reformation has not received sufficient attention. In a European context, the years following the Reformation have often been thoroughly discussed and investigated,[5] and in many countries there is great interest in historical archaeological studies. In Danish archaeological research, however, the period has to some degree been neglected. Most excavations have been concerned with medieval remains and only a few active investigations into the period after the Reformation have been made. At some larger urban excavations conducted during the course of the twentieth century, post-me-

---

3   Larsen (2018), pp. 15-17.
4   Larsen (2018), pp. 17-20.
5   Cf. Ericsson (1995); Andrén (1997), pp. 11-18.

dieval layers were simply dug away, often because of tight excavation budgets.[6] However, in recent years, scholarly emphasis on the archaeology of the recent past has spawned an interest in the period after the Reformation and has called attention to this important field of research. Like medieval archaeology, Renaissance archaeology as a recognized academic discipline is fairly young, yet studies in the material culture of the period have been conducted for several years.[7]

Despite the fact that only a few friary sites are preserved, most of the lost complexes have been the subject of several archaeological investigations during the past century. In some cases, the material evidence from post-medieval structures on the grounds of former friaries can be very extensive, as seen in the Swedish example of Jönköping, where the Franciscan friary after the Reformation was converted into a royal castle, or in the Franciscan friary of Flensburg, where a large part of the demolished friary was used as a churchyard – the preserved parts of the complex were converted to a hospital.[8]

In earlier research, there has been some tendency not to acknowledge the extensive use of some of the Franciscan friaries after their closure, often with dubious interpretations of (supposedly) medieval deposits. In Copenhagen, the Franciscan friary was to some extent converted into a noble estate after the Reformation (the so-called Ulfeldt's Manor). In the past century, almost twenty smaller excavations have unearthed remains of the complex and in several cases, the cultural deposits have been uncritically interpreted as remains of the medieval friary.[9] However, due to extensive use of the so-called 'Flensborgsten' (a small size of bricks used primarily during the Danish Renaissance) combined with artefacts corresponding with the period's material culture, the remains should probably be seen in relation to the site's post-Reformation use.

The same tendency can be seen with the Franciscan friary of Randers, where large excavations of the church and east range were carried out during the 1970s.[10] The excavation material was of poor quality; it was a composite site with a complex stratigraphy, where post-medieval use as a royal manor in particular complicated matters, since this greatly changed the medieval complex. Among unconvincing interpretations is the claim that there was a crypt beneath the friary church, a feature completely unknown in medie-

---

6 Mårtensson (1976), p. 13.
7 Svart Kristiansen (2006), pp. 474-476.
8 Witte (2003), pp. 113-117; Pettersson (2014), p. 99.
9 Liisberg (1901), pp. 63-67; Rosenkjær (1906), pp. 37-40; Ramsing (1940), pp. 133-139.
10 Hyldgård (1996), pp. 95-96.

val Franciscan architecture and probably the result of the massive rebuilding during the Danish Renaissance.[11]

The politics of reuse

As mentioned above, King Frederik I vowed in his charter of 1523 to protect the Church against Lutheranism, a guarantee that was more or less renewed in 1527 at a Diet in Odense (*Herredagen*).[12] The following years, however, proved crucial in the expulsion of the mendicants and the king did nothing to prevent this action. In reality, he sanctioned what happened.

The question of when malcontent arose is an interesting one. In 1521, the last Franciscan convent was established (the nunnery in Odense) with the queen dowager Christina as founder.[13] Material evidence suggests that construction works on the friaries initiated by the convents themselves seemed to continue well into the sixteenth century. It is well-known that the late Middle Ages saw growing criticism of the Church as such, but also specifically of monasticism.[14] During the fifteenth century, most of the Danish Franciscan convents were reformed. Even though the friars were aware of internal conflicts in the Church, they apparently did not expect such rapid conflict and change. Otherwise, their building activity probably would not have been so intense.[15]

The attacks on the mendicants might also find an explanation in the policy of the king, Frederik I and his attempts to consolidate his rule. He was crowned after his nephew, Christian II, was deposed and in the years prior to his kingship had ruled the duchies of Schleswig-Holstein, a region to which he also in later life felt closely attached. His reign was unstable, as Christian II sought refuge and assistance from his Habsburg brother-in-law, Charles V, in his attempts to regain the throne. Fortunately for King Frederik, the Habsburg Emperor had problems controlling his own vast dominion and the aid to Christian II was of a more symbolic character. Apart from the rejected nephew, Frederik also had problems with the nobility and clergy forming the Council of the Realm as well as the lower classes of society – peasantry and patricians – with whom King Christian had had a good relationship. Political turmoil and uncertainty gave rise to periods of civil and political unrest

---

11   Cf. Krongaard Kristensen (2013) p. 180.
12   Larsson (2010), pp. 210-211.
13   Nybo Rasmussen (2002), pp. 116-117.
14   Lausten (1987), pp. 13-14.
15   Larsen (2018), pp. 144-146.

during the new king's (and his successor's) reign, draining the country's finances.[16]

It was in these chaotic years that the majority of the Franciscan convents disappeared. During the period 1528-32, at least fifteen Franciscan friaries were dissolved.[17] In many cases, King Frederik decided that when the friars had left their houses, the remaining buildings should be given to the townspeople – often with a specific purpose. Thus, the king handed over the initiative to the local townsmen, in some cases aided by his counsellor Mogens Gøye, by which manoeuvre the king retained a 'neutral' role. The remaining friaries who survived the first purge more or less continued in existence until the actual Reformation, after which they were finally closed.

Whether or not Frederik I was a convinced Lutheran shall not be discussed, but he probably saw Lutheranism as a positive means of consolidating his throne, taking control of the politically influential Church and obtaining valuable lands and estates. Also, he probably understood the political significance of handing over the confiscated friaries to the patricians, who would have been pleased with his action.

Frederik I's reign lasted no more than a decade; he died in 1533 and the long-term consequences of his church policy can be difficult to decipher. After an interregnum of about a year, his son Christian formed an alliance with a part of the realm in 1534 and began a conquest of Denmark. He was a devoted Lutheran, having been with Martin Luther at the Diet of Worms and after a few years he carried through the Reformation.

The fate of the friars

The mendicant orders were in many ways caught in the crossfire of Reformation politics. Although the Danish Reformation was not in the same way a religious *war* as was the case elsewhere in Europe, the mendicant brethren were in several cases actively driven out by force. In the account commonly known as 'The Chronicle of the Grey Friar's Expulsion' (*De Expulsione Fratrum Minorum*), some of these events are described in detail. In the descrip-

---

16 Lyby (1993), pp. 32-43; Grell (1995), pp. 3-4.
17 By 1532, the friaries of Flensburg, Viborg, Tønder, Malmö, Copenhagen, Kolding, Aalborg, Randers, Trelleborg, Køge, Halmstad, Ystad, Næstved, Kalundborg and Horsens were dissolved – *De Expulsione Fratrum Minorum* (1922), pp. 331-367. Also the friaries of Husum, Schleswig, Nykøbing and Torkö were probably dissolved by 1532. Surviving until the second half of the 1530s were the friaries of Lund, Ribe, Odense, Svendborg, Nysted, Elsinore and Roskilde – Nybo Rasmussen (2002), pp. 500-508.

tion from the friary in Ystad, it is mentioned that the townspeople took the friary by storm and drove the brothers out of their dormitory, while maiming some of them.[18] In Viborg, a Danish Evangelical, Hans Tausen, began his Lutheran preaching in the Franciscan friary church in 1527. The Catholic bishop Jørgen Friis disapproved and sent armed men to arrest Tausen, but the number of Lutheran followers was huge and the bishop's men withdrew for 'fear' of bloodshed. The following year, the friars probably also felt ill at ease regarding the church that they shared with the Lutherans and retired to a chapel within the actual friary – and by 1530 they had probably left the friary for good.[19] Public discontent is often seen as a reaction to the incongruence between the mendicant ideals of poverty and the wealthy and extravagant friary complexes.[20]

The account was written as counter-propaganda in favour of the mendicants clearly described as the victims of heretical crimes and in the case of the dissolution of the friary in Aalborg, the perpetrator, Axel Gøye is characterised as a "rude heretic". Also Mogens Gøye, in the account of the friary in Randers, is described as "the protector of heretics" as well as "the worst of all heretics". In some cases, the dissolution appears to have been a non-violent event. In Kalundborg, the Franciscan guardian Melchior Jensen negotiated the friary's dissolution with the king's bailiff and a peaceful agreement was probably found. Naturally, the Chronicle of the Grey Friar's Expulsion provided the guardian with a poor posthumous reputation![21] Also, the end appears to have been peaceful in Ribe, where the friars left their house with a letter of recommendation from the mayors of Ribe and the bailiff at Riberhus.[22]

From the Church Ordinance of 1537/39, it is clear that the mendicants were more harshly treated than other monastic communities – they were completely banished from the realm and only the very sick and ailing brothers were allowed to remain.[23] And what happened to the rest of the Franciscan community? Most friars probably sought refuge south of Denmark, but in some cases it is evident that they adapted to the changes and converted to Lutheranism. Thus, the last guardian of the friary in Kalundborg, Melchior Jensen, became a Lutheran pastor.[24]

---

18   *De Expulsione Fratrum Minorum* (1922), pp. 359-364; cf. *Krøniken om Graabrødrenes fordrivelse fra deres klostre i Danmark* (1967), pp. 63-70.
19   *De Expulsione Fratrum Minorum* (1922), pp. 336-339; Ingesman (1998), pp. 208-210.
20   Larsson (2010), p. 220.
21   *De Expulsione Fratrum Minorum* (1922), pp. 365-366; cf. *Krøniken om Graabrødrenes fordrivelse fra deres klostre i Danmark* (1967), pp. 72-73.
22   Nielsen (1985), p. 143.
23   *Kirkeordinansen 1537/39* (1989), pp. 192-193.
24   McGuire (2013), pp. 221-223.

The immediate change

A large number of the mendicant friaries disappeared during the first few decades after the Reformation; however, in some cases the buildings (or parts of them) were given a new function. As mentioned above, the king often explicitly dictated that the friaries were to be given to the townspeople with a specific purpose, which in some cases came to pass – in other cases not.

The buildings as such were converted into a variety of uses that in many ways did not resemble their former functions. With regards to the churches and cloister walks, their physical appearance more or less dictated their use. The church was a distinctive building and would have been difficult to convert to other uses. Thus, most churches which were not torn down came to function as parish churches. The same applies to the cloister walks – they were difficult to utilise after the Reformation and in many cases were gradually demolished.[25] The friary buildings, however, were not distinctive building types and thus it was possible in many cases to utilize the remaining buildings.

The character of the friary buildings as well as the vast extent of most friary complexes meant that they were often split up into several segments or cadastres. In Odense, the Franciscan church was converted into a parish church, whereas the friary buildings were made into a hospital – and had its own church inserted into the former east range of the friary.[26] In Viborg, the friary church was already in 1529 turned into a parish church and the northern part of the friary was in 1541 converted into a hospital. Also the town mayor, Jesper Simonsen, owned parts of the complex in the years following the Reformation.[27]

In most cases, only parts of the former friaries were actively reused. The reason for this should probably be understood in light of the fact that the friary buildings were erected throughout the entire period of the order's existence in Denmark. Some friary buildings were thus several hundred years old by the time of the Reformation. Those which are still preserved and obviously found use in the post-medieval period were typically among the youngest in the complex, often erected in the latter part of the fifteenth or the beginning of the sixteenth century.

---

25 Larsen (2018), p. 105.
26 Larsen (1939), p. 25-27.
27 Ørberg (1986), pp. 22-23.

Abandonment and destruction

In some cases, we have almost no knowledge as to what happened to the buildings after the Reformation. For the most part, we can assume that this is due to the fact that the buildings were torn down. It is probable that neither Frederik I nor Christian III wanted this outcome, but most of the friaries were eventually destroyed. In one case, however – the Franciscan friary of Ribe – King Christian III dictated that the buildings should be demolished, due to their location close to the royal castle of Riberhus. The king feared that the friary might be strategically well placed during a potential siege. The entire complex was nonetheless not immediately destroyed and the east range was sold to a local man named Ruprecht Geispuscher in 1542.[28] During the sixteenth century, there was also some discussion about moving the town hall to the remains of the friary, or using the space for a new market square. Finally, the buildings were demolished.[29]

The buildings belonging to the friars were built for specific purposes and in relation to a plan structured in accordance with the friars' needs. This very characteristic pattern of a building complex may have proven difficult to utilise without extensive remodelling and thus it may have been easier simply to demolish the complex and perhaps reuse the building material elsewhere. This fate is not solely related to monastic institutions, but had implications for several ecclesiastical buildings in the urban context. During the late 1530s, a man known as 'kerken brecker' (i.e. 'the church demolisher') was active in the town of Ribe, where he is mentioned in relation to the demolition of some of the medieval parish churches – and maybe also the mendicant friaries.[30] In Nykøbing, where the church and the west range are still preserved, the east and north range were probably torn down already in the sixteenth century. It is known that Knud Gyldenstierne in 1532 got royal permission to demolish a wooden house belonging to the friary.[31]

Parish churches

During the years of Reformation, several Franciscan churches were converted into regular parish churches. This happened in Viborg, Horsens, Odense, Svendborg, Nykøbing and Ystad.[32] The friary churches were typically large,

---

28 *Danske Kancelliregistranter 1535-1550* (1881-1882), p. 220.
29 *Danske Kancelliregistranter 1535-1550* (1881-1882), p. 315; *Danmarks Kirker*, Ribe Amt, p. 847.
30 Nielsen (1985), p. 142.
31 *Kong Frederik den Førstes danske Registranter* (1879), p. 463.
32 *Diplomatarium Vibergense* (1879) p. 170; *Kong Frederik den Førstes danske Registranter* (1879), pp. 273, 301, 316, 337; *Danske Kancelliregistranter 1535-1550* (1881-1882), p. 89.

hence making them suitable for large numbers of parishioners and they were constructed to facilitate preaching, which was essential to the Lutheran Church. Also, by the time of the Reformation, some of the churches had recently undergone massive rebuilding and restoration and were probably in good repair. This may have been the case in Viborg, where several smaller medieval parish churches were taken out of use during the years of the Reformation and the town area was divided into two large parishes. The northern parish was centred on the Franciscan church, whereas the southern parish was orientated toward the Dominican church.[33]

The form and functions of the medieval church were changed to suit the new practices of the Lutheran service and thus large parts of the interior fittings were markedly altered. The church buildings gained new rooms, due to changing liturgical needs. In many cases, a fundamental shift can be seen in the addition of a porch building to one of the main doors to the church. In many cases, the porch is interpreted as a late medieval addition, but the architectural form as well as the social, practical and religious functions of the building are centrally linked to the liturgy of the parish church and should probably be seen as additions dating to the years immediately after the Reformation, as is known from the Franciscan church of Odense.[34] Another significant change was the tendency to incorporate the adjoining cloister walk as a side aisle, thereby increasing the size of the church nave and making space for a larger congregation. This change can be seen in the Franciscan churches of Odense, Nykøbing and Horsens,[35] as well as in the Dominican counterparts of Holbæk and Viborg.

A large selection of the Franciscan church furnishings and interior fittings were made obsolete during the Reformation. Side altars, lectoria, chancel screens and choir stalls had no use in the Lutheran service and were often either sold or destroyed in the following years. In some cases, however, they found a new function in the Lutheran church. In Horsens, a great deal of the late medieval church furnishings is preserved, comprising an elaborate altarpiece as well as some of the medieval choir stalls. Despite the pronounced Franciscan iconography on both altarpiece and stalls, they found use after the Reformation.[36] Also a large part of the grand memorial complex in the Franciscan church in Odense was preserved after the Reformation, consisting of a large altarpiece, chancel crucifix, memorial tablets and grave stones

33   Krongaard Kristensen (1987), pp. 105-106.
34   Wangsgaard Jürgensen (2012), pp. 250-252; Larsen (2013), p. 39.
35   *Danmarks Kirker*, p. 207; *Danmarks Kirker*, Århus Amt, p. 5716; Larsen (2013), p. 67.
36   Plathe (1999).

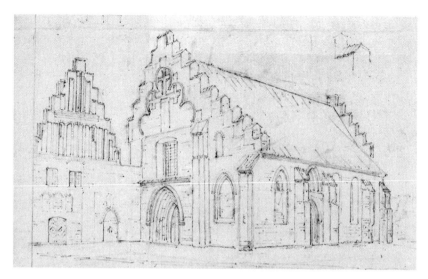

The Franciscan church of Svendborg, drawn in 1828 by C.F. Thorin on the eve of demolition. After the Reformation, the friary church was converted into a church for parish use, until it was rendered redundant in the beginning of the nineteenth century. To the left, the south gable of the late medieval west range can be seen, which was reused as a public school. Drawing in the National Museum of Denmark

for the royal family and choir stalls. The fittings were preserved in the church until it was demolished in the early nineteenth century and even after that, many of the fittings (altarpiece, memorial tablets and royal graves) were moved to the cathedral church in Odense.[37] The choir stalls disappeared by this event and the same tendency can be seen in Svendborg, where the Franciscan church was demolished around the same date. A large number of the medieval furnishings were kept when the friary was abandoned, but most of them were given over to other churches to be preserved. Much of the original furnishings, however, disappeared in the following years.[38]

Odense and Svendborg are in many ways curious cases. Their friary churches were both maintained and initially intended to be used as parish churches. In Svendborg, the town was already divided into two parishes and the Franciscan church was therefore only used for burials and special services.[39] In Odense, the Franciscan church functioned as a parish church until the early seventeenth century, when the parish was incorporated into that of

---

37 Cf. Bøggild Johannsen (2014).
38 Krongaard Kristensen (1994), pp. 74-81.
39 Reinholdt (1992), p. 99.

the cathedral church – probably due to the cathedral's poor economy. There-after, the Franciscan church was used only for special services until gradual decay doomed the building to demolition.[40] In Svendborg, the reason for the long preservation might be seen in relation to the noble family of Harden-berg, who took interest in the abandoned friary by erecting a burial chapel and establishing a hospital in some of the remaining buildings. In Odense, however, the royal burials (King John, Queen Christina and their sons) from the early sixteenth century may have made the difference in securing preser-vation in the centuries after the Reformation.

Hospital

Most notable is the reuse of friaries as hospitals or similar social institutions taking care of the poor, weak and elderly. The interest in converting men-dicant estates into social institutions might also be seen as a way to comply with a growing problem of the general welfare and care of the population, since the late medieval concept of almsgiving was transformed during the course of the Reformation.[41] Poul Helgesen (*Paulus Helie*), the contemporary Carmelite scholar, even wrote harshly that a typical act by Lutherans was to convert churches and monasteries into hospitals.[42]

In 1532, Frederik I conveyed a large part of the friary in Ystad to the town for use as a hospital.[43] In Odense, the Franciscan friary as a whole (with the exception of the church) was in 1540 given over to the function of a hospi-tal.[44] The same happened to parts of the friary in Viborg in 1541.[45] Also, the friary in Schleswig functioned as a hospital in the years following the Refor-mation.[46] In Svendborg, the king initially wanted the buildings converted into a hospital, but this was not realised until decades later.

Other public institutions

In Nykøbing Falster, a part of the west range of the friary was by royal decree converted into a town hall – with a prison in the cellar.[47] Also in Schleswig, the friary church was converted into a town hall in 1529 and functioned as

---

40   Larsen (2013), p. 10.
41   Dahlerup (1979-81), pp. 207-208.
42   *Skrifter af Paulus Helie* 6 (1937), p. 172.
43   *Kong Frederik den Førstes danske Registranter* (1879), p. 332.
44   *Danske Kancelliregistranter 1535-1550* (1881-1882), pp. 89, 127.
45   *Danske Kancelliregistranter 1535-1550* (1881-1882), pp. 203-204.
46   Lafrenz (1985), p. 132.
47   *Kong Frederik den Førstes danske Registranter* (1879), p. 316; Holm (1916), pp. 9-10.

such until 1793.[48] In Ribe, it was originally the intention to place the town hall in the abandoned friary, but the plan was never realised.[49]

In a few cases, it is known that the remaining friary buildings were reused as public schools. In Nykøbing, a part of the lower floor of the former west range of the friary was converted into a school, where the school's headmaster had an apartment on the upper floor.[50] The decision to convert part of the west range into a school was not the king's and must have been an idea generated by the town officials in the years after the takeover. The same happened to the west range in Svendborg, where the king in 1530 and 1532 had intended to establish a hospital. This did not take place until 1586 and then it was on the initiative of the noble family of Hardenberg.[51] In 1541, however, a school was started in the west range and continued to exist until well into the eighteenth century.[52]

Residence

In Randers, the friary was initially given by the king to the nobleman Mogens Gøye, steward of the realm, but already in 1544 the friary was again in the Crown's possession.[53] During the following years the complex was heavily rebuilt and transformed into a royal castle ('Dronningborg'). The same happened to the Franciscan friary in Copenhagen, where the Renaissance town residence of 'Ulfeldt's Manor' was erected on the remains of the friary buildings, although it is unknown to what degree the friary buildings were incorporated. In Viborg, Christian III made an addition to the Franciscan friary in preparation for personal residence, today known as 'Kongens Kammer' (the King's Chamber) and 'Dansesalen' (the dance hall). The initiative was probably made already in one of the king's first years as a regent, while the fate of the buildings had not yet been decided. This took place in 1539, when the precinct was divided between different parties. By then, the king had obtained the former bishop's manor in Viborg, which he probably preferred as residence while staying in the town.[54] In Aalborg, King Frederik already early in the 1530s split the Franciscan friary's precinct into smaller plots and sold them to different citizens – in one case the king reserved the right to revoke

---

48   Lafrenz (1985), p. 132; Mehlhorn (2007), p. 203.
49   Nielsen (1985), p. 143.
50   Holm (1916), pp. 9-10.
51   Krongaard Kristensen (1994), p. 12.
52   *Kong Frederik den Førstes danske Registranter* (1879), p. 272-273, 336; *Danske Kancelliregistranter 1535-1550* (1881-1882), p. 204.
53   *Kong Frederik den Førstes danske Registranter* (1879), p. 246.
54   Krongaard Kristensen (1987), p. 107; Vellev (1996).

the deed in case the friary was to be rebuilt, as a castle.[55] Apparently, this outcome did not come to pass, since a new castle, Aalborghus, was erected in the following years.

In one case, the reuse probably did not require a large rebuilding process. When Frederik I gave the friary of Ystad to the burghers for use as hospital and parish church, he added a note that he reserved the right to have personal quarters within the friary precinct, as his forefathers had had before him.[56]

Implications on urban topography

The changes caused by the Reformation in some cases had influence beyond the friary precinct. The destruction of several friaries could make it possible to reshape urban topography. In Næstved, the friars were driven out in 1532 and the buildings were given to the town.[57] It was apparently difficult to utilise the buildings (despite the noble intention of establishing a hospital) and in 1553, the burghers received permission to demolish the church and establish a large town square ('Axeltorv'), thereby significantly altering the urban topography.[58]

Active reuse in some cases also had indirect influence on the shaping of the urban layout. When the mendicant friaries in Viborg were converted into two parish churches ('Nørresogn' and 'Søndresogn'), the numerous existing medieval parish churches were taken out of use and demolished, thereby changing the geography of the town.[59]

The long-term perspective

Friaries, as we have seen, were given new functions after the Reformation. In the long term, they also saw several changes. One notices Frederik I's interest in using friary buildings as political leverage, but change did not always take place in accordance with the king's wishes. Soon, new political interests and practical reasons reshaped the abandoned friaries.

In the case of the nunnery of St Clare in Copenhagen, the king initially (in 1530) decided that the nuns could stay, but already in 1535 or 1536, they had apparently left the nunnery buildings, probably due to the turmoil in the

---

55 *Kong Frederik den Førstes danske Registranter* (1879), p. 255.
56 *Kong Frederik den Førstes danske Registranter* (1879), p. 301.
57 *Kong Frederik den Førstes danske Registranter* (1879), p. 332.
58 *Kancelliets Brevbøger*, 1551-1555, p. 213 (1553 January 29th)
59 Krongaard Kristensen (1987), pp. 105-109.

wake of the siege of Copenhagen.[60] In 1543, a royal mint was established on the nunnery precinct; in 1558, it is known that the buildings were used for storage; while in 1573, the nunnery was once again used for spiritual purposes when the German community in Copenhagen needed a church. A few decades later (in 1585), however, it moved to the Church of St Peter and now the nunnery buildings were converted into a canon foundry.[61] A few years later – in 1610 – the complex was finally demolished and the last remains of the medieval site disappeared by 1616 at the latest.[62] Despite the initial intentions during the years of Reformation, the politics of reuse often dictated other solutions.

Concluding remarks

Despite their attempts during the latter part of the fifteenth century to reorganise the order in search of a stricter ideal, the Franciscan friars were among the first to be confronted with the realities of the Lutheran Reformation. The general view that the friars did not live in accordance with their ideals probably had a negative effect, when the Lutheran teachings gained ground.

In this tense religious climate, King Frederik I and his son Christian III probably saw an opportunity to gain control of segments of a church that was slowly losing its grip on the people. They used the friaries as political leverage in relation to a class of patricians and other townsmen, of growing political influence – and vice versa. Also abandoned friaries could help compensate after the dissolution of different medieval welfare institutions.

Despite Frederik I's attempts to utilise the remaining buildings, he in many cases did not succeed, or the new institutions had a relatively short life span. Shifting interests combined with practical problems in actively reusing the abandoned friaries meant that most complexes were gradually torn down in the decades immediately after the Reformation. However, in a few cases the buildings survived – even until today.

---

60 *Kong Frederik den Førstes danske Registranter* (1879), p. 269.
61 Bobé (1925) pp. 176-178, 295.
62 *Danmarks Kirker*, København By, p. 32.

Bibliography

Andrén, Anders, *Mellan ting och text. En introduktion till de historiska arkeologierna* (Stockholm, 1997).

Bobé, Louis, *Die Deutsche St. Petri Gemeinde zu Kopenhagen, ihre Kirche, Schulen und Stiftungen 1575-1925* (Copenhagen, 1925).

Bøggild Johannsen, Birgitte, 'Gråbrødre Klosterkirke i Odense', in *Danske Kongegrave 2*, ed. Karin Kryger (Copenhagen, 2014), pp. 173-195.

Dahlerup, Troels, 'Den sociale forsorg og reformationen i Danmark', *Jyske Samlinger* 13:1-2 (1979-81), pp. 195-208.

Danmarks Kirker, København By, 1, eds. Jan Steenberg et al. (Copenhagen, 1954-1988).

Danmarks Kirker, Maribo Amt, 8, eds. Aage Roussell et al. (Copenhagen, 1948-1951).

Danmarks Kirker, Ribe Amt, 19, eds. Elna Møller et al. (Copenhagen, 1979-2003).

Danmarks Kirker, Svendborg Amt, 10, eds. Marianne Goral Krogh Johansen et al. (Copenhagen 2010-).

Danmarks Kirker, Århus Amt, 16, eds. Kjeld de Fine Licht et al. (Copenhagen, 1968-2008).

Danske Kancelliregistranter 1535-1550, eds. Kristian Erslev and William Mollerup (Copenhagen, 1881-1882).

'De Expulsione Fratrum Minorum', in *Scriptores Minores Historiæ Danicæ Medii Ævi 2*, ed. M. Cl. Gertz (Copenhagen, 1922).

Diplomatarium Vibergense. Breve og Aktstykker fra ældre viborgske Arkiver til Viborg Bys og Stifts Historie 1200-1559, ed. A. Heise (Copenhagen, 1879).

Ericsson, Ingolf, 'Archäologie der Neuzeit. Ziele und Abgrenzungen einer jungen Disziplin der archäologischen Wissenschaft', *Ausgrabungen und Funde* 40:1, (1995), pp. 7-13.

Grell, Ole Peter, 'Introduction', in *The Scandinavian Reformation. From evangelical movement to institutionalization of reform*, ed. Ole Peter Grell (Cambridge, 1995), pp. 1-11.

Holm, Viggo, 'Nykøbing Kirke og dens Omgivelser I', *Lolland-Falsters Historiske Samfund. Aarbog* (1916), pp. 1-21.

Hyldgård, Inger Marie, 'De arkæologiske spor efter Gråbrødre Kloster i Randers', *hikuin* 23 (1996), pp. 95-106.

Ingesman, Per, 'På vej mod reformationen', *Viborgs Historie. Oldtid-1726*, eds. Henning Ringgaard Lauridsen and Lars Munkøe (Viborg, 1998), pp. 179-222.

Kancelliets Brevbøger vedrørende Danmarks indre Forhold i Uddrag, eds. C. F. Bricka et al., 39 vols. (Copenhagen, 1885-2005).

Kirkeordinansen 1537/39, ed. Martin Schwarz Lausten (Copenhagen, 1989).

Kong Frederik den Førstes danske Registranter, eds. Kristian Erslev and William Mollerup (Copenhagen, 1879).

Krongaard Kristensen, Hans, *Middelalderbyen Viborg* (Aarhus, 1987).

Krongaard Kristensen, Hans, *The Franciscan Friary of Svendborg* (Svendborg, 1994).

Krongaard Kristensen, Hans, *Klostre i det middelalderlige Danmark* (Højbjerg, 2013).

Krøniken om Graabrødrenes fordrivelse fra deres klostre i Danmark, trans. Henning Heilesen (Copenhagen, 1967).

Lafrenz, Deert, *Kirchen, Klöster und Hospitäler. Die Kunstdenkmäler der Stadt Schleswig, 3* (Berlin/München, 1985).

Larsen, Morten, *Franciskanerklosteret i Odense. En arkæologisk undersøgelse af det middelalderlige bygningskompleks* (Højbjerg, 2013).

Larsen, Morten, *Danmarks middelalderlige tiggerklostre* (Højbjerg, 2018).

Larsen, Svend, *Graabrødre Hospital og Kloster i Odense* (Copenhagen, 1939).

Larson, James L., *Reforming the North. The Kingdoms and Churches of Scandinavia, 1520-1545* (Cambridge, 2010).

Lausten, Martin Schwarz, *Reformationen i Danmark* (Copenhagen, 1987).

Liisberg, H.C. Bering, 'Fra Ulfelds Plads og Graabrødretorv', *Architekten* 4, (1901), pp. 63-67, 77-84.

Lyby, Thorkild C., *Vi Evangeliske. Studier over samspillet mellem udenrigspolitik og kirkepolitik på Frederik I's tid* (Aarhus, 1993).

McGuire, Brian Patrick, 'Kalundborgs franciskanerkloster og Raklev Kirke. Kirkens reformationer i lyset af Melchior Jensens historie', in *Menneskers veje – kulturhistoriske essays i 100-året for Kalundborgs Museum*, ed. L. Pedersen (Kalundborg, 2013), pp. 221-240.

Mehlhorn, Dieter J., *Klöster und Stifte in Schleswig-Holstein. 1200 Jahre Geschichte, Architektur und Kunst* (Kiel, 2007).

Mårtensson, Anders, *Uppgrävt förflutet för PKbanken i Lund* (Lund, 1976).

Nielsen, Ingrid, *Middelalderbyen Ribe* (Aarhus, 1985).

Nybo Rasmussen, Jørgen, *Die Franziskaner in den nordischen Ländern im Mittelalter* (Kevelaer, 2002).

Pettersson, Claes, 'Fram i ljuset – utgrävningar på Jönköpings slott', in *Stormaktsstaden Jönköping. 1614 och framåt*, eds. Ann-Marie Nordman, Michael Nordström and Claes Pettersson (Jönköping, 2014), pp. 99-127.

Plathe, Sissel F., 'Franciskansk ikonografi: Horsens klosterkirke', in *Billeder i Middelalderen. Kalkmalerier og altertavler*, eds. Lars Bisgaard et al (Odense, 1999), pp. 51-76.

Ramsing, H. U., *Københavns Historie og Topografi* 3 (Copenhagen, 1940).

Reinholdt, Helle, *Middelalderbyen Svendborg* (Aarhus, 1992).

Rosenkjær, H. N., *Fra det underjordiske København* (Copenhagen, 1906).

Samling af danske Kongers Haandfæstninger og andre lignende Acter (Copenhagen, 1856-1858 [1974]).

Skrifter af Paulus Helie, vol. 6, eds. Marius Kristensen and Hans Ræder (Copenhagen, 1937).

Svart Kristiansen, Mette, 'Renæssance, arkæologi – og bønder', in *Renæssancens Verden. Tænkning, kulturliv, dagligliv og efterliv*, eds. Ole Høiris and Jens Vellev (Aarhus, 2006), pp. 473-490.

Vellev, Jens, "Kongens Kammer" og 'Dansesalen'. Indrettet i Viborg Gråbrødrekloster', *hikuin* 23 (1996), pp. 191-198.

Wangsgaard Jürgensen, Martin, *Changing Interiors. Danish village churches c. 1450 to 1600* (Copenhagen, 2012).

Witte, Frauke, *Archäologie in Flensburg. Ausgrabungen am Franziskanerkloster* (Flensburg, 2003).

Ørberg, Paul G., *Når nøden er størst. Viborg Gråbrødre Klosters historie fra reformationen til nutiden* (Viborg, 1986).

A
Regional
Perspective

The Monasteries in Sweden during the Reformation

Martin Berntson

In December 1595, a group of visitors entered the Brigittine abbey in Vadstena. Most noticeable among the visitors were the Archbishop Abraham Angermannus (d. 1607), well known for his Lutheran orthodox stance, and Duke Charles (later Charles IX) (1550-1611). According to a written account by the historian Johannes Messenius (d. 1636), the nuns were given a choice. They could either accept the Lutheran faith and remain in the convent, or refuse conversion and cause its closure. According to the same source, the nuns chose to remain Catholics and left the convent. They stayed in the city until the summer when most of them left for a nunnery of the same order in Gdańsk.[1] Two young convent sisters stayed in the city of Vadstena and Sweden for several decades.[2]

The dissolution of Vadstena Abbey, the sole surviving monastery in Sweden at this time, is usually related to the turbulent political situation in Sweden during the 1590s. The kingdom of Sweden was ruled by King Sigismund (his rule lasted from 1592 until 1599), who was a Catholic by birth and favoured the abbey. Sigismund was also king of Poland, and in his absence from the Swedish realm, his uncle Duke Charles was elected steward of the kingdom in October 1595. In practice, he was thereby given charge of the kingdom. As part of the process of creating a more firm political position, he accepted the demands from the orthodox Lutheran clergy to close all Catho-

---

1   The most famous account of this dissolution is found in Messenius, *Scondia* 8 p. 31. The same author also gives a short account of this event in Messenius, CSB, pp. 242-243. In Knut Persons chronicle on King Charles IX from 1616, the dissolution is described from another point of view, see HSH 10 p. 41.

2   Berntson (2003), p. 252.

lic institutions in the kingdom that were protected by King Sigismund.[3] This rebellious policy would eventually lead to civil war between the duke and the king, a war which ended with the victory of Duke Charles in 1598.

However, with the dissolution of Vadstena Abbey, the last monastery in Sweden was closed. A process that had been initiated nearly eighty years earlier had come to an end.

The state of the monasteries and mendicant houses in Sweden before the Reformation

Around the year 1520, there were about 50 monasteries and mendicant houses in the kingdom of Sweden.

In comparison with Denmark, where, as mentioned in the introduction to this volume, 116 monastic foundations existed at the time of the Reformation, the number of monasteries in Sweden must be regarded as relatively low. While the number of monasteries and mendicant houses in the Archdiocese of Lund was 24, the corresponding number in the Archdiocese of Uppsala was only seven.[4] There were actually more monastic foundations in the diocese of Linköping than in the Archdiocese. In comparison with Denmark, there were (at least not formally) no Benedictine abbeys in Sweden at this time. Instead, we find a number of Cistercian nunneries. The oldest Cistercian monasteries for men in Sweden were Alvastra in Östergötland and Nydala in Småland, both of which were, according to tradition, founded in 1143.[5] Both were daughter houses to Clairvaux. During the latter half of the twelfth century, Alvastra founded two daughter houses: Varnhem in Västergötland and Julita in Södermanland.[6] The oldest nunnery in Sweden, Vreta Abbey, may according to some historians have existed as a monastic institution as early as 1100.[7] Under all circumstances it became a Cistercian nunnery in 1162. Vreta became mother house of Askeby in Östergötland and of Riseberga in Närke, which were established during the latter half of the twelfth century. During the following decades, three additional Cistercian nunneries were founded: Gudhem in Västergötland, Sko in Uppland and

---

3   Berntson (2003), p. 249
4   See Berntson (2016a), pp. 29–35.
5   Ortved (1933), pp. 53, 56, 141; Johansson (1964), pp. 91-92; France (1992), p. 3, 8.
6   Ortved (1933), pp. 56, 225, 256; France (1992), pp. 29, 35-36, 38-40.
7   For a critical discussion on this matter, see Nilsson 2008.

Vårfruberga in Södermanland. A last Cistercian house, Gudsberga, was established in the southern part of the province of Dalarna in 1486. This house was to become the northernmost monastery in Sweden.[8]

During the late twelfth century, a Hospitaller house was established in Eskilstuna. Another house belonging to the same order was established in Kronobäck in Småland 1479.[9]

The spiritually and culturally most influential monastery in Sweden during the Late Middle Ages was Vadstena Abbey, which was consecrated in 1384, the first house of the Brigittine Order. Another Brigittine house, Naantali in Finland (which was a Swedish province at this time), was founded in 1440.[10]

One of the latest monastic institutions that was founded in Sweden before the Reformation was *Pax Mariae* (*Mariefred*), which was to become the only house in Scandinavia belonging to the Carthusian Order. The monastery was situated on an estate called Gripsholm which the regent of the kingdom, Sten Sture the elder, donated to the Carthusian brethren in the 1490s.[11] As we shall see, this house was also the first monastery to be dissolved. However, *Pax Marie* was not the very last monastic house to become established in Sweden. During the last decades preceding the Reformation, the Order of the Holy Ghost was established in the kingdom. One house belonging to this order had been established in Söderköping 1510[12] and another monastery was planned to be built at Lindholmen on the peninsula Kålland in Västergötland.[13]

Among the mendicant houses, sixteen were Franciscan. Of these, nine were established during the thirteenth century and six during the fifteenth century. Most of these houses were situated in towns. However, there were two exceptions: Krokek in the forest of Kolmården and Kökar in the south eastern archipelago in Finland.[14] In Stockholm, a house belonging to the Order of St Clare was also established.[15] Eleven mendicant houses belonged to the Dominican Order. The majority of these were founded during the thirteenth century. The only exceptions were the convent in Stockholm, which

---

8   Ortved (1933), pp. 316, 323, 363, 401, 483-485, 519; Johansson (1964), pp. 74-85; McGuire (1982), pp. 186-187; France (1992), pp. 42, 151-152, 157-158, 169-173, 420; Larsson (1998) p. 87; Lovén (2001), p. 247.
9   Reitzel-Nielsen (1984), pp. 80, 205, 210, 212, 221-226; Pernler (1992), p. 34; Konow (1995), pp. 66-67.
10   Cnattingius (1963), pp. 21-23, 14-17, 26, 69; Klockars (1979), p. 13; Nyberg (1991), pp. 78, 116-118, 130.
11   Collijn (1935), pp. 149-150; Hallberg (1968), p. 2.
12   Hedqvist (1893), pp. 109-110; Lindbæk et al. (1906), p. 65; Gallén (1961) p. 313; see also Berntson (2016c).
13   Berntson (2003), p. 35.
14   Samzelius (1965) p. 103; Gallén (1989), p. 32; Gustavsson (1994), pp. 494, 497, 501-503.
15   On the Franciscan houses, see Leinberg (1890), p. 104; Gallén (1989), p. 32, 47; Rasmussen (1994), p. 5, 23; Rasmussen (2002), pp. 500-517.

was founded in the 1340s, and the convent in Vyborg, which was established as late as the early fifteenth century.[16] Among the mendicants we also count the Hospital Brothers of St Anthony who had a house in Ramundeboda situated in a forest between the provinces of Närke and Västergötland, which functioned as a guesthouse for travellers.[17] Finally, the Carmelite order had but one convent in Sweden, situated in the city of Örebro, a house which was established in the 1450s.[18]

When it comes to describing the state of the monasteries at this time, there has been a tendency in previous research to focus on the number of their estates and sort the houses into the categories of "rich" and "poor".[19] This method, I suggest, is problematic since the number of estates does not say anything about the wealth of the houses. Furthermore, how do we define a "rich" or a "poor" monastery? The fact that a monastery owned several estates does not say anything about its actual surplus. During good periods, a monastery could have a good income, but it also had expenses.[20] Nevertheless, one economic tendency is noticeable. For many monasteries there had been a decline in terms of donations. Lars-Arne Norborg has argued that this trend, which is discernible from the late fifteenth century, may be part of a struggle by the nobility to decrease the wealth of the Church.[21]

---

16   Leinberg (1890), p. 71; Gallén (1946), pp. 12, 21-22, 37-40, 43, 55, 137, 183, 188-195; Gallén (1958), pp. 178-179, 183-184.
17   See Hallberg (1968), p. 11; see also Bednar (2007).
18   Grandinson (1933), p. 56; Dahlerup (1963), p. 298; Pernler (1992), p. 41.
19   Collijn (1935), p. 157; Stensland (1945), p. 40; Pernler (1992), p. 35; Larsson (1998), pp. 85-86.
20   Berntson (2003), pp. 41-43.
21   Norborg (1958), pp. 66-70.

Monasteries and nunneries

Cistercians	Carthusians (male)
Monasteries	Gripsholm
Alvastra	
Husby	**Hospitallers (male)**
Julita	Eskilstuna
Nydala	Kronobäck
Varnhem	(Stockholm)
Nunneries	**Brigittines**
Askeby	Naantali (Nådendal)
Gudhem	Vadstena
Riseberga	
Sko	**Order of the Holy Ghost (male)**
Vreta	Söderköping
Vårfruberga	(Lindholmen)

Mendicant houses

Dominicans	Franciscans
Brethren	*Brethren*
Kalmar	Arboga
Lödöse	Enköping
Sigtuna	Jönköping
Skara	Krokek
Skänninge	Kökar (Hamnö)
Stockholm	Linköping
Strängnäs	Nyköping
Vyborg (Viborg)	Nylödöse
Västerås	Rauma (Raumo)
Turku (Åbo)	Skara
	Stockholm
Sisters	Söderköping
Skänninge	Uppsala
	Vyborg (Viborg)
Antonites (male)	Växjö
Ramundeboda	
	Sisters
Carmelites (male)	Stockholm
Örebro	

In both old and recent studies, we sometimes find the claim that the monastic houses at the end of the Middle Ages were in decay and had lost their "spiritual ardour".[22] In the very few cases where these arguments have been supported, the facts have mostly come from the letters of the bishop of Linköping Hans Brask and his criticism of the Franciscan order. In 1524, Bishop Hans Brask wrote to the Franciscans and claimed that the whole order was in decay. Because of disagreements and greediness among the brethren, their perambulations in the countryside should be forbidden.[23] Many of his accusations may correspond to actual problems. Yet, this criticism should also be related to long term tensions between bishops and mendicants concerning jurisdiction in the dioceses. Since the mendicants were not subordinated to the leadership of the parish, it was not unusual to have

---

22 Hall (1907), p. 19; Westman (1918), p. 78; Holmquist: I (1933), p. 36; Larsson (1998), p. 85; Larsson (2002), pp. 121-122.
23 See the cited sources in Berntson (2003), p. 58; Stobaeus (2010), pp. 166-170.

conflicts between bishops and Franciscans in Europe.[24] Furthermore, many of the authors that refer to such "decay" seem to believe that the number of monastic "scandals" had increased in the years preceding the Reformation, but examples of monks and nuns that disobeyed the monastic rules are found throughout the whole history of monasticism. Furthermore, since there are no objective means of defining the term, the question of "spiritual ardour" is a value expression difficult to use in an academic study.

We do know, however, that many orders were affected by the tensions resulting from the waning union among the three Scandinavian states. The so-called Kalmar Union, which had been established in 1397 among the three Scandinavian kingdoms of Denmark, Norway and Sweden, was opposed during the fifteenth century by parties and associations in Sweden who were unwilling to accept Danish rule. These tensions sometimes resulted in civil war. The warfare between the kingdoms affected some of the houses materially. For example, some houses were damaged or set on fire.[25] Furthermore, in the Cistercian convent in Nydala, some monks were murdered by the Danish King Christian II as part of his attempt to silence political opposition.[26] There were also tensions in the relations between Swedish and Danish houses. For example, there seem to have been disagreements between Danish and Swedish Franciscans concerning adherence to the Observant movement. The Observants had since the early fifteenth century emphasized the poverty ideal, in opposition to the Conventuals who were more open to ownership and income from estates. In 1517, the Observants gained a superior position in relation to the Conventuals. In practice, the Conventuals became a subject minority.[27] In the Franciscan province of Dacia, as a rule, the provincial ministers were alternately to come from Denmark and from Sweden/Norway. In practice, the ministers were usually Swedes or Danes.[28] While the Danish Franciscan houses became Observant, the Conventual Franciscans seem to have had a stronghold in Sweden where the Observant movement was seen as a Danish affair.[29] When the Danish provincial minister Jens Mogensen died in 1515, he was – according to the rule – replaced by a Swedish brother, Lars Johansson. Since all Danish Franciscan convents had joined the

24   Lawrence (1984), pp. 213-214; Stobaeus (2010), p. 167.
25   Berggren (1902), pp. 63-64; Gallén (1958), pp. 183-194; Torbrand (1968), pp. 80, 83-84.
26   See GR I, pp. 14, 23.
27   Lindbæk (1914), pp. 50, 55–65, 74-75; Westman (1918), pp. 79-80; Gallén (1959), sp. 570; Gallén (1989), pp. 48-49.
28   Lindbæk (1914), p. 50.
29   Lindbæk (1914), p. 65; Westman (1918), pp. 79-80; Gallén (1989), pp. 48-49.

Observants in 1517, he was only to retain authority over the Swedish (and perhaps also the Norwegian) Franciscan convents.[30] Likewise, the Swedish Hospitallers for many years refused to obey their motherhouse Antvorskov in Denmark. The conflict between the Hospitaller houses in Eskilstuna and the motherhouse in Antvorskov had existed since the middle of the fifteenth century. For example, between 1457 and 1460 the brethren in Eskilstuna on two occasions expelled the newly appointed – Danish – priors. The second time, they were accused of having used arms to expel the prior.[31] It is possible that the Swedish Hospitallers wanted to create an independent priory in Sweden. The reason behind the Swedish monks' animosity toward the Danes could be related to the fact that the house in Eskilstuna had good relations with the leading figures in the anti-union groups.[32] This would not be surprising. It was natural for a monastic order to be loyal to the secular authorities, not least since military protection as well as various donations from the regent and the council were needed.[33]

Just as in Denmark and Germany, Swedish Reformation theologians expressed negative opinions about monastic life. The leading Swedish Lutheran theologian, Olaus Petri (d. 1552), criticized monasticism in a series of books during the latter half of the 1520s. He also wrote a whole book directed against monastic life: *Een liten boock j huilko closterleffwerne forclarat warder* (A small book in which monastic life is explained) (1528). If we compare Martin Luther's discussions of the problems of monasteries and monastic vows with the opinions of his disciple Olaus Petri,[34] we notice a slight difference in emphasis. Luther emphatically emphasized monastic vows as one form of good works falsely regarded as a means to salvation. Olaus Petri shared Luther's view on justification by faith alone, but this was not a very important topic for him. Instead Olaus Petri focused on the lack of biblical foundation for both monastic vows and monastic life.[35] According to Olaus Petri, the monastic life in its present form had no basis in the Bible. Instead, the monastic movement was thought to have begun more than two hundred years after the time of the apostles, with desert hermits such as St Paul and

---

30 See Lindbæk (1914), pp. 74-75; Gallén (1989), pp. 48-49; Rasmussen (1994), pp. 8-9.
31 Hatt Olsen (1961), pp. 324-327; Hatt Olsen (1962), pp. 104-105; Reitzel-Nielsen 1984, pp. 310-311; see also Berntson (2006), pp. 60-61.
32 Reitzel-Nielsen (1984), pp. 263-264; 310-312; Gallén et al. (1962), sp. 602; Konow (1995), p. 64.
33 The same tensions between Swedish and Danish monastic houses might also be noticed in other orders, for example among the Dominicans and the Order of the Holy Ghost, see Berntson (2003), p. 52.
34 For Luther's view on monastic vows, see for example Lohse (1963), pp. 344-355.
35 On the theological debate concerning monasteries in Sweden, see Berntson (2003), pp. 190-198.

St Anthony.[36] Olaus Petri also criticized the idea that the prophets in the Old Testament and the "devout men" mentioned in Acts 2:5 should be interpreted as monastics.[37] As in the writings by Martin Luther and Philipp Melanchton, much of Olaus Petri's criticism was aimed at monastic vows. According to Olaus Petri, these vows violated those given at baptism and the evangelical freedom articulated in the Bible. Furthermore, the vows were, according to Olaus Petri, impossible to uphold since it was difficult for a man to live in chastity without committing fornication or other sins.[38] Just like Martin Luther, Olaus Petri claimed that man was not created to live in virginity. Man's nature contained sexual desire, which could only be controlled through marriage. Not even nuns or monks had, according to Olaus Petri, received the grace to live in a chaste manner, something that he found evident in the daily life of monasteries. For example, he noted that nuns tended to be eager to speak and write to men and often wanted to provide them with various gifts such as wreaths and handkerchiefs. These examples were "certain signs that they have yearnings and lust for men, and a natural desire yearning in their own bodies" (my translation).[39]

However, Olaus Petri did not reject the entire monastic tradition. Just like many of the German reformers, Olaus Petri held the Church Fathers in high esteem, and in full accordance with Luther and Melanchton, Olaus Petri appreciated the early monastic movement, which had neither vows nor monastic rules. Rather, the first monastics followed the biblical "rule" and created "Bible-schools". According to this version of history writing, degeneration started with the Rule of Benedict and reached its climax with the coming of the mendicant friars in the thirteenth century.[40]

Even though this opinion was never explicitly articulated by Olaus Petri, his appreciation of the early monastic movement made possible a transformation rather than an abolition of the monasteries. Although Olaus Petri was in many ways highly critical of the contemporary monastic life, he could express a will to turn the monasteries into "Christian schools".[41] As we shall see, this view agreed with the government's policy of transforming the monastic houses into institutions of various kinds.

---

36 OPSS I, pp. 278-279.
37 OPSS I, pp. 280-281.
38 See OPSS I, p. 485; see also Ingebrand (1964), p. 319; Berntson (2003), pp. 193-195.
39 OPSS I, pp. 347-348, 522-523.
40 See OPSS I, p. 279-280; 478-479; Ingebrand (1964), p. 58; Christensen (1973), p. 71; Berntson (2003), pp. 195-197.
41 See OPSS I, p. 197-198; see also Berntson (2003), pp. 197-198.

Intensified state control of the monasteries

After the war of independence from the union, Gustav Vasa was elected king of the independent kingdom of Sweden in June of 1523. His regime is often associated with the introduction of the Lutheran Reformation in the kingdom. The regime lacked economic resources and it also needed ideological and theological legitimization. The Reformation in its Lutheran form would provide the regime with both. First of all, the kingdom needed material resources and it was in many ways natural to seek the solution to this challenge in the wealth of the Church and the monasteries, not least because, as already noted, there had been attempts by the nobility to limit the increasing economic wealth of the Church for decades.

In some earlier research, there is a tendency to regard all of Gustav Vasa's early aggression towards the monasteries as part of an explicit "plan" to dissolve all monasteries.[42] However, before 1527 it is hard to perceive an explicit "plan" where various acts of aggression took place in a well-planned manner in order to dissolve the monasteries.[43] It is unlikely that Gustav Vasa at the time of his accession to the throne could have imagined the possibility of a complete dissolution of the monasteries (something that, furthermore, was not accomplished during his long reign). But even though it is not possible to discern any explicit "plan" to dissolve *all* the monasteries during the first four to five years after King Gustav Vasa's accession to the throne in 1523, in practice his government did in various ways work towards a *subordination* of the Church and the monasteries during the years before the Diet in Västerås in 1527. It is important, however, to note that subordination and state control of monasteries did not necessarily imply a *dissolution* of all of them.

One of the earliest infringements by the Swedish State on the monasteries was a series of confiscations of silver during the years 1523-24. Since they were actually justified along with a defence of evangelic preaching, these confiscations became a first step towards state control of the monasteries.[44] Another step in this direction was the establishment in 1524 of so-

---

42 Holmquist: I (1933), p. 101; Härdelin (1998), p. 133.

43 A misreading by Werner (2003), p. 244, has given rise to the misunderstanding that I would claim that there *never* existed any plan or intention to dissolve the monasteries, see Stobaeus (2010) pp. 200-201. It needs to be noted that what I do claim is that it is difficult to find any explicit plan to dissolve all the monasteries *before the time of the Diet in Västerås 1527*, see for example Berntson (2003), p. 82.

44 Berntson (2003), p. 74. However, it should be noticed that confiscations of silver and other valuables was not something new, neither in Sweden nor in the rest of Europe, see the discussion in Berntson (2003), pp. 69-70.

called *borgläger*, i.e. the practice of quartering royal soldiers and their horses in the monasteries.[45] The perhaps most important step towards royal control of the monasteries was taken in January 1526, when Gustav Vasa claimed the property of Gripsholm (belonging to the Carthusian order), which was said to be his inheritance. Even though the justification for this claim had a weak foundation, the act was to set a precedent. At the Diet of Västerås in 1527, the nobility used the royal move as a warrant for the right of any nobleman to claim family estates from the churches and monasteries.[46]

All these infringements on the monasteries as well as the levying of taxes and silver confiscations from various churches were criticized during the uprisings in the province of Dalarna in 1525 and 1527.[47] In a letter from the inhabitants of the province of Dalarna 1525, for example, the king was accused of having confiscated treasures from churches and monasteries devoted to "Service of the Lord", such as monstrances, chalices and reliquaries.[48] During the second uprising in Dalarna 1527, complaints were made against the regime because of the destruction of churches and monasteries and the establishment of *borgläger* in the monasteries and in other places.[49] In order to secure his government, the king therefore gathered a Diet in Västerås 1527.[50] At the Diet, the clergy was not allowed to contribute to the decisions made. The other estates (burghers, peasants and nobility) pledged allegiance to the king. Among the decisions made, three had immense consequences for the monasteries and mendicant houses: limitations of the friars' movements in the country, the right to reclaim monastic estates and the secular administration of the monasteries.

The dissolution of the mendicant houses

At the Diet in Västerås 1527, mendicant peregrinations in the countryside were regulated and limited. The official reason was the participation of a few Franciscans and Dominicans in the two uprisings. Because of this, the king accused the mendicants of spreading of propaganda.[51] According to the

---

45   Berntson (2003), pp. 74-75.
46   GR IV, p. 217.
47   Berntson (2010a), pp. 53-55, 98, 230-231.
48   HSH 23, p. 17.
49   Samuelsson (1925), pp. 96-97; GR IV, pp. 170-171.
50   Berntson (2003), pp. 93-94.
51   See GR IV, p. 225; see also Berntson (2003), pp. 94-95.

Diet, the mendicant friars should only be allowed to leave their houses for ten weeks a year. The official reason was that the mendicants spread "deceit" (*bedregerj*) and "lies" (*lygn*) around the country.[52] Eventually, this regulation would lead to a depopulation of the mendicant houses in Sweden, not least since their economy was in many cases based on alms collected during these travels.[53]

Most of the mendicant houses were depopulated during the latter half of the 1520s and the earlier half of the 1530s. Some of these houses were closed fairly quickly after the Diet. The Dominican houses in Stockholm and Västerås were brought to an end already in 1528 and the Franciscans in Arboga left their house only one year later.[54] In many cases, we do not know exactly how and when the friars' houses were closed or decimated. However, on the basis of rare notices and records of exhaustive confiscations of monastic properties, it can be concluded that most of the mendicant houses were closed during the first three to four years after the Diet. In some cases, the houses were slowly drained of personnel, with only elderly or sick brethren remaining. For example, a "sick monk" lived in the Franciscan house in Skara as late as 1539, and in the Franciscan house in Krokek, elderly brethren stayed on as late as 1544.[55] In some instances the houses were not simply closed down, but rather transformed into new institutions. These conversions can be seen as part of a larger process aimed at improving the structure of almshouses and hospitals in Sweden.[56] At the Diet in Strängnäs in 1529, these changes were regulated and it was claimed that the religious houses could be maintained if they took care of poor and sick people.[57] This policy was in practice only maintained for mendicant houses. In some cases, the friars were invited to stay in the houses and tend the sick and the poor.[58] The Franciscans of Jönköping and Enköping were offered to stay and tend the sick.[59] However, it is possible to discern clear continuity between abbey and hospital in only one case. The Clares in Stockholm, who had moved to the abandoned (male) Franciscan house at Gråmunkeholmen (nowadays Riddarholmen) in 1527, were supposed to stay in this house after it was converted into a charitable institution (*helgeandshus*) in 1531. It is likely that some of the Clares still be-

---

52 The decision known as Västerås Ordinantia is printed in GR IV, pp. 242-243
53 Berntson (2003), pp. 95-112; see also Jakobsen (2007) pp. 179-184.
54 Berntson (2003), pp. 96-97.
55 Berntson (2003), p. 98
56 Berntson (2003), pp. 99-105.
57 GR VI, p. 148; see also Ivarsson (1970), pp. 19-20
58 Berntson (2003), pp. 100-102.
59 Berntson (2003), pp. 101-102.

longed to this house (which moved to Danviken in 1551) as late as the 1570s. It is also likely that they still kept some of the old orders, for example keeping an "abbess" as superior.[60]

Secular administration of the monasteries

At the Diet in Västerås 1527, the Church and its leaders were accused of being wealthier than the Crown and the nobility. In his introductory speech at the Diet, the king gave an overview concerning the economic problems in the kingdom, for example the "weakened" nobility and Crown. The reason for this "weakness" was, according to the king, that its possessions had fallen under the Church.[61] At the Diet, it was decided that all estates given to churches and monasteries after the 1450s could be handed back to the donors' families.[62] Invoking this decision in the years that followed the Diet, the nobility reclaimed several monastic estates. However, it is difficult to investigate in what way these claims affected the economic situation of the monasteries. Likewise, it is unclear what consequences they had for the actual dissolution. To start with, due to scant source material, the loss of one estate does not say anything about the extent of this loss. Furthermore, it is usually very difficult to account for the range of the monastic estates before the Diet. Also, it is probable that estates were retaken from some monasteries without mention in the source material. These circumstances indicate that the handing back of estates may have been a factor – among many others – behind some dissolutions.[63]

A more important decision when it comes to explaining the reasons behind the dissolution of the monasteries concerns the question of how the monasteries were to be governed. At the Diet of Västerås, the nobility suggested that the king should pass all the monasteries to representatives of the nobility. However, it was also emphasised that the monks and nuns should remain in the monasteries and be provided with food.[64]

Although a few monasteries came to be governed by lay persons after the Diet, most retained authority over their estates through their tenants. During

---

60 See GR IV, pp. 209, 218, 221, 225; GR VII, p. 252; see also Klockhoff (1935), pp. 120-121 and Berntson (2003), pp. 102-103.
61 Berntson (2003), pp. 211-213.
62 GR IV, p. 230.
63 Berntson (2003), pp. 125-129.
64 GR IV, p. 230.

the first four to five years after the Diet, the monasteries had more influence over their own economy than what earlier research has suggested.[65] In comparison with the male convents, the nunneries came to enjoy an even higher degree of freedom concerning their economy. But eventually they would also lose it. It could be argued that one important practical reason for the depopulation of the monasteries and nunneries was the result of problems arising from monks and nuns losing administrative control of their own economies and thereby also the possibility of providing food and repairing and renovating their buildings. This is partly shown by the fact that the monasteries and nunneries seem to have been abandoned *after* they lost control of the monastic economy.[66] Around the year 1560, when all the mendicant houses and the male monasteries had been closed, four nunneries still existed in Sweden: the Cistercian abbeys in Sko and Vreta and the Brigittine abbeys in Naantali and Vadstena. The main reason for their survival was the fact that they had managed to establish agreements with the State concerning purveyance.[67]

After the abbess in Vadstena lost control of the administration of the monastic estates in the early 1530s, the nunnery had to rely on smaller donations. These were given by common people as well as nobles, for example by Gustav Vasa's queen Margareta Leijonhufvud.[68] After a series of complaints from the abbess, yearly provisions were supplied for the nunnery from the late 1540s until it was closed in 1595.[69] From the late 1530s until 1549, Vreta Abbey was governed by Ebba Eriksdotter (Vasa), a devout Catholic and the king's second cousin as well as his mother-in-law. After 1549, the government was responsible for food supplies to Vreta, which was inhabited by nuns until at the latest 1582.[70] The situation was similar in Sko Abbey, which may have had the right to administer itself until the early 1550s.[71] Due to the abbess' and the convent's ability to claim the right to supplies and protection from the king, the government supported the abbey until 1587. In Naantali Abbey, after an agreement with the king, the abbess was responsible for its economic administration from 1530 until the early 1550s. Thereafter, the government took over control. As late as 1558, there were still fifteen nuns and six brethren living in Naantali,[72] but in 1576, only four nuns still remained. Between

65   See Berntson (2003), pp. 132–157.
66   Berntson (2003), pp. 144-157.
67   Berntson (2003), pp. 157-160.
68   See Nyberg (1991), pp. 390-391.
69   Berntson (2003), pp. 149-157.
70   See Berntson (2003), pp. 144-145; Berntson (2010c), pp. 372-375.
71   Berntson (2003), pp. 145-146.
72   Ivarsson (1970), pp. 87-88.

1581 and 1592, the abbey was inhabited by only one nun, Elin Knutsdotter, and her servants.[73]

In earlier research, the survival of the nunneries has been explained in three ways. According to one version, the nunneries were not regarded as a "political threat" against the State, and therefore they were allowed to remain.[74] This theory, however, has no support in the source material and should be seen as mere speculation. Actually, according to letters from the king to his bailiffs in the 1540s, the Dominican sisters in Skänninge were to remain in their house since there was danger that they would spread lies and propaganda among the peasants if the house were dissolved.[75] Consequently, the house survived, until the sisters were moved to Vadstena 1544, because the sisters were seen as a "political threat". Another explanation claims that Vadstena Abbey was spared since it was seen as a "national monument".[76] However, this theory and the use of the term "national monument" have no support in the source material. Furthermore, it could be regarded as an anachronism. Lastly, it has been suggested that the nunneries survived because the nobility wanted to use them as places to house unmarried daughters.[77] This theory has been used especially regarding Vadstena. This explanation is interesting since it corresponds to similar explanations concerning the survival of nunneries in Denmark and Germany. However, unlike the Danish and German situations, this argument is never explicitly used in the Swedish material. Also, this explanation is founded on the assumption that the majority of the nuns of Vadstena came from the nobility. However, it is probable that, at the time of the Reformation, only a minority of the nuns of Vadstena came from the nobility and the number of daughters of noble descent seems also to have been in decline at the time of the Reformation.[78] However, this explanation need not be abandoned altogether. The abbesses came from the nobility and through their status and contacts they may have held a strong position when it came to defend their monasteries.

I argue that the main reason for the relatively long survival of the nunneries was the agreements mentioned concerning provisions to be supplied. However, why were these agreements made with the nunneries? It is likely that the main reason for these understandings between the State and the

---

73 Ivarsson (1970), pp. 92-94.
74 Lindblom (1961), p. 1; Ivarsson (1970), p. 30.
75 GR XVI, p. 214.
76 Nyman (1997), p. 223; Hidal (2000), p. 56
77 Holmquist:I (1933), p. 333; Wiking (1949), p. 66; Andrén (1999), p. 129; Fritz (2000), p. 202.
78 See Wallin (1991), p. 314; see also Jacobsen (1989), p. 49.

nunneries is to be found in the social problems that would arise for a nun who had to leave her secluded existence in the monastic house. This theory actually also corresponds to explanations for the relatively long persistence of some nunneries in Germany.[79] While the monks could function as clergymen or teachers, most of these occupations were unavailable for women. Moreover, it could be difficult for an ex-nun to marry since she might either be too old or feel bound by the vow of chastity she had given.[80] Unlike many of the theories mentioned above, this explanation is supported by the source material. For example, the king explicitly let the abbess in Naantali administer the estates belonging to the nunnery since the old brethren and sisters would have nowhere to go if it closed.[81] Likewise, in a letter from the remaining aged Cistercian monks in Gudsberga, brother Joakim showed his gratitude toward the king since he had provided the monastery with "bread and protection" and he pleaded for continued supplies since the monks were old and sick and therefore could not serve as vicars or chaplains.[82] Likewise, in the year 1533, the archbishop Laurentius Petri wrote in his explanation for decisions regarding Västerås that the monasteries were maintained, since otherwise the old monks and nuns would not be able to take care of themselves.[83]

Resistance against the dissolution of the monasteries

The Reformation in Sweden is sometimes regarded as a relatively smooth process in which the reformers hesitated to make radical changes in traditional church life.[84] Although this picture might be true in many ways, it is not easy to reconcile it with the known facts about the *rather* fast dissolution of the monasteries. Not only was this process rather rapid; it was also regarded by many of its contemporaries as a disruption of traditional pious life.[85]

In four of the revolts that occurred during Gustav Vasa's reign, the rebels described the dissolution of the monasteries as an expression of an unchris-

---

79   Wiesner (1988), p. 154; Wiesner (1989), pp. 10-11; Roper (1991), pp. 214, 220, 235, 237; Oliva (1998a), pp. 87-88, 97-98; Oliva (1998b), pp. 201-202.
80   Berntson (2003), pp. 159-160.
81   See GR VII, p. 118.
82   This source is discussed in Berntson (2003), p. 160.
83   HSRK pp. 76-77, 93-94.
84   See Eckerdal (2007), p. 82; Lavery (2011), pp. 127, 137; see also Lavery (2012a), pp. 60, 67; Lavery (2012b), p. 11.
85   See also the discussion in Berntson (2016b).

tian political agenda that they opposed. In the argumentation this disruption was described as severe because it meant that the "Service of the Lord" (Sw. *Guds tjänst*) was limited or even abolished. In the letters from the rebels during the rebellion in Västergötland and Western Småland in 1529, it was stated that one cause of the rebellion was the fact that the "Service of the Lord" had disappeared from the monasteries.[86] This term should be related to the obligation of monks and nuns to spend much of their time praying, especially in the form of prayers in the office and masses for the souls of the departed. The relations between monastery and society were in many ways based on the principle of giving and taking. The monasteries needed the income and protection from society, and society needed the prayers. The importance of this "Service of the Lord" should be understood as a covenant, based on the idea that the people of God received gifts and grace, but were also supposed to give something back. The expression "Service of the Lord", which in some cases may have been a common way of describing the services performed by priests and monks, could denote both the celebration of the mass and the prayers of the monastic office and also pilgrimage. Consequently, it was not only priests that performed the "Service of the Lord", but also nuns and pilgrims.[87] According to this perspective, a disruption or avoidance of the "Service of the Lord" meant that the covenant was broken, something which could lead to eternal damnation as well as punishment in this world in the form of famine and other disasters.[88] In some sources we can see a connection between the dissolution of the monasteries and the threat of God's vengeance, i.e. pestilence, starvation and flooding. According to this view, God punished the nation because it broke the covenant. We have an example in the letter mentioned above, issued 1525 by inhabitants in the province of Dalarna to the king. The authors criticized the confiscation of silver from churches and monasteries by claiming that the king stole treasures that were devoted to the "Service of the Lord" (monstrances, chalices and reliquaries): For this act they feared God's vengeance: "For Your harsh acts, we strongly fear that God's wrath and revenge will strike the kingdom and ourselves, if penance is not performed" (my translation).[89] It deserves to be mentioned that the foundation of a monastery and donations to it could be perceived as a means of lessening the wrath of God.[90] From this perspective, it is not

---

86 GR VI, p. 358.
87 Berntson (2003), pp. 292–311; Berntson (2010a), pp. 282– 286; Berntson (2012), pp. 52–59.
88 On the impact of God's vengeance, see Malmstedt (1994), pp. 211–213; see also the discussions in Berntson (2003), pp. 299–303; Stobaeus (2008), pp. 118–122; Berntson (2010a), pp. 296–301.
89 HSH 23, pp. 17-18; see also Berntson (2003), p. 302.
90 See for example Berntson (2003), pp. 301-302.

surprising to find that the dissolution of the monasteries was thought to have the opposite effect.[91]

In answering the criticism of the disappearance of the "Service of the Lord", the king revised the content of this expression in a polemical manner. According to the king the – true – "Service of the Lord" should be understood as an obligation of all Christians, not only monks and priests. Rather, the expression was made to denote an ethical manner of action.[92] Olaus Petri expressed a similar view and claimed that the true "Service of the Lord" meant being a good neighbour, rather than keeping up with old customs.[93] According to the king, the true "Service of the Lord" was not to 'roar in the monasteries' (i.e. singing mass and/or the hours),[94] but rather to love and help the needy. Consequently, the king, in his aim to protect the people and the kingdom through confiscations of silver belonging to churches and monasteries, was cultivating the "Service of the Lord". This pursuit could be compared with "lazy" monks and bishops who, according to the king, did not care about their neighbour, but were only thinking about themselves.[95] Even though we could regard this discussion as a mere rhetorical word game, it also reflects a theological or ecclesiological change. The traditional use of the expression "Service of the Lord", which associated it with mass celebration, devotion to saints and singing the hours, can be related to a spirituality where the road to salvation was delivered by the visible earthly church, which existed in symbiosis with the Church instituted by Christ. This ecclesiology was questioned by the reformers, whose definition of the "Service of the Lord", can be related to a way of describing the Church as primarily an invisible community of believers where the value of visible and material forms of devotion was relativized. The traditional emphasis in the outward material and ritualized forms of "Service of the Lord" tended, according to this perspective, to diminish the importance of the immaterial meeting between man and the Word of God and the moral consequences of this meeting.[96] It is in light of this revision of the expression "Service of the Lord" that we can see the transformation of certain mendicant houses into social institutions, and the reformation of the activities in certain nunneries where the nuns were supposed to teach and tend the sick and the poor.[97]

---

91 Berntson (2003), pp. 300-303; Berntson (2010a), pp. 296-301.
92 Berntson (2003), pp. 305-306.
93 OPSS I, pp. 270-272. We find a similar perspective in Peder Laurentsen's discussion in *Malmøbogen*, see Berntson (2012), pp. 55-56.
94 This expression was according to Peder Svart's chronicle used by the king, see PS, p. 94.
95 Berntson (2003), p. 305; Berntson (2010a), pp. 333–343.
96 Berntson (2012), pp. 58-59.
97 Berntson (2003), pp. 310-311.

Did evangelical communities exist in Sweden?

During the 1540s, the Swedish government articulated its adherence to the evangelical faith in a more explicit way than it had done during previous decades. Even though this adherence was not expressed in a confession or in an official church order, in practice it drew the consequences of the decisions from the Diet in Västerås 1527, which stipulated that the Word of God should be preached in a "pure" way. It was also of importance for the government to suppress expressions of Catholic ritual that were thought not to correspond to this decision.[98] A conservative reaction against this evangelic turn was articulated for example during the Dacke rebellion in Småland 1542-43, the most serious of all revolts opposing Gustav Vasa's reign. During the uprising, the rebels demanded a return to the old forms of the mass, and they also criticized the confiscations of silver from churches. Peasants in Småland demanded a reintroduction of holy water, blessed salt and blessed palms.[99] Once the rebellion had been overcome, the king used the reactionary Catholic stance in order to clarify the kingdom's evangelical status. In the rhetoric of the king, all revolts against his regime had been instigated by Catholic bishops and Catholic priests.[100] Therefore it was important to suppress their political influence.

A way of limiting the "threat" from the Catholics was to force them to become evangelical. This policy also affected the monasteries. In Germany and Denmark, some nunneries survived the Reformation through being transformed into evangelical communities. By the Danish Church Ordinance (*Kirkeordinansen*), issued in its first version 1537, monastic life in a Lutheran form was explicitly given a place in the church structure.[101] However, in some of the remaining Danish monasteries and nunneries, a Catholic spirituality was preserved for many decades. In the former Brigittine abbey of Maribo, which during the 1550s was turned into an institution for daughters of noble standing, traditional Catholic piety seems to have lingered for many decades and was regarded as a problem as late as the 1590s. The community was not closed until the summer of 1621.[102] Interestingly, a Brigittine spirituality seems to have prevailed in Maribo Abbey for many decades after the Reformation. Even the younger sisters, who were often in conflict with their elder

---

98   Berntson (2010a), pp. 240-242.
99   GR XV, pp. 287-288; see also Berntson (2014), pp. 91-98.
100 SRA 1:1, pp. 342-344; Berntson (2010a), pp. 260-261.
101 *Kirkeordinansen* 1537/39, pp. 139-140.
102 Haugner (1937), pp. 76-77; see also Knudsen (1919); Rübner Jørgensen (2001); Berntson (2010b).

superiors, were suspected of deviating from the evangelical faith through their devotion to St Birgitta. According to one of the complaints against Maribo made by the bishop of Odense, Niels Jespersen (1518-87), there seems to have been an agreement between both younger and elder nuns concerning their attitude to St Birgitta. According to Niels Jespersen's accusations, the nuns maintained their rule (implicating the *Regula Salvatoris*) and read books of St Birgitta. Even the younger nuns are reported to make "impious and deformed invocations" to St Birgitta.[103] Furthermore, even though the old habit was abolished, according to Niels Jespersen the nuns still wore "crowns or mitres" in a form that had been abolished by the king.[104] These words indicate that the sisters wore a Brigittine or some kind of semi-Brigittine habit.

It may be possible that the *idea* of evangelical communities also existed in Sweden during the sixteenth century. The government seems to have worked towards making the remaining nunneries evangelical. In Vadstena Abbey, the king tried to make both the nuns and the brethren convert to the evangelical faith.[105] According to the Jesuit Antonio Possevino (1534-1611), who visited Vadstena Abbey in 1580, the nuns had been obliged for several years to listen to evangelical preaching in the abbey church. In a letter to Rome, he also mentioned rumours that they had accepted communion *sub utraque*, under both species.[106] According to the same source, the nuns had put wax and cotton in their ears to avoid listening to heretical preaching.[107] According to Rasmus Ludvigsson's chronicle of the reign of Gustav Vasa, written during the 1570s, those nuns who wanted to remain in the convent and serve God in the correct way, were to adopt right and pure evangelical teaching. After instructing the nuns on matters of faith and after teaching them to sing hymns and songs in Swedish, they were said to have adopted this faith.[108] Johannes Messenius, who was a Catholic, wrote around fifty years later that some of the inhabitants of Vadstena Abbey adopted the Lutheran faith.[109] In the contemporary material, two brethren from Vadstena Abbey were said to have promised to stand firm in the evangelical faith.[110] After Bishop Mikael Agricola's visitation in 1554 in Naantali Abbey, both monks and nuns were said to have promised to become "evangelical persons" in life and teaching. They

---

103 See Pontoppidan (1747), p. 394.
104 Pontoppidan (1747), p. 394.
105 Berntson (2003), pp. 224-225.
106 Theiner (1839), p. 29.
107 See Berntson (2003), p. 226.
108 HH 20, pp. 101-102.
109 Messenius, *Scondia* 5, p. 103; Messenius, CSB, pp. 234-235.
110 GR XIX, p. 96.

were also forbidden to sing or read St Birgitta's revelations and were only allowed to celebrate mass in Swedish or in Finnish, not in Latin. The abbey was supposed to be responsible for teaching children and young women.[111] Furthermore, in Sko Abbey, the nuns were obliged to abolish all Catholic ceremonies and listen to evangelical sermons in the abbey church. Just as in Naantali, they were supposed to teach children and young women. However, no more women should be allowed to enter the abbey and become nuns.[112] In the Brigittine abbey Marientaal in Tallinn, the nuns were informed by the Swedish regime in 1561 that they could remain if they abandoned Catholic ceremonies and their false "Service of the Lord".[113] In Vadstena, Naantali, Sko and Marientaal, there were attempts to make the nuns (and brethren) adopt evangelical teaching. Yet, only Vadstena and Naantali yield indications that these attempts should be considered successful.

The fact that the government tried to make nuns and brethren turn evangelical does not imply that the nunneries became evangelical communities. Firstly, it is not certain whether this was a temporary policy. The conversion process could be a way of making the nunneries acceptable until the old nuns died out. Secondly, it remains unclear whether or not the nuns really accepted the new regime. It is, nevertheless, clear that the *concept* of evangelical communities was a living idea in Sweden from the 1540s until the 1570s.[114]

I would suggest that there is one striking similarity between Maribo and Vadstena, and that is the preservation of Brigittine spirituality. It is likely that many of the nuns in Vadstena preserved this devotion during the Reformation. Even though the cowl, at least for the monks, was abolished in 1544,[115] Brigittine spirituality seems to have lived on until the dissolution. This orientation is shown not least in the fact that most of the remaining nuns migrated to another Brigittine abbey in Gdańsk after the dissolution.

John III and the remaining monasteries

The reign of King John III (*Johan*, r. 1568-92) meant a revival for many of the remaining nunneries in the kingdom. The king explicitly aimed to restore convent buildings and ceremonies that had been abandoned during the

---

111 HTH VIII, p. 70; see also Leinberg (1890), pp. 281-282; Ivarsson (1970), p. 30; Klockars (1979), p. 187.
112 See Ivarsson (1970), p. 26.
113 See Leinberg (1890), pp. 286-287; Ivarsson (1970), p. 26.
114 Berntson (2003), p. 228.
115 VD, pp. 460-461.

past decades. In 1575, a new church ordinance was issued, known as *Nova Ordinantia*. According to one of its articles, the monasteries were to be restored in a reformed manner. The monastic houses were said to house old clergy and other persons who wanted to maintain a distance to the "world". In the monasteries, they could live a life of prayer and godliness, preaching and singing the Word of God. Furthermore, elderly women and maidens who did not want to marry could also live there. These reformed monasteries could also function as schools where orphans could learn to read, write, sing and sew. However, no monastic vows were to be permitted.[116] Some still extant monasteries, like Naantali, Vreta and Vadstena, and also some buildings belonging to dissolved monasteries, like the abbey churches in Alvastra and Gråmunkeholmen, were renovated.[117] In Vreta Abbey, the church, the convent buildings and the walls were renovated.[118] In Vadstena, the so-called *Sanctum Sanctorum*, also known as St Birgitta's prayer chamber, was decorated with a detailed painting (which still exists) depicting for example St Birgitta and her daughter Katarina (dressed in the Brigittine habit).[119] John III also fostered the acceptance of new nuns in Vadstena and Naantali and permitted Catholic priests to be sent to Vadstena Abbey.[120]

John III's general church policy as well as his attitude toward the monasteries is often thought to have had a "Catholic bearing", which does not necessarily always correspond to medieval or Tridentine Catholicism. Rather, it is probable that John III was inspired by irenical theology, seeking peace and reconciliation.[121] In addition, the support of the monasteries, provision of supplies to the nuns and the admission of new nuns to the remaining nunneries need not, especially if we consider the existence of evangelical communities in some German states as well as in Denmark, be seen as Catholicism in either its late medieval, irenical or Tridentine form.

Epilogue

After Antonio Possevino's visits, Vadstena Abbey developed into what could be called a Catholic zone amid a kingdom where the church policy moved

---

116 HRSH 2:II, p. 349.
117 Ivarsson (1970), pp. 106-108, 112-119, 125-140.
118 Ivarsson (1970), pp. 116-117, 244; see also Berntson 2010c, pp. 375-379.
119 See Lindblom (1961), pp. 8-9, 21, 37.
120 Ivarsson (1970), pp. 71, 80, 93.
121 Holmquist:I (1933), pp. 16, 36, 41; Strömberg-Back (1963), pp. 194-195; Serenius (1966), p. 336; Andrén (1990), p. 339; Montgomery (1995), pp. 148-152; Andrén (1999), p. 156.

toward an orthodox Lutheran manner of articulating the faith. At the Diet in Söderköping, held in October 1595, it was decided that the "misuse" of the abbey and the people living there should be removed.[122]

The monasteries in Sweden were caught in a dilemma. They turned out to be all too Catholic to be accepted by Lutheran orthodoxy, and as reformed institutions they failed to find a place in the structure of the Lutheran Church in Sweden. Even though there was an option, granted by both Luther and Olaus Petri, that monasticism could endure in a reformed way, this possibility was not realized. And why did this happen? I think James France has a point when he says that when monastic life was invested with a new role, for example teaching and nursing, it eventually became obvious that those activities could be better performed elsewhere.[123] When the monasteries were deprived of monasticism, they had difficulty in finding a function in early modern society.

---

122 SRA III, p. 615.
123 France (1992), p. 472.

Bibliography

Andrén, Åke, 'Den liturgiska utvecklingen i Sverige under reformationstiden', in *Reformationens konsolidering i de nordiska länderna 1540-1610* (Skrifter utgitt av Nordiskt institut för kyrkohistorisk forskning, 6), ed. Ingmar Brohed (Oslo, 1990), pp. 327-350.

Andrén, Åke, *Sveriges kyrkohistoria 3. Reformationstid* (Stockholm, 1999).

Bednar, Helmut, 'Antonitklostret i Ramundeboda', in *Kloster och klosterliv i det medeltida Skara stift*, ed. Johnny Hagberg (Skara, 2007), pp. 201-252.

Berggren, Per Gustav, 'Kalmar nunnekloster', *Meddelanden från Kalmar läns fornminnesförening* 3 (Kalmar, 1902), pp. 33-65.

Berntson, Martin, *Klostren och reformationen. Upplösningen av kloster och konvent i Sverige 1523-1596* (Skellefteå, 2003).

Berntson, Martin, 'The Dissolution of the Hospitaller houses in Scandinavia', in *The Military Orders and the Reformation. Choices, State Building and the Weight of Tradition*, ed. Helen Nicholson, Klaus Militzer and Hans Mol (Hilversum, 2006), pp. 59-77.

Berntson, Martin, 'Västergötlands kloster och reformationen', in *Kloster och klosterliv i det medeltida Skara stift* (Skara stiftshistoriska sällskaps skriftserie, 33), ed. Johnny Hagberg (Skara, 2007), pp. 253-281.

Berntson, Martin, *Mässan och armborstet. Uppror och reformation i Sverige 1525-1544* (Skellefteå, 2010a).

Berntson, Martin, 'Reformation and counter-culture in Maribo abbey', in *Saint Birgitta, Syon and Vadstena. Papers from a Symposium in Stockholm 4-6 October 2007*, ed. C. Gejrot, S. Risberg and M. Åkestam. (Kungl. Vitterhets Historie och Antikvitets Akademien Konferenser 73) (Stockholm, 2010b), pp. 216-226.

Berntson, Martin, 'Vreta kloster och reformationen', in *Fokus Vreta kloster. 17 nya rön om Sveriges äldsta kloster* (The Museum of National Antiquities, Stockholm. Studies, 14), ed. Elisabet Regner and Göran Tagesson (Stockholm, 2010c), pp. 369-383.

Berntson, Martin, 'Reformationsmotstånd och en kyrkosyn i förändring', in *Auktoritet i förvandling. Omförhandling av fromhet, lojalitet och makt i reformationstidens Sverige* (Opuscula Historica Upsaliensia 49), ed. Eva-Marie Letzter (Uppsala, 2012), pp. 33-69.

Berntson, Martin, 'Striden om herr Ambjörn. En ingång till liturgisk förändring i Skara stift under 1540-talet', in *Vägen mot bekännelsen. Perspektiv på organisation, bekännelsebildning och fromhetsliv i Skara stift ca 1540-1595* (Skara stiftshistoriska sällskaps skriftserie, 79), ed. Martin Berntson (Skara, 2014), pp. 91-122.

Berntson, Martin, 'Klostrens upplösning i Lundastiftet under reformationstiden', in *Lunds stift i världen. Från mission till emigration* (Stiftshistoriska sällskapet i Lunds stift. Årsbok), ed. Stig Alenäs, Ingmar Brohed & Anna Minara Ciardi (Lund, 2016a), pp. 29–57.

Berntson, Martin, 'Popular Belief and the Disruption of Religious Practices in Reformation Sweden', in *Re-forming Texts, Music, and Church Art in the Early Modern North*, ed. Tuomas M.S. Lehtonen & Linda Kaljundi (Amsterdam, 2016b), pp. 43–68.

Berntson, Martin, 'Söderköpings kloster och reformationen', in *S:t Ragnhilds Gille. Årsbok 2016* (Söderköping, 2016c), pp. 12–22.

Christensen, Th. Lyby, 'Paulus Helie og Olavus Petri om bibelens auktoritet', in *Reformationen i Norden. Kontinuitet och förnyelse* (Skrifter utgitt av Nordiskt institut för kyrkohistorisk forskning, 3), ed. Carl-Gustaf Andrén (Lund, 1973), pp. 61-75.

Cnattingius, Hans, *Studies in the order of St. Bridget of Sweden I. The crisis in the 1420's* (Stockholm, 1963).

Collijn, Isak, 'Kartusianklostret Mariefred vid Gripsholm och dess bibliotek', in *Nordisk tidskrift för bok- och biblioteksväsen* 22 (1935), pp. 147-178.

Dahlerup, Troels, 'Karmeliterordenen', in *Kulturhistoriskt lexikon för nordisk medeltid från vikingatid till reformationstid*, vol. 8 (Malmö, 1963), sp. 298-299.

Eckerdal, Lars, 'Kommunionssång i Svenska kyrkan', in *Hjärtats tillit. Trosförmedling i luthersk tradition* (Svenskt gudstjänstliv 82) (2007), pp. 82-130.

France, James, *The Cistercians in Scandinavia* (Cistercian studies series, 131) (Kalamazoo, 1992).

Fritz, Birgitta, 'Klostret under och efter reformationen', in *600 år i Vadstena. Vadstena stads historia från äldsta tider till år 2000*, ed. Göran Söderström (Stockholm, 2000), pp. 198-207.

Gallén, Jarl, *La province de Dacie de l'ordre des frères prêcheurs. I. Historie générale iusqu'au grand schisme* (Helsinki, 1946).

Gallén, Jarl, 'Dominikanorden', in *Kulturhistoriskt lexikon för nordisk medeltid från vikingatid till reformationstid*, vol. 3 (Malmö, 1958), sp. 174-185.

Gallén, Jarl, 'Franciskanorden', in *Kulturhistoriskt lexikon för nordisk medeltid från vikingatid till reformationstid*, vol. 4 (Malmö, 1959), sp. 563-573.

Gallén, Jarl, 'Helgeandsorden', in *Kulturhistoriskt lexikon för nordisk medeltid från vikingatid till reformationstid*, vol. 6 (Malmö, 1961), sp. 312-313.

Gallén, Jarl, 'Kökar, klosterbröderna och havet', in *Maritima medeltidsstudier* (Jungfrusund 2), ed. Christoffer H. Ericsson and Kim Montin (Åbo, 1989), pp. 15-97.

Gallén, Jarl et al., 'Johannitorden', in *Kulturhistoriskt lexikon för nordisk medeltid från vikingatid till reformationstid*, vol. 7 (Malmö, 1962), sp. 600-606.

GR = *Konung Gustaf den förstes registratur* I, IV, VI, VII, XV, XVI, XIX (Stockholm, 1861, 1868, 1875, 1877, 1893, 1895, 1901).

Grandinson, Karl Gustaf, 'Bidrag till kännedomen om Vårfruklostret i Örebro', in *Meddelanden från Föreningen Örebro läns museum* 11 (1933), pp. 55-64.

Gustavsson, Kenneth, 'Franciskanerklostret på Kökar. Nytt ljus över medeltiden i Skärgårdshavet', in *Historisk Tidskrift för Finland* 79 (1994), pp. 494-518.

Hall, Frithiof, 'Jönköpings kloster', in *Meddelanden från Norra Smålands fornminnesförening* 1 (Jönköping, 1907), pp. 22-42.

Hallberg, Svante et al., 'Kartusianernas och antoniternas ämbetssigill i det medeltida Sverige', in *Kyrkohistorisk Årsskrift* 68 (1968), pp. 1-21.

Hatt Olsen, Thomas, 'The Priorate of Dacia of the Order of Saint John of Jerusalem', in *V:e Congrès International des Sciences Généalogique et Héraldique* (Stockholm, 1961), pp. 301-330.

Hatt Olsen, Thomas, *Dacia og Rhodos. En studie over forholdet mellem Johannitterstormesteren på Rhodos og prioratet Dacia i de 14. og 15. Århundrede med særligt henblik på Juan de Carduna's visitation (-1476)* (Copenhagen, 1962).

Haugner, C. C., *Maribo historie* 1 (Maribo, 1937).

Hedqvist, Vilhelm, *Den kristna kärleksverksamheten i Sverige under medeltiden* (Strängnäs, 1893).

HH = *Historiska Handlingar* 20 (Stockholm, 1904-1905).

Hidal, Sten, 'Den katolska kyrkans historia i Sverige', in *Vägen till katolska kyrkan i Sverige*, ed. Holmquist, Hjalmar, *Svenska kyrkans historia III. Reformationstidevarvet I-II* (Stockholm, 1933).

HRSH = *Handlingar rörande Sveriges historia* 2:II (Stockholm, 1872).

HSRK = *Handlingar till Sveriges reformations- och kyrkohistoria under konung Gustaf I* I-II (Handlingar rörande Sveriges inre förhållanden under konung Gustaf I, I) (Stockholm, 1841-1845).

HSH = *Handlingar rörande Skandinaviens historia* 10, 23 (Stockholm, 1822, 1839).

HTH = *Handlingar till upplysning af Finlands häfder* VIII, ed. A. I. Arwidsson (Stockholm, 1856).

Härdelin, Alf, *Kult, kultur och kontemplation. Studier i medeltida svenskt kyrkoliv* (Skellefteå, 1998).

Ingebrand, Sven, *Olavus Petris reformatoriska åskådning* (Studia doctrinae Christianae Upsaliensia, 1) (Uppsala, 1964).

Ivarsson, Gustaf, *Johan III och klosterväsendet* (Bibliotheca theologiae practicae, 22) (Lund, 1970).

Jacobsen, Grethe, 'Nordic women and the Reformation', in *Women in Reformation and Counter-Reformation Europe. Public and private worlds*, ed. Sherrin Marshall (Bloomington, 1989), pp. 47-67.

Jakobsen, Johnny Grandjean Gøgsig, 'Dominikanerne i Västergötland. Konventerne i Skara og (Gamla) Lödöse betragtet som en del af prædikantordenens nordiske provins Dacia', in *Kloster och klosterliv i det medeltida Skara stift*, ed. Johnny Hagberg (Skara, 2007), pp. 159-184.

Johansson, Hilding, *Ritus cisterciensis. Studier i de svenska cisterciensklostrens liturgi* (Bibliotheca theologiae practicae, 18) (Lund, 1964).

Kirkeordinansen 1537/39, ed. Martin Schwarz Lausten (Copenhagen, 1989).

Klockars, Birgit, *I Nådens dal. Klosterfolk och andra c. 1440-1590* (Skrifter utgivna av svenska litteratursällskapet i Finland nr 486) (Helsingfors, 1979).

Klockhoff, Axel, *Danviks hospital. Dess rättsliga ställning* (Uppsala, 1935).

Knudsen, Gunnar, 'Fra Maribo klosters Nedlæggelse', *Lolland-Falsters historiske Samfund Aarbog* 8 (1919), pp. 52-61.

Konow, Jan von, 'Johanniterorden i Sverige. Tidigare verksamhet omkring 1180-1527', in *Johanniterorden i Sverige*, ed. Jan von Konow (Stockholm, 1995).

Larsson, Lars-Olof, 'Från Nydala klosters undergång till klosterkyrkans pånyttfödelse', in *Nydala kloster. Andligt centrum och maktfaktor i det medeltida Småland* (Meddelande, Växjö stiftshistoriska sällskap, 20), ed. Lars Aldén (Växjö, 1998), pp. 85-99.

Larsson, Lars-Olof, *Gustav Vasa. Landsfader eller tyrann?* (Stockholm, 2002).

Lavery, Jason, 'The Reformation in Finland – A historiography of continuities', in *Religion and Identity in Russia and the Soviet Union. A Festschrift for Paul Bushkovitch*, ed. Nikolaos A. Chrissidis, Cathy J. Potter, David Schimmelpenninck van der Oye, and Jennifer B. Spock (Bloomington, 2011), pp. 127–43.

Lavery, Jason, 'A frontier of reform. Finland in the Reformation era', in *Migration und Kulturtransfer im Ostseeraum während der frühen Neuzeit* (Acta Bibliothecae Regiae Stockholmiensis 80), ed. Otfried Czaika and Heinrich Holze (Stockholm, 2012a), pp. 60–75.

Lavery, Jason, 'The Swedish Kingdom and Europe's Age of Reform 1523–1611', in *Luther, reformaatio ja kirja* (Suomen Kirkkohistoriallisen Seuran toimituksia 220), ed. Tuija Laine (Helsinki, 2012b), pp. 9–14.

Lawrence, Clifford Hugh, *Medieval monasticism. Forms of religious life in Western Europe in the Middle Ages* (London and New York, 1984).

Leinberg, Karl Gabriel, *De finska klostrens historia* (Skrifter utgivna av svenska litteratursällskapet i Finland nr 14) (Helsinki, 1890).

Lindbæk, Johannes, *De danske franciskanerklostre* (Copenhagen, 1914).

Lindbæk, Johannes et al., *De danske helligaandsklostre* (Copenhagen, 1906).

Lindblom, Andreas, *Johan III och Vadstena nunnekloster* (Antikvariskt arkiv 16) (Stockholm, 1961).

Lohse, Bernhard, *Mönchtum und Reformation. Luthers Auseinandersetzung mit dem Mönchsideal des Mittelalters* (Göttingen, 1963).

Lovén, Christian, 'Kloster, klosterliknande inrättningar och klostertraditioner', in *Fornvännen* 96 (2001), pp. 243-266.

Malmstedt, Göran, *Helgdagsreduktionen. Övergången från ett medeltida till ett modernt år i Sverige 1500-1800* (Avhandlingar från Historiska institutionen i Göteborg, 8) (Göteborg, 1994).

McGuire, Brian Patrick, *The cistercians in Denmark. Their attitudes, roles and functions in medieval society* (Cistercian studies series, 35) (Kalamazoo, 1982).

Messenius, CSB = Johannes Messenius, *Chronologia Sanctae Birgittae*, ed. Ann-Mari Jönsson (Lund, 1988).

Messenius, *Scondia* = Johannes Messenius, *Scondia illustrata* (Stockholm, 1700-1705).

Montgomery, Ingun, 'The institutionalisation of lutheranism in Sweden and Finland', in *The Scandinavian Reformation. From evangelical movement to institutionalisation of reform*, ed. Ole Peder Grell (Cambridge, 1995), pp. 148-152.

Nilsson, Bertil, 'Det tidigaste klostret i Vreta', in *Kyrkohistorisk årsskrift* 108 (2008), pp. 47-58.

Norborg, Lars-Arne, *Storföretaget Vadstena kloster. Studier i senmedeltida godspolitik och ekonomiförvaltning* (Lund 1958).

Nyberg, Tore, *Birgittinsk festgåva. Studier om heliga Birgitta och birgittinorden* (Skrifter utgivna av Svenska kyrkohistoriska föreningen, II:46) (Uppsala, 1991).

Nyman, Magnus, *Förlorarnas historia. Katolskt liv i Sverige från Gustav Vasa till drottning Kristina* (Uppsala, 1997).

Oliva, Marilyn, 'Unsafe passage. The state of the nuns at the dissolution and their conversion to secular life', in *The vocation of service to God and neighbour. Essays on the interests, involvements and problems of religious communities and their members in medieval society* (International medieval research 5), ed. Joan Greatrex (Turnhout, 1998a), pp. 87-104.

Oliva, Marilyn, *The convent and the community in late medieval England. Female monasteries in the diocese of Norwich 1350-1540* (Woodbridge, 1998b).

OPSS = Olavus Petri, *Samlade skrifter* I (Uppsala, 1914).

Ortved, Edward, *Cistercieordenen og dens klostre i Norden II. Sveriges klostre* (Copenhagen, 1933).

Pernler, Sven-Erik, 'Klosterordnarna och Strängnässtiftet. Ett kyrkopolitiskt spänningsfält', in *Öppna gränser. Ekumeniskt och europeiskt i Strängnäs stift genom tiderna* (Skrifter utgivna av Samfundet Pro fide et christianismo, 14), ed. Samuel Rubenson (Stockholm, 1992), pp. 33-46.

Pontoppidan, Erich, *Annales ecclesiae danicae diplomatici* 3 (Copenhagen, 1747).

PS = Peder Svart, *Konung Gustaf I:s krönika*, ed. Nils Edén (Stockholm, 1912).

Rasmussen, Jørgen Nybo, *Franciskanerne i Norden* (Aelnoths skriftserie nr. 3) (Grenaa, 1994).

Rasmussen, Jørgen Nybo, *Die Franziskaner in den nordischen Ländern im Mittelalter* (Franziskanische Forschungen, 40) (Kevelaer, 2002).

Reitzel-Nielsen, Erik, *Johanniterordenens historie, med særlig henblik på de nordiske lande. I. Tiden før Rhodos* (Copenhagen, 1984).

Roper, Lyndal, *The holy household. Women and morals in Reformation Augsburg* (Oxford, 1991).

Rübner Jørgensen, Kaare, 'New Wine into Old Bottles. Maribo Abbey after the Reformation', *Birgittiana* 12 (2001), pp. 121-153.

Samuelsson, Sixten, 'Daljunkern och Värmland', *Värmland förr och nu* 1925, pp. 93-99.

Samzelius, Margareta, 'Krokeks kloster eller Vårfrukloster på Kolmården', *Kolmården 1* (Motala, 1965), pp. 102-114.

Serenius, Sigtrygg, *Liturgia Svecanae ecclesiae catholicae et orthodoxae conformis. En liturgihistorisk undersökning med särskild hänsyn till struktur och förlagor* (Acta Academiae Aboensis. Ser. A, Humaniora, 33:1) (Åbo, 1966).

SRA = *Svenska riksdagsakter jämte andra handlingar som höra till statsförfattningens historia*. 1:1-3 (Stockholm, 1887-1900).

Stensland, Per G., *Julita klosters godspolitik* (Sörmländska handlingar nr. 10) (Stockholm, 1945).

Stobaeus, Per, *Hans Brask. En senmedeltida biskop och hans tankevärld* (Skellefteå, 2008).

Stobaeus, Per, *Från biskop Brasks tid* (Skellefteå, 2010).

Strömberg-Back, Kerstin, *Lagen, rätten, läran. Politisk idédebatt i Sverige under Johan III:s Tid* (Bibliotheca historica Lundensis, 11) (Lund, 1963).

Theiner, Augustin, *Schweden und seine Stellung zum heiligen Stuhl* II (Augsburg, 1839).

Torbrand, Dagny, 'Klara kloster i Stockholm. Ett exempel på agrar stordrift under medeltiden', in *Geografiska annaler, series B. Human geography vol. 50B* (1968), pp. 75-85.

VD = *Vadstenadiariet*, ed. Claes Gejrot (Stockholm, 1996).

Wallin, Curt, 'Vadstenanunnornas sociala proveniens', in *Birgitta. Hendes værk og hendes klostre i Norden* (Odense University studies in history and social sciences, 150), ed. Tore Nyberg (Odense, 1991), pp. 291-322.

Werner, Yvonne Maria, ' [Review of] Martin Berntson, Klostren och reformationen. Upplösningen av kloster och konvent i Sverige 1523-1596", in *Kyrkohistorisk Årsskrift* 103 (2003), pp. 241-244.

Westman, Knut B., *Reformationens genombrottsår i Sverige* (Uppsala, 1918).

Wiesner, Merry, 'Women's response to the Reformation', in *The German people and the Reformation*, ed. R. Po-chia Hsia (Ithaca and London, 1988), pp. 148-171.

Wiesner, Merry, 'Nuns, wives and mothers. Women and the Reformation in Germany', in *Women in Reformation and Counter-Reformation Europe*, ed. Sherrin Marshall (Bloomington, 1989), pp. 8-28.

Wiking, Bo Sture, 'Linköpings stift under medeltiden', in *Linköpings stift i ord och bild* (Stockholm, 1949), pp. 31-68.

Thrown to the Wolves?

The Fate of Norwegian Monasteries after the Reformation

Øystein Ekroll

Introduction

In the history of European monasticism, Norway constitutes a small chapter. Compared to most other European countries, monasticism never became a very dominant force in medieval Norwegian society. Inside the country's medieval borders, which included the county of Bohuslän ceded to Sweden in 1658, 31 monastic foundations are known.[1] The majority of them were concentrated in and around the few towns that existed in this period and only a few had a rural setting. In a European perspective, most of these foundations were small and insignificant, but in a Norwegian perspective, some of them were important and relatively wealthy. Today, most of them exist as ruins or they are buried under later streets and houses, and only a couple of monasteries have a continuous history of occupation from the Middle Ages until today.

It can hardly be a surprise that most of the attention paid to the monasteries by historians, architects and archeologists since the nineteenth century has concentrated on the medieval history of these buildings and building complexes. During the various excavations and restorations of them, traces or remains of the post-medieval phases were often at best only documented before being removed, or they were unceremoniously removed without any kind of documentation. Any post-medieval use of these buildings was regarded as a degradation of their original purpose, and the dominant restoration view from the mid-nineteenth century until well into the twentieth century

---

1   The best introduction to the history of Norwegian monasticism is still Lange (1st edition 1847, 2nd edition 1856). The Society for the Preservation of Ancient Norwegian Monuments' (*Foreningen til norske fortidsminnesmerkers bevaring*) 1987 yearbook was also dedicated to monasteries.

was that the post-Reformation features distorted the features of the original building and consequently should be removed. This attitude led to the loss of important historical material in both the ruins and the preserved buildings, and the question of how the monasteries were used after their dissolution attracted little interest.

A short overview of monasticism in Norway

The most important monastic orders established themselves in Norway in successive waves.[2] The first wave began in the first three decades of the twelfth century with the Benedictine Order, followed by the Cistercian Order in the 1140s. Then, during the next five decades after the establishment of the Norwegian archbishopric in Nidaros/Trondheim in 1153, the orders of the Augustinians, the Premonstratensians and the Hospitallers arrived in the country, so that by c. 1200, twenty-one monasteries were established in the country. Like Christianity itself, monasticism in Norway was founded with the help of British monks, e.g. the Cistercian abbeys were daughters of abbeys in Yorkshire and Lincolnshire.

The second wave of foundations began in the 1220s with the mendicant orders of the Franciscans and the Dominicans. During the thirteenth century, these two orders established ten male houses between them in various Norwegian towns (six Franciscan and four Dominican), most of them by the help of royal or aristocratic patronage. Unlike the first wave where the British Isles were important, these houses were founded by mendicants arriving in Norway via Germany and Denmark.[3]

After the mid-fourteenth century, when the Black Death struck Norway and killed off at least half the population, the monastic movement was halted. Until the Reformation almost two hundred years later, there were hardly any new foundations, so perhaps we can not speak of a third wave, perhaps more a ripple. However, in the country's largest town, Bergen, which was the only Norwegian town that grew and expanded during the late Middle Ages, a couple of old monasteries were taken over by new orders. In 1426, the Brigittine Order took over the buildings and the land holdings of the old Benedictine Abbey of St Michael (*Munkalif*), which had long been in decline.[4] In 1507, the

---

2   Gunnes (1987), pp. 49-85.
3   Ekroll (1993), pp. 135-154; Hommedal (1993), pp. 154-174.
4   Lange (1856), pp. 289-315.

Order of the Hospitallers of St Anthony took over the Benedictine nunnery of Nonneseter, which by this time seems to have become empty and deserted.[5]

In the rest of the country, after the Black Death, many of the older establishments clearly fell into decline with a steadily falling number of inhabitants and some, like the Benedictine abbey of St Alban at Selja Island, seem to have been deserted already in the fifteenth century.

Many of the oldest institutions stagnated with little evidence of any new development, and after the Black Death, several of them clearly fell on bad times, with the number of inhabitants steadily decreasing. Many monasteries owned a large number of farms or parts of farms, but due to the decline in population after the Black Death, the annual income from the land rent was reduced with as much as 80 %, causing an economic loss for the landowners. The landowners had to compete for tenants who could now demand better conditions, and a large number of the more marginal farms were therefore abandoned and not repopulated until the seventeenth century; some remained abandoned. In addition, the monastic land holdings were not concentrated into large single estates but spread over sizable areas, and it was therefore a costly business to administer the estate, collect the land rent and find new tenants. Still, even if the extensive land holdings were not very profitable at the time, they remained a potential resource for the future in terms of timber, minerals, hunting and fishing.

As witnessed by the two Bergen examples, from the fifteenth century onwards the greater part of the monastic movement in Norway had clearly lost its impetus. The exception seems to be the mendicant orders in Bergen and Oslo that were closely connected to the guilds, especially in Bergen which had a large colony of North German Hanseatic merchants, and in their wills many of these merchants left gifts for the guild altars. Around 1500, the Dominicans in Bergen were even able to rebuild their whole convent in stone, an indication that they had access to rich economic resources.

The first period of monastic secularization

In the early sixteenth century, we see two different attempts to redraw the monastic landscape in Norway, both of which are well-known in other countries. The first took place within the Catholic Church and was a kind of reform movement led by the bishops trying to bring the fossilized monastic movement into the modern era or at least weed out the worst excesses. This

5   Lange (1856), pp. 320-323.

is an interesting movement of which we have some examples, but in hindsight they are not relevant in the present context.

The second effort can be called the first period of secularization when lay men and women, usually belonging to the nobility, tried and often succeeded in having themselves installed as guardians or protectors of a monastery. This often happened by staging an election among the monks or nuns and thus in reality achieving full control of the institution's economy. In many instances, these nobles also managed to obtain royal confirmation of their election as guardians. Their argument was often that one of their ancestors had founded the institution and that they thus had a right to ensure that the family's donation was properly managed for the benefit of the institution. This overture could lead to the eventual takeover of the abbey and its property, pensioning off the last inhabitants or providing them with jobs or a new livelihood.

This process started in Norway in the 1520s and it met with fierce opposition from the church hierarchy, but the bishops often lacked the physical power or spiritual authority to prevent the development, as the new lay guardians often cooperated with corrupt abbots or priors. As some of the orders were moreover exempt from episcopal visitations, the bishops also had limited canonical authority to prevent this process.

One good example is what took place in Archbishop Olav Engelbrektsson's own diocese of Nidaros with its eight monastic foundations. The leading noble family in the diocese was headed by Lady Ingjerd Ottesdotter, widow of the Lord High Steward of Norway, Nils Henriksson (Gyldenløve), and her six daughters, all of whom were married to Danish noblemen such as Vincent Lunge, Peder Litle, Niels Lykke and Jens Bjelke. This family was in almost constant opposition to the archbishop, who tried to prevent them from extending their power over ecclesiastical institutions. The whole family's strong Lutheran sympathies, obvious already in the 1520s, did not improve the relationship.

In 1531, Lady Ingjerd made the nuns of Rein Abbey (see p. 162) elect her as guardian (*forstanderinde*) of the abbey claiming that it had been founded by her ancestors.[6] Lady Ingjerd promised to keep the abbey buildings well maintained, to keep the sisters well dressed and fed and to ensure that the abbey was properly run. However, before she could take control of the abbey, the archbishop had its valuables and its seal removed to Trondheim, an act which caused a bitter conflict between him and Ingjerd's family.[7]

---

6   Lange (1856), p. 250.
7   Ree & Wallem (1916), pp. 15-24.

The same year, through a secret deal with its abbot Matthias Henriksson, a former monk of Sorø Abbey in Denmark, Lady Ingjerd's son-in-law, Niels Lykke, took control of Tautra Cistercian abbey by becoming its guardian. Niels Lykke managed to obtain a royal confirmation of this arrangement from King Frederik I. The agreement said that the abbot and each monk were to get a solid payment, and the abbot would receive a generous annual pension for the rest of his life.[8]

This was a deal unacceptable to Archbishop Olav Engelbrektsson just a few miles away in Trondheim. The Cistercian abbey was formally independent of the archbishop and only answered to the abbot of Sorø Abbey, Henrik Tornekrans, the head of the Cistercian province of Dacia. The archbishop nevertheless arrested the abbot in 1532 and put him on trial in a consistory court. Niels Lykke was arrested for committing incest with his sister-in-law and was executed in 1535. The archbishop took charge of the abbey and used it at first for incarcerating his political enemies, and it seems soon after to have been deserted by the last monks.

The revenging arm of the archbishop also caught up with Niels Lykke's brother-in-law, Vincent Lunge, who was a member of the Council of the Realm. In 1528, King Frederik I gave him the Antonine abbey of Nonneseter in Bergen, formerly a Benedictine nunnery, which Lunge converted into a private residence named Lungegård. The abbey was a royal foundation, so the king clearly believed he acted within his powers. This move caused much resentment by the archbishop who bided his time. Eight years later, in early January 1536, ten days after the execution of Niels Lykke, the archbishop's men murdered Vincent Lunge in Trondheim.[9]

As mentioned, the first efforts by lay persons to take control of monasteries and their property took place from 1527 to 1532, but this was concentrated on the dioceses of Bergen and Nidaros/Trondheim. In the diocese of Oslo in southeast Norway, the demise of the monastic houses during the same years was mainly caused by disturbances during the fighting linked to the effort of the exiled King Christian II to reconquer Denmark by establishing a bridgehead in Norway. This attempt led to the plundering and destruction of almost all monastic houses in the diocese of Oslo, possibly with the exception of the three houses in the town of Oslo that were better protected from enemy action.

---

8   Lange (1856), p. 244; Ekroll (1996), pp. 32-53.
9   Ree & Wallem (1916), p. 23.

In Bergen, the fear of an attack from King Christian II in 1530-31 led to demands for stronger defenses of the royal castle. This caused a domino effect, which brought about the end of several monastic houses in Bergen. The entire ecclesiastical centre of Bergen, encompassing Christchurch Cathedral, the bishop's palace, the canons' residences and the Dominican friary, was situated on the small island or peninsula of Holmen next to the entrance to the harbour of Bergen, a location they shared with the royal castle and its Church of the Holy Apostles. In order to modernize the old castle and make it possible to defend it with cannons, the new governor, Eske Bille, demanded and got permission to demolish all buildings around the royal castle that obstructed the shooting range, including the churches. The Dominican friary was removed, and as compensation for his demolished cathedral and residence, the bishop was given the Brigittine Abbey of St Michael (*Munkaliv*) on the hilltop across the harbour as his new cathedral and residence.

However, already in 1536, this building complex also came to be regarded as a potential danger to the royal castle in case of armed conflict, and the governor decided to demolish it as well. The bishop, or now rather the Lutheran superintendent, was moved to the newly closed Franciscan friary, whose church is the cathedral of Bergen today. The superintendent moved into the convent buildings, which became the episcopal residence until 1835, when it was demolished and replaced by the new Cathedral School building.[10]

The second period of monastic secularization

This period marks the final dissolution of the last monasteries in 1536-37. In the town of Trondheim, the archbishop exercised full military control and the five monastic foundations within the town continued to function until Archbishop Olav Engelbrektsson had to flee the country in 1537. Very fittingly, the archbishop spent his last night on Norwegian soil in the Benedictine Abbey of Nidarholm before his three ships left Norway for the Netherlands on April 1, never to return.

During the summer of 1537, King Christian III, who now exercised full military control of Denmark and had all the Catholic bishops arrested, consolidated his power in Norway. The last Norwegian bishops were taken into custody and the remaining monasteries in Bergen and Oslo were dissolved. After the bloodless surrender of the archbishop's castle of Steinvikholm on May 30, there is no evidence of armed resistance or any violence connected

---

10   Berg (1928), pp. 55-64.

with this last purge. The king was not interested in confrontation, and like almost all parish priests, the monks accepted the realities of the new situation.[11] Only a handful of people preferred to leave Norway and go to a country that was still Catholic.

The attraction of the monastic properties

So, what kind of values did the Norwegian monastic foundations present to contemporaries and how could they be utilized by other interested parties?

First, the monastic buildings represented little value as buildings *per se*. However, the carved stones had high value as building material. In many cases, the monastic buildings were used as quarries for the rebuilding and extension of new royal castles and fortresses in Norway and Denmark. Carved stones, e.g. from the cathedral and the surrounding churches in Bergen that were demolished in 1530-31, were shipped to Denmark to be used in royal building projects such as Gottorf Palace in Schleswig. In 1578, shiploads of carved stones from the abbeys of Lyse and Nonneseter were sent to Kronborg in Elsinore and, as late as 1642, there was still a demand in Denmark for carved stones from Bergen. Some of the royal servants also pilfered stone for their private building projects, such as Governor Eske Bille who used stones from the Bergen churches for his private residence at Månstorp near Malmö.[12]

Especially urban monastic churches were demolished soon after the dissolution, while rural churches were used for storage or as barns until the roofs fell in and they were abandoned. Many were also situated in places that made them unsuitable for new purposes. In addition, many of the monastic buildings in Norway were built of wood and these timber houses could easily be dismantled, moved to new locations and rebuilt there. A good example of this occurred at Tautra Abbey, where the abbot in 1532 sold to Niels Lykke a new wooden house of three floors, perhaps a 'loft', to be moved to a new location.[13] The monastic archives and libraries were usually lost, as only the cadastres or land registers detailing the institutions' properties and incomes were of interest to the new owners. Even in the last phase of the monasteries, the libraries were not always cared for: the sole mention of books in the inventory of Tautra Abbey in 1532 is '70 old books in the attic'.[14]

---

11 Lange (1856), p. 190.
12 Lidén (1980), pp. 138, 147, 162.
13 Ekroll (1996), p. 45.
14 Ekroll (1996), p. 50.

The real and durable wealth of the abbeys was of course their land holdings and thereby the rights to their natural resources. One abbey could own as many as two or three hundred farms that were scattered over a large region, but the abbey could often claim only a part of a farm's annual produce, as one farm could have more than one owner. After the Black Death, the land rent had been reduced by up to 80% and it stayed low during the Late Middle Ages. The sharply reduced income partly explains the decline of the monasteries during this period. But the land holdings also comprised large areas of forest, lakes and coastal stretches and they contained other possible mineral resources such as gold, silver, copper and iron. The monasteries, however, lacked the skills or economy to exploit these dormant resources by actively establishing sawmills, iron mines, copper mines or large-scale fisheries to produce or process goods for export to the Continent and the British Isles. The first sawmills and iron mines were established in Norway in the 1490s, but the monasteries took no part in this early industrial development.

The growing class of urban merchants and the internationally oriented aristocracy, on the contrary, clearly saw the commercial potential of this dormant fortune. By 1500, the religious institutions owned c. 40% of the Norwegian farms, including enormous tracts of forest. The lay world dearly wanted to lay their hands on these possessions, but this could only be done by crushing the power of the Church. Only the monarchy had the strength to do so, and the emerging schism headed by Martin Luther and Jean Calvin presented an opportunity to overwhelm church institutions. Supporting the Protestant cause and the monarchy of King Christian III was therefore the best means of breaking the power of the Catholic hierarchy and obtaining control of a share of the Church's property.

In many ways, we can say that the Reformation and the ensuing redistribution and regeneration of a large part of the Church's property, including the destruction of the large stone-built complexes that dominated the towns and occupied a large part of the town area, was a precondition for the introduction of post-Reformation Scandinavia's new civilian society. Vast properties which had been owned by ecclesiastical institutions and not changed hands for centuries, the profit of which had benefited very few, now became available. A great part of these holdings ended up in the hands of the new class of capitalists, who knew how to make a profit. This development bears some resemblance to the rampant 'Gordon Gekko capitalism' of the 1980s, when old financial structures and companies were ruthlessly stripped of their assets and then bankrupted and discarded without considering the interests or feelings of their employees and former owners.

The dissolution and destruction of the urban monasteries released large tracts of space in the densely built-up towns, space that gave room for new streets, marketplaces, workshops or residences. The freshly available urban space literally opened up the townscape for new groups. The release of these areas, hitherto reserved for monastic buildings, gardens and cemeteries, onto a commercial market created a property boom in the towns. Within a few years, the sites of many former monasteries and redundant churches were covered with houses and streets, and only some traces and a few names survived as memories. One good example of this development is the town of Trondheim, where the two mendicant convents and 10-12 churches were made redundant in the 1530s. Two churches were converted into private residences, and the Franciscan church later became the town hall of Trondheim.[15]

The last wave of monastic destruction in Norway took place during the Nordic Seven Year War from 1563 to 1570, when both the Oslo region and the Trondheim region suffered an invasion by Swedish forces that led to much plundering and destruction. Some of the monastic houses that had been converted into residences were destroyed during this war, e.g. Elgeseter and Bakke in Trondheim and Nonneseter in Oslo, while others were abandoned at the same time (Lyse). Broadly, we can say that what survived the Seven Year War continued in use for several centuries.

Comparison with the neighbouring countries

Comparing the Norwegian situation with Denmark, Sweden or other countries, it is noticeable that very few of the Norwegian monastic houses were turned into private residences. One part of the explanation was that many of the monastic buildings were built of wood and thus not as durable as stone buildings. Also, wooden buildings could easily be moved to another location, as we observed at Tautra Abbey, where the last abbot sold to Niels Lykke a large wooden building with three floors.

Another part of the explanation was that the Norwegian agricultural system, with no villages and only scattered individual farms separated by forests, lakes and fjords, permitted very few large estates where it was possible or necessary to live and keep up an aristocratic lifestyle. The owner could therefore live anywhere and just employ bailiffs to collect the land rents and other income. A third reason was that the new owners of the old monastic estates

---

15   Ekroll (1989).

often did not live in Norway at all, but resided in Denmark, working in the service of the king. In addition, many of the new owners did not belong to the nobility, but were administrators or officials who received these estates as a part of their income. They had therefore no obligation to keep up an aristocratic lifestyle.

After the Reformation, the Norwegian nobility declined in numbers to a small group, and the Danish kings clearly favoured Danish or German noblemen over Norwegians for holding fiefs or official positions in Norway. Most of these were not interested in keeping up a nobleman's lifestyle in Norway, and they were clearly more interested in maximizing the income from their estates than in spending money on a lavish lifestyle. Also, many already had family estates in Denmark where they preferred to invest their profits, like building splendid new houses.

Unlike elsewhere, no Norwegian nunneries continued as or were turned into women's convents after 1600. One or two nunneries functioned until the 1560s, but no new institutions were established. In 1548, the Norwegian nobility petitioned King Frederik II for the establishment of a nunnery for noble maidens to save them from poverty or marrying below their class.[16] There is no indication that this wish was fulfilled, probably because of the weak position of the Norwegian nobility with its smaller numbers, which meant that there was no real basis for a separate institution for widows and unmarried daughters.

Nor were any Norwegian monasteries converted into royal residences or official seats for royal servants. The main reason for this situation was that the kings resided in Denmark and rarely visited Norway. On these rare occasions, they stayed in the royal castles or in the largest private houses. The royal administration of Norway was very limited with only a minimum of officials to rule the population. The need for large, permanent residences was therefore non-existent.

Only two monastic houses were converted for public purposes. The Franciscan church in Oslo became a hospital in 1538, and the same year the north wing of the Dominican friary in Oslo was given to the Cathedral School. In 1552, King Christian III gave the Augustinian Abbey of St John in Bergen to the town as a new town hall, but the building was destroyed by fire before the offer was accepted.[17] The Franciscan church of St Olav in Trondheim became the town hall in 1669 after more than a century in private hands.[18]

---

16   Vea (1987), p. 209.
17   Lidén (1980), p. 143.
18   Ekroll (1989), p. 10.

Oslo Hospital in 1699, painting by Jacob Coning. The former Franciscan church is whitewashed and has a tiled roof, and on the north side a wooden corridor and a wooden building have been added. In the foreground the wooden bridge Geitabru (Goat Bridge) across the river Alna. Photo: Rune Aakvik/ Oslo Museum

Only four of the monastic churches were still used as churches after the Reformation: Utstein Augustinian Abbey Church became a parish church, Bergen Franciscan Church became a combined parish church and cathedral, Oslo Franciscan Church became a hospital church and Marstrand Franciscan Church became a parish church.[19]

Five case studies

As case studies, I will present five former monastic institutions, three rural abbeys and two urban convents, that as a group serve as illustrations of the fate of those monastic houses in Norway that were not immediately demol-

---

19   Ekroll (1993), pp. 135-154.

have survived until today because its solid walls protected the later wooden manor houses built inside the former church from the strong western winds. The abbey buildings were probably made of wood and they have left no visible traces.[21] The oldest building dates to the seventeenth century and it occupies the site of the presumed east wing of the abbey. It contains reused timbers dating to the fifteenth century, perhaps deriving from one of the abbey houses. The present manor house dates from 1866 and it occupies the presumed site of the south wing of the abbey. The abbey well in the cloister garth still supplies the manor with water and never runs dry.

Reinskloster today presents a situation, which is rarely preserved in Norway, with the medieval ruins directly connected to the later manor building still occupied by the private owners.

Halsnøy Abbey

Halsnøy Augustinian Abbey of the Holy Spirit in Sunnhordland south of Bergen was the richest abbey in Norway, with an annual income equivalent to 10 tonnes of butter or 1320 barrels of grain. The abbey and its property were confiscated by the king in 1537, and in 1539, they were given to the royal servant Jens Spliid as a fief in lieu of an annual payment to the king. The property was a fief until 1664 when it became part of the new Bergenhuus Amt. The abbey estate passed into private hands in 1744 when it was sold to a Stavanger merchant, and since 1758, the manor has been owned by the Juel family, the first of which was the bailiff Andreas Juel.[22]

The monastic buildings were converted into a manor house, while the abbey church stood as a roofless ruin. These buildings were demolished in the 1840s and the stone used to construct a new manor house on the site, while the monastic outhouses still exist. The abbey was depicted in a 1654 painting by the Bergen artist Elias Figenschou, the oldest known Norwegian landscape painting. The abbey buildings were fortunately mapped in the 1830s ahead of their destruction, so that the ground plan of the abbey can be reconstructed. The medieval cloister well is incorporated into the basement of the new manor house and still provides the manor with excellent water.

The farms belonging to the abbey were gradually sold to the tenants, leaving only the farmland surrounding the abbey. The remaining ruins of the monastic buildings were sold to the local museum in 1956 and the church site was excavated in the 1960s.

---

21   Berg (1969), p. 107.
22   Lidén (1967), pp. 1-44; Lidén (2013), pp. 39-69.

Halsnøy Manor seen from the north in 1656, painting by Elias Figenschou. The painting belongs to Skokloster Museum, Sweden. The roofless abbey church is easily recognized and behind it the gable of the new manor house built by Otte Krag, who held the fief from 1646 to 1651. It was he who commissioned the painting. The other structures are medieval outbuildings and most of them still exist. Photo: Skokloster Museum

Utstein Abbey

Utstein Augustinian Abbey of St Lawrence on Mosterøy Island near Stavanger was a manor house until the twentieth century, and the abbey church is still a chapel for the island's inhabitants. After its dissolution in 1537, the abbey and its property were given as a fief to various royal servants until it was sold to a group of seven Danish noblemen in 1665 to cover a royal debt. In 1700, Johan Frimann, the bailiff of Halsnøy Abbey, bought Utstein Abbey and his descendants still own the abbey farm, first the Garman family and today the Schanche family.[23]

The chancel of the abbey church doubled as manor chapel and parish church, while the nave of the church stood as a roofless ruin until the 1950s. The west wing was demolished in 1630 and replaced by a timber building, which became the main residence of the manor, while the old dormitory in

23   Weidling (2005), pp. 291-343.

the east wing became a granary. After 1700, the manorial residence was established in the east and south wing of the abbey. The private owners tried to convert the abbey buildings into a baroque residence by establishing a new central axis leading from the landing quay by the sea through a new entrance in the south wing and directly to the staircase leading up to the entertaining rooms in the old dormitory in the east wing.[24]

In 1933, the Schanche family sold the old abbey buildings and the garden to a newly established foundation, which aimed to restore the complex. The buildings were excavated from 1937 onwards, and the buildings were restored from 1950 until 1965 . Today, the abbey is a museum and conference center.

Oslo Franciscan Convent

The Franciscan convent in Oslo was closed down in 1537 and the following year King Christian III established Oslo Hospital in the convent buildings as a home for the poor and sick.[25] The institution still exists, but today as a psychiatric clinic.[26]

The hospital buildings were burnt down by Swedish forces in 1567 and during its rebuilding, if not already in 1538, the polygonal chancel of the large abbey church was converted into dwellings for the inhabitants. The oldest illustrations of the hospital show that the chancel was divided into two floors and its large windows were replaced by two rows of small windows, while the nave still had its tall windows and was clearly the hospital's chapel with a small steeple on top. In 1737, a new 21m long hospital building as high and wide as the church was added to its west façade, thus making it a c. 75m long and 12m wide building.[27]

The church burned in 1794 and was rebuilt with a different design, but the lateral walls still incorporate some medieval masonry. The polygonal medieval chancel was demolished and new hospital buildings erected for the patients.

Oslo Dominican Convent

The Dominican convent of St Olav in Oslo was situated next to the cathedral of Oslo. It was closed down in 1537 and its buildings were soon transformed for new purposes.[28] The south wing containing the church was soon

---

24   Ekroll (2005), pp. 215-263.
25   Lange (1856), p. 464.
26   Semmingsen (1939), pp. 1-131.
27   Berg (1939), pp. 150-170.
28   Lange (1856), pp. 441-442; Hommedal (1987), pp. 129-155; Hommedal (1993), pp. 154-174.

demolished, the north wing became the cathedral school and dwellings for its teachers, the east wing was given to the new superintendent, Frans Berg, as his private residence, and the vaulted rooms in the west wing were let out to merchants as fireproof storage cellars. In 1622, the superintendent's residence was bought by the state from Berg's descendants and has ever since been the official residence of the bishop of Oslo. In 1622-23, it was restored in Renaissance style with arcaded gables, as shown on the oldest images of Oslo.

Most of Oslo was destroyed by fire in 1624, and King Christian IV subsequently moved the town across the harbour and named it after himself – Christiania. The newly restored bishop's residence escaped the fire and the bishop was therefore not permitted to move with the rest of the town's inhabitants, but stayed behind in what became rural isolation. The cathedral school moved to Christiania, and the remaining school buildings and cellars were demolished and the bishop's garden laid out over the remains. In the 1820s, the house was given a neoclassical façade, and in 1882-83, it was rebuilt in neo-Gothic style, which it retains today. The medieval ground floor containing vestry, chapter house and scriptorium is restored and these rooms retain much of their original character.

Conclusion

If we sum up our knowledge concerning the secularization of the monasteries in Norway, it took place in two main waves. The first dates to 1527-32 when about one third of the monasteries were secularized or ceased to exist, usually as the result of war or a forced takeover by noble men or women. The second wave came with the Lutheran Reformation in 1536-37 when the last fifteen houses were closed. The rural monasteries were often converted into manor houses while the urban houses became bishops' residences, schools, town halls and hospitals.

A few nunneries, which mainly housed the daughters and widows of the nobility, survived for some decades until the nuns died. The last surviving nuns were often taken in by the local bishops and lived for the remainder of their lives in the bishops' residences as house guests. The last mention of old nuns is made in Oslo as late as 1586, half a century after the Reformation.

Looking at the thirty monastic houses, two thirds of them found no continuing use except as stone quarries or agricultural storage buildings until the roofs fell in and they were left as ruins and subsequently also used as quarries. There were several reasons for this outcome, the most important being that the monastic buildings were situated so far off the beaten track that they were of no use. Most of the urban monasteries fell prey to the many urban conflagrations in the sixteenth and seventeenth centuries. They gradually disappeared beneath new streets and houses when the towns were rebuilt. Fortunately, some of the monastic buildings are still partly preserved as ruins and form an important part of the medieval cultural heritage of Norway.

Bibliography

Berg, Arne, 'Klosterruinen på Rein i Rissa', *Foreningen til norske fortidsminnesmerkers årbok*, 124 (1969), pp. 100-108.

Berg, Arno, 'Bergens bispegaard', *Bergens historiske forening skrifter*, 34 (1928), pp. 55-63.

Berg, Arno, 'Hospitalets bygningshistorie', in *Oslo Hospitals historie*, eds. Ingrid Semmingsen, Gerhard Fischer and Arno Berg (Oslo, 1939), pp. 150-170.

Ekroll, Øystein, 'Olavskyrkja. 8 fragment blir monument', *Arkeologiske undersøkelser i Trondheim nr. 3* (1989), pp. 1-78.

Ekroll, Øystein, 'Norske fransiskanarkonvent', *Tverrfaglige seminarer i Tønsberg, rapport nr. 1* (1993), pp. 135-154.

Ekroll, Øystein, 'Abbed Matthias og Tautra kloster', *Nord-Trøndelag historielag årbok for 1996*, 73 (1996), pp. 32-53.

Ekroll, Øystein, 'Bygning og bruk', in *Utstein kloster – og Klosterøys historie*, ed. Eldbjørg Haug (Stiftelsen Utstein kloster, 2005), pp. 215-263.

Gunnes, Erik, 'Klosterlivet i Norge. Tilblivelse – økonomi – avvikling', *Foreningen til norske fortidsminnesmerkers årbok*, 141 (1987), pp. 49-85.

Hommedal, Alf Tore, 'Olavsklostret i Oslo', *Foreningen til norske fortidsminnesmerkers årbok*, 141 (1987), pp. 129-155.

Hommedal, Alf Tore, 'Olavsklostret i Oslo og dei andre norske dominikanaranlegga i mellomalderen. Opprettinga av konventa og utforminga av ordenshusa', *Tverrfaglige seminarer i Tønsberg, rapport nr. 1* (1993), pp. 154-174.

Lange, Christian C.A., *De norske Klostres Historie i Middelalderen. Anden omarbeidede Udgave* (Christiania, 1856).

Lidén, Hans-Emil, *Halsnøy kloster*, Fortidsminner 54, Utgitt av Foreningen til norske fortidsminnesmerkers bevaring (Oslo, 1967).

Lidén, Hans-Emil, *Norges kirker, Bergen*, 1 (Oslo, 1980).

Lidén, Hans-Emil, 'Bygningane på Halsnøy kloster', in *Halsnøy kloster. Til kongen og Augustins ære*, eds. Bård Gram Økland, Jane C.S. Jünger, Ingvild Øye (Oslo, 2013), pp. 39-69.

Ree, Lorentz Harboe and Wallem, Fredrik B., *Østraat* (Trondhjem, 1916).

Semmingsen, Ingrid, 'Hospitalets almindelige historie', in *Oslo Hospitals historie*, eds. Ingrid Semmingsen, Gerhard Fischer and Arno Berg (Oslo, 1939), pp. 1-131.

Vea, Erik, 'Var Nonneseter kloster eslet til adelig jomfrukloster?', *Foreningen til norske fortidsminnesmerkers årbok*, 141 (1987), pp. 209-213.

Weidling, Tor, 'Klostret som verdslig len 1537-1664' and 'Under dansk konsortsium 1664-1700', in *Utstein kloster – og Klosterøys historie*, ed. Eldbjørg Haug (Stiftelsen Utstein kloster, 2005), pp. 291-343.

Monasteries and Collegiate Chapters in the Duchies of Schleswig and Holstein and the Reformation

Oliver Auge

The Reformation profoundly changed the monastic situation in the region of Schleswig-Holstein and elsewhere – although admittedly not immediately in 1517. Consequently, the anniversary in 2017 can merely claim limited, if any, relevance for Schleswig-Holstein. The changes set in slowly and progressed by degrees until the end of the sixteenth century.[1] The last monastery to be dissolved in Schleswig-Holstein was the Cistercian monastery in Reinfeld in 1582; in fact, the four nunneries in Itzehoe, Preetz, Uetersen and Schleswig outlasted the Reformation and still exist today as Protestant noblewomen's convents.

The volume at hand, entitled "The Dissolution of Monasteries – The case of Denmark in a Regional Perspective", promises to be the first to deliver a comprehensive account of those days' events for the Danish area. Certainly, it stands to reason to include the situation in Schleswig and Holstein in these considerations, as both were – at least partly – ruled by the king of Denmark since the famous Treaty of Ribe (March 1460); this personal union ended in 1864.[2] It seems all the more obvious to include Schleswig-Holstein considering that the department of regional history at the University of Kiel will shortly publish the "Klosterbuch für Schleswig-Holstein und Hamburg",

---

1   For a general overview, cf. Seegrün (1993), pp. 140-164; Lange (2003), pp. 166-173; Rathjen (2004); Hoffmann (1990), pp. 394-469; Hoffmann and Reumann (1986), pp. 92-106; Göbell, Hoffmann, Hauschild et al. (1982).

2   Cf. Auge and Büsing (2012), also for further references.

which, for the first time, provides a valid and compact basis for such an account as the following contribution will provide.[3]

While the "Klosterbuch" takes into account all monasteries, collegiate chapters and convents located in present-day Schleswig-Holstein (including Dithmarschen, North Frisia, the Duchy of Lauenburg and Lübeck), in Hamburg and in North Schleswig, which was ceded to Denmark in 1920, the following contribution adheres to the objective of these proceedings by merely covering those monasteries, nunneries and collegiate chapters which were part of the duchies of Schleswig and Holstein at the time of the Reformation.

The monasteries in Dithmarschen – a region only affiliated to the duchies since its conquest in 1559[4] – will not be considered, as their Reformation occurred under completely different circumstances and took a different course; therefore, to include them here would not make much sense. Also, the cathedral chapter of Schleswig, with its particular role both during and after the Reformation, cannot be taken into account.[5]

I. The end of the monasteries 1526–1582: A chronological outline

In the course of the Middle Ages, a complex network of monasteries and collegiate chapters developed in the duchies of Schleswig and Holstein (the latter being a county until 1474) below the level of the episcopal sees of Schleswig, Bremen-Hamburg and Lübeck. Shortly before the Reformation, the situation was as follows:[6]

The Augustinian canons regular belong to the oldest institutions in the country. They date back to the days of St Vicelinus, the missionary who, in a joint effort with Emperor Lothair III, founded a collegiate chapter of Augustinian canons in Segeberg in 1134. At that point, he had already established a similar institution in Neumünster. While the latter was relocated to Bordesholm in 1327/32, the first remained in Segeberg until the sixteenth century, in fact experiencing a second heyday under the influence of the Windesheim monastic reform. Approximately a hundred years later, the

---

3   Auge and Hillebrand (2019), [in press].
4   Lange (2003), pp. 166-173; Hoffmann, Reumann and Kellenbenz (1986), pp. 17-26.
5   Rausch and Nawrocki (2019).
6   Cf. Auge (2019b); id. (2011), pp. 13-17; for the individual monasteries, cf. their respective articles in Auge and Hillebrand (2019), [in press] and the relevant pages in Auge and Hillebrand (2017), pp. 22-33 and 99-108.

Order of Saint Benedict settled in Schleswig-Holstein: In the second quarter of the thirteenth century, Benedictines founded a convent in Cismar, which, however, had its roots in Lübeck. A women's convent was established in Preetz in 1211/12. The Cistercian monasteries were more numerous: The oldest of their communities consisted of the former Benedictines of Seem, who had been relocated to Løgum by order of the bishop of Ribe as part of a reform in 1175. In 1186/90, Count Adolf III of Schauenburg initiated the foundation of a Cistercian monastery in Reinfeld. In 1209/10, another community of Cistercians, who had originally settled in Guldholm in 1191, was moved to Ryd Abbey. Nunneries that adopted the Cistercian way of monastic life, but stood apart from the strict structures of the order existed, in Reinbek from 1226/29 onwards, in Itzehoe from 1230 and in Uetersen from 1235. The Mendicant orders, too, were particularly widespread, although, interestingly, only their male branches: Dominican communities settled in Schleswig and Haderslev in 1235 and 1273, respectively; Franciscan monasteries existed in Flensburg from 1232/33 or 1263 onwards, in Schleswig from 1234, in Tønder from 1238, and in Kiel from c. 1240. Moreover, an episcopal collegiate chapter was founded in Haderslev in c. 1266 and a Carthusian monastery in Ahrensbök in 1397. Lastly, three houses of the so-called Sisters of the Common Life were established in connection with the late medieval movement for religious reform called *devotio moderna*: in Neustadt in 1461 – probably originating from a previous community of Augustinian canonesses regular – in Plön in 1468 as a subsidiary of a community in Lübeck and in Neumünster in 1498, again as a subsidiary of the house in Plön.

Apparently, the collegiate chapter in Haderslev was the first pre-Reformation institution to fall victim to the Reformation.[7] It appears to have been dissolved before May 1526, following the retirement of the former provost Christian Wulf, who was replaced in 1526 by Eberhardt Weidensee from Magdeburg as the chapter's new provost and Johan Wenth from Wittenberg as its new lector. The collegiate chapter's early dissolution seems surprising at first, considering that these kinds of institutions tended to be more tenacious and resilient than other monastic establishments and in many cases persisted longer, undisturbed by the Reformation. This is why Peter Moraw once referred to collegiate foundations as the index fossils of ecclesiastical history in the Middle Ages and the Early Modern Period.[8] In this regard, the continuation of the Prince-Bishopric of Lübeck's collegiate church in Eutin until 1803 should be mentioned.[9] Searching for the cause of this phenom-

---

7   Cf., also with regard to the following, Madsen (2019a), § 2.1.3., [in press].
8   Moraw (2003), p. 71.
9   Röpcke and Hillebrand (2019), [in press].

enon, one meets Junker Christian (1503-59), Frederik I's (1471-1533, Duke of Holstein, King of Denmark from 1523) eldest son.[10] The districts of Haderslev and Tørning Len had been appointed to him in the spring of 1525 to maintain him and his (future) wife; also, this appointment was supposed to give Christian some practical experience regarding administration and politics for his future duties as king and duke.[11] Christian was a known follower of Martin Luther and his teachings. In this spirit, he actively reorganised the ecclesiastical structures within his realm, creating something of a role model and having some effect on the development in the whole of Schleswig and Holstein. Consequently, it is certainly no coincidence that it was the collegiate chapter of Haderslev, which was secularised first of all the monastic institutions in the duchies, considering that it was located in the area to which Christian had been sent by his father.

Next up for secularisation were all the houses of the Mendicant orders. Considering what has just been said, it is hardly surprising that, as far as we know, the Dominican monastery in Haderslev was dissolved first.[12] According to a sixteenth century source, the monks were expelled from their monastery by Junker Christian after mass on Epiphany in 1527. However, evidence of the further existence of the establishment exists up until April 1528, casting doubt on the popular tale about the abrupt end in early 1527. On 26th April 1528, the guardian and the monks gained permission to leave their monastery and travel to any monastery of their choice that was willing to take them in. Shortly afterwards, the Dominican monastery in Schleswig, too, was dissolved.[13] Around 1528/29, the Reformation preacher Reinholt Westerholt supposedly swept out (*"genßlichen uthgefegheth"*) the last monks who had stayed on and ravaged the monastery (*"de kloster gewostett"*).

The same treatment meted out to the community of Franciscans in Schleswig. With King Frederik I's permission, the monastery buildings were transferred to the Heilig-Geist-Hospital and St. Jürgen Hospital, while the church was given to the city council, which soon turned it into a new town hall.[14] The Franciscan monastery in Flensburg, too, was dissolved in favour of an almshouse.[15] On 8th January 1528, Frederik I entrusted his Steward of the Realm, Mogens Gøye, a Danish nobleman, with this task. Shortly afterwards, the

---

10   Lange (2003), pp. 167f.; Kämmel (1881), pp. 690-692; Voss (1974), pp. 660f.
11   Cf. Madsen (2008), pp. 112-114.
12   Madsen (2019b), § 2.1.3., [in press]. Also concerning the following.
13   Rathjen (2019), § 2.1.3., [in press]. Also concerning the following.
14   Ommen (2019), § 2.1.3., [in press]. Also concerning the following.
15   Kraack (2019), § 2.1.3., [in press]. Also concerning the following.

mayor and the city council compiled an inventory of the monastery's treasures and furnishings, which they sent to the king. After a first attempt to drive out the monks on 6th April 1528 had been thwarted by the spirited resistance of Wolf Pogwisch (c. 1485-1554), bailiff and castle commander in Flensburg, the second attempt on 7th June 1528 was successful: By order of Gøye, a priest named Sven forced his way into the monastery, accompanied by a large group of citizens from Flensburg and equipped with a deed signed by the king, and demanded Guardian Stig Nielsen and the convent, who were occupied in their morning prayer, hand over the keys. Eventually, the monks left their monastery, but only after they and the intruding citizens had used up the convent's remaining provisions. The buildings – with the exception of the arboretum, the refectory and the kitchen – were transferred to the city of Flensburg by King Frederik I and turned into an almshouse. In 1536, eight former monks were still living there. Ultimately, this almshouse merged with the city's other poorhouses and infirmaries in 1545 by royal consent and deed.

In Tønder, the dissolution of the Franciscan monastery did not favour the poor and old but the preservation of the castle.[16] The end of the monastery came when the king visited Tønder castle on 8th September 1530. However, the *Chronicle of the Expulsion of the Greyfriars* mentions that the convent had, at that point, already been subjected to drastic violations of monastic autonomy: The bailiff of the castle, Jasper Rantzau, had seized large parts of the monastery buildings and begun using them as food storage – probably with the king's consent. Only the choir, the dormitory and the small refectory had been left to the monks. The chronicle also mentions that a Lutheran sermon was being preached in the church of the friary during the king's visit. After that, the guardian approached the king, asking him in the name of the community for permission to stay and serve God. According to the chronicle, Frederik I was evasive at first; later, when the guardian mentioned the issue a second time, the king refused his request with reference to the maintenance requirements of the castle. Lastly, on 13th October 1530, Frederik I granted the city of Kiel the right to dissolve the Franciscan friary within its city walls and to assimilate its property.[17] The church treasures, including 15 gilded cups, a monstrance of silver and several paraments (liturgical cloth hangings), as well as all furnishings, amongst others six beds from the guest chamber and the hospital, were to be given to the magistrate for safekeeping. However, the king instead arranged for these items to be brought to Gottorp.

---

16   Eigenbrod and Madsen (2019), § 2.1.3., [in press].
17   Auge (2019c), § 2.1.3., [in press]. Also concerning the following.

In a letter of 3rd April 1531, he then expressly forbade the expulsion of the remaining eight friars, which the magistrate seems to have had in mind. The monastic buildings served the city as a municipal school until 1556, from 1556 to 1665 they housed a hospital (*Heiliggeistkloster*) and from 1665 onwards the newly founded university took up quarters in the old building.[18] A year before the dissolution of the Franciscan monastery in Kiel, the nunnery in Reinbek had been secularised as the first of the Cistercian communities within the duchies, when by 7th April 1529 all nuns had left the monastery.[19] Earlier, they had appealed to the king to release them from their "Babylonian prison".

Compared with this, the dissolution process of the remaining monasteries and collegiate chapters took much longer. Having first belonged to Christian III's domain, the Cistercian house in Løgum became part of his younger brother John (*Hans*) the Elder's (1521-1580) territory in 1544.[20] During his reign, the last abbot of the monastery was elected in 1546; the abbot, however, died only two years later. Subsequently, the monastery was administered by the prior, and from 1553 onwards, all traces of the convent are lost. A few years later, the Cistercian Ryd Abbey near Flensburg ceased to exist.[21] In 1553, the abbey's last abbot, Johannes Hildebrandt, who himself had turned to the Protestant faith, had asked the king for permission to re-sign, which the king granted him. Nevertheless, he apparently remained in office for some time. In 1557, the Protestant priest of St Nikolai in Flensburg, Gerhard Slewart (c. 1490-1570), mentioned the abbot's frailty and poor state of health, and requested the appointment of a successor. Slewart was a former Augustinian hermit from Magdeburg, who was strongly influenced by Luther's and Melanchthon's writings. He and two other priests from Flensburg had been instructed to introduce Protestant services in the monasteries of Løgum and Ryd in 1541. In 1559, Slewart himself was appointed provost of Ryd Abbey, marking the end of its monastic era. Under his direction, a school was established in the monastery buildings. Because the school was intended to prepare the students for their theological studies, it seems likely that former monks were initially involved in providing instruction. This likelihood, however, cannot be proven.

In the years between 1526 and 1530, the duchies thus saw a first wave of secularisation. After a pause lasting around twenty years, the 1560s turned into a second heyday of dissolutions of monasteries in Schleswig and Hol-

---

18   Auge (2017b), p. 121; Beuckers (2015), pp. 177f.; cf. also Krüger and Künne (1991), pp. 111 and 124f.
19   Grabkowsky (2019b), § 2.1.3., [in press]. Also concerning the following.
20   Kragh (2019), § 2.1.3., [in press]. Also concerning the following.
21   Jensen and Salonen (2019), § 2.1.3., [in press]. Also concerning the following.

stein. The first institution to be hit by this second wave, not counting the above-mentioned Ryd Abbey, was the Benedictine monastery in Cismar.[22] Its finances were in a bad state due to tax burdens imposed by the sovereign. This, however, was not uncommon, as the other rural monasteries still in existence found themselves in the same situation. The abbot of the monastery is last mentioned in the sources in 1559; he probably died shortly afterwards. On 28th January, the sovereign instructed Benedikt von Ahlefeldt to compile an inventory of the monastery's possessions. Around this time, the monastery ceased to be a manorial entity and was instead incorporated into the sovereign's property; the monastery was thus secularised.

The Carthusians in Ahrensbök met the same fate: The end of the monastery came in 1564, after it had already suffered from severe looting during The Count's Feud and even more so from the abovementioned financial burdens imposed by the sovereign.[23] Moreover, the pressure on the Carthusians had noticeably increased under Christian III in the 1540s, although the king obviously did not want the dissolution at that time.[24] During a visitation in 1541, Christian had expressly requested the prior to swear that he would carry out the management of the monastery more efficiently, especially by economising on wood, and that he would not sell or give in pawn monastic property, except in instances of greatest need. The prior, however, seems to have violated this oath; in 1561, he received a written warning by Christian's successor Frederik II (1534–88). When the prior took ill, already advanced in years, in 1562, the king and Heinrich Rantzau (1526–98) decided to end the autonomous administration of the friary and to transfer its property into the sovereign's charge. The prior, however, failed to do them the favour of dying quickly but lived far longer than expected. Thus, it was the division of the territory in 1564 which dealt the monastery the final blow, in that it was transferred to John (*Hans*) the Younger (1545-1622), King Frederik II's brother.[25] On their mother's (Dorothea of Saxe-Lauenburg, 1511–71) initiative, who included Ahrensbök in her dower, the Carthusian monastery was then immediately dissolved, although Frederik II unsuccessfully protested against this step. A bailiff was appointed to manage the property. The old prior was promised maintenance for life. The last monk, Heinrich Breide (†1587), who was accused of document forgery and of unauthorized assumption of authority, fled the monastery to avoid capture and, in fact, carved out a remarkable prebendary career in Lübeck until he died in 1587.[26]

---

22 Grabkowsky (2019a), § 2.1.3., [in press]. Also concerning the following.
23 Auge (2019a), § 2.1.3., [in press]. Also concerning the following.
24 Cf. section III.
25 Adriansen (2008), p. 210; Lange (2003), p. 177.
26 For more information on Heinrich Breide, cf. Prange (2009).

At the same time, the two long-standing communities of Augustinian canons in Segeberg and Bordesholm were facing their end. In Segeberg, Lutheran parish services had already been held in the nave of the collegiate church since the end of the 1520s, while the collegiate chapter was still using the church choir for their liturgical tasks.[27] By the beginning of the 1560s, the chapter had lost all its canons through death or flight, except for one professed monk adhering to the Windesheim monastic reform, still documented after 1563. Some canons were taken in by the Cistercians in Reinfeld. Also, King Frederik II appointed a monk named Eberhard as the chapter's new provost after the last prior had died; however, Eberhard was deposed from his office only a year later, because the Reformation was now to be introduced there ("gemelts closter in vorenderung zu bringen"). The last canon, Dirich Schyndell, passed the institution on to Heinrich Rantzau, and thus it ceased to exist. Schyndell received a pension of 20 Thalers as well as free clothing and nourishment. The relevant deed dates from 27th June, but the year is not specified; therefore, it is impossible to say whether the dissolution occurred in 1564, 1565 or 1566. In any case, the chapter's property was consequently managed by Rantzau, who paid the king an annual 3,500 Thalers of the proceeds. Rantzau, who was interested in humanism, transferred parts of the chapter's library to his castle in Breitenburg.

The community of Augustinian canons in Bordesholm existed until 1566.[28] Having already been exposed to growing political and financial strain imposed by the sovereign for quite some time, in 1561, John the Elder directly interfered with the canons' affairs when he sent magister Erasmus Heinsen, who had been educated in Wittenberg, to Bordesholm to give sermons and convert the canons to the Lutheran faith. After the dissolution of this chapter, a newly established Latin school moved into the buildings, which was funded by the chapter's former property. This institution then formed the basis for the foundation of the University of Kiel in 1665.[29]

The house of the Sisters of the Common Life in Neumünster was dissolved comparatively late, in 1570, after the community in Neustadt had already been transformed into a Folwark in 1546.[30] In the 1560s, at the latest, the Sisters' house had already begun to suffer from severe economic difficulties and surely would have been closed down earlier, had it not been for the financial support and deliveries of grain from Bordesholm. This can be deduced from

27 Bünz (2019), § 2.3.1., [in press]. Also concerning the following.
28 Schnabel (2019), § 2.3.1., [in press]. Also concerning the following.
29 Pauls (1955), pp. 11f.; Piotrowski (2015), pp. 21-30.
30 Piotrowski (2019a), § 2.3.1., [in press]; Hillebrand (2019), § 2.3.1., [in press].

the correspondence between the Sisters and the subprior and procurator of Bordesholm as well as the bailiff of Rendsburg and Bordesholm, Christoff Rantzau. Duke Adolf I had the buildings in Neumünster demolished and a lordly house erected in its place, which later housed the local district offices and gaol. The last community of Sisters of the Common Life in Plön was dissolved in 1578.[31] Their house had been heavily damaged by a fire ravaging the city in 1570, forcing the last *mater* to sell the buildings to Duke John the Younger. In February 1584, they were demolished by order of the duke. In the sources, reform efforts within this convent can be detected, especially around 1517/20, leading not quite to a complete but to a strong orientation towards the monastic life, which may be the secret of this community's comparatively long existence.

The last larger monastery to be dissolved was the Cistercian community in Reinfeld.[32] Reinfeld's secularisation was connected to another division of territory between King Frederik II and his younger brother John II of Schleswig-Holstein-Sonderburg (1545–1622) in 1581.[33] In order to gratify the latter's forcefully asserted claims to a larger share, the king secularised the long-standing institution. On 10th March 1582, its last abbot, Johannes Kule, ceded the monastery to the king, who was represented by a secularisation committee. Officially, the appropriation by the king happened on 13th March 1582. The monastery was thus dissolved. At the end of June the same year, the so-called "Klosteramt Reinfeld" was transferred to Duke John II, who had the monastery buildings – with the exception of the church – demolished in 1599 and replaced with a new castle complex during the following two decades.

II. A compromise with the nobility: Nunneries are turned into Lutheran women's convents

Unlike the above-mentioned monasteries, collegiate chapters and convents, the four nunneries in Itzehoe (Cistercians), Preetz (Benedictines), Uetersen (Cistercians) and Schleswig (Benedictines) did not have to face complete dissolution[34]: The *Christlyke Kercken Ordeninge* of 1542, in this aspect copying Christian III's Lutheran church ordinance for Denmark, Norway and

---

31 Piotrowski (2019b), § 2.3.1., [in press].
32 Cf. Schröter (2019), § 2.3.1., [in press]. And, more comprehensively, id. (2012), pp. 553-599.
33 For a general overview, cf. Adriansen (2008), p. 217; Lange (2003), p. 177.
34 See, for the following, Auge and Hillebrand (2017), pp. 109-114.

The church of the Protestant noblewomen's convent in Itzehoe. Photo: Katja Hillebrand

Schleswig-Holstein of 1537, paved the way for the continuation of the remaining chapters and monasteries in Schleswig and Holstein.[35] The church ordinance revoked the binding quality of the profession, allowing every occupant of a monastery to leave their convent if they wished to do so. A Protestant advisor was appointed to oversee the remaining occupants, to hold the Evangelical service and, ideally, to transform the monks into Lutheran pastors. Regarding nuns and *"kloster Junckfrouwen"*, the church ordinance ruled that they would in the future be free to leave the monastic community with their relatives' consent. Those women, however, who wanted to stay in the nunnery *"scholen se gehorsam syn / erer auersten edder priorissen nicht vthteen edder varen / sonder eerliken lenen [live] / alletidt etwas tho donde hebben / lesen / unsern hemmlischen Vader anropen ym namen Christi / Dat se horen Lectien uth der Schrifft / uth dem Cathechismo unde predigen / Desgleichen ock leren de rechte art des gelouens yn Christum"*.[36] According to this ordinance, the character of the services in the remaining monastic institutions was to change, while, at the same time, they were meant to continue to be places of devout community life. Thus, the four medieval nunneries were, in a formal sense, replaced by Lutheran women's convents, each of which was characterised by close association of its inhabitants, lasting until the seventeenth century.[37] The prescriptions of the church ordinance concerning monasteries and their convents in principle applied to all monastic institutions still existing in 1542. However, only the four women's convents mentioned above actually continued to exist, while the friaries – with the exception of the Cistercian monastery in Reinfeld, which was dissolved in 1582 only – were all deprived either personnel or finances, and/or were subjected to divisions of territory by their sovereign and were, eventually, dissolved. Interestingly, two of the three houses of the Sisters of the Common Life, too, continued to exist for a comparatively long time, until 1570 or 1578, respectively; they closed down merely because of an obvious lack of personnel or, even more importantly, evident financial difficulties.

The significant difference was that, firstly, these four nunneries did not belong to a specific sovereign after the territorial divisions, but were located in the part of the duchies which was ruled collectively and in which consent

---

35 Bugenhagen (1986 [1542]).
36 "... Are supposed to obey their superior or prioress, not to defy or effervesce, but live honestly, always having something to do, read, call to our heavenly Father in the name of Christ; they are supposed to listen to readings from the Holy Scripture, from the Cathecism and Sermons, and also learn the right kind of faith in Christ.", Bugenhagen (1986 [1542]), pp. 196-199, especially p. 198.
37 Auge (2014), pp. 317-346; Posselt (1894).

to rule was imperative. Consequently, from the start they did not, at least only in rare cases, become the target of a sovereign's efforts of secularisation. On the other hand, the growing significance of the nobility, especially of the *Equites Originarii* (*Schleswig-Holsteinische Ritterschaft*), within provincial government and politics apparently enabled the nobles to secure and expand their historically established influence on the four nunneries, which they used as a comparatively problem-free manner of housing their unmarried daughters. Similar efforts on the part of the citizenry of Plön or Neumünster regarding their houses of Sisters of the Common Life are not recorded. In this light it is hardly surprising that, at the State Diet in 1564, the *Equites Originarii* strongly advocated the preservation of the women's convents in Itzehoe, Uetersen, Preetz and St Johannis in Schleswig. And, indeed, on 25th October 1564 King Frederik II confirmed all "*privilegia, fryheiden, begnadungen, herlicheiden und gerechticheiden, olde und nie, so se van unsen forfaren lofflicher und milder gedechtnusse immer gehatt und noch hebben*" of the convent in Itzehoe.[38]

It is still disputed when exactly the Lutheran convents were, in fact, turned into exclusively aristocratic institutions. One of the central statements from an older contribution on this question by Volquart Pauls is that the *Equites Originarii* had already cultivated such close contacts with the four nunneries Itzehoe, Preetz, Uetersen and Schleswig even before the Reformation. Also, after the introduction of the Reformation, the nunneries were almost inevitably perceived as the *Equites'* annex.[39] "This connection […] has not been established in the course of the Reformation, but […] can be traced back to the Catholic era during the Middle Ages. The Equites' monastic rights are older than the Reformation; they have not been granted the Equites as a show of gratitude for services to state and sovereign, but are the recognition and confirmation of rights, which the Equites had already been exercising as their customary rights for a long time." Pauls justifies his claim by stating that the nobility had been involved as devout founders and that, by the end of the Middle Ages, the management of the monasteries, i.e. the monastic offices of the prioress, abbess and provost, had almost exclusively been taken into the hands of the nobility; noble influence, he continues, also increased within the nunneries, especially due to the levying of an entry fee for novices, which could hardly be afforded by members of other social groups. In this fashion, monasteries had already been turned into institutions designed for the ac-

---

38 Pelc (2019), § 2.3.1., [in press]. "... privileges, liberties, endowments, territories and rights old and new, as they from our ancestors' worthy and meek memory always have and always will possess.",

39 Pauls (1949), pp. 87-118, including the following quotations, translated from German into English; for critcism on Pauls's interpretation cf. Auge (2014), pp. 322-326.

The church of the Protestant noblewomen's convent in Preetz. Photo: Katja Hillebrand

commodation of the nobility's unmarried daughters prior to the Reformation. According to Pauls, this relationship had then been further intensified during the Reformation when nobles on a large scale availed themselves of the monasteries' financial assistance. Considering the nobility's longstanding privileges and their foundations for the benefit of the Church, Christian III had agreed to allow the four nunneries to continue without any changes in their organisation and legal status, not as Catholic monasteries but as spiritual institutions of the Protestant faith. Changes were limited to the actual form of the services, states Pauls who also claims that the overall purpose of the monastic institutions did not change after they had been turned into Lutheran women's convents.

There is good reason to doubt Pauls' claims, although less so when it comes to his assessment of the monasteries as a way for the nobles to accommodate their unmarried daughters. Still, in his study on the monastery in Preetz and its manorial system, focusing on the years leading up to 1550, Johannes Rosenplänter emphasises that the characterisation of Preetz as a place of noble accommodation is inadequate[40] as this was only one reason for the nobility to send their daughters into monastic life, while their concern for the family's intercession and salvation as well as their sense of identity – with monasteries being perceived as an integral part of noble culture in Holstein – were of equal importance.[41] In fact, Pauls himself concedes that, even in the post-Reformation era, the monasteries were not merely a way for the *Equites* to accommodate their unmarried daughters, but only acquired this exclusive purpose in the course of time.[42] Rather, their main purpose was religious service, calling upon God in the name of the authorities and the whole state (*Gott mit andechtigen Gebete für die Obrigkeit und ganze Landschafft anzuruffen*).[43]

What we have to question, however, is Pauls' statement of the chronology of noble exclusivity. Joachim Stüben, for instance, casts doubt on the nobles' monastic privileges before the Reformation in his study on the provost of Uetersen named Johann Schomburg (died after 1511). Stüben notes that, although the landed gentry emerged in Schomburg's era[44], the bourgeois element was still present in the convent in Uetersen in the sixteenth century. The minutes of a trial from 1618 state that many foreign maidens and many daughters of citizens from Hamburg had entered (the monastery), and that their coats of arms were still visible in the (monastery's) windows ("*viel auslendische Junfern, ja viel Bürger aus Hamburg Töchter (ins Kloster) hineingenommen, deren Wappen annoch in den Fenstern (im Kloster) vorhanden [seien]*").

Louis Bobé's study from 1918 also expresses a view differing from Pauls': Prior to the Reformation, the *Equites Originarii* do not seem to have enjoyed any privileges regarding the acceptance of their daughters into the monasteries. Unlike in German monasteries, no documentary proof of noble birth including an authenticated pedigree was necessary. The daughters of renowned and affluent citizens were admitted, too, but due to the obligatory admittance fee, it was chiefly noble maidens who were accepted.[45] Markus Posselt discusses the question of monastic rights in more detail and states that, in pre-Reformation time, a limitation of the right to the monasteries to

---

40   Rosenplänter (2009), pp. 237-242.
41   Cf. Auge (2013), pp. 115f.
42   Pauls (1949), p. 109.
43   Ibid., p. 110, with reference to the regulations in the monastery order of 1620; cf. also Michelsen and Johannßen (1773), p. 308 (cf. also for the quotation).
44   Stüben (2011), p. 116. Also concerning the following.
45   Bobé (1918), p. 58.

The church of the Protestant noblewomen's convent in Uetersen. Photo: Katja Hillebrand

the *Equites Originarii* was out of the question.[46] Rather, Posselt tries to show that the *Equites* themselves only perceived the monasteries as theirs towards the end of the sixteenth century.[47] In fact, the sovereigns did not at all accept this claim at that time and even actively contested it between 1610 and 1613. For instance, the sovereign resolution of 15th April 1613 expressly states that the monasteries are not affiliated to the *Equites Originarii*, but to the sovereign.[48] It was only at the State Diets in Kiel (1636) and Flensburg (1637) that the *equites* were able to gain the exclusive right to the monasteries, more or less unchallenged by royalty.[49] Therefore, it is not by chance that the first paragraph of the royal monastic order of 1636 states that the monasteries had been allowed to persist in order to accommodate adult noble maidens.[50]

---

46 Posselt (1894), p. 36.
47 Ibid., p. 37.
48 Posselt (1894), p. 41.
49 Cf. especially Posselt (1894), p. 42; cf. also Auge (2012), pp. 170-177.
50 Posselt (1894), pp. 44, 48. – Michelsen and Johannßen (1773), p. 537, § 1: „[…] nachdem in unsern Fürstenthümben etzliche Jungfrawen Clöster gelegen, welche hierumb in esse gelassen, darmit darin erwachsene Adeliche Jungfrawen, in dem Stande, die Zeit deren Lebens ihrem Gott dienen, und Unterhalt haben könten, die jungen Jungfrawen aber in wahrer Gottesfurcht und guten Sitten auferzogen werden möchten, darauff ein wachendes Auge zu haben, daß darin gute Ordnung und Erbarkeit zu halten, alle Unordnung und Unartigkeit aber abgeschaffet werde."

On the basis of these observations it seems reasonable to date the noble exclusivity in the context of nunneries in Schleswig and Holstein in accordance with Bobé and Posselt: Only at the State Diets in 1636-37 did the *Equites* claim their exclusive right to the monasteries, after the daughters of foreign nobles had received entitlement and elevation.[51]

III. The role of royalty

Of course, the attitude of royalty towards the new faith was of crucial importance for the spread of the Reformation in the territories in general and in the monasteries in particular. On the one hand, kings were indeed motivated by their personal faith, but on the other hand, they also pursued tangible material goals and advantages, as, for example, when the assets of a dissolved monastery or foundation were surrendered directly to them. The land belonging to the former Dominican monastery in Haderslev, for instance, was directly assigned to the castle administration of Haderslevhus,[52] and, similarly, the dissolved Franciscan monastery in Tønder was partly used to satisfy the needs of local castle maintenance.[53] In Bordesholm, a princely Latin school was established.[54] The proceeds from the dissolution of the Carthusian monastery in Ahrensbök were used for the princely dower.[55] In Reinfeld, the king ordered the dissolved monastery to be knocked down and erected a castle in its place.[56] With regard to the peasants who changed from ecclesiastical to secular manorialism due to the Reformation, royalty gained four fifths, while the nobles only gained one fifth, according to calculations by Ulrich Lange.[57] Thus, royalty became the major winner of the Reformation era. Of course, nobles belonging to the royal entourage were profiteers, too, especially in the prominent case of Heinrich Rantzau and the assets of the secularised Augustinian canons regular in Segeberg.[58]

At the same time, urban municipalities utilised the secularisations of mendicant institutions to meet charitable or educational needs by establishing hospitals and schools – under municipal direction – in abandoned build-

---

51 Bobé (1918), p. 58.
52 Madsen (2019b), § 2.3.1., [in press].
53 Eigenbrod and Madsen (2019), § 2.3.1., [in press].
54 Schnabel (2019), § 2.3.1., [in press].
55 Auge (2019a), § 2.3.1., [in press].
56 Schröter (2019), § 2.3.1., [in press].
57 Lange (2003), p. 173.
58 Bünz (2019), § 2.3.1., [in press].

ings.[59] The need for these kinds of establishments seems to have been vast, which at least partly explains the early dissolution of especially the urban monasteries.

The attitudes of the respective sovereigns were by no means uniform. Frederik I (1471-1533) seems to have been indifferent;[60] however, scholars still have reason to debate his faith: While he can be viewed as a Catholic-reformist, aiming to enforce a sovereign church regime of pre-Reformation character, his active role in the dissolution of the mendicants' monasteries and in the case of Reinbek cloister in the years from 1527 onwards seems to contradict this view. He benefited financially from the decisions of the Diet (*Herredag*) in Odense in 1526 directed against the Curia which renders it audacious to deduce from it a pro-reformary attitude of Frederik. On the contrary, his hands were probably also tied by his charter which he had to confirm to the initially anti-reforming estates of Danmark as his electors at the enthronement to profess the Reformation straightforwardly. Therefore, in individual cases it remains unclear who was actually the driving force. Frederik I could have acted in the spirit of the Reformation and dissolved the monasteries of the mendicant orders to purge himself of the almost overwhelming municipal pressure at that time on this matter. It must be emphasised that it was strong financial need, afflicting him since his accession to the Danish throne in 1523, which dictated his first steps towards the reformation of the monasteries. This interpretation is confirmed by the events at the State Diets in 1525 and 1526, when royalty pushed through an extraordinary tax of tremendous proportions.[61] In 1526 alone, this tax amounted to the staggering sum of 60,000 Marks lübisch. The Danish example, too, with which he became better acquainted when he was king of Denmark than when he had been duke, will have had an influence on him.[62]

More clearly on the side of the new faith – albeit less definitely and evidently than some want to believe – was his son Christian III.[63] He facilitated the carrying out of the Reformation, first in the districts of Haderslev and Tørning Len, which had been ceded to him prior to his maturity, and later, when he had succeeded his father as king and duke, in the remaining territories.[64] This seems a plausible explanation for the unusually early disso-

---

59   Lange (2003), p. 168.
60   Krüger (2017). Also concerning the following.
61   Leverkus (1840). Also concerning the following.
62   Lange (2003), p. 168.
63   See now Auge (2017a).
64   Göbell, Hoffmann, Hauschild et al. (1982).

lution of the foundation in Haderslev, which has been described above. As early as 8th April 1529 he, still a prince, together with Johannes Bugenhagen (1485–1558) led the disputation on the right faith and its concrete manifestation, which was held in Flensburg in the church of the former Franciscan monastery in front of over 400 listeners.[65] King Frederik left this task to his son, although he was staying in Flensburg at the exact same time – again, he appears indifferent in his personal attitude. According to Detlev Kraack, the disputation contributed substantially to the promotion of Luther's teachings in Schleswig and Holstein. Still, Christian III's pro-Reformation attitude did not equal a categorical rejection of monastic culture as such. In fact, he acted more carefully, maybe even generally more sensitively, than his father when it came to the issue of the monasteries: While the Kiel Diet of 1533 allowed the members of all monastic institutions to leave their monastery and instructed all those remaining in their institutions to elect an evangelical preacher, Christian, in return, expressly promised the nobility and the prelates of the territories the continuation of the landed property of all rural monasteries and nunneries. It seems, however, that Christian III was primarily concerned with the religious aspect rather than economic or financial motives. Johannes Bugenhagen's *Ordinatio Ecclesiastica* for Denmark, Norway and Schleswig-Holstein, completed in 1537, reiterated the regulation from 1533 allowing members of monastic establishments to leave their institutions, but not forcing them to do so if they only led a life in accordance with the evangelical teachings, and if a learned and capable preacher, living in secular circumstances, was assigned to and accommodated by each monastery.[66] On this normative basis, which the edict of the church ordinance of Schleswig-Holstein in 1542 was supposed to round off, the priests commissioned, Rudolph von Nimwegen (†1542) and Johann Meiger (†1561), were charged with the task of visiting the monasteries and ecclesiastical foundations in order to fully prepare the way for their transformation to Lutheranism.[67] In April 1541, they reported that most monasteries had submitted to the royal order.

Christian III's concrete handling of the situation regarding the monasteries becomes apparent in the example of the Cistercians in Itzehoe, regarding whom he was ready to compromise:[68] In 1538, it transpired that some

---

65 Kraack (2019), § 2.3.1., [in press]. Also concerning the following.
66 Kirchenordnung (1934).
67 Bugenhagen (1986). Also concerning the following.
68 Pelc (2019), § 2.3.1., [in press].

The Protestant noblewomen's convent in Schleswig seen from the South West. Photo: Katja Hillebrand

citizens had stolen and sold ornaments and other objects from St Laurentii Church in Itzehoe. The city council had, apparently, already employed an evangelical preacher without being legally allowed to do so. When the abbess issued a complaint about this matter, Christian III's reply of 29th April 1538 included the following instructions: The objects which had been removed were to be kept together, and the perpetrators were to be punished; a preacher – who may be Lutheran – must only be employed with royal consent; he must be accommodated by the monastery, the city and the other inhabitants of the *Kirchspiel*. In this fashion, the king and duke promoted the introduction of the Reformation in Itzehoe, while at the same time leaving the monastery the contested patronage and seeing to the preservation of his acquisition.

Christian III's attempt at "organically" converting the existing monasteries to the new evangelical church ordinance is also apparent in his correspondence with the Carthusians in Ahrensbök.[69] In a letter to the prior, dating from 1549, in which he discusses the visible decrease in members, Christian emphasises that he does not like seeing the monasteries "*dergestalt erledigt und verwustet*" – i.e. in such a desolate state. Rather, he wanted them

---

69   Auge (2019a), § 2.3.1., [in press].

to recruit more "*christliche und fromme Personen*" – i.e. devout Christians. But when monks who had been expelled from the Carthusian monastery Marienehe near Rostock and from other places came to Ahrensbök and were admitted into the monastery, the king expressly requested that they should be asked whether they would be willing to live in accordance with his Christian church ordinance and the Reformation. He was unwilling to condone their "*eigene Abgotterey und Muncherey*" – their specific idolatry. So this was Christian III's line of demarcation: Monasteries and their members were allowed to remain where they were, but not under the unacceptable auspices of the old faith.

Under Christian III's son and successor, Frederik II, the attitude towards the remaining monastic institutions grew increasingly uncompromising, which explains the wave of dissolutions in the 1560s. These were caused by the dynastically and strategically motivated territorial divisions of 1564 and 1581. The dissolution of the monasteries served to keep the peace within the dynasty by satisfying the king's younger brother John's additional demands. Of course, as a member of the third Reformation generation, Frederik II must have seen the ecclesiastical developments much clearer than his grandfather and father had been able to. Therefore, it must have been far easier for him to bid farewell to the traditional institution of the monasteries than for his predecessors.

IV: Between resistance and adaptation: The inhabitants of the monasteries

Up until this point, the actual inhabitants of the monasteries as actors during the Reformation era have been mentioned only in passing. In fact, many works on Reformation history create the impression that monks and friars were only passive objects during the events. On closer inspection, however, the monasteries – as a whole or at least partly – emerge as actors who either welcomed the Reformation and its results, or tried to put up a fight against it.

In the convent of Benedictine nuns in Schleswig under prioress Drude Pogwisch, the Reformation was introduced towards the end of the 1520s without any apparent resistance.[70] In Preetz, the transformation seems to have been similarly smooth.[71] Also, there is no notable mention of opposition

---

70   Greinert (2019), § 2.3.1., [in press].
71   Rosenplänter (2019), § 2.3.1., [in press].

in our sources for the dissolution of the mendicant monasteries in Schleswig and Holstein. In Tønder, the guardian at least tried to appeal to the king in order to come to an amicable settlement – although he was not successful.[72] Possibly, in this context the composition of the convents from non-local monks proved a burden, because, other than in the case of the women's convents, the Mendicants did not have many local contacts to the secular surroundings. At least, the sources suggest that not all Mendicants left their houses immediately, so that not all convents dissolved straightaway. In 1531, Kiel, for instance, was still home to eight – old and frail – Franciscans.[73]

Especially with regard to the Cistercians in Reinbek, sources have survived which show that the nunnery unanimously welcomed the Reformation and its consequences. In a letter to Martin Luther by Johannes Bugenhagen, dating from 9th October 1528, we learn that the prioress and two nuns listened to several of his sermons, had two conversations with him and sat with him once.[74] It further states that monastic life in Reinbek was at that point – although this was against the provost's will – limited to the wearing of the habit and the singing of the psalms, with the latter not even conforming to the Rule of Saint Benedict any longer. Six nuns had already been released by the prioress in order to get married; the prioress was intending the same path for all of the remaining nuns, or at least as many as possible, after which she wanted to leave the monastery herself. Thus, the self-induced dissolution of the nunnery was merely a question of time. On 29th March 1529, King Frederik I informed the nobleman Luder Schack from Lauenburg in a long letter that his four daughters living in the nunnery were allowed to leave the monastery as all other nuns after an examination of their consciences, so that he, the father, was to take his daughters back. Each of them would be endowed with 300 marks, although none of them had paid this amount upon entering the nunnery. On 7th April 1529, it seems that all remaining nuns did indeed leave the monastery. Shortly before, the convent had ceded the monastery and its landed possessions with all affiliations, except for the assets and claims located in Lauenburg to the king and duke for 12,000 Marks. In the respective document, the prioress and the forty listed sisters give their reasons for this step: Most of them had been given to the monastery against their will when they were still children in order to create bigger shares of the inheritance for their siblings. Through their own reading of the Holy Bible they

---

72 Eigenbrod and Madsen (2019), § 2.3.1., [in press].
73 Auge (2019c), § 2.3.1., [in press].
74 Grabkowsky (2019b), § 2.3.1., [in press]. Also concerning the following.

had realised that the monastic statutes did not comply with Scripture. In order to be released from their "Babylonian prison" they had, through friends, sought the advice of their sovereign, King Frederik I, who supported their request and provided each of them with 300 Marks for their future subsistence, for which they were grateful. Of their own free will and with the consent of their parents, friends and relatives they now wanted to leave the nunnery and never return. A farmer reported in 1569 that he had eye-witnessed the nuns leaving the monastery with seven carts, accompanied by drum rolls. In the same year, the eighty year old former scribe of the last provost explained that the king had expelled the nuns after taking the monastery into his possession. Apparently, not all the nuns were content with leaving their convent and thus abandoning their monastic way of life.

We know that the Reformation caused a deep division within the convent in Itzehoe.[75] 28 nuns sent a letter to King Christian III on 21st February 1538, asserting that they all were already devoted to the new faith, but that they were kept from holding evangelical services by their unrelenting abbess and thirteen other nuns who were on her side. However, even this strong opposition to Protestantism could only delay but not prevent the transformation of their nunnery into an evangelical women's convent. Whether or not the attested discord between sisters and *mater* in the house of Sisters of the Common Life in Neumünster, which the queen dowager attempted to settle amicably, had a confessional background can only be surmised.[76]

The Augustinian canons regular in Bordesholm and Segeberg fluctuated between resistance and adaptation, as can be seen from a letter sent by the prior of Windesheim to provost Bernhard in Bordesholm on 11th October 1541. Having been asked how to handle the new conditions and the sovereign's demands to adapt, the prior recommended giving way as much as possible, but to adhere to the three unalterable vows of poverty, obedience and chastity.[77] If mass were not to be celebrated publicly anymore, the divine office were not to be conducted and the saints were not to be cultivated any longer, the prior further recommended withdrawing the canons from parish churches, holding service behind closed doors, hiding the administration of the sacrament to the so-called sick people (= the Protestants, O.A.) and conducting the divine office individually and, if possible, employing someone of the old faith as lector.

---

75 Pelc (2019), § 2.3.1., [in press].
76 Cf. Hillebrand (2019), § 2.3.1. [in press].
77 Bünz (2019), § 2.3.1., [in press]; Schnabel (2019), § 2.3.1., [in press].

The Cistercians in Reinfeld, too, attempted the difficult balancing act of remaining loyal to their sovereign and monastic authorities while at the same time maintaining central elements of their monastic life and the previous form of service.[78] For instance, they delayed markedly in employing a Lutheran lector as prescribed by the church ordinance of 1542. Moreover, they kept several elements of monastic life as it had been prior to the Reformation, something which visitators criticised again and again.

The Carthusians in Ahrensbök turned out to be even more adamant. In 1541, the visitators reported that the prior was refusing to give up mass, sacraments and holy water, and that the monks were unwilling to remove their habits.[79] In 1544 and again in 1557, it was required that the king finally impose a ban on the continuing celebration of mass in Ahrensbök and forbid the monks to wear their habits. In 1558, Frederik II indeed ordered that the idolatrous altar and pictures be removed from the monastery's church. Moreover, the monks should no longer pay levies to the general of their order. Still, the convent kept in contact with the Order of the Carthusians, a bond which the king wanted to sever. Subsequently, the Carthusians often violated the king's strict rules for more efficient management. In 1561, it transpired that the prior had taken out money and pledged monastic property without permission. Was this a form of resistance or an act of sheer need? Either way, Frederik II reacted by sending a written warning and demanding better administration. The last Carthusian monk, Heinrich Breide, who is referred to in the sources as "*verloffener Kirchendieb und garstiger leichtfertiger loser Bube*" and as "*ein boser mensch*" – i.e. as a thief of church property, a frivolous, reckless boy and a bad person – violated several laws, committing document fraud and unauthorised assumption of authority, for instance, before he fled the monastery. From today's as well as the past's perspective, this behaviour can hardly be perceived as resistance, but rather as personal failings. In Lübeck, for example, he sold treasures and cups which he had stolen together with copies of privileges and other documents from the monastery.

Interesting, and at the same time revealing, is the case of the Cistercians in Uetersen, which will be the last to be considered here.[80] They, too, resisted the introduction of the Reformation. During the visitation of the monastery in 1541, the convent justified this behaviour by claiming that they were subject to a different authority. They were referring to Count Adolf XIII of

---

78 Schröter (2019), § 2.3.1., [in press].
79 Auge (2019a), § 2.3.1., [in press].
80 Stüben (2019), § 2.3.1., [in press].

Holstein-Pinneberg (1511-56). In order to emphasise his demand that the Cistercians adopt the Reformation, Christian III appeared in the monastery in person shortly afterwards, and Provost von der Wisch received a message telling him that two evangelical pastors were to be employed in Uetersen. Indeed, we know of a Lutheran priest, Balthasar Schroeder (1517-83), who lived in Uetersen until he went to Segeberg in 1548. However, Christian III had thus disregarded the Schaumburgers' rule, leading to a dispute between him and Count Adolf XIII, which was fought out through letters. Probably for this reason, negotiations were conducted in Uetersen in 1543 and 1546 in the presence of representatives of the king. The negotiations seem to be connected to Schroeder's departure, which in all probability cannot be attributed to the resistance of the monastery, but rather to the introduction of the Interim at that time. They were resumed later by the Schaumburgers and the royal Danish side. In 1544, Provost von der Wisch died. Christian III then recommended Otto Rantzau (around 1500–after 1580) as his successor. The monks passed this recommendation on to Count Otto IV of Holstein-Pinneberg (1517-76), who in turn passed it on to his *Drost* Hans Barner. Barner then negotiated the employment of Otto Rantzau with the monastery and Rantzau himself. Under this provost, and Prioress Mette von der Wisch (1535–72), the Reformation was finally introduced in Uetersen and the monastery was – allegedly in 1555 – turned into an evangelical women's convent. However, even now the king of Denmark was not able to prevail as the institution's sole authority. In 1564, King Frederik II confirmed the convent's property and privileges; two years later, Count Otto IV followed suit.

V. Monasteries and collegiate chapters in Schleswig-Holstein and the Reformation: A conclusion

As has been described above, the dissolution of monasteries and collegiate chapters located in Schleswig-Holstein took place from 1526 until 1582. Especially two waves of dissolutions shaped the events. The first mainly affected the mendicant orders in the cities and lasted from 1526 until 1530. The second wave occurred under King Frederik II in the 1560s and affected all remaining institutions except for Reinfeld, which was dissolved very late, in 1582. In 1570 or 1578, respectively, the last two houses of the Sisters of the Common Life in Neumünster and Plön were dissolved. The four remaining nunneries, however, continued to exist, and, in a lengthy process of transformation, were turned into evangelical women's convents under the aegis of the nobles; in this form they still exist today. Thus, it can be stated that the introduction of the Reformation as a process of factual transformation of church practices took a long time in Schleswig-Holstein and must therefore be viewed and evaluated in terms of its diversity.

Acting in favour of the Reformation were mostly the sovereigns and the urban municipalities profiting from the dissolution of the monasteries. The nobility's attitude towards the Reformation was inconsistent; obviously, they took an interest in preserving their property and privileges, or even successfully used the situation to build up and expand both. The nobles contented themselves with compromise in that they preserved the monasteries in Itzehoe, Preetz, Uetersen and Schleswig.

The three sovereigns Frederik I, Christian III and Frederik II played dominant roles due to their positions and thanks to their interventions, although on second look the first two should not necessarily be characterized as generally pro-Reformation. Christian III, especially, turned out to be a careful actor, who was aiming for a smooth transformation of the monasteries to Protestantism rather than pursuing the total eradication of monastic culture as such. Frederik II was far more rigorous for practical dynastic reasons. He belonged to the third generation after the beginning of the Reformation; consequently, the situation he was facing was much clearer and more definitive than it had been for his two predecessors. They had lived through the advent of the Reformation, during which everything was still in a state of flux.

The inhabitants of the monasteries acted similarly inconsistently. Some welcomed the introduction of the Reformation as an act of liberation and happily abandoned their monasteries, while others passively endured whatever came and a third group openly or covertly resisted the Reformation. Consequently, the introduction of the Reformation in the monasteries and collegiate chapters in Schleswig-Holstein took place in a manner that is far from consistent and smooth. In this regard, earlier descriptions of Reformation history certainly need to be corrected.

Bibliography

Adriansen, Inge, 'Herzog Hans der Jüngere', in *Die Fürsten des Landes: Herzöge und Grafen von Schleswig, Holstein und Lauenburg*, eds. Carsten Porskrog Rasmussen, Elke Imberger, Dieter Lohmeier and Ingwer Momsen (Neumünster, 2008), pp. 208-231.

Auge, Oliver, 'Wer? Wann? Wo? Eine kurze Einführung in die schleswig-holsteinische Klostergeschichte', in *Glauben, Wissen, Leben: Klöster in Schleswig-Holstein*, eds. Jens Ahlers, Oliver Auge and Katja Hillebrand (Kiel, 2011), pp. 13-17.

Auge, Oliver, 'Zur Rolle von Klerus und Städten auf den Schleswig-Holsteinischen Landtagen bis zur Mitte des 16. Jahrhunderts', in *Der Vertrag von Ripen 1460 und die Anfänge der politischen Partizipation in Schleswig-Holstein, im Reich und in Nordeuropa: Ergebnisse einer internationalen Tagung der Abteilung für Regionalgeschichte der CAU zu Kiel vom 5. bis 7. März 2010*, eds. id. and Burkhard Büsing. Kieler Historische Studien, 43; Zeit + Geschichte, 24 (Ostfildern, 2012), pp. 155-177.

Auge, Oliver, 'Begegnungsstätten von Kirche und Welt: Monastische und klerikale Einrichtungen in Schleswig-Holstein im Wirkungsfeld territorialer oder städtischer Herrschaft', in *Klöster, Stifte und Konvente: Zum gegenwärtigen Stand der Klosterforschung in Schleswig-Holstein, Nordschleswig sowie den Hansestädten Hamburg und Lübeck*, eds. id. and Katja Hillebrand. Quellen und Forschungen zur Geschichte Schleswig-Holsteins, 120 (Neumünster, 2013), pp. 101-146.

Auge, Oliver, 'Frauenklöster als konstitutive Bestandteile der Adelskultur des 17. und 18. Jahrhunderts im nordelbischen Bereich', in *Neue Räume – neue Strukturen: Barockisierung mittelalterlicher Frauenstifte*, eds. Klaus Gereon Beuckers and Birgitta Falk. Essener Forschungen zum Frauenstift, 12 (Essen, 2014), pp. 317-346.

Auge, Oliver, 'Christian III., König von Dänemark und Norwegen (1503-1559)', in *Luthers Norden*, eds. Kirsten Baumann, Joachim Krüger and Uta Kuhl (Petersberg, 2017a), pp. 131f.

Auge, Oliver, *Kiel in der Geschichte. Facetten einer Stadtbiografie*. Sonderveröffentlichungen der Gesellschaft für Kieler Stadtgeschichte, 86 (Kiel/Hamburg, 2017b).

Auge, Oliver, 'Ahrensbök, Kartäuser', in *Das Klosterbuch für Schleswig-Holstein und Hamburg: Klöster, Stifte und Konvente von den Anfängen bis zur Reformation*, eds. id. and Katja Hillebrand (Regensburg, 2019a), [in press].

Auge, Oliver, 'Einführung', in *Das Klosterbuch für Schleswig-Holstein und Hamburg: Klöster, Stifte und Konvente von den Anfängen bis zur Reformation*, eds. id. and Katja Hillebrand (Regensburg, 2019b), [in press].

Auge, Oliver, 'Kiel, Franziskaner', in *Das Klosterbuch für Schleswig-Holstein und Hamburg: Klöster, Stifte und Konvente von den Anfängen bis zur Reformation*, eds. id. and Katja Hillebrand (Regensburg, 2019c), [in press].

Auge, Oliver and Büsing, Burkhard (eds.), *Der Vertrag von Ripen 1460 und die Anfänge der politischen Partizipation in Schleswig-Holstein, im Reich und in Nordeuropa: Ergebnisse einer internationalen Tagung der Abteilung für Regionalgeschichte der CAU zu Kiel vom 5. bis 7. März 2010*. Kieler historische Studien, 43; Zeit + Geschichte, 24 (Ostfildern, 2012).

Auge, Oliver and Hillebrand, Katja (eds.), *Das Klosterbuch für Schleswig-Holstein und Hamburg: Klöster, Stifte und Konvente von den Anfängen bis zur Reformation* (Regensburg, 2019), [in press].

Auge, Oliver and Hillebrand, Katja, *Klöster in Schleswig-Holstein. Von den Anfängen bis zur Reformation* (Kiel/Hamburg, 2017).

Beuckers, Klaus-Gereon, 'Gebaute Bildungspolitik: Die architektonische Entwicklung der CAU', in *Christian-Albrechts-Universität zu Kiel: 350 Jahre Wirken in Stadt, Land und Welt*, ed. Oliver Auge (Kiel/Hamburg, 2015), pp. 175-215.

Bobé, Louis, *Die Ritterschaft in Schleswig und Holstein von der ältesten Zeit bis zum Ausgange des Römischen Reiches 1806: Geschichtliche Darstellung in Umrissen* (Glückstadt, 1918).

Bugenhagen, Johannes, *Die Schleswig-holsteinische Kirchenordnung von 1542*, ed. Walter Göbell (Neumünster, 1986).

Bünz, Enno, 'Segeberg, Augustiner-Chorherren', in *Das Klosterbuch für Schleswig-Holstein und Hamburg: Klöster, Stifte und Konvente von den Anfängen bis zur Reformation*, eds. Oliver Auge and Katja Hillebrand (Regensburg, 2019), [in press].

Eigenbrod, Philipp and Madsen, Lennart S., 'Tønder, Franziskaner', in *Das Klosterbuch für Schleswig-Holstein und Hamburg: Klöster, Stifte und Konvente von den Anfängen bis zur Reformation*, eds. Oliver Auge and Katja Hillebrand (Regensburg, 2019), [in press].

Göbell, Walter, Hoffmann, Erich, Hauschild, Wolf-Dieter et al., *Schleswig-holsteinische Kirchengeschichte, vol. 3: Reformation.* Schriften des Vereins für Schleswig-Holsteinische Kirchengeschichte, Reihe 1, 28 (Neumünster, 1982).

Grabkowsky, Anna-Theresa, 'Cismar, Benediktiner', in *Das Klosterbuch für Schleswig-Holstein und Hamburg: Klöster, Stifte und Konvente von den Anfängen bis zur Reformation*, eds. Oliver Auge and Katja Hillebrand (Regensburg, 2019a), [in press].

Grabkowsky, Anna-Theresa, 'Reinbek, Zisterzienserinnen', in *Das Klosterbuch für Schleswig-Holstein und Hamburg: Klöster, Stifte und Konvente von den Anfängen bis zur Reformation*, eds. Oliver Auge and Katja Hillebrand (Regensburg, 2019b), [in press].

Greinert, Melanie, 'Schleswig, Benediktinerinnen', in *Das Klosterbuch für Schleswig-Holstein und Hamburg: Klöster, Stifte und Konvente von den Anfängen bis zur Reformation*, eds. Oliver Auge and Katja Hillebrand (Regensburg, 2019), [in press].

Hillebrand, Katja, 'Neumünster, Schwestern vom gemeinsamen Leben', in *Das Klosterbuch für Schleswig-Holstein und Hamburg: Klöster, Stifte und Konvente von den Anfängen bis zur Reformation*, eds. Oliver Auge and Katja Hillebrand (Regensburg, 2019), [in press].

Hoffmann, Gottfried Ernst, Klauspeter Reumann and Hermann Kellenbenz, *Die Herzogtümer von der Landesteilung 1544 bis zur Wiedervereinigung Schleswigs 1721.* Geschichte Schleswig-Holsteins, vol. 5, ed. Olaf Klose (Neumünster, 1986), pp. 17-26.

Hoffmann, Erich, *Spätmittelalter und Reformationszeit.* Geschichte Schleswig-Holsteins, vol. 4, part 2, ed. Olaf Klose (Neumünster, 1990), pp. 394-469.

Jensen, Kurt Villads and Salonen, Kirsi, 'Rudekloster, Zisterzienser', in *Das Klosterbuch für Schleswig-Holstein und Hamburg: Klöster, Stifte und Konvente von den Anfängen bis zur Reformation*, eds. Oliver Auge and Katja Hillebrand (Regensburg, 2019), [in press].

Kämmel, Heinrich Julius, 'Juncker, Christian', in *Allgemeine Deutsche Biographie*, vol. 14 (Leipzig, 1881), pp. 690-692.

Die lateinische Kirchenordnung König Christians III. von 1537, nebst anderen Urkunden zur Schleswig-Holsteinischen Reformationsgeschichte, ed. Verein für Schleswig-Holsteinische Kirchengeschichte. Schriften des Vereins für Schleswig-Holsteinische Kirchengeschichte, 18 (Kiel, 1934).

Kraack, Detlev, 'Flensburg, Franziskaner', in *Das Klosterbuch für Schleswig-Holstein und Hamburg: Klöster, Stifte und Konvente von den Anfängen bis zur Reformation*, eds. Oliver Auge and Katja Hillebrand (Regensburg, 2019), [in press].

Kragh, Line, 'Løgum, Zisterzienser', in *Das Klosterbuch für Schleswig-Holstein und Hamburg:*

Klöster, Stifte und Konvente von den Anfängen bis zur Reformation, eds. Oliver Auge and Katja Hillebrand (Regensburg, 2019), [in press].

Krüger, Joachim, 'Friedrich I., König von Dänemark und Norwegen (1471-1533), in *Luthers Norden*, eds. Kirsten Baumann, Joachim Krüger and Uta Kuhl (Petersberg, 2017), pp. 129f.

Krüger, Kersten and Künne, Andreas, 'Kiel im Gottorfer Staat (1544 bis 1773', in *Geschichte der Stadt Kiel*, eds. Jürgen Jensen and Peter Wulf (Neumünster, 1991), pp. 65-136.

Lange, Ulrich, 'Stände, Landesherr und Grosse Politik: Vom Konsens des 16. zu den Konflikten des 17. Jahrhunderts', in *Geschichte Schleswig-Holsteins: Von den Anfängen bis zur Gegenwart, 2nd ed.*, ed. Ulrich Lange (Neumünster, 2003), pp. 153-266.

Leverkus, Wilhelm, 'Berichte über die schleswig-holsteinischen Landtage von 1525, 1526, 1533, 1540', in *Archiv für Staats- und Kirchengeschichte der Herzogtümer Schleswig, Holstein, Lauenburg und der angrenzenden Länder und Städte, vol. 4*, ed. Andreas Ludwig Jacob Michelsen (Altona, 1840), pp. 451-505.

Madsen, Lennart S., 'Haderslev, Kollegiatstift', in *Das Klosterbuch für Schleswig-Holstein und Hamburg: Klöster, Stifte und Konvente von den Anfängen bis zur Reformation*, eds. Oliver Auge and Katja Hillebrand (Regensburg, 2019a), [in press].

Madsen, Lennart S., 'Haderslev, Dominikaner', in *Das Klosterbuch für Schleswig-Holstein und Hamburg: Klöster, Stifte und Konvente von den Anfängen bis zur Reformation*, eds. Oliver Auge and Katja Hillebrand (Regensburg, 2019b), [in press].

Madsen, Lennart S., 'Junker Christian und Herzog Hans der Ältere', in *Die Fürsten des Landes: Herzöge und Grafen von Schleswig, Holstein und Lauenburg*, eds. Carsten Porskrog Rasmussen, Elke Imberger, Dieter Lohmeier and Ingwer Momsen (Neumünster, 2008), pp. 111-141.

Michelsen, Nicolaus Christian and Johannßen, Carl Hinrich (eds.), *Sammlung der hauptsächlichsten Schleswig-Holsteinischen gemeinschaftlichen Verordnungen* (Glückstadt, 1773).

Moraw, Peter, 'Stiftskirchen im deutschen Sprachraum: Forschungsstand und Forschungshoffnungen', in *Die Stiftskirche in Südwestdeutschland: Aufgaben und Perspektiven der Forschung*, eds. Sönke Lorenz and Oliver Auge. Schriften zur südwestdeutschen Landeskunde, 35 (Leinfelden-Echterdingen, 2003), pp. 55-71.

Ommen, Brechtje, 'Schleswig, Franziskaner', in *Das Klosterbuch für Schleswig-Holstein und Hamburg: Klöster, Stifte und Konvente von den Anfängen bis zur Reformation*, eds. Oliver Auge and Katja Hillebrand (Regensburg, 2019), [in press].

Pauls, Volquart (ed.), *Die Anfänge der Christian-Albrechts-Universität Kiel: Aus dem Nachlaß von Carl Rodenberg* (Neumünster, 1955).

Pauls, Volquart, 'Das Klosterrecht der Schleswig-Holsteinischen Ritterschaft: Seine Entstehung, Entwicklung und rechtliche Bedeutung', in *Zeitschrift der Gesellschaft für Schleswig-Holsteinische Geschichte* 73 (1949), pp. 87-118.

Pelc, Ortwin, 'Itzehoe, Zisterzienserinnen', in *Das Klosterbuch für Schleswig-Holstein und Hamburg: Klöster, Stifte und Konvente von den Anfängen bis zur Reformation*, eds. Oliver Auge and Katja Hillebrand (Regensburg, 2019), [in press].

Piotrowski, Swantje, 'Die Finanzierung der Christiana Albertina in der Frühen Neuzeit 1665 bis 1800', in *Christian-Albrechts-Universität zu Kiel: 350 Jahre Wirken in Stadt, Land und Welt*, ed. Oliver Auge (Kiel/Hamburg, 2015), pp. 107-140.

Piotrowski, Swantje, 'Neustadt, Schwestern vom gemeinsamen Leben', in *Das Klosterbuch für Schleswig-Holstein und Hamburg: Klöster, Stifte und Konvente von den Anfängen bis zur Reformation*, eds. Oliver Auge and Katja Hillebrand (Regensburg, 2019a), [in press].

Piotrowski, Swantje, 'Plön, Schwestern vom gemeinsamen Leben', in *Das Klosterbuch für Schleswig-Holstein und Hamburg: Klöster, Stifte und Konvente von den Anfängen bis zur Reformation*, eds. Oliver Auge and Katja Hillebrand (Regensburg, 2019b), [in press].

Posselt, Markus, *Die Schleswig-Holsteinischen Klöster nach der Reformation* (Itzehoe, 1894).

Prange, Wolfgang, 'Das Ende des Kartäuserklosters Ahrensbök und sein letzter Mönch', in *Zeitschrift der Gesellschaft für Schleswig-Holsteinische Geschichte* 134 (2009), pp. 59-94.

Rathjen, Jörg, 'Schleswig, Dominikaner', in *Das Klosterbuch für Schleswig-Holstein und Hamburg: Klöster, Stifte und Konvente von den Anfängen bis zur Reformation*, eds. Oliver Auge and Katja Hillebrand (Regensburg, 2019), [in press].

Rathjen, Jörg, 'Die Reformation in den Herzogtümern Schleswig und Holstein', in: *Nordost-Archiv* 13 (2004), pp. 173-200.

Rausch, Wolf Werner and Paul Nawrocki, 'Schleswig, Domkapitel', in *Das Klosterbuch für Schleswig-Holstein und Hamburg: Klöster, Stifte und Konvente von den Anfängen bis zur Reformation*, eds. Oliver Auge and Katja Hillebrand (Regensburg, 2019), [in press].

Röpcke, Andreas and Katja Hillebrand, 'Eutin, Kollegiatstift', in *Das Klosterbuch für Schleswig-Holstein und Hamburg: Klöster, Stifte und Konvente von den Anfängen bis zur Reformation*, eds. Oliver Auge and Katja Hillebrand (Regensburg, 2019), [in press].

Rosenplänter, Johannes, *Kloster Preetz und seine Grundherrschaft: Sozialgefüge, Wirtschaftsbeziehungen und religiöser Alltag eines holsteinischen Frauenklosters um 1210-1550*. Quellen und Forschungen zur Geschichte Schleswig-Holsteins, 114 (Neumünster, 2009).

Rosenplänter, Johannes, 'Preetz, Benediktinerinnen', in *Das Klosterbuch für Schleswig-Holstein und Hamburg: Klöster, Stifte und Konvente von den Anfängen bis zur Reformation*, eds. Oliver Auge and Katja Hillebrand (Regensburg, 2019), [in press].

Schnabel, Kerstin, 'Bordesholm, Augustiner-Chorherren', in *Das Klosterbuch für Schleswig-Holstein und Hamburg: Klöster, Stifte und Konvente von den Anfängen bis zur Reformation*, eds. Oliver Auge and Katja Hillebrand (Regensburg, 2019), [in press].

Schröter, Martin J., *Kloster Reinfeld: Eine geistliche Institution im Umfeld der Hansestadt Lübeck 1186/90-1582: Bd. 1 Geschichte*. Quellen und Forschungen zur Geschichte Schleswig-Holsteins, 117 (Neumünster, 2012).

Schröter, Martin J., 'Reinfeld, Zisterzienser', in *Das Klosterbuch für Schleswig-Holstein und Hamburg: Klöster, Stifte und Konvente von den Anfängen bis zur Reformation*, eds. Oliver Auge and Katja Hillebrand (Regensburg, 2019), [in press].

Seegrün, Wolfgang, 'Schleswig-Holstein', in *Die Territorien des Reichs im Zeitalter der Reformation und Konfessionalisierung: Land und Konfession 1500-1650: Der Nordosten*, vol. 2, 3rd edn., eds. Anton Schindling und Walter Ziegler. Katholisches Leben und Kirchenreform im Zeitalter der Glaubensspaltung, 50 (Münster, 1993), pp. 140-164.

Stüben, Joachim, 'Johann Schomburg – ein schauenburgischer spelebroder als Propst von Uetersen', in *Pfarrer, Nonnen, Mönche: Beiträge zur spätmittelalterlichen Klerikerprosopographie Schleswig-Holsteins und Hamburgs*, eds. Klaus-Joachim Lorenzen-Schmidt und Anja Meesenburg. Schriften des Vereins für Schleswig-Holsteinische Kirchengeschichte, 55; Studien zur Wirtschafts- und Sozialgeschichte Schleswig-Holsteins, 49 (Neumünster, 2011), pp. 87-116.

Stüben, Joachim, 'Uetersen, Zisterzienserinnen', in *Das Klosterbuch für Schleswig-Holstein und Hamburg: Klöster, Stifte und Konvente von den Anfängen bis zur Refomation*, eds. Olivier Auge und Katja Hillebrand, (Regensburg, 2019), [in press].

Voss, Jürgen, 'Juncker, Christian', in *Neue Deutsche Biographie*, vol. 10 (Berlin, 1974), pp. 660f.

The Individual Orders

Alive and Well—for a While

The Danish Cistercians in their Last Century 1480-1580

Brian Patrick McGuire

Modern views of the monks at the end of the Middle Ages

The Cistercians were monks who belonged to the first well-organized order of the medieval Christian Church. There were monks and nuns from the earliest medieval centuries, and from the eighth century most of them belonged to monasteries that followed the Rule of Saint Benedict.[1] But the Rule dealt only with the functioning of individual monasteries and made no provision for bonds among monasteries. The independence of monasteries from each other fitted a society whose institutions were fragile and vulnerable, and which were prone to invasion and political instability. But by the time the abbey of Cîteaux in Burgundy began sending out groups of monks to found daughter houses in the first decades of the twelfth century, it was possible to set up a structure that maintained regular contacts between mother and daughter houses and thus create a well-defined monastic order.[2] The third abbot of Cîteaux, Stephen Harding, was a genius at creating practices that secured such contacts, as in annual visitations and in the requirement that all abbots meet once a year in September for the General Chapter at Cîteaux.[3] This eventually became a legislative body, but the main purpose of the Chapter was to ensure that abbots could keep each other informed about the situation of their monasteries and encourage each other to follow the Rule of Saint Benedict and the constitutions of the Cistercian Order.

Historians of the Cistercians have since the end of the twelfth century

---

1   For background, see McGuire (2014), pp. 53-55.
2   Burton and Kerr (2011), pp. 32-35.
3   McGuire (1995), pp. 402-405.

been discussing when the original zeal and commitment began to decline. Already in the *Exordium Magnum Cisterciense* from the 1190s, Conrad of Eberbach warned against *negligentia*, the lack of care and concern for the Rule that he feared was creeping into the Order to which he belonged.[4] Later historians have perhaps been more generous and have seen the departure from original ideals and practices as coming later than the thirteenth century. Since the nineteenth century, however, most observers have agreed that the Cistercians went into decline in the later Middle Ages.[5] In the fourteenth century war and plague made it almost impossible for many abbots to attend the General Chapter, and the Great Western Schism of the Church, with rival popes, meant that for a period there were also two rival general chapters. It was thus difficult to maintain the bonds among monasteries and attachments among abbots and monks that had characterized the Cistercians in the twelfth and thirteenth centuries.

In Northern Europe the Protestant Reformation came to mean the end of Cistercian monasticism, but as this paper will show, this culmination came not with the proverbial bang but with a relatively soft and prolonged whimper. In spite of the fact that the monks were allowed to continue for many decades after the coming of the official Reformation in Scandinavian countries, later attitudes have not been kind to monastic life and practices. The negative view is reflected in the hymn *Lover Gud, I kristne fromme* (Praise God, you good Christians), written by the controversial and talented theologian and author N. F. S. Grundtvig in 1817 and still included in the official Danish hymn collection as late as the 1980s. The second verse can be roughly translated as follows:

> The Lord's book was left on the shelf
> In the church fairy tales were told.
> For a coin, for pure payment
> They put Heaven up for sale.
> The light of truth and the word of the cross
> Had as it were been buried in the earth,
> For they would not at all condemn
> Papal lies and monkish dreams.[6]

---

4   Conrad of Eberbach (2012), pp. 541-549 (Book 6, Chapter 10).
5   Lekai (1977), pp. 91-93.
6   *Den Danske Salmebog* (Copenhagen, 1984), nr. 302: Herrens bog var lagt på hylden,/ eventyr i kirken lød;/ for en krone, for en gylden/ Himmerig til fals de bød;/ sandheds lys og korsets ord/ var som sunket ned i jord,/ at de skulle ej fordømme/ paveløgne og munkedrømme.

The term *munkedrømme* probably refers to Grundtvig's idea that monks were living empty lives, full of false *eventyr*, the exemplum stories that had come to characterize sermons that Grundtvig believed lacked grounding in Scripture.

Not everyone in nineteenth century Denmark was quite as negative about medieval monasticism. Grundtvig's contemporary, the theologian and philosopher Kierkegaard, recognized in the institution some value,[7] but certainly the general point of view was that the Reformation cleared away a form of life that was not in harmony with the Gospels. At the beginning of the twentieth century, however, a partial reevaluation of the value of monastic life came in Denmark, as in the work of the cultural historian Valdemar Vedel.[8] But even Roman Catholic scholars seemed to think that the last medieval centuries manifested a departure from original monastic ideals, as seen in the work of Edward Ortved, a Catholic priest who spent many years on what was meant to be a treatment of the Cistercians in Scandinavia. Ortved completed only the first two volumes, on the Order in general and on the Swedish houses. Towards the close of the first volume's final chapter, 'Period of Decline' (*Nedgangstid*), Ortved described how the 'softer times' of the later Middle Ages did not allow 'the strictness of the first age': 'Thus it was quite natural, that an age of decline for the Order had to come and came'.[9]

The judgment of Ortved is echoed in a recent study of the development of the Cistercian Order in the North, *The Cistercians in Scandinavia* by James France, published in 1992. He points out in his chapter 'Twilight Existence' that the Cistercians in their last medieval century lost 'many of the features which had originally distinguished them from other religious'.[10] As the Cistercians had gained wealth, they fought to maintain their position and privileges and became 'indistinguishable' from other religious: '…with a few notable exceptions, they no longer possessed the vitality with which they had in the past invariably defended themselves'.[11]

In France's work, as that of Ortved, the Cistercians in Scandinavia enjoyed a golden age in the twelfth and first part of the thirteenth centuries, followed by one of slow decline and departure from original ideals and practices. Thus the Reformation came as a logical outcome of the monks' failure to maintain their 'vitality' through international contacts, regular meetings, and disciplinary measures.

---

7   Heiberg (1927), p. 218. I am grateful to James France (1992), p. xv for this reference.
8   Vedel (1911), pp. 418-431.
9   Ortved (1927), p. 195: 'Og således var det aldeles naturligt, at tilbagegangstiden for ordenen måtte komme og kom'.
10   France (1992), p. 430.
11   France (1992) , pp. 430-431.

Recent treatments of the Danish Cistercians at the Reformation

James France has provided the fullest overview of the outcome of the Reformation for the Cistercians in Denmark. His study is especially valuable because he compares what happened in Denmark with developments in Sweden and Norway. He asks why many of the Danish houses were allowed to continue for several decades after the official adoption of the Reformation by the monarchy in 1536. France points out 'the relative mildness with which the religious houses were treated in comparison with England or Sweden…'. He explains this development as a reflection of 'a pragmatic approach… careful to avoid extreme solutions' which 'favours accommodating opposites', something he finds to be 'very much part of the Danish national character'.[12] France knows Denmark well because he grew up here and experienced the Occupation, during which, at least until August 1943, the government tried to find a *modus vivendi* with the Germans. It is perhaps James France's experience of the Occupation which made the relatively gentle Danish Reformation seem understandable.

I would hesitate, however, to use the term 'Danish national character'. Such characterizations of a people are problematic for the historian, even though I take the point that non-violent solutions have been reached at times of crisis and change in Denmark. But we should remember that while the Cistercians were not turned out of their monasteries, the Franciscans were forcibly removed. The Cistercians lived in relative isolation in the countryside and provided no threat to the Reformation preachers, while the mendicants in their city churches were rivals to the new faith and their sermons and agitation were considered to be a danger to Luther's Danish proselytizers.[13]

Besides the relative harmlessness of the Cistercians, James France also emphasizes the king's desire to maintain control of the monasteries and their properties instead of letting the noble families that once had given their lands to the monasteries take control of them again. As France writes, '…the interests of the king were better served by allowing these monasteries that remained to retain their independent existence than further to strengthen the position of the nobility and thereby possibly endanger his own supreme position'.[14] It might be added that Denmark had just experienced a period of civil war (*Grevens Fejde*) in the 1520s, and it was paramount for the king to

---

12   France (1992), p. 465.
13   'De Expulsione Fratrum Minorum', pp. 325-368.
14   France (1992), p. 465.

exercise power, both political and religious, in showing that it was up to him to decide on how the Reformation was to be carried out.

In a new treatment of the last years of the Cistercian Esrum Abbey in Northern Zealand, tracing its survival into the 1560s, Johnny Gøgsig Jakobsen adopts this same explanation, the desire of the king to limit the power of the nobility.[15] Both James France and Johnny Jakobsen are dependent on a classic study from 1924 of Sorø Abbey by Poul Nørlund, once head of the National Museum and a brilliant historian who made Denmark's medieval "golden altars" internationally known. Nørlund devoted attention to the next-to-last abbot of Sorø, Henrik Christensen Tornekrans (1508-38), who as we shall see in this article played a central role in protecting his monastery in the midst of religious and political change. Nørlund's portrait probably encouraged James France to make use of him as the last of his portraits of medieval Danish Cistercians, where we usually have no more than names and can only rarely trace careers, to say nothing of inner lives. According to Nørlund, 'the new age does not come at once, but was prepared over a long time before the actual Reformation and is brought to completion much later'.[16] Nørlund traces the fate of Sorø Abbey under its last abbot, Morten Pedersen: 'As late as 1570 the abbot seems to have tried to assert the old privileges of the monastery'.[17]

In 2003 Bo Gregersen, then head of the Øm Kloster Museum, wrote about the Reformation at Øm in terms of 'greatness before the fall' (*Storheden før faldet – Øm Kloster på reformationstiden*). He showed how 'the activity of the monastery as administrative center for large areas of land … continued in spite of the Reformation, and the relationship between royal power and the monastery was characterized by a pragmatic approach…' [18] Gregersen together with Carsten Selch Jensen also published the Øm Abbey Inventory of 1554, which includes a list of the books in the monks' and abbot's libraries. I wrote about this collection in 1976 and showed how it indicated that Abbot Peder Sørensen (c. 1523-54) apparently was trying to keep abreast of the new Protestant theology.[19] Now Birgitte Langkilde has skilfully analysed the contents of this library, as can be seen from her article in the present volume.

---

15 Jakobsen (2015), pp. 26-27.
16 Nørlund (1924), p. 125: '…at den nye Tid ikke kommer med ét Slag, men allerede forberedes længe før selve den egentlige Reformation og først fuldbyrdes langt senere'.
17 Nørlund (1924), p. 128: 'Saa sent som i 1570 synes Abbeden at have forsøgt at gøre Klostrets gamle Rettigheder gældende'.
18 Gregersen (2003), pp. 198.
19 McGuire (1976), pp. 128-136.

My own study from 1982, *The Cistercians in Denmark*, stopped in the early fifteenth century because I found that it was here that the monks departed from their earlier asceticism and ideals and became almost landed gentry.[20] But I did qualify this evaluation by pointing to the Esrum Altar from 1496, now in the National Museum in Copenhagen. In one corner of the altar, in great contrast to the central crowded crucifixion scene, is found Bernard of Clairvaux, with a tiny model of his monastery behind him. He is being embraced by Jesus, who is bending down from the cross. This *amplexus* theme is well known in later medieval art,[21] but its inclusion in the Esrum Altar shows that the abbot who had the altar made, Peder Andersen, was familiar with the story to be found in the *Exordium Magnum Cisterciense* and was asserting an attachment to a tradition of Cistercian spirituality.[22] I tried to go deeper into the last medieval century at Esrum in an article from 2000 where I looked at the sources for the monastery in terms of "the spirituality of the late Middle Ages".[23] I will return to some of these materials in this article.

My thesis in what follows is that the Danish Cistercians in their final century cannot be dismissed as decadent. They were not the same type of monks as they had been in the twelfth century, for they no longer cultivated the international bonds that had made the Cistercians into a monastic order separate from all others. The monks had originally settled far from towns and had distanced themselves from the lay population. By the fifteenth century they had made themselves and their monasteries more accessible to the laity, and the last abbots participated much more willingly in the politics of secular power, as we will see with Henrik Tornekrans. But the Cistercians showed a remarkable adaptability to changing times, while they did their best to continue the traditions that were their foundation in the Rule of Saint Benedict and the daily *opus dei*, by praying and singing the Psalms of David. It should always be remembered that monks and nuns existed primarily in order to praise the Lord and not for the sake of material acquisitions. The prayer life of the Cistercians leaves little trace in the sources available to us, but it remained the foundation of Cistercian spirituality and practice, right to the very end in 1580 when the last monk left Sorø, the last monastery.

---

20 McGuire (1982) , ch. 7, 'Complexity, Isolation and Vitality, 1357-1414 and beyond', pp. 221-233.
21 France (2007), pp. 179-204.
22 Conrad of Eberbach (2012), pp. 136-137 (Bk 2, ch. 7).
23 McGuire (2000), pp. 264-281.

In the remainder of this article, I will divide the last century, 1480-1580, into three stages:

C. 1480-1520—The last period of consolidation and growth

C. 1520-1541 –Seeking accommodation with the new faith

C. 1541-1580—Disappearing from view

The last period of consolidation and growth: 1480-1520

For the Danish Cistercians one great problem was how to come to terms with their international obligations. From the last decades of the thirteenth century the monasteries were required to make contributions to the abbey of Cîteaux for the expenses of holding the General Chapter. A study of the tax books of the Cistercian Order reveals how the Danish abbeys were assessed, but also how both Esrum and Sorø at different times were enlisted to collect funds from other houses, not only in Denmark but also in Sweden and Norway.[24] In 1451 the General Chapter accused Sorø and Esrum of failing to carry out their duties in this area and the task was handed over to the abbots of Øm and the North German monastery of Reinfeld. By 1487, however, Esrum and Sorø were again collecting contributions from Scandinavian Cistercian houses.[25]

It looks as if in the fifteenth century Danish Cistercian abbots had more or less stopped attending the General Chapter, for presence there would inevitably have brought demands for contributions. But we are not to think of the monasteries as destitute. The excavations at Øm Abbey in the 1970s revealed that there was a great deal of building in this period.[26] The cloister was finally enclosed and given stone vaulting, and a significant building just outside the monastic precinct has been interpreted as a hospital, built as late as 1495 and likely to have been intended for lay persons as well as for monks.[27] At the same time the monks profited from the fact that in the nearby town of Ry, there was a place of pilgrimage that attracted many lay persons. In the traditional Cistercian mould the monks would have had nothing to do with such people, but in the Late Middle Ages there seems to have arisen more contact between pious pilgrims and Cistercian monks.

---

24 France (1992), pp. 386-387.

25 France (1992), p. 391.

26 Olsen (1979), pp. 8-10; Gregersen (2003), pp. 193-195.

27 Kristensen (2003), p. 189.

Not all the monasteries did well economically. Knardrup, founded in 1326 by King Christopher II at his own estate west of Copenhagen, had already then met opposition from local families. Its monks were driven out and the monastery had to be refounded in 1343. It remained small and insignificant, the second-to-the-last Cistercian foundation in Scandinavia.[28] Two other monasteries, Herrevad in Scania and Holme (Brahetrolleborg) on the island of Funen, left behind so few sources that it is impossible to know what state they were in at the Reformation. As for the two monasteries for Cistercian nuns in Denmark, in Roskilde and Slangerup, we also have a dearth of sources. We can assume that the Monastery of Our Lady in Roskilde benefited from pilgrimages to the tomb of the local saint figure Margaret of Højelse.[29] In the Late Middle Ages the choir of the monastic church was extended to the east, presumably to make more room for pilgrims who wanted to pray at Margaret's tomb.[30] As at Øm, the nuns at Roskilde seem to have allied themselves with lay persons who expressed their faith through pilgrimage. In the process monastic houses must have gained much-needed income to support their building funds.

Esrum in Northern Zealand was traditionally the leading Danish Cistercian house, with five daughter houses, four of which in turn had daughters. Peder Andersen, abbot from at least 1473 until 1500,[31] as already mentioned, gave the abbey church the high altar reredos which is found today at the National Museum. In 1488 Pope Innocent recognized the contribution of Johannes Oxe to an altar in Esrum's church, presumably that of the Eleven Thousand Virgins. An indulgence was given to all those who visited the altar on feast days, an indication that lay persons were now allowed inside the abbey church.[32] Cistercian churches had formerly been closed off to lay persons, but such documents indicate that the monks were opening at least part of the nave to lay persons. I think it likely that the section of the nave once reserved for lay brothers, who had long since disappeared, was now being made available to the laity.[33]

In 1485 Abbot Peder Andersen drew up a letter for the nobleman Poul Laxmand and his wife Inger. In return for their donation to Esrum they were to be included in all the spiritual benefits the benefactors of Esrum shared

---

28 McGuire (1982), pp. 194, 227; France (1992), pp. 362-364.
29 'Vetus Chronica Sialandie', p. 56.
30 McGuire (2005), pp. 24-28.
31 France (1992), p. 507.
32 *Codex Esromensis* (1973), nr. 265, pp. 286-287.
33 France (2012), pp. 300-322.

with the monks. They would be allowed to choose 'a suitable confessor from our monastery' (...*ydoneum confessorem de nostro monasterio*), who would be able to absolve them from sin and even from all ban of excommunication on their deathbed. The long statement emphasizes that Laxmand and his wife would gain in the Cistercian Order: '...full participation in life and in death, so that when your deaths, would they be happy in the Lord, be announced to us, there you be solemnly absolved and for you, as for our own brothers and benefactors of our order and friends customarily is done every year, also prayers be said'.[34]

In 1492 a citizen of Elsinore, Jens Andersen, also entered the confraternity of the Cistercian Order at Esrum. He, together with 'my dear wife Berit's complete assent and consent' gave the monastery 'our farm, placed in Elsinore at Sletten by the Chapel of the Holy Cross'. In return 'abbot and convent in the same place should take us into their confraternity and allow us to share in all the good deeds that are done night and day in the named Esrum Abbey'.[35] The document, copied into the Esrum Book which was drawn up by Abbot Peder Andersen himself to record all the holdings of the monastery, was written in Danish, as were most of the legal deeds of the monastery after the middle of the fifteenth century. Thus the confraternity of Esrum to which citizen Jens Andersen now belonged is called *theres brøthrescap*.

Elsewhere I have called this union between a Cistercian monastery and a lay donor an indication of a "liturgical spirituality" in which the monks' prayer life was joined to that of the lay person.[36] Abbot Peder Andersen seems to have encouraged the local nobility and townsmen to come to the monastery and there find spiritual guidance in confessors and liturgical celebration on saints' feast days, as with the 11,000 Virgins thought to have been martyred with Saint Ursula in Roman times and remembered on 21 October. At the same time the abbot was making his own contribution to Cistercian spirituality and liturgical life with his own altar reredos. And finally he was rationalizing the land holdings of the monastery by drawing up the Esrum Book or *Codex Esromensis*, containing copies of papal, royal and other charters going back to the mid-twelfth century and arranged according to the

---

34 *Codex Esromensis* (1973), nr. 264, pp. 285-286: '...plenam in vita pariter et in morte vobis concedimus participacionem, vobis concedentes, ut cum obitus vestri, utinam in domino felices, nobis fuerint nunciati, iibidem solempniter absoluamini et pro vobis, sicut pro propriis fratribus et benefactoribus nostri ordinis et amicis annuatim fieri eciam fiant et iniunguntur oraciones'.

35 *Codex Esromensis* (1973), nr. 246, p. 255: '...at her abbet oc conuent in sammesteth schulle annamme oss I theres brøthrescap oc vnde oss bothe lothtagne oc deelacktighe at bliffwe I alle the gothe giærninger, som giøres nath oc dagh i fornæffnde Esromscloster...'.

36 McGuire (2000), p. 279.

geographical location of the monastery's properties. The Esrum Book might be looked upon as the result of the abbot's fear that the day was coming when the monks' ownership would be challenged, but it is probably more accurate to see its creation as an expression of a dynamic abbot's desire to rationalize ownership and organize monastic holdings. Certainly Abbot Peder could have believed that, with his donors, his altarpiece and his property book, Esrum would continue to thrive in spiritual and material terms. There is no hint that he feared the end was near.

The evidence we have of the abbatial career and concerns of Peder Andersen of Esrum indicate that he was a busy, committed churchman who did his best to strengthen the position of his monastery. His successor, Henrik Christiernsen, known as Tornekrans from his family seal showing Christ's crown of thorns, is much better known and documented, and with him we pass through the last medieval decades and into the Protestant Reformation. He matriculated as "brother Henrik Christiernsen from the diocese of Aarhus" at the University of Greifswald in 1490.[37] Probably already then a Cistercian monk, he lived up to the intention of the Cistercian General Chapter to see to it that the most able monks got a university education.[38] It had already been decided back in the mid-thirteenth century that such monks would attend university, and Greifswald seems to have become the goal for scholastically-minded Cistercians in the North of Europe.[39] In 1494 Henrik was elected abbot of Vitskøl. As James France points out in his superb portrait 'Abbot Tornekrans of Sorø', his family estate was located at Livø, not far from Vitskøl, so his election as abbot probably reflects his family's local prominence.[40] At Vitskøl he arranged for the abbey's royal and episcopal charters to be transcribed, just as Peder Andersen was doing at Esrum.[41]

Abbot Henrik was apparently able to combine his position at Vitskøl with a larger political involvement, for he became a member of *Rigsrådet*, the Council of the Realm, an office not usually held by an abbot of a monastery of secondary importance. Vitskøl was a significant foundation in the north of Jutland, but it remained in the shadow of Esrum and Sorø. Henrik Tornekrans bore witness to this difference by accepting election, probably in 1502, as abbot of Esrum. He now headed what traditionally had been the leading Cistercian house in Denmark and even in Scandinavia, and yet

---

37 Andersen (1943), p. 206.
38 Lekai (1977), pp. 78-83.
39 McGuire (1982), p. 254.
40 France (1992), p. 482.
41 McGuire (1982), pp. 26-27.

he transferred in 1508 to become abbot of Sorø. This move indicates that Sorø had greater importance than Esrum, even though it had originally been founded as a daughter house of Esrum. But in terms of landed wealth and political influence, Sorø had long become the most influential Cistercian house in Denmark, and it is here Abbot Henrik remained until his death in 1538.

Henrik Tornekrans was given the title *visitator ac reformator* of all Cistercian monasteries in Sweden, Norway and Denmark and received contributions to the Order from the abbeys[42]. He also remained on the Council of the Realm and was present at the accession of Christian II in 1513. His name is found immediately after those of the Danish bishops, as if to indicate his elevated rank.[43] He was clearly a figure who functioned in the highest political circles, and his success and that of his predecessor at Esrum, Peder Andersen, demonstrates that the Cistercians were by no means marginalized in the late fifteenth and early sixteenth century. They could have problems, as when the bishop of Roskilde Niels Skave in the late fifteenth century attacked the interests of Sorø Abbey and brought upon himself the censure of the Cistercian Order.[44] But in general this was a prosperous period, with abbeys such as Øm having an ambitious building program and abbots such as Henrik Tornekrans close to the centre of political power.

As late as 1511 we still find Esrum Abbey negotiating with a prominent family to establish two weekly masses at the altar of the Eleven Thousand Virgins: 'on Mondays for all Christian souls' and 'on Thursdays...for Niels Bradhe's and his dear wife's souls...'. Abbot and brothers promised to carry out this function 'in an eternal service' (*en ewighe thienisthe*).[45] Neither the monks nor their patrons seem to have realized that this mode of religious life was soon to come to an end. It is important to point out that, for people who live through periods of great historical change, the very thought of giving up their way of life can be quite alien.

Seeking accomodation with the new faith: 1520-41

Henrik Tornekrans provides a bridge between the last medieval decades and the coming of the Protestant Reformation. In 1523 he transferred his allegiance from Christian II to Frederik I. Already at this time in Sweden Cis-

---

42   Kalkar (1845), p. 103.
43   France (1992), p. 483.
44   McGuire (1982), p. 236.
45   *Codex Esromensis* (1973), nr. 269, p. 290.

tercian houses were suffering from heavy royal taxation,[46] and Henrik may have seen the writing on the wall and decided to support Frederik. He was rewarded with a royal confirmation for the privileges of Sorø, and in September of that year the king at Kalundborg issued a letter recognizing Henrik's prerogative 'to visit the Order of Saint Bernard in the kingdom and the duchy of Schleswig'. Royal officials were asked 'to be helpful towards him'.[47]

The term *Sancti Bernardi orden* is already found in a document drawn up for Esrum in 1494, where the terms 'Saint Bernard' and 'Cistercian' are combined: *sancti Bernardi orden Cistercij*.[48] Elsewhere in Scandinavia the term 'The Order of Saint Bernard' is also used,[49] but in the Esrum documents from this period it is common not to mention the Cistercian Order as such but to speak of 'The Abbey of Our Lady in Esrum'.[50] I wonder, however, whether the reference to Saint Bernard in the royal letter of 1523 was meant to link Esrum with one of the few medieval figures whom Martin Luther genuinely admired. However little he accepted monastic life, Luther saw in Bernard a churchman whose independence of mind and intense spiritual life attracted him.[51]

Like Peder Andersen at Esrum, Henrik Tornekrans at Sorø contributed to the inventory of his abbey church. In 1527 he commissioned Claus Berg to make what to this day is the largest crucifix in Denmark. It was originally above the altar of the Holy Cross at the west end of the monks' choir but was in 1641 placed above the crossing between nave and choir.[52] In 1536 he commissioned a new tombstone for Archbishop Absalon, who is seen in pontifical dress.[53] The Renaissance style of the grave is matched by Henrik's own stone.[54] Absalon was placed directly behind the high altar, a reminder of his importance for the foundation of the monastery and for the history of the Danish monarchy. Tornekrans thus allied himself and his efforts with the glorious tradition of Absalon and the Hvide family, which had been so central to the rise of the Danish monarchy in the twelfth century. Sorø became almost

---

46   France (1992), p. 444.

47   *Kong Frederik den Førstes danske Registranter* (1879), p. 22: 'Henricus abbas Sorensis ffick breff, att handt maa vistere Sancti Bernardi ordenn her om uti riiget och Slesuiig furstendom, och k. Maits fogether og embitzmenndt sculle vere hannum behiellpelige…'.

48   *Codex Esromensis* (1973), nr. 267, p. 288.

49   As in a property gift to the Cistercian nunnery in Øster Götland, Riseberga, from 19 November 1409: *sancti Bernardi orden*. See SDHK nr: 17376 (No. 1216 in print version).

50   As *Codex Esromensis* (1973), nr. 268, p. 289.

51   Lohse (1994), pp. 271-301. For Luther on the monastic life, see Euan Cameron's article in this volume.

52   *Danmarks Kirker*, Sorø Amt, p. 68.

53   *Danmarks Kirker*, Sorø Amt, pp. 79-80.

54   *Danmarks Kirker*, Sorø Amt, pp. 91-92.

a national temple, a monument to what later historians have called *Valdemar-ernes storhedstid*, the great age of the Valdemars.[55]

Henrik Tornekrans could not reverse the fact that the body of Queen Margaret I, originally buried at Sorø, had been taken by force in 1414 to Roskilde Cathedral. But Sorø did have the bones of two kings, the hapless Christopher II and his successor, the capable and brilliant Valdemar Atterdag. In Tornekrans's day there may still have been hope that Sorø would resume its place as the burial church of the Danish monarchy. In any case, his attention to the tomb of Absalon indicates a desire to demonstrate to the world that Sorø was not only a Cistercian abbey church. It was the burial place of a Danish hero, an outstanding churchman and the founder of the abbey of Sorø. By linking his own age with that of Absalon, Henrik Tornekrans may well have hoped that, in spite of the new religious allegiance, the abbey would be allowed to continue, thanks to its place in Danish history.

Another sign of an apparently conscious strategy for preserving Sorø is Abbot Henrik's compilation of a list of the graves of the founders and benefactors of the abbey, with a guide to where in the church they were buried.[56] Tornekrans also contributed to the collection of copies of charters for the abbey known as the Sorø Book. This had apparently been drawn up by Henrik's predecessor as a result of the bad treatment of the monastery by Bishop Niels Skave of Roskilde.[57] Henrik brought it up to date, and at the same time showed an interest in the records of other Cistercian houses. He sponsored a necrology for Løgum Abbey, and thus Henrik seems to have taken charge of organizing the records of the Danish Cistercians.[58] He had started his campaign as abbot of Vitskøl and now continued at Sorø.

Henrik must have seen where his world was heading. In the words of James France, he 'showed an acute awareness of the dangers that lay ahead'.[59] But his strategy was not to return to the sources of Cistercian spirituality. It was to emphasize the importance of his political position in the Danish kingdom and to influence developments. James France criticized Tornekrans for having become 'too absorbed by the pleasures and concerns of this world' in maintaining a high standard of living: 'Even Abbot Henrik's successors, who no longer enjoyed the prestige of their pre-Reformation predecessors,

---

55 Erslev (1898).
56 *Scriptores Rerum Danicarum* IV (1878), pp. 539-545.
57 McGuire (1982), p. 25.
58 McGuire (1982), p. 252.
59 France (1992), p. 486.

are known to have had four or five liveried servants to serve at their table'.[60] We are clearly far from the ascetic ideals of Stephen Harding and the first Cistercians, but for Abbot Henrik it seems to have been natural and necessary to demonstrate his position in society in order to preserve and protect the heritage of Sorø Abbey.

In the process, of course, the Cistercian character of the place must have disappeared. On 4 May 1534 the abbot of Cîteaux wrote to Count Christopher of Oldenburg and asked him to look after the interests of the Cistercians in Denmark. The abbot pointed to the dire situation of the Cistercian houses in Germany but said that 'the exceptions, we hear, are to be found in your province'. And so the abbot of Cîteaux commended the monks to the mercy of the count, and he singled out 'the venerable father of our Order's monastery of Sorø, the General Commissary, Inspector and Reformer in Denmark'.[61] He was referring, of course, to Henrik Tornekrans, whom Cîteaux must have seen as providing hope that the Cistercian houses would be protected.

It was all in vain. Duke Christopher soon lost out to Duke Christian of Schleswig, and with his coming the Lutheran Reformation was officially carried out in 1536. There were no more contacts between Cîteaux and Denmark. But Abbot Henrik survived the storm and was present at the royal assembly (*Rigsdag*) in that year after the imprisonment of the Catholic bishops and so must have given his consent to the new situation.[62] In 1538 King Christian III described Tornekrans as 'our man and councillor' and accepted him as head of the remaining Cistercian abbeys: Sorø, Esrum, Herrevad, Vitskøl and Øm.[63]

A few weeks later, on 30 December 1538, Tornekrans died. The inscription on his grave in Sorø Abbey Church speaks of his 'outstanding family' but 'more outstanding virtue'. His tenure at Vitskøl, Esrum and Sorø is mentioned, but nothing at all about his belonging to the Cistercian Order. He is shown holding a crozier and with a mitre above his family coat of arms, a grand depiction that in death represents what he tried to be in life. A far cry from the humble Cistercian roots of the twelfth century, but a fitting monument to a man who did his best to preserve Cistercian monasteries in the midst of the Protestant Reformation and especially to look after the interests of Sorø.

---

60   France (1992), p. 487.
61   Text in Kalkar (1845), p. 103. Translated by France (1992), p. 439.
62   France (1992), p.490.
63   *Danske Kancelliregistranter 1535-1550* (1881-82), p. 68. Nørlund (1924), pp. 116-117.

As abbot of Sorø Henrik Tornekrans had to accept the result of the Diet (*Herredag*) in Odense in 1527, where King Frederik I allowed monks who decided to leave their monasteries to remain outside and also to marry.[64] In 1536, with the king's official acceptance of the Lutheran Reformation, monasteries were allowed to continue to exist until the king should decide otherwise. Monks and nuns, as in 1527, were free to leave their monasteries, but if they stayed on, they were to live in a manner 'worthy of Christian men' (*christianis hominibus digna*) and accept having the Gospel preached to them by advocates of the Lutheran faith.[65]

Perhaps one reason the monasteries were to be allowed to continue was in order that they become places of learning for the new faith. Each monastery was to have a theologian who knew the Scriptures and would preach to the brethren. Young men studying at the monastery should 'lead a life of chastity, honesty, prayer and study and should sing every day and read in the choir'.[66] They were to wear monastic dress, which is carefully described: 'It is well that they should be distinguished by the cowl while they remain in the monastery'.[67] This provision attempted to combine classic monastic ways with Scriptural study. It would not be long before the new university in Copenhagen would take over theological instruction and become the only place of training for the new priesthood, but in an interim phase the old monasteries were considered to be suitable educational institutions. This is not surprising, at least for the remaining Cistercian houses, since their brethren had been studying at European universities probably already since the thirteenth century. In 1541 twelve monasteries, including Sorø, Herrevad, Vitskøl, Esrum and Øm, were told to find the most promising students and to supply them with sufficient means to study at the University of Copenhagen.[68] Thus emphasis was already at this point shifting away from the monasteries as houses of study to monasteries as the economic basis for university studies.

When Henrik Tornekrans died in 1538, his successor at Sorø, Niels Jespersen, was appointed to replace him as abbot responsible for the five re-

---

64 France (1992), p. 457.
65 Kidd (1911), p. 327: 'Monachis liberum concessumque esto ex Monasteriis exire, quotquot in iis nolunt ulterius aetatem degere : qui vero porro cupiunt ibidem commorari, superioribus suis, Abbatibus, Prioribus aut Praepositis monasteriorum obedientes…'.
66 Rørdam (1883), p. 39, '…debent esse subditi majoribus et agere in castitate, honestate, oratione et studiis, et canere quotidie, ac legere in choro…'. Trans. in France (1992), pp. 467-468.
67 Rørdam (1883), p. 39 ('esseque induti habitu monachali, quamdiu ibi fuerint'), trans. in France (1992), pp. 467-468. Also Nørlund (1924), p. 117.
68 Rørdam (1883), p. 187.

maining Cistercian houses.[69] New abbots at the other Cistercian houses were to be chosen with his consent and were to declare allegiance to the king. Thus Cistercian monasticism in Denmark became Lutheran, and the monks had become a part of the new Lutheran dispensation of learning. On the surface everyday life in the monasteries could continue as before, with prayer, work and schooling. The teaching of Lutheran theology, however, could much better be carried out at the reorganised university in Copenhagen, and thus the monasteries would eventually lose the new role the king had assigned to them. I have chosen 1541 as a decisive date for the end of the Danish Cistercian attempt to adjust to the new times because it was in this year the monasteries were made to support the new university's students. From this time onwards the remaining abbeys were looked upon by the royal authorities as sources of income.

Disappearing from view: 1541-80

After the death of Henrik Tornekrans there was no longer a prominent figure to represent the Cistercians and their monasteries at the national level. At the same time the king preyed upon the monasteries as sources of income. Poul Nørlund calculated that Sorø's estates were diminished by about seventeen percent from 1536 to 1568, and when the new school was founded in 1586 after the monastery had been closed, only sixty-two percent of the original estates was intact.[70] One royal exaction after another was decreed not only on Sorø but also on the other remaining Cistercian abbeys.[71] Sorø was used as a place for difficult people who did not fit in with Reformation Denmark: recalcitrant Catholic priests, a mentally unbalanced university professor and other problematic individuals.[72] The wealth of Sorø must have seemed tempting to a monarchy in constant need of funding, while other abbeys provided prime real estate for king and nobility in their passion for hunting. This was the fate of Øm Abbey after Frederik II came to the throne in 1559, when it became a royal hunting lodge for a year. When archaeologists excavated the monastic precinct in the 1970s, they found a significant layer of broken glass

---

69   Nørlund (1924), p. 117.
70   Nørlund (1924), pp. 129-130.
71   Jakobsen (2015), pp. 28-29.
72   Nørlund (1924), p. 121-123.

and concluded that it was the result of drinking parties that had taken place during this brief period.[73]

As late as 1551 Sorø and Esrum were ordered to provide for a lecturer (*læsemester*) to instruct in Scripture '*for the wunge brødre oc the anndre wnnge personner som ther i closterit ere*' ('for the young brothers and the other young persons who are in the monastery').[74] The idea of the monasteries as places of learning in Scripture had not been abandoned, but their economic basis for looking after their inhabitants was being eroded. In 1580 the last monks of Sorø were transferred to what once had been the Benedictine house at Ringsted. By now the terms "Benedictine" and "Cistercian" no longer had meaning, and it had become clear that monasticism was a disappearing institution. At the same time, however, there had been two Cistercian houses for women, at Roskilde and Slangerup on Zealand. In 1562 the monastic church at Slangerup was handed over to the town as its parish church, an indication that the last nun had died or left.[75] In 1570 Roskilde Our Lady monastery was given by the king to a nobleman, Franz Banner, and subsequently the monastic buildings were torn down.[76] We can assume that some of the nuns remained until that time. It was a general practice to leave nuns in peace, probably not so much out of respect for women but because their institutions were usually much less wealthy than the men's houses, so there was no hurry to get hold of their modest incomes.

How did the monks and nuns of the sixteenth century experience the change in faith and the end of their international links with the Cistercian Order? We do not know, even though it would seem likely that some of them did take advantage of the permission granted those who wished to leave their monasteries. But at all the Cistercian houses, sizeable groups of monks remained, even though there seems to have been no recruitment of new members. There was no prohibition against joining a monastery, but ambitious young men of the period seem to have realized that there was no future in becoming a monk. At the last surviving Cistercian houses of Esrum, Sorø, Vitskøl, Øm and Herrevad, the monks got older and were not replaced. As long as they accepted the new regime and listened to Lutheran sermons, they could continue in their old round of prayer and work.

---

73 This information I received from archaeologists after the excavations in the 1970s. See also Gregersen (2003), pp. 201-202.
74 Rørdam (1862), p. 758.
75 Jørgensen and Thomsen (2004), p. 244.
76 Jørgensen and Thomsen (2004), p. 240.

It would be wonderful if we had a memoir from the period in which an aged monk or nun looked back on his or her life and recalled how he or she had experienced the changes that had come. But there is no such source, in spite of the fact that Danish historians have done everything possible to comb not only their own libraries but also European ones in order to find new sources for medieval and Reformation Denmark.[77] But we do have one indication of how the new faith was received. We can return to the Esrum Altar and note that the figure of Abbot Peder Andersen, placed in the middle of the Crucifixion scene, no longer appears in Cistercian garb but as a Lutheran pastor, ruff and all.[78] At some time after the Reformation, when the altarpiece had long since left Esrum Abbey, and perhaps in the seventeenth century, Peder Andersen was "converted" into a Lutheran. As such, he could remain in the altar, and Bernard could also stay at Clairvaux and be embraced by Christ from the cross.

Generations of Danish churchgoers, first at St Olai Church in Elsinore, and later at Holme Olstrup Church near Næstved, had an opportunity to contemplate a work of profound Cistercian spirituality, but no one seems to have minded that the altarpiece was the remnant of a way of life far removed from Lutheran practices. In this way the medieval heritage and the Cistercian presence were preserved. Even though it is centuries since the monks and nuns departed the scene, they left behind such reminders of the life they lived and loved. And their Lutheran successors have for the most part been mild and understanding in preserving this heritage.

---

77   The church historian of the nineteenth century Holger Fr. Rørdam (1830-1913) was a tireless investigator of archives in Denmark and abroad.
78   Plathe (1997), pp. 151-152.

Bibliography

Andersen, J. O., 'Henrik Christiernsen Tornekrans', in *Dansk Biografisk Leksikon* 24 (1943), p. 206.

Burton, Janet and Kerr, Julie, *The Cistercians in the Middle Ages* (Woodbridge, Suffolk, 2011).

Codex Esromensis. Esrum Klosters Brevbog, ed. O. Nielsen (Copenhagen, 1973).

Conrad of Eberbach, *The Great Beginning of Cîteaux*, trans. Benedicta Ward and Paul Savage, ed. E. Rozanne Elder (Collegeville, Minnesota, 2012).

Danmarks Kirker, Sorø Amt, 5:1 (Copenhagen, 1936).

Danske Kancelliregistranter 1535-1550, eds. Kristian Erslev and William Mollerup (Copenhagen, 1881-1882).

'De Expulsione Fratrum Minorum', in *Scriptores Minores Historiae Danicae Medii Ævi*, vol. 2, ed. M. Cl. Gertz (Copenhagen, 1970), pp. 325-368.

Den Danske Salmebog (Copenhagen, 1984).

Erslev, Kristian, *Valdemarernes Storhedstid* (Copenhagen, 1898).

France, James, *The Cistercians in Scandinavia* (Kalamazoo, Michigan, 1992).

France, James, *Medieval Images of Saint Bernard of Clairvaux* (Kalamazoo, Michigan, 2007).

France, James, *Separate but Equal: Cistercian Lay Brothers 1120-1350* (Collegeville, Minnesota, 2012).

Gregersen, Bo, 'Storheden før faldet—Øm Kloster på reformationstiden', in *Øm Kloster: kapitler af et middelalderligt cistercienserabbedis historie*, eds. Bo Gregersen and Carsten Selch Jensen (Odense, 2003), pp. 191-204.

Heiberg, P.A., Kuhr, V., and Torsting, E. (ed.), *Søren Kierkegaards Papirer*, vol. 10, part 3 (Copenhagen, 1927).

Jakobsen, Johnny Grandjean Gøgsig, 'Esrum Klosters nedlæggelse', in *Esrum Klosters storhed og fald*, eds. Jens Anker Jørgensen and Bente Thomsen (Esrum Kloster, 2015), pp. 11-37.

Jørgensen, Jens Anker and Thomsen, Bente, *Gyldendals bog om danske klostre* (Copenhagen, 2004).

Kalkar, Christian (ed.), *Aktstykker henrørende til Danmarks Historie i Reformationstiden* (Odense, 1845).

Kidd, B. J., (ed.), *Documents Illustrative of the Continental Reformation* (Oxford, 1911).

Kong Frederik den Førstes danske Registranter, ed. Kristian Erslev and William Mollerup (Copenhagen, 1879).

Kristensen, Hans Krongaard, 'Hospitalet i Øm', in *Øm Kloster: kapitler af et middelalderligt cistercienserabbedis historie*, eds. Bo Gregersen and Carsten Selch Jensen (Odense, 2003), pp. 177-189.

Lekai, Louis, *The Cistercians: Ideals and Reality* (Kent State, Ohio, 1977).

Lohse, Bernhard, 'Luther und Bernhard von Clairvaux', in *Bernhard von Clairvaux. Rezeption und Wirkung im Mittelalter und in der Neuzeit*, ed. Kaspar Elm (Wiesbaden, 1994), pp. 271-301.

McGuire, Brian Patrick, *Conflict and Continuity at Øm Abbey* (Copenhagen, 1976).

McGuire, Brian Patrick, *The Cistercians in Denmark* (Kalamazoo, Michigan, 1982).

McGuire, Brian Patrick, 'Who Founded the Order of Cîteaux?', in *The Joy of Learning and the Love of God*, ed. E. Rozanne Elder (Kalamazoo, Michigan, 1995), pp. 389-413.

McGuire, Brian Patrick, 'Esrum kloster i 1400-tallet og senmiddelalderens spiritualitet', in *Danmark og Europa i senmiddelalderen*, eds. Per Ingesman and Bjørn Poulsen (Aarhus, 2000), pp.264-281.

McGuire, Brian Patrick, 'Roskilde i europæisk middelalderperspektiv', *Historisk Samfund for Roskilde Amt* (2005), pp. 13-36.

McGuire, *Det kristne Europas fødsel: Sankt Bonifacius* (Frederiksberg, 2014).

Nørlund, Poul, 'Klostret og dets Gods', in *Sorø, Klostret, Skolen, Akademiet gennem Tiderne*, 2 vols. (Copenhagen, 1924-1931), 1, pp. 53-131.

Olsen, Olaf, 'Krønike og udgravning. Øm kloster i historisk og arkæologisk belysning', *Convivium* (Aarhus, 1979).

Ortved, Edward, *Cistercieordenen og dens Klostre i Norden* (Copenhagen, 1927).

Plathe, Sissel F., 'Altertavlen i Esrum klosterkirke', in *Bogen om Esrum Kloster*, eds. Søren Frandsen, Jens Anker Jørgensen, Chr. Gorm Tortzen (Hillerød, 1997), pp. 150-167.

Rørdam, Holger Fr., 'Bidrag til den danske Reformationshistorie 8: Om Reformationen af Herreklostre', *Kirkehistoriske Samlinger* 2:2 (1862), pp. 736-765.

Rørdam, Holger Fr., ed. *Danske Kirkelove*, 3 vols. (Copenhagen, 1883-1889), 1.

Scriptores Rerum Danicarum, ed. Jakob Langebek (Copenhagen, 1878).

SDHK = *Svenskt Diplomatariums huvudkartotek över medeltidsbreven*. Available online at: https://riksarkivet.se/sdhk

Vedel, Valdemar, *Bag Klostermure. Et Forsøg i Kulturpsykologi* (Copenhagen, 1911).

'Vetus Chronica Sialandie', in *Scriptores Minores Historiae Danicae Medii Ævi*, vol. 2, ed. M. Cl. Gertz (Copenhagen, 1922), pp. 20-72.

Fighting for the Faith

The Hospitallers and their Monasteries after the Reformation in Denmark

Janus Møller Jensen

When the Reformation was introduced in Denmark in 1536/37, the Hospitallers were one the richest monastic orders in the kingdom. After the Reformation, the monasteries of the order were confiscated by the crown, but decades later several houses were still functioning as monasteries with their own priors and rights, albeit with royal governors. The Hospitallers prospered in the second half of the fifteenth and the first decades of the sixteenth century, like some of the other monastic orders in Denmark. The Franciscan order for instance flourished in the 1520s and was the object of royal patronage and support, but came to an abrupt end with the Reformation. In contrast, the Hospitallers apparently experienced what could be interpreted as a prolonged afterlife compared to other orders. This is usually explained with reference to the hospital function of the order, but it should also be seen in light of its military role as a crusading order, which appealed to both sides of the confessional divide in sixteenth century Europe. Several young Danish Protestant nobles continued to take part in the Hospitallers' wars against the Ottoman Empire in the sixteenth and seventeenth century, some even in the eighteenth century. However, not everyone would agree that the Hospitallers were treated very differently from other monastic orders after the Reformation. The purpose of this article is to investigate and describe what happened to the Hospitallers in Denmark during the Reformation period and to determine whether their continued popularity was due to continuing crusades in the sixteenth century and to ask what the Reformation in Denmark meant in this context.

History of the order

The Knights of Saint John or the *Hospitallers* was a military monastic order. Its origins are a bit obscure, but the order is generally said to have been founded in the eleventh century by Italian merchants as a hospital in the Muristan neighbourhood in Jerusalem near the Saint John the Baptist Monastery. At first it was not a monastic order, but was made up of brothers who took care of the sick and poor and lived by the Rule of Saint Augustine. Only after the First Crusade, which conquered Jerusalem in 1099 and the establishment of the first Latin kingdom of Jerusalem, the Hospitallers were made into an order with its own rule. During the twelfth century, the order further became militarized to meet the military demands of the established Christian states in the Middle East.

The order quickly received donations and lands across Europe that supplied the resources to fight for the faith in the Holy Land where the order together with the Templars, and from the end of the twelfth century also the Teutonic knights, formed the backbone in the defense and military campaigns in the Christian states. When the last Christian castles in Outremer surrendered and the Christian states were conquered by the Mamluks in 1291, the order managed to conquer Rhodes during the first decade of the fourteenth century after temporarily having taken up residence in Cyprus. The Hospitallers became victims of the same criticism for the failure to defend the Holy Land as the other military orders, but towards the end of the fourteenth century, the order became wealthy and began to flourish economically again. The order had its headquarters in Rhodes until 1522 when the island was conquered by the Ottoman Turks. The order then moved to Malta, where it resided from 1530 until Napoleon conquered the island in 1798.

The demands on the military aspects of the order required a strict organization and the steady provision of funds and materials from its possessions in Europe to finance its wars in the Holy Land and the Mediterranean. During the thirteenth century, the order was divided into a system of provinces and/or bailiwicks that were grouped together in so-called *lingua* – languages – which were represented in the convent surrounding the grand master of the order. The smallest unit was the commandery headed by a prior. The order had three serving classes: knights, priests and lay-brothers. It never forgot its origins as a hospital order and it was just as important to care for the sick, not only in the great hospital in Jerusalem, but also in the houses and monasteries of the order across Europe. The order also had a female branch, but apparently not in Denmark.[1]

---

1   For a general introduction to the history of the order, see Riley-Smith (1967); Luttrell (1995);

The Hospitallers and Denmark

The Hospitallers came to Denmark probably around 1170, but perhaps as early as the 1150s, as argued by Kurt Villads Jensen.[2] The order received its first monastery at Antvorskov on Zealand. It was most likely at the behest of the Danish king who granted a tax of one *penning* from every household in Denmark to go to the order.[3] The order probably played a part in the Danish crusades in the Baltic, if not directly through use of its military branch and expertise as in other frontier regions of Latin Christendom, then at least indirectly as part of the formation of the royal crusade ideology. Shortly afterwards, the order also came to Sweden and Norway. Eskilstuna in Sweden was founded between 1170 and 1185 and it is possible that the order's house in Varna in Norway (near Oslo) was also founded as early as around 1170 by the king and by nobles who where all associated with the crusading movement and the Danish king.[4]

Together, Denmark, Norway and Sweden-Finland formed the province of Dacia within the order with its motherhouse at Antvorskov. At least from the thirteenth century, the province of Dacia had become part of the German *lingua*. During the period between coming to Denmark and the Reformation the order established nine monasteries in Dacia as well as several houses that probably did not turn into monasteries, although some of them were rather wealthy, for instance the house it received in Nyborg in 1441.[5] It might at one point have turned into a proper monastery. In Denmark, the monasteries were beside Antvorskov: Viborg, Odense, Ribe, Horsens and Dueholm on Mors. In Sweden, they were Eskilstuna and Kronobäk, and in Norway only Varna. The order further had residences in Nyborg on Funen, Svenstrup on Zealand and in Lund in Denmark as well as in Stockholm and Köpinge in Öland in Sweden. There is thus a tendency that the order acquired a prescence in growing cities, as Nyborg and Stockholm. It gained possessions in other areas related to trade, for instance with the hospital at Köpinge and properties in Dragør.[6]

    Riley-Smith (1999); Nicholson (2003); Luttrell & Nicholson (2006); Bronstein (2005). Cf. Mitchell (2005); Boas (2006).

2   Møller Jensen (2003); Jensen (2011), pp. 365–371.

3   *Diplomatarium Danicum*, ser. 1, vol. 7, no. 156.

4   If not, it was probably around 1270, cf. Svandal (2006), pp. 15–33. For Sweden, cf. Carlsson (2010).

5   On this house, see Sørensen (2015).

6   For a general overview, even if it is in many respects outdated, see Reitzel-Nielsen (1984-1991).

Historiography of the order in Denmark

The history of the order and its houses in Dacia has received a great deal of scholarly interest through a number of studies dedicated to the individual houses, historically and archaeologically.[7] Tore Nyberg has through a life-long career enhanced our understanding of the history of the order in Scandinavia in general, especially with regard to its earlier history.[8] Thomas Hatt Olsen studied the relationship between the convent in Rhodes and Dacia with special regard to the fifteenth century.[9] Recently, Christer Karlsson has studied the economic history of the order from an archaeological perspective in the Late Middle Ages from 1291 until 1536 and demonstrated how the growing wealth of the order during the fifteenth century is witnessed in its building activity.[10] Trond Svandal has written a dissertation on the monastery of Varna debating the role and impact of the Hospitallers in Norwegian society until Varna was dissolved in 1532. He similarly found a continued and even increased support of the order in the fifteenth and early sixteenth centuries and suggested that the reason for this could perhaps be found in the military aspects of the order that continued to appeal especially to the kings, but also to the nobility.[11]

The most recent scholarship has been influenced by the studies of the impact of crusading in late medieval Scandinavia by the new Danish crusade historiography that, in turn, is part of a growing awareness of the influence of crusading on late medieval Europe in international crusade scholarship, including the history of the military orders. The general conclusions are that crusading continued to be of great importance politically, religiously and ideologically, and so did the role of the military orders fighting for the faith in the fifteenth and early sixteenth centuries. It is therefore not surprising that the more recent studies of the order have found that, in Denmark, the Hospitallers flourished and grew in importance and wealth during the fifteenth century, with a peak in donations to the monasteries of the order in the period up until 1523. But so far, little attention have been paid to the Hospitallers after the Reformation, especially in Scandinavia.[12]

---

7   Beside the overview in Reitzel-Nielsen (1984-1991) and the references below, cf. for an overview of the building history of the monasteries, Daugaard (1830); Lorenzen (1927); Krongaard Kristensen (2013).
8   Cf. for instance Nyberg (1985); Nyberg (1990).
9   Hatt Olsen (1960); Hatt Olsen (1962).
10   Carlsson (2010).
11   Svandal (2006).
12   Cf. Møller Jensen (2007).

In older historiography, it was said that the order left Denmark after the Reformation as silently as it had come in the twelfth century. In the huge work in three volumes from the 1980s and early 1990s on the history of the order from its founding to the present, with special regard to its Scandinavian history, Erik Reitzel-Nielsen, however, described the history of the order after the Reformation in more detail. He demonstrated, based on his great compilation of sources, how many of the houses in Denmark continued to function after the Reformation. Some did so for rather a long period of time. He further argued that the order was never really dissolved by the Danish king. On the contrary, it was deliberately preserved as a military order in the evangelical state and lay dormant until revived in the twentieth century.[13] Recently, the Swedish historian Martin Berntson has questioned this claim and argued convincingly that the order did, in fact, follow the pattern of the other monastic orders in Denmark that became Lutheran institutions with the church ordinance of 1537/39. He concluded that it is difficult to see that the order was treated separately. To argue that it was maintained by the Danish state is simply misleading. According to Berntson, the monks of the order who wanted to leave the monastery were free to do so. Instead, the monasteries functioned as schools for priests based on Luther's conception of the original monastic ideal. Berntson did wonder, however, why the process apparently took so long in Denmark, which was solidly Lutheran compared, for instance, to Sweden where the order was dissolved in the 1520s and abandoned in the 1530s, even though the Reformation as such was gradual process, but he left the question unanswered.[14]

I will not challenge Martin Berntson's general conclusion, which I think is correct, but instead suggest that it should be qualified. There can be little doubt that the growing interest in the order in the fifteenth century was explicitly linked as much to its role as fighting for the faith as to caring for the sick. Perhaps the former may have been even more pronounced in Denmark than has previously been believed right up to the Reformation and maybe even beyond. In Danish historiography, it has generally been assumed that crusading came to an end with the Reformation – and probably long before that. This view has recently been challenged. Modern crusade scholarship has at least suggested that crusading and the military orders continued to have an appeal on both sides of the confessional divide in Europe.[15] Recent studies of the military orders during the Reformation period show, however,

---

13   Reitzel-Nielsen (1984-1991) and Reitzel-Nielsen (1976).
14   Berntson (2006).
15   Maier (1998), pp. 355-62. Cf. in general Møller Jensen (2007); Tyerman (2011).

that the picture is not at all uniform. In some places, the order was dissolved and in other cases, such as Denmark, this was a prolonged process. Here, I intend to propose a more complex picture of the dissolution of the order in Denmark than Berntson draws and suggest that its role as a crusading order at least partly explains why, at the Reformation, the order was not simply dissolved and had all of its lands confiscated.

The Hospitallers, fighting for the faith and the king

With the Reformation in Denmark, the king, Christian III, at the crowning ceremony underlined his role as protector of the faith.[16] What did this mean for the role of the Hospitallers in defending the faith in Denmark? If we compare the situation in Denmark with England, for instance, Henry VIII inherited the title as protector of the order in England and apparently supported the order as long as it obeyed him and his royal policy. In 1540, however, he dissolved the order completely. That the order should disappear was perhaps not as evident as has sometimes been suggested. As the English historian Gregory O'Malley has demonstrated, Henry VIII's breach with Rome did not result in any royal rejection of defending the faith or by implication undermine the order's activities in this direction.[17] Rulers had throughout the fourteenth and especially the fifteenth centuries been wary of letting funds for the crusade leave the country without at least some part of them going into the royal coffers – also in Denmark.[18] But when the loyalty between the order and the king was tested, problems arose. From 1529-40, this test took place in England when, in the end the king lost patience and dissolved the order, confiscated its lands and prohibited its members to meet in their former houses. This treatment was not due to the Hospitallers' function as a military order. No one could have foreseen this development in 1509 when Henry ascended the throne, nor was it obvious after 1529 that it would end with the prohibition of the order in England.[19]

The situation was of course different in Denmark. The English kings had traditionally been associated with the founding of the order and saw themselves as protectors of especially the English *langue*. The English *langue* had an explicitly military function and its role as translators, mediators and am-

---

16 *Danske Kongers Haandfæstninger*, pp. 1-150, at pp. 83, 95-96, and 103. Cf. Schwartz Lausten (1987), especially pp. 13-16.
17 O'Malley (2005).
18 Cf. Reitzel-Nielsen (1976), pp. 35-40.
19 Cf. Phillips (2011).

bassadors traditionally made the monarchs interested in the order in a way that is perhaps not mirrored in Denmark, even though the order had a place in the Danish royal council. The king was, however, also instrumental in introducing and maintaining the order in Denmark all through the Middle Ages. So, how was the role of the order as fighting for the faith influenced by the Reformation in Denmark?

Taking care of the sick and fighting for the faith

The crusading role of the order also appears to have been one of the main reasons for the support it received in Scandinavia in the fifteenth century. There can be little doubt that the hospital function of the order was important both for the leaders of the order and the Danish kings. Grandmaster Pedro Zacosta wrote in a letter concerning future visitation of Dacia that the order should strive in every monastery to take care of the poor.[20] When Christian I (r. 1448-81) founded the monastery on Öland, he underlined the necessity for a leprosy hospital similar to the one at Antvorskov.[21] We know that several of the other monasteries had hospital functions or ran hospitals in connection with the monasteries. It appears that the monastery of Dueholm continued to have its hospital function according to the original rule even as late as the 1560s, but other Catholic practices continued at that house, so it might not be representative.[22] When Kronobäk was dissolved in the late 1520s, only the hospital continued whereas the monastery was abandoned and the brethren apparently all left for Eskilstuna, which, however, was dissolved in the 1530s.[23] The function of taking care of the sick and poor was part of the order in Denmark until the Reformation and in some instances even later. The order also received donations to that purpose both before and after the Reformation.

However, it appears to have been the military function of the order that really made it attractive to donors. Apparently, most of the many donations in the second half of the fifteenth century came from the nobility. There is very little to suggest that crusading mattered less in Danish society in the fifteenth century than in the High Middle Ages. Crusading resembled a modern multimedia show: It was preached, formed part of the church liturgy and

---

20   Cf. the letters edited in Hatt Olsen (1962).
21   *Diplomatarium Christierni I*, no. 148.
22   *Dueholms Diplomatarium*; Cf. Reitzel-Nielsen (1984-1991), 2.
23   Cf. Reitzel-Nielsen (1984-1991), 1, p. 314.

mass, crusade literature was read, church bells were rung to remind of the danger of the Turks and negotiations for new pan-European crusades formed the background to the international politics of the Danish kings, especially concerning the relationship to Sweden after the continuous breakups of the union in the second half of the fifteenth century. The order's continued resistance to the Ottomans greatly improved its prestige and won for it the support of the Danish kings, particularly after the 1450s. Both Christian I and King John (r. 1481-1513) used the negotiations for the international crusade in their own politics and royal ideology, as did Christian II (r. 1513-23), and their support of the order should most likely also be seen in this context.[24]

The Hospitallers were active in collecting money for the crusades besides paying yearly duties to the convent in Rhodes. After the visitations by Juan de Cardona in 1460 and 1470, the amounts were said to be 140 Golden.[25] The sums the order collected must have been rather big. In the early fourteenth century, the order was in charge of collecting all of the crusade tithes from Scandinavia and making sure that the money reached Rome. At least the amounts were big enough for the papacy to send cost expensive legations to Denmark to collect the money.[26] The crusade was supported on all levels of society, if we can judge by surviving letters of indulgence: rich and poor, lay and ecclesiastics, men, women and children.[27] The preaching of the crusade followed the same pattern as in the rest of Europe and the Hospitallers continued to play a prominent role.

The first book that was printed in Scandinavia was the Vice-chancellor of the Knights of Saint John William Caoursin's story of the Turkish siege of Rhodes in 1480. William Caoursin was a French humanist and not a member of the order, but besides fulfilling his obligations as vice-chancellor, he was employed to function as the Order's historian. Caoursin's history was, as argued by Theresa Vann, "a humanistic text that was part of a political program designed to win Christendom's support for the Hospitallers of Rhodes in the fight against the Turks". It was only part of a "diplomatic corpus" that was created by Caoursin and the master of the Order from 1478, Pierre d'Aubusson, and "circulated throughout Europe to raise money to defend Rhodes".[28] The Hospitaller Juan de Cardona, who made a visitation to Dacia in 1463, came to Lübeck in 1480 with some of this material, not least the bull of Pope Sixtus IV

---

24 Møller Jensen (2007), pp. 148-157.
25 Hatt Olsen (1962).
26 Cf. Jensen (2000); Møller Jensen (2011).
27 Møller Jensen (2007), pp. 121-127.
28 Vann (2001), pp. 109-20, quotations at p. 112. Cf. Setton (1976-84), 2, pp. 346-363.

declaring indulgences for those who aided the defence of Rhodes.[29] It cannot be stated as a fact that he came to Denmark, but the messages and indulgences he carried with him undoubtedly did. In 1481, the prior of Antvorskov, Hans Mortensen, handled a large amount of money collected in Dacia for the defence of Rhodes. Papal legates came to Denmark in 1481 and 1482 to negotiate Danish participation in the crusade with letters describing the great danger from the Turks.[30] The chroniclers in Lübeck also used newssheets describing the atrocities of the Turks during the siege,[31] which naturally must have been widespread in Denmark as well. Caoursin's history was printed in the Danish city of Odense in 1482 by the German printer Johan Snell, who also printed letters of indulgence both in Denmark and in Sweden.[32] It was translated into Danish and printed in 1508 by Gotfred of Ghemen, who also printed indulgence letters.[33] In the late 1520s or early 1530s, the Danish reform-Catholic Poul Helgesen (*Paulus Helie*) wrote in his so-called Skibby Chronicle concerning the Hospitallers' crusade preaching:

"That year [1502] a Danish doctor by the name of Herman, who belonged to the Knights of Saint John, came to Denmark as papal legate to preach a so-called crusade ("cruciata") against the Turk, but by his letters and bulls of indulgence – that is pure and simple audacity – he eradicated much piety. Because these kinds of legates and their vicars did not teach the people to show real remorse, but to sin without fear, and hence the window was opened allowing Lutheranism to come in. And never has the Turk been mightier than when people started preaching crusades against him ... because this preaching is not the result of piety but of greed".[34] But apparently it worked.

There is only one reference to nobles actually becoming fully professed knights of the order within Scandinavia. In 1417, a note in the letter-book of the Grand Master states that the prior of Dacia, Hemming Laurentzen, was allowed to receive six noblemen into the order as knightly brethren (*fratres milites*). These noblemen, born in lawful wedlock, were accepted provided they would proceed to the convent of Rhodes with horses and arms if neces-

---

29   *Die Chroniken der niedersächsischen Städte*, 4, pp. 223-224, 226-227, 233-236.

30   *Repertorium* 3, pp. 190-191 (no. 4936); *Acta Pontificum Danica* 7, pp. 481-485, 496-499 (no. 6015, 6033).

31   Vogtherr (1997), pp. 103-125, at pp. 122-23. Cf. also the description in the chronicle of Reimar Koch from the middle of the sixteenth century, MS Copenhagen, GkS 2293 4°, 2:200ʳ-201ʳ.

32   Caoursin (1982), pp. 10-12, 145; Venge et al. (1982); Lange (1906), pp. 1-23 with pl. II; Collijn (1905-1912), 2, pp. 49-55; Collijn (1934-1938), pp. 41-46.

33   *Tyrkens Tog til Rhodos*; Cf. Fjeldstrup (1910); Lange (1906), pp. 25-46.

34   Helie (1932-1948), 6, p. 69.

sary.[35] The papal legations of the early fourteenth centuries did, in fact, hire the Hospitallers as bodyguards on their journey in Scandinavia – but it is not entirely clear whether the knights actually came from Denmark.[36] The order also contributed to what is perhaps a unique Danish facet of the international crusade movement: When a new brother entered the monastery at Antvorskov, it was celebrated with the customary "crusade beer" (*kors øøll*).[37] However, the fight against the Ottomans was at the forefront of the minds of the Danish nobility. Most supported the war by providing spiritual weapons in the form of prayers, liturgical services and donations to, for instance, the Hospitallers. Others went in person, like the noble "her Hennik" who was one of the leaders of the army that saved Belgrade from the Turks in 1456, even if they did not become Hospitaller knights.[38] Such activity is undoubtedly to be seen as the immediate background to the growing support for the order until the Reformation, aside from its hospital function. The order prospered, as is reflected in its building activities just before the Reformation.

The Reformation and the Hospitallers in Denmark

Some of the Hospitaller brethren in Denmark became Lutheran and were actively involved in the Reformation, the most famous probably being Hans Tausen. He had been a monk at Antvorskov, but became a Lutheran after studies in Wittenberg in 1523. After the Reformation, the monasteries became Lutheran, although according to the recess of 1536 and the church ordinance of 1537/39, the monks were allowed to stay and were to be provided for. Most of the monasteries became secularized relatively shortly afterwards. Dueholm was bestowed to the nobleman Niels Lange in 1539, but, as mentioned, Catholic practices continued in the monastery, such as the celebration of mass. This became increasingly important there after it became impossible to allow the Catholic mass in Viborg once the Reformation was begun there in 1529. In 1558, Niels Lange was instructed to have the practice stopped. From the late 1530s onwards, the houses in Viborg, Odense and Horsens were given to noblemen who performed services for the king. The houses were to provide food and clothes for students and a teacher was to be employed. That provision, however, had to be repeated in 1551. At what point

---

35   Hatt Olsen (1962), pp. 26-27.
36   Jørgensen & Saletnich (1999), pp. 91-99.
37   *Dueholms Diplomatarium*, pp. 23-24.
38   Gille & Spriewald (1968-1972), 2, pp. 674-705 (no. 328), at p. 703

the last brethren actually left the houses cannot be stated with certainty. Antvorskov was the last monastery to be secularized. The last prior was elected in 1580 and the buildings turned into a castle in 1582.[39]

The order was very popular with the kings, who all renewed its privileges until the Reformation.[40] Antvorskov was the richest of all monasteries in Denmark, second only to the Cistercian Abbey of Sorø at the Reformation.[41] Although the headquarters of the Order in Scandinavia, Antvorskov, was made a royal fief at the Reformation and the monastery church went into decay, several Hospitaller houses functioned for more than fifty years after 1536. There is little doubt that Berntson is right in pointing out that, at first sight, the order's history is very similar to some of the other monastic orders, but is it possible that the Hospitallers' long afterlife is connected to the continued fight for the faith against the Ottomans? It is clear that the order still appealed to Lutheran nobles, and Malta was a popular station for young Danish nobles on their educational travels around Europe.[42]

Protestant crusaders and the Hospitallers

Christopher Tyerman has drawn attention to the fact that Protestant nobles from England continued to take part in the crusades in the sixteenth century.[43] The same applies to the nobles of the Danish realm. Some, for instance, visited the Holy Sepulchre in Jerusalem and some were knighted there. In 1509, for example one of the admirals of King John's fleet that commanded the violent sacking of the city of Åbo went to Jerusalem later the same year, but died on the way in Bavaria in 1510.[44] In 1518, the two nobles Holger Gregersen Ulfstand and Johan Oxen went to Jerusalem of which they left an account.[45] Another early sixteenth century account of a journey to Jerusalem is preserved in the same manuscripts.[46] In 1520, the nobleman Mogens Gyldenstierne was knighted by King Christian II for his part in the conquest

39   See Reitzel-Nielsen (1984-1991), vol. 2. Cf. Carlsson (2010).
40   Cf. Reitzel-Nielsen (1976), pp. 35-40.
41   Reitzel-Nielsen (1976).
42   Cf. Reitzel-Nielsen (1984-1991), 2, pp. 468-83.
43   Tyerman (1988).
44   Bech (1979-1984), 12, p. 460; Helgesen (1890-1891), pp. 44-45 n. 1.
45   MS Copenhagen, GkS 844 2°, fols. 235ᵛ-239ʳ. Another copy is preserved in MS Copenhagen, NkS 540 2°, fols. 11ʳ-16ʳ.
46   MS Copenhagen, GkS 844 2°, fols. 240ᵛ-245ᵛ; MS Copenhagen, NkS 540 2°, fols. 17ᵛ-21ʳ. They have been edited by Holger Fr. Rørdam, Rørdam (1901-1903), pp. 481-492.

of Stockholm. Afterwards, he went to Jerusalem where he was knighted at the Holy Sepulchre.[47] Henrik Nielsen Rosenkrantz (†1537) was knighted in Jerusalem in 1522 and his letter of knighthood has been preserved.[48] This practice continued after the Reformation.

In the 1580s and early 1590s, the nobleman Otto Skram visited Jerusalem and was knighted at the Holy Sepulchre. His letter of knighthood gave him the privilege to carry "the insignia and coat-of-arms of the Holy Cross, the Holy Sepulchre and Saint George,[49] secretly and in public according to his own will. Hereafter, as a brave and legitimate knight he is privileged to enjoy and use all the liberties, rights and privileges as other knights of the Holy Sepulchre usually do".[50] Sigvard Grubbe met Christian Barnekow and Jacob Ulfeldt (1567-1630) in Venice in the 1580s while they were embarking on a trip to the Holy Land. Sigvard was keen to join them, but he had already made other arrangements. He tried to make a change of plans but was bound by his word of honour, and despite trying to be released from his former agreement, he had to wave goodbye from the shore while his Danish friends sailed off.[51] He missed some interesting travels indeed. Christian Barnekow went all the way to Ethiopia after having seen Jerusalem.[52] Ulfeldt went on to Syria and Egypt. The nobleman Henrik Rantzau (1599-1674) visited Jerusalem and Egypt in 1623, but his travel account was not published until 1669.[53] Apparently, he was not knighted at the Holy Sepulchre, but he took great interest in crusading history. In Acre, he spent time looking at what he believed to be the great ruins of the palace of the Grand Master of the Temple and the Church of Saint John. At the church of the Holy Sepulchre, he saw the tombs of Godfrey of Bouillon and Baldwin I. At least some connection was seen in the sixteenth century between being knighted at the Holy Sepulchre and the cre-

---

47 Rothe (1753), 1, p. 657.
48 *Diplomatarium til Familien Rosenkrantz's Historie,* 2, pp. 54-55 (no. 45).
49 Cf. Mennenius (1613), p. 42: "S. Crucis Sanctissimique Christi Sepulchri ac S. Georgii insignia deferre".
50 MS Copenhagen, GkS 3084 4°, fols. 26ʳ ᵛ: "Före det Hellige Korse[s: NB! from MS Copenhagen, Kallske Saml. 678 8°, fol. 131], den Hellige Gravs og Sti: Georgii insignia og Vaaben, hemmelig og offentlig, som det hannem selv got siynes, og Han her efter som en tapper og lovlig Ridder med billighed og ret at maa nyde og bruge alle de friiheder, Höiheder, og privilegier, som andre den Hellige Gravs riddere pleier at nyde og bruge"; MS Copenhagen, Kallske Saml. 128 2°: "decernentes insuper Dominum Ottonem Schram à Dano, de cetero libere deferre posse, Sanctæ crucis, Sancti Sepulchri ac Sancti Georgii insignia, secrete aut publice, prout sibi videbitur, nec non in futurum ut verum ac legittimum Militem omni dignitate, Jure optimo frui valere ac debere, omnibus et singulis immunitatibus, præeminentiis ac privilegiis, quibus ceteri Milites Sancti Sepulchri uti ac frui consverere".
51 *Sigvard Grubbes Dagbog,* p. 376.
52 Bricka & Gjellerup (1874-1913), 2, pp. 2-20.
53 Rantzau (1669).

ation of *Equites Aurati* – Golden knights – the common term for knighthood in Denmark. At his coronation in 1559, Frederik II dubbed several "golden knights".[54] Sigvard Grubbe wrote in his diary that the nobleman Jørgen Lykke of Overgaard was an *Eques Auratus* and the last of this order in Denmark towards the end of the sixteenth century.[55] Johan Rantzau "received the dignity of a golden knight" when he was knighted in Jerusalem.[56]

Several of the nobles also visited the residence of the Hospitallers in Malta and some even fought in their ranks. Jacob Ulfeldt visited Malta between 1588 and 1592 on the journey that took him to Jerusalem, but also included visits to Constantinople, Rhodes, Cyprus, Syria and Egypt. Christian Friis of Borreby (1556-1616), who later became Christian IV's chancellor, visited Malta in 1579 during a stay in Padua. He actually became *lensmand* at Antvorskov in 1589. When the later bishop of Copenhagen, Hans Resen, had to flee for his life from Turkish corsairs in the 1590s, he was on his way to see the residence of the Knights of Saint John in Malta.[57] Henrik Ernst (1603-65), who was a legal expert, travelled to Malta in 1630 and the scholar Thomas Bartholin visited the island around 1644. In 1699, the nobleman Frederik Rostgaard (1671-1745) also visited the residence of the Knights. Several nobles took an active part in the Hospitallers' war against the infidels. For instance Jacob Ulfeldt fought in the order's ranks against the Turks. So did the nobles Christian Skeel (1623-88), who took part in a six weeks expedition at sea in 1648, and Christian Nielsen Holberg (†1686), who served both the Knights and the Venetians against the Turks in the 1650s. And in 1677, Frederik Walter (1649-1718) also fought with the Knights against the Muslims.

A knightly order fighting for the Protestant cause was in no way inconceivable. The Teutonic Order, for instance, was reformed and continued as a Protestant order. As Christoph Maier has pointed out, the military orders were considered orders of secular chivalry as much as religious orders of the Church on both sides of the confessional divide. In addition, they fought not only for the defence of the Catholic Church, but also for the whole of Christian Europe.[58] Shortly after the battle of Lepanto in 1571, during which the

---

54 Hogenbergius (1589), pl. 6; Bircherod (1706), pp. 22-23.

55 *Sigvard Grubbes Dagbog*, p. 367.

56 Cimber (1570), pp. 258-59. Magnus Madsen wrote in his *Regum Daniæ Series* from the sixteenth century concerning Valdemar IV that he fought against the Lithuanians in Prussia, and that he went on a pilgrimage to Jerusalem where he was knighted, "which we call golden knight", by count Erik of Saxony, Madsen (1873-87), pp. 131-32.

57 Rothe (1753), 2, p. 142. On the following individuals, cf. the articles in Bricka (1887-1905) and Bech (1979-1984).

58 Maier (1998), pp. 358-59, 362.

Hospitaller fleet distinguished itself, Erasmus Lætus, who was professor of theology in Copenhagen, wrote to the Grand Master of the Knights of Saint John in Malta and warned him of the dangers of fighting for the Catholic faith. He explained that the reason for the Turkish power and advances was the contempt shown for the word of God and outright insults to his son, Jesus Christ, by which he meant Catholicism. The order had hitherto been successful in defeating its enemies. The knights had to understand this outcome as an expression of God's unique mercy towards them, for which they should be aware of their enormous debt to God. He then encouraged them to fight for Protestantism instead of error and idolatry. If they did so, he assured them, they would feel the salvation of God's presence and the freedom of a clear conscience would strengthen them in combat. As a result, Christ would support their plans and their faith in the Son of God would bring the enemy to fall and take away his strength.[59] Although the knights did not mend their ways, Protestant nobles from Denmark fought, as indicated, in the service of the Knights of Saint John against the Turks well into the seventeenth century. The religious military orders thus continued to have an influence upon the minds of Lutheran nobles well into this time.

Martin Luther had also promulgated the war against the Turks and even suggested that the Protestant soldiers who fell in this battle, if they fought with the right intention and not to win profit and honour, would become martyrs.[60] Luther almost paraphrased the statute of the Council of Clermont declaring the indulgence to be gained by taking part in the First Crusade.[61] Even if Luther, like modern theologians, would not have liked the comparison,[62] it appears that the idea was perceived in this manner by the Protestant nobles who fought in the wars of religion in the sixteenth century.

Two cases from the king's court of the 1590s are very interesting in this respect. Jørgen Høeg received the death penalty for the murder of the mayor in the city of Skive in 1592, but was pardoned on condition that he left the country within six weeks and "let himself be used against the Turk". In 1594, a warrant for his arrest was issued, when the king learned that the *written* conditions Høeg had signed – that he would leave the country within six weeks and serve in the war against the Turks for four years – had not been fulfilled

---

59 *Erasmus Lætus*, pp. 334-37.
60 Martin Luther, *Ob Kriegsleute auch in seligem Stande sein können?*, pp. 653-58. Cf. Martin Luther, *Heerpredigt wider den Türken*, p. 174.
61 Somerville (1972), p. 74: "Whoever for devotion alone, not to gain honour or money, goes to Jerusalem to liberate the church of God can substitute this journey for all penance".
62 Møller Jensen (2007), 220-257.

at all. Not only had he stayed in Denmark for more than the six weeks, but he never went to fight against the Turks. Instead, he moved to Sweden – something that especially upset the young King Christian IV – and re-married. In July 1594, Christian wrote to King Sigismund III of Sweden and Poland that he wanted Høeg executed.[63] It is perhaps important to note that Høeg's case is only known because he did *not* go to fight the Turks. Others did, however. In October 1599, Frederik Rosenkrantz was condemned at the king's court in Copenhagen in the presence of Christian IV to lose his noble title as well as two of his fingers for having impregnated one of the queen's maidens. He, too, was pardoned on the condition that he went to Hungary to fight the Turks. The terms of the agreement must have resembled those of Jørgen Høeg. Frederik went to Hungary and soon distinguished himself in the war against the Turks. His superiors begged his pardon from Christian IV, who refused to give permission for Frederik to return to Denmark. Frederik was shortly afterwards killed in an attempt to separate two duellists and was buried in Prague.[64] To commute the penalty for a crime against the Danish king by fighting the Turks could almost be seen as the final stage in the development of the Lutheran secularized crusade indulgence.

Contemporaries also read about crusading history. In 1584, the Danish historian Anders Sørensen Vedel wrote a preface in Latin to a twelfth-century copy of the chronicle of Robert of Rheims, which he planned to publish. There can be no doubt that his purpose in issuing the chronicle was to incite to war against the Turks. Apparently, his work was never published, but the foreword still exists in manuscript bound together with the chronicle.[65] Vedel dedicated his work to a young nobleman named Erik, probably the alchemist Erik Lange, and encouraged him to follow the example set by the first crusaders when they won the palms of martyrdom in the Holy Land in battle against the Turks and especially the history of the Danish prince, Svend, who was killed while on his way to Jerusalem during the First Crusade.

---

63   *Kancelliets Brevbøger*, 1593-1596, pp. 241, 267-68.
64   *Danske Domme, 1375-1662.* 6, pp. 100-104 (no. 783-84).
65   MS Uppsala, UUB: C691. Edited by Ellen Jørgensen, Jørgensen (1909-1911), pp. 771-86, at pp. 777-85 and in *Recueil des historiens des croisades*, 3, pp. lii-lv. I would like to thank Karen Skovgaard-Petersen for initially providing me with a copy of the manuscript. See now Skovgaard-Petersen (2018)

According to the German chronicler Albert of Aachen, who wrote his chronicle of the First Crusade at the beginning of the twelfth century on the basis of testimonies of returned crusaders, the Danish Prince Svend died in an ambush together with his Burgundian fiancée Florina and 1500 men in Asia Minor on his way to Jerusalem during the First Crusade.[66] The story was made famous in the sixteenth century by the crusade poem *Gerusalemme liberata* by Torquato Tasso, which was considered an authoritative source for the First Crusade.[67] In forewords to the various editions and translations of the poem it was hoped that this story would "once more inspire to erect the theatre of Mars at the gates of Jerusalem".[68] Tasso described how the sword of Prince Svend was found after the battle by a Danish knight named Karlo. He passed it on to Godfrey of Bouillon, who in turn gave it to a German knight by the name of Rinaldo, ordering him to avenge the death of Svend. This Rinaldo set out to do and in his hand the sword of Svend became the first Christian sword to enter the walls of Jerusalem when the city fell to the crusaders in 1099. The story gave Denmark a special role in the history of the First Crusade, which was fully exploited during the reign of Christian IV who had a painting of the scene of the recovery of Prince Svend's sword commissioned.

In Denmark, official historiography developed a national Danish crusading past and the kings took great pride in their ancestors fighting for the faith, both in the Holy Land and in the Baltic. The national symbols of the Danish flag and the white heraldic cross in the coat of arms of Denmark were both believed to have originated during the crusades in the Baltic and to the Holy Land, respectively. In the sixteenth century, new royal orders of chivalry were created, such as the Order of the Elephant and the Order of the Armed Arm from the early seventeenth century. Both were explicitly linked to crusading history and the Order of the Elephant was directly associated with Danish participation in the first crusade. The Order of the Armed Arm symbolized the fighting for the faith through an armour-clad arm holding a sword standing on a Bible with a candle symbolizing the evangelical light. It has been suggested that the sword might even be the sword of Prince Svend.[69]

---

66 Albert of Aachen (2007), pp. 222-225. Albert's chronicle was edited by Jacques Bongar in 1611. Cf. Jensen (2001); Møller Jensen (2000), 285-328, at pp. 295-96.

67 Tasso (1581) [(Bari, 1930)], chan. 8, st. 2-42.

68 *Godfrey of Bovlogne or The Recouerie of Iervsalem*, introduction, not paginated. Cf. Tyerman (1988), p. 369.

69 Møller Jensen (2007), pp. 317-18, 321-31.

Crusading ideals were thus directly linked to Protestant knighthood. The crusading past was deliberately used to explain national symbols and individual crusaders used as role-models for Lutheran nobles. It is therefore understandable that the Danish nobles wanted to visit the order and to take part in its fighting for the faith, even if the order was in the end dissolved. And it might just explain why the order had a prolonged afterlife in Denmark.

Conclusion

There are numerous reasons why the Hospitallers never became Protestant. The economic basis for the order had to some extent been removed with the Protestant Reformation. Contact with the papacy was probably not relevant to the Danish king, who in the last decades of the sixteenth century and the early seventeenth century carved out a Protestant crusading past in which there was no room for the knightly orders. They were not chosen for that role, although this could probably easily have happened. Instead, a Protestant crusading past was deliberately invented for the new royal orders of chivalry. And fighting for the faith under the Lutheran king for the Protestant cause could be seen as earning the palms of martyrdom, just like the first crusaders had done. The sources do not allow any firm conclusions on whether this development was the main reason for the prolonged existence of the order in Denmark. I do not want to claim that the order simply continued as a crusading order in Denmark and maintained itself in this manner. But to merely claim that the order was treated in the same way as the other monastic orders – although this is essentially true – would miss a fundamental aspect of the Hospitallers' existence and role in the Late Middle Ages. The order continued beyond the Reformation, even though it took on a different guise. It contributed to the religious life of young Protestant nobles and of the king as part of Protestant knighthood and in the royal knightly orders. Focusing on the dissolution of the order and simply relegating its post-Reformation history to the general history of the monastic institutions in Denmark in the sixteenth century, as Berntson does, will cloud the fact that some of the ideals and ideas of the order, such as fighting for the faith, continued in other forms – like the royal orders of chivalry – and in their continued appeal to Protestant nobles even after the Reformation.

Manuscript sources

MS Copenhagen, Royal Library, GkS 3084 4°, 'Otto Skram's Beretning om hans Udlandsrejse 1587-92'.

MS Copenhagen, Royal Library, GkS 2293 4°, 'Reimar Kocks Predicker to St Peter Croniken van der Kaiserlichen Stadt Lübeck in 2 Theilen'.

MS Copenhagen, Royal Library, GkS 844 2°, '['Anna Krabbes Kopibog'] En Bog med gamle Domme, Adels-Testamenter, Gavebreve, Aarfeider, Leidebreve, samt andre Documenter og historiske Optegnelser af det 14de, 15de, 16de og 17de Seculo og deriblandt Holger Gregersen's og Johan Oxe's Reiser til den hellige Grav 1518'.

MS Copenhagen, Royal Library, NkS 540 2°, 'Et Bind med Afskrivter af adskillige Breve, kongelige Anordninger mm, meest Danmarks indvortes Historie angaaende, tildeels ey trykte. Skreven i 17de Aarhundrede'.

MS Copenhagen, Royal Library, Kallske Saml. 678 8°, 'Peder Skram's Historie; Hr. Otte Skram's Rejsebeskrivelse'.

MS Copenhagen, Royal Library, Kallske Saml. 128 2°, 'En Pakke Miscellanea til dansk Personalhistorie'.

MS Uppsala, University Library, UUB: C691, 'Robertus Monachus'.

Bibliography

Acta Pontificum Danica = Acta Pontificum Danica. Aktstykker vedrørende Danmark 1316-1536, ed. L. Moltesen, Alfred Krarup & Johannes Lindbæk, 7 vols. (Copenhagen, 1904-1943).

Albert of Aachen, Historia Hierosolymitana. History of the Journey to Jerusalem, ed. Susan B. Edgington (Oxford, 2007).

Bech, Sv. Cedergreen (ed.), Dansk Biografisk Leksikon, 16 vols., 3rd ed. (Copenhagen, 1979-1984).

Berntson, Martin, 'The Dissolution of the Hospitaller houses in Scandinavia', in The Military Orders and the Reformation. Choices, State Building and the Weight of Tradition, ed. Helen Nicholson, Klaus Militzer & Hans Mol (Hilversum, 2006), pp. 59–77.

Bircherod, Janus, Breviarium Equestre (Copenhagen, 1706).

Boas, Adrian, Archaeology of the Military Orders (Routledge, 2006).

Bricka, C. F. (ed.), Dansk Biografisk Leksikon, 19 vols. (Copenhagen, 1887-1905).

Bricka, C. F. & Gjellerup, S. M. (eds.), Den danske Adel i det 16de og 17de Aarhundrede. Samtidige Levnetsbeskrivelser uddragne af trykt og utrykte Ligprædikener, 2 vols. (Copenhagen, 1874-1913).

Bronstein, Judith, The Hospitallers & the Holy Land: financing the Latin East, 1187-1274 (Woodbridge, 2005).

Caoursin, Guillelmus, Descriptio obsidinonis urbis Rhodie, facsimile ed. of Johan Snell's edition in Odense 1482, trans. Jacob Isager (Odense, 1982).

Carlsson, Christer, Johanniterordenens kloster i Skandinavien 1291-1536. En studie av deras ekonomiske förhållanden utifrån historiskt och arkeologiskt material, Unpublished ph.d.-dissertation, University of Southern Denmark (Odense, 2010).

Cimber, Christianus Cilicius, *Belli Dithmarsici* (Basel, 1570).

Collijn, Isak, *Ettbladstryck från femtonde Århundradet*, part I: *Text*, 2 vols (Stockholm, 1905-1912).

Collijn, Isak, *Sveriges Bibliografi indtill år 1600*, vol. 1: *1478-1530* (Uppsala, 1934-1938).

Danske Domme, 1375-1662. De private domssamlinger, ed. Erik Reitzel-Nielsen with Ole Fenger, 8 vols (Copenhagen, 1978-87).

Danske Kongers Haandfæstninger og andre lignende Acter, in *Aarsberetninger fra det Kongelige Geheimearchiv*, 2 (Copenhagen, 1856-1860), pp. 1-150.

Daugaard, Jacob B., *Om de danske Klostre i Middelalderen* (Copenhagen, 1830).

Die Chroniken der niedersächsischen Städte, 5 vols. in 6, Die Chroniken der deutschen Städte vom 14. bis ins 16. Jahrhundert, 19, 26, 28, 30-31 (Leipzig, 1884-1911).

Diplomatarium Christierni I, ed. Hans Knudsen (Copenhagen, 1856).

Diplomatarium Danicum, ed. Franz Blatt et al., ser. I-, vol. 1- (Copenhagen, 1938 ff.).

Diplomatarium til Familien Rosenkrantz's Historie = *Diplomatarium til Familien Rosenkrantz's Historie, II, 1500-1572*, in Konrad Barner, *Familien Rosenkrantz's Historie*, 2 vols. (Copenhagen, 1874-1882).

Dueholms Diplomatarium, ed. O. Nielsen (Copenhagen, 1872).

Erasmus Lætus = *Erasmus Lætus' skrift om Christian IVs fødsel og dåb (1577)*, ed. and trans. Karen Skovgaard-Petersen & Peter Zeeberg (Copenhagen, 1992).

Fjeldstrup, August, *Gotfred af Ghemens Udgave af Historien om Jon Præst* (Copenhagen, 1910)

Gille, Hans & Spriewald, Ingeborg (eds.), *Die Gedichte des Michel Beheim*, 3 vols. in 4, Deutsche Texte des Mittelalters, 60, 64, 65/1-2 (Berlin, 1968-1972).

Godfrey of Bovlogne or The Recouerie of Iervsalem. Done into English Heroicall vers by Edward Fairefax, 2nd edn. (London, 1624).

Hatt Olsen, Thomas, 'The Priory of Dacia in the Order of Saint John of Jerusalem', *Annales de l'Ordre Souverain Militaire de Malte*, 18/4 (1960), 20-33.

Hatt Olsen, Thomas, *Dacia og Rhodos. En studie over forholdet mellem Johannitterstormesteren på Rhodos og prioratet Dacia i de 14. og 15. Århundrede med saerligt henblik på Juan de Carduna's visitation (-1476)* (Copenhagen, 1962).

Helgesen, Poul, *Historiske Optegnelsesbog: sædvanlig kaldet Skibykrøniken*, ed. A. Heise (Copenhagen, 1890-1891).

Helie, Paulus, *Chronicon Skibyense*, in *Skrifter af Paulus Helie*, 7 vols., eds. P. Severinsen et al. (Copenhagen, 1932-1948), 6, pp. 51-149.

Hogenbergius, *Res gestæ serenissimi potentissimique potentissimique principis ac Domini Frederici II. etc.* (n.p., 1589).

Jensen, Kurt Villads, 'Korstogstanken i dansk senmiddelalder', in *Danmark og Europa i senmiddelalderen*, eds. Per Ingesman & Bjørn Poulsen (Aarhus, 2000), pp. 39-63.

Jensen, Kurt Villads, 'Myten om Prins Svend', *Skalk* 2 (2001), pp. 20-25.

Jensen, Kurt Villads, *Korstog ved verdens yderste rand. Danmark og Portugal ca. 1000 til ca. 1250* (Odense, 2011).

Jørgensen, Ellen, 'Fra svenske Biblioteker', *Kirkehistoriske Samlinger*, 5:5 (1909-1911), pp. 771-786.

Jørgensen, Torstein & Saletnich, Gastone, *Brev til Paven. Norske forbindelser med Den hellige stol i senmiddelalderen* (Stavanger, 1999).

Kancelliets Brevbøger = *Kancelliets Brevbøger vedrørende Danmarks indre Forhold i Uddrag*, eds. C. F. Bricka et al., 39 vols. (Copenhagen, 1885-2005).

Krongaard Kristensen, Hans, *Klostre i det middelalderlige Danmark* (Højbjerg, 2013).

Lange, H. O., *Analecta Bibliographica* (Copenhagen, 1906).

Lorenzen, Wilhelm, *De danske johannitterklostres bygningshistorie* (Copenhagen, 1927).

Luthers Werke = M. Luther, *Werke: Kritische Gesamtausgabe*, 58 vols. plus indexes [many vols. subdivided] (Weimar, 1883-1948).

Luther, Martin, *Ob Kriegsleute auch in seligem Stande sein können?*, in *M. Luther, Werke: Kritische Gesamtausgabe*, 58 vols. (Weimar, 1883-1948) 19, pp. 616-662.

Luther, Martin, *Heerpredigt wider den Türken*, in *M. Luther, Werke: Kritische Gesamtausgabe*, 58 vols. (Weimar, 1883-1948) 30-2, pp. 149-197.

Luttrell, Anthony, 'The Military Orders, 1312-1798', in *The Oxford Illustrated History of the Crusades*, ed. Jonathan Riley-Smith (Oxford, 1995), pp. 326–364

Luttrell, Anthony & Nicholson, Helen J. (eds.), *Hospitaller Women in the Middle Ages* (Routledge, 2006)

Madsen, Magnus, *Regum Daniæ Series*, in *Monumenta Historiæ Danicæ. Historiske Kildeskrifter og Bearbejdelser af dansk Historie. Især fra det 16. Aarhundrede*, ed. Holger F. Rørdam, 4 vols. (Copenhagen, 1873-87), 2/2, pp. 81-246.

Maier, Christoph T., 'Strategies of Survival: The Military Orders and the Reformation in Switzerland', in *The Military Orders*, vol. 2: *Welfare and Warfare*, ed. Helen Nicholson (Aldershot, 1998), pp. 355-362.

Mennenius, Franciscus, *Deliciæ equestrium ordinum* (Köln, 1613).

Mitchell, Piers D., *Medicine in the Crusades. Warfare, Wounds, and the medieval surgeon* (Cambridge, 2005).

Møller Jensen, Janus, 'Danmark og den hellige krig. En undersøgelse af korstogsbevægelsens indflydelse på Danmark, ca. 1070-1169', *Historisk Tidsskrift* (Copenhagen) 100 (2000), pp. 285-328.

Møller Jensen, Janus, '*Sclavorum Expugnator*: Conquest, Crusade and Danish Royal Ideology in the Twelfth Century', *Crusades* 2 (2003), pp. 55–81.

Møller Jensen, Janus, *Denmark and the Crusades, 1400-1650* (Leiden, 2007).

Møller Jensen, Janus, 'Politics and Crusade. Scandinavia, the Avignon Papacy and the Crusade in the XIVth Century', in *La papauté et les croisades/The Papacy and the Crusades*, ed. Michael Balard, Crusades – Subsidia 2 (Ashgate, 2011), pp. 269-285.

Nicholson, Helen, *The Knights Hospitaller* (Woodbridge, 2003)

Nyberg, Tore, 'Zur Rolle der Johanniter in Skandinavien. Erster Auftreten und Aufbau der Institutionen', in *Die Rolle der Ritterorden in der mittelalterlichen Kultur*, ed. Zenon Hubert Nowak, Ordines militares. Colloquia Torunensia Historica, 3 (Torun, 1985), pp. 129-144

Nyberg, Tore, 'Skandinavisches Königtum, Papsttum und Johanniter: Versuch einer Charakterisierung', in *Die Ritterorden zwischen geistlicher und weltlicher Macht im Mittelalter*, ed. Zenon Hubert Nowak, Ordines Militares. Colloquia Torunensia Historia, 5 (Torun, 1990), pp. 127–142.

O'Malley, Gregory, *The Knights Hospitaller of the English Langue, 1460-1565* (Oxford, 2005).

Phillips, Simon, *The Prior of the Knights Hospitaller in Late Medieval England* (Rochester, 2011).

Rantzau, Henrik, *Reise-Buch auff Jerusalem/Cairo in Ægypten und Constantinopell* (Copenhagen, 1669).

Recueil des historiens des croisades = *Recueil des historiens des croisades. Historiens occidentaux*, ed. Académie des Inscriptions et Belles-Lettres, 5 vols. (Paris, 1844-1895).

Reitzel-Nielsen, Erik, *The Danish Order of Saint John since the Reformation* (Copenhagen, 1976).

Reitzel-Nielsen, Erik, *Johanniterordenens historie med særligt henblik på de nordiske lande*, 3 vols. (Copenhagen, 1984-1991).

Repertorium = *Repertorium diplomaticum regni Danici mediævalis*, ser. 2, ed. William Christensen, 9 vols. (Copenhagen, 1928-1938).

Riley-Smith, Jonathan, *The Knights of St John in Jerusalem and Cyprus, c.1050-1310* (London, 1967)

Riley-Smith, Jonathan, *Hospitallers. The History of the Order of St John* (London, 1999)

Rothe, Caspar Peter (ed.), *Brave Danske Mænds og Quinders Berømmelige Eftermæle*, 2 vols. (Copenhagen, 1753).

Rørdam, Holger Fr., 'Danskes Rejser til det hellige Land', *Kirkehistoriske Samlinger* 5:1 (1901-1903), pp. 481-492.

Schwarz Lausten, Martin, *Christian den 3. og kirken 1537-1559* (Copenhagen, 1987).

Setton, Kenneth M., *The Papacy and the Levant (1204-1571)*, 4 vols., Memoirs of the American Philosophical Association, 114, 127, 161-62 (Philadelphia, 1976-1984).

Sigvard Grubbes Dagbog, ed. Holger F. Rørdam, *Danske Magasin*, 4:2 and 4:4 (1873 and 1878), pp. 361-406 and 4-83.

Skovgaard-Petersen, Karen, 'A Lutheran appropriation of the First Crusade. The Danish historian Anders Sørensen Vedel's apology for an Edition of Robert of Rheims, in *Fighting for the Faith – The Many Crusades*, eds. Kurt Villads Jensen, Carsten Selch Jensen & Janus Møller Jensen (Stockholm, 2018), pp. 317-329.

Somerville, Robert, *The Councils of Urban II, vol. I, Decreta Claromontensia*, Annuarium Historiae Conciliorum, suppl. 1 (Amsterdam, 1972).

Svandal, Trond, *Johannitterordenen. En ridderorden ved verdens ytterste grense* (Oslo, 2006).

Sørensen, Claus Frederik, *Korsbrødregården: "Sankt Hans Gård" – 600 års Nyborghistorie* (Nyborg, 2015).

Tasso, Torquato, *Gerusalemme liberata* (Ferrara, 1581) [a cura di Luigi Bonfigli (Bari, 1930)].

Tyerman, Christopher J., *England and the Crusade 1095-1588* (Chicago, 1988).

Tyerman, Christopher J., *The Debate on the Crusades* (Oxford, 2011).

Tyrkens Tog til Rhodos = *Tyrkens Tog til Rhodos, Godfred af Ghemens Udgave af 1508*, facsimile ed. (Copenhagen, 1910).

Vann, Theresa M., 'Guillaume Caoursin's *Descriptio obsidione Rhodiae* and the Archives of the Knights of Malta', in *The Crusades and the Military Orders. Expanding the Frontiers of Medieval Latin Christianity*, ed. Zsolt Hunyadi & Jósef Laszlovszky (Budapest, 2001), pp. 109-120.

Venge, Mikael et al. (eds.), *Skrift, Bog og Billede i Senmiddelalderens Danmark*, (Odense, 1982) [= *Bogvennen*, 1982].

Vogtherr, Thomas, 'Wenn hinten, weit, in der Türkei … Die Türken in der spätmittelalterlichen Stadtchronistik Norddeutschland', in *Europa und die osmanische Expansion im ausgehenden Mittelalter*, ed. Franz-Reiner Erkens [= *Zeitschrift für Historische Forschung, Beiheft*, 20] (Berlin, 1997), pp. 103-125.

New Wine into Old Bottles

Maribo Abbey after the Reformation[1]

Kaare Rübner Jørgensen

> Get thee to a nunnery
> *Hamlet 3.1 (1602)*

Monasticism cannot be confirmed by Holy Writ. The lives of monks and nuns, their ceremonies are self-invented and contrary to Scripture. Their vows are disagreeable to God because, denying the merits of Christ, they express a false belief that man can justify himself. They are inconsistent with the commandment of love and against the freedom of a Christian, and they cannot be binding.

Such Protestant statements were formulated by the reformers during the Diet of Copenhagen in 1530. Six years and a civil war later, they became the official policy of the king and his government towards monasteries, monks and nuns.[2] In practice, the authorities were, however, rather lenient. King Christian III (1534-59), a devoted Lutheran, was prudent enough to realise that no one can change religion overnight. As he did not want any martyrs, Denmark did not become a place to breathe "the delicate flavour of burned flesh, so common in the history of the Reformation".[3]

Apart from the mendicants' houses, the monasteries were allowed to exist, but as royal estates. They were endowed to noblemen who might be a deposed Catholic bishop or even the monastery's own former abbot. These

---

1   This is a revised version of my paper, published in *Birgittiana, Rivista internazionale di Studi Brigidiani* 12, (Naples, 2001), pp. 121-153. A more comprehensive Danish version is printed in *Kirkehistoriske Samlinger* 2015.
2   *Kirkeordinansen 1537/39* (1989), pp. 139-140, 237-238.
3   Dahlerup (1987), p. 65.

then had to pay for the livelihood of the remaining monks or nuns whose number, owing to the prohibition of new admissions, gradually declined due to deaths. Generally, the king looked pragmatically at the monasteries. If the monastic buildings could be used as a castle or their rural possessions for hunting, the monks and nuns were transferred to another monastery. The same might happen when the number of inhabitants was reduced to three or four, even though several monasteries were not closed until the last monk or nun passed away.

The Brigittine abbeys at Maribo ("The Home of Mary") on the island of Lolland in Southern Denmark and Mariager ("The Field of Mary") in Jutland were still, however, allowed to receive daughters of the nobility after the Reformation in 1536.[4] Not much is known about Mariager, which was closed in 1588,[5] but at Maribo, the entry of the last nun is recorded in September 1620, just four months before King Christian IV (1588-1648) decided to close the monastery.[6]

But what kind of life did the nuns have at Maribo after the Reformation? Was it a new wine that was consumed, or was it still the old Brigittine bottles with "their sweet and delicious wine" that were uncorked? At first, it might seem like new wine because the parameters within which the nuns lived before 1536 were set by the *Regula Salvatoris* of St Birgitta, while now it was the Church Ordinance of 1537/39, supplemented by later royal charters and letters, that laid down the guidelines for their life after the Reformation. Reality was, in fact, not that simple. The nuns at Maribo did not change their religion overnight. Similar to the Brigittine nuns at Vadstena, they continued to live their traditional monastic life, at least until they were ordered to change their habits.[7] In what follows, I will analyse the charters, decrees and letters from the royal chancellery to the abbey, as well as other letters from the period, in an attempt to answer the question of old and new wine, of continuity and discontinuity at Maribo.

---

4   In 1562, the nobility made a petition to King Frederik II for the establishment of at least two new nunneries in Jutland so that they were not forced to marry their daughters to men of common lineage, but the king did not grant the request; Pontoppidan (1747), p. 383.

5   Dahlerup (1882), p. 26. On the history of the abbey, see Rübner Jørgensen (1991), pp. 231-279.

6   KBB 1616-1620, pp.792, 954.

7   On Vadstena, see Cnattingius (1970), pp. 46-102; Härdelin (1998), pp. 37-62.

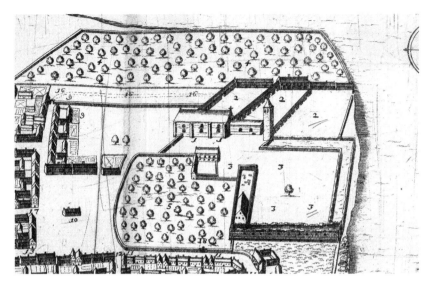

Maribo Abbey c. 1670. 1. The church; 2. The male monastery; 3. The female monastery. Photo: Reproduced from Resen

From a dual monastery to a nunnery

To St Birgitta, a key monastic principle was the idea of a dual monastery: a combination of a male and a female convent inside the same monastic complex.[8] After the Reformation, Maribo Abbey continued as such a monastery. The Franciscan friar Vincent Kampe, titular bishop of Garðar (Greenland), and an unknown number of monks and friars of other orders were transferred to Maribo in the autumn of 1536.[9] These asylum monks, as they were called, seem not, however, to have entered the Order of St Birgitta, but only to have had their board paid by the abbey, just like two worn-out Lutheran clergymen who were sent to Maribo in 1576.[10]

Without new vocations, the community of monks gradually died out. In 1547, we still hear about the existence of the sisters' and the brothers' convents, but in 1551, only that of the sisters, so the dual monastery must have ceased to exist by then - most likely as a consequence of the king's order of

---

8   Cf. Nyberg (1974a), pp. 43-60; (1981), pp. 195-222, both reprinted in Nyberg (1991), pp. 69-89 and 146-178.
9   Petrus Olai (1918-1920), p. 307; cf. Rørdam (1867), p. 133; Kornerup (1959), p. 46.
10   On June 7, 1532, Maribo Abbey had been granted papal permission to accept monks and nuns of other orders, including mendicants, but it is not known whether this actually happened, APD VII (1943), p. 789-790, no. 6464. On the Lutheran priests in 1576, see Rørdam (1889), p. 270.

January 21, 1551, that the confessor, Mathias, should be moved to the Cistercian abbey at Sorø.[11] Subsequently, Maribo became a convent exclusively for women of noble birth.[12]

After 1536, the abbey continued to be governed by an abbess, who, as in the Middle Ages, came from the top of the society: Anne Hardenberg, mentioned 1520-35,[13] Birgitte Brahe, mentioned 1538-46,[14] Margrethe Jensdatter (Juel?), confirmed July 12, 1547,[15] Mette Marsvin, confirmed July 15, 1551, died 1564,[16] Margrethe Urne, elected 1564, died August 9, 1582,[17] Sophie Gyldenstierne, elected 1582, deposed August 5, 1596,[18] Margrethe Norby, confirmed September 18, 1596, died February 6, 1602,[19] Else Huitfeldt, confirmed March 14, 1602, died November 29, 1602,[20] and Margrethe Hardenberg, elected 1602.[21]

Whereas the first seven had been nuns for numerous years at the time of their election (between the ages of 18 and 43), the last two had only lived at Maribo for four and a half and three years, respectively, when they were elected. Furthermore, it was not until the election of Sophie Gyldenstierne in 1582 that a nun who had entered the convent after the Reformation became its mother superior.

The nuns living behind the walls during the period 1520-1620 came from noble families, such as Baad, Basse, Brahe, Brand, Bielke, Bild, Bille, Falster, Friis, Galde, Gyldenstierne, Gyntersberg, Gøye, Hack, Hardenberg, Heidensdorph, Huitfeldt, Juel, Kaas, Lange, Lindenov, Lykke, Marsvin, Norby, Oxe, Parsberg, Pogwisch, Pors, Rosenkrantz, Rønnow, Sandberg, Sehested, Skinkel, Thott, Urne, Walkendorff and Venstermand. These were, by and large, the same families from which the nuns had been recruited before the Reformation. And as in those days, they often had a sister, a cousin, an aunt or another relative already in the convent. Thus, in regards to both leadership and social recruitment, there was clear continuity from the Catholic to the Protestant era.

---

11 Rørdam (1883), pp. 305-306; KBB 1551-1555, pp. 5-6. The monks left Vadstena in 1550, at Mariager they died out between 1554 and 1559, and at Nådendal (Finland) between 1558 and 1560, Silfverstolpe (1895-1898), p. 197; Cnattingius (1970), p. 46-47; Dahlerup (1882), 24; Klockars (1979), p. 188.

12 Confirmed by a royal decree of October 1, 1556, Rørdam (1883), p. 497; KBB 1556-1560, pp. 45-46.

13 DAA (1897), p. 17.

14 DAA (1888), pp. 102; (1950), p. 11.

15 DAA (1927), p. 25.

16 DAA (1904), p. 276; KBB 1551-1555, p. 41.

17 DAA (1904), p. 492; *Danmarks Kirker*, Maribo Amt, p. 74.

18 DAA (1926), p. 24.

19 DAA (1906), p. 321.

20 DAA (1887), p. 220.

21 DAA (1897), p. 25.

The admission of new nuns

St Birgitta had decided that no one should take vows and enter religious life before their eighteenth year.[22] The pope could, however, waive this rule, as he did in 1478 with a permission to Maribo and Mariager, allowing them to receive girls as young as nine in order to avoid that they be seduced, deflowered or began having dreams of marriage.[23] Out of nearly seventy nuns living at Maribo after the Reformation and known by name, a year of birth can be assigned to only a few, but at least three were between eleven and twelve years of age and two between fourteen and sixteen when they took the veil. Another was an unmarried woman of about forty. Four others were widows and one was divorced. The latter was Margrethe Norby who became a nun in 1564, eight years before her husband's death.[24] When the nuns elected her as their superior in 1596, they thus disregarded the advice of St Birgitta that the abbess should be a virgin.[25]

In the years immediately after 1536, there could presumably still be pious motives behind a woman's wish to enter the convent, but it is an open question whether this factor remains the case in the second half of the century. In 1585, Cæcilie Gyntersberg wanted to enter "because of her weakness and feebleness", and in 1590, her sister Sophie asked for admission owing to "her miserable condition and broken heart" after the execution of her husband, the freebooter Mogens Heinesen.[26] Although permission was granted in both cases by the chancellery, Lady Sophie did not become a nun because the following year, when she was endowed with the Crown's grain tithe from the parishes of Nørre Tranders and Sønder Tranders, she was living in Aalborg.[27] And Miss Cæcilie soon sailed to Norway and got married.[28] So the two sisters must have found other ways to recover from deep-felt grief and feebleness.

But some had to be sent to the nunnery. In 1590, Anne Sehested wrote to the king that, in her house, she had a niece, Politta, who on the advice of her friends and relatives wished to take the veil. The reason was that God had given her parents many children and her mother had recently died.[29]

---

22 *Regula* XXII, § 231.
23 APD IV (1910), pp. 188-189, no. 2723.
24 DAA (1906), p. 321.
25 *Reuelaciones extrauagantes* (1956), p. 131, ch. XXI.
26 KBB 1584-1588, p. 309-310; 1588-1592, p. 440. The motive of the latter was against *Regula* X, § 101, which refused entrance caused by "grief over secular disappointment and hardship".
27 KBB 1588-1592, p. 634; DAA (1941), p. 14.
28 DAA (1941), p. 15.
29 KBB 1588-1592, pp. 420, 421.

The same motive may have lain behind the entrance of Margrethe Rønnow, Ermegaard and Sophie Gyldenstierne in the 1560s, Johanne Falster in 1568, Inger Rosenkrantz in 1589, Anne Parsberg in 1602, Lisbeth and Berte Skinkel in 1609 and 1612 and Ingeborg Lange in 1618.[30] The nunnery was obviously a home for the nobility's surplus daughters[31] in the same way as it had been before the Reformation.[32] And this practice continued right up until modern times in Catholic parts of Europe.[33]

In the Middle Ages, the abbess and the convent were able to decide for themselves whom they wanted as their fellow-sisters. This, however, was not the case after the Reformation, where it was often the king who gave the abbess an order to admit a particular woman. Whether this was a new practice is uncertain because, even in pre-Reformation times, it must have been difficult to turn down a postulant, supported by the king or by another influential benefactor. The first woman placed at Maribo by the king was Johanne Falster in 1568. After her, there was a pause, but from 1582 onward royal requests became prevalent. Over the last forty years of the nunnery's existence they were distributed as follows: 1581-90: four, 1591-1600: five, 1601-10: five, 1611-20: six.

Some of these requests were not to the abbess' liking. This seems to have been the case already with the first request in 1568 because the king had ordered her to provide Johanne Falster with a room with a chimney and permit her to have her own maid and to wear her own dress.[34] Deeply upset, the

---

30 Margrethe Rønnow was out a family of eleven children, Ermegaard and Sophie Gyldenstierne out of one of twenty-two, twelve of which, including seven girls, reached the age of discretion. Inger Rosenkrantz, Anne Parsberg and Ingeborg Lange were each out of families of nine, Lisbeth and Berte Skinkel out of one of eight and Johanne Falster out of one of seven, DAA (1913), p. 487; (1926), pp. 24-25; (1910), p. 424; (1901), p. 266; (1910), p. 443; (1916), pp. 449-455; (1892), p. 128.

31 Cf. *Charter 1596*, p. 11: the purpose of the monastery was to provide "a convenient place to which the nobility could send their daughters, either because they had too many of them, and therefore were unable to provide for them, or because the daughters were afflicted with some weakness".

32 The abbesses Birgitte Brahe and Margrethe Urne came from families of ten and seven children, and Inger Urne from one of sixteen. Furthermore, the father of Drude and Agnete Friis had eleven and the father of Dorothea and Karen Sandberg five daughters, DAA (1888), p. 99-103; (1904), pp. 491-492; 467-492; (1886), p. 133; (1902), p. 448.

33 Hsia (1998), p. 34. In Florence, for instance, there were 441 male and 2,786 female religious out of a population of 59,000 in 1552. The higher number of cloistered women was not, however, caused by their deeper religious devotion, but by the heavily increased amount of money that the upper- and middle classes had to pay as dowry for their daughters, Wiesner (1993), p. 61. The same was the case in Venice where, in the mid-seventeenth century, there were fifty nunneries with more than 3,000 nuns and where about half of the city's noble women lived in convents. Here, it seems that among the upper classes the birth of a baby girl always posed the question: *maritar ò monacar* (to marry or to a monastery), Laven (2002), pp. xxii, 24, 33.

34 KBB 1566-1570, p. 389.

young nun Sophie Gyldenstierne wrote to her father that this arrangement would only create an atmosphere of envy within the community.[35] Thus, it might be assumed that the abbess had opposed the acceptance of Miss Johanne. But in vain. On February 13, 1569, another letter was issued by the king, reasserting her rights in the convent.[36] Later, when Sophie Gyldenstierne herself became abbess, she tried twice to prevent an admission. The first in 1582 when the king ordered her to receive the widow Lene Gøye, the second in 1590 when the regency for the infant-king Christian IV wanted the above-mentioned widow Sophie Gyntersberg to live in the nunnery. In the first case, the abbess suggested another solution by promising Lady Lene board and pension anywhere else but Maribo.[37] Although the king accepted her proposal, which was accompanied by a little present, Lady Lene seems to have entered the convent, since, together with another widow, Margrethe Huitfeldt, she received a royal order to leave the nunnery in 1595.[38] In the last case, however, the abbess succeeded in preventing the admission, for, as we have seen, Sophie Gyntersberg got her maintenance, paid by the Crown, in Jutland.

As in the Middle Ages, entrance into the convent was intended to express the woman's own, free will. In real life it was, however, the family which made the decision. This was only natural, the prioress wrote to Mogens Gyldenstierne, because young girls must realise "that a father and a mother always take the best interests of their children into consideration".[39] Furthermore, St Birgitta had decided that the nun's family should provide for her living in the nunnery.[40] Therefore, in the Middle Ages, the practice was that a woman's entrance was followed by a copyhold farm or two, donated as *proventa* to the abbey by her family.[41] Apart from the cases where the king had ordered an admission, a fee seems to have been paid also after the Reformation. Although in 1563 Prioress Drude Pogwisch declared that Mogens Gyldenstierne himself could decide how much he would pay for his daughters' entrance, she did not fail to mention that Eiler Rønnow had given the abbey 100 *daler* (i.e. 300

---

35   MG III (1941), p. 293.
36   KBB 1566-1570, p. 424.
37   KBB 1580-1583, p. 569.
38   KBB 1593-1596, p. 510.
39   MG II (1936), p. 402.
40   *Regula* XX, § 205.
41   In the sixteenth century, the *proventa* often seems to have been paid in cash, e.g. in 1509 Tyge Brahe paid 100 mark for Angenete Eriksdatter and 40 mark for her food at the nunnery, Vedel Simonsen (1845), p. 71. At Vadstena, the fee was between 40 and 50 mark, although there are examples of payments of 100 and 133 marks, Silfverstolpe (1895-1898), pp. 18, 92, 97, 101, 116, 132.

mark) and the nuns two *daler* each, in addition to a little more to the abbess and the prioress for the admission of his daughter Margrethe. In the same letter, she informed the family of what else the two daughters should bring with them: each should provide a slip and a gown, two coats, five *alen* of fine linen (about 3 meters, presumably for the veil), linen for underwear, pinafores and scarves. Furthermore, a bed with ten pairs of sheets, two cushions, two pieces of canvas for the bed-curtains, four big wash bowls, two kettles, two jugs, six pewter dishes, two plates, two butter-dishes, small name-plates for her chair in the choir and in the hall and a ring of gold.[42] Apparently, it was not the custom for a novice to inherit the bed, clothes and other personal belongings from a deceased nun.[43]

As in the Catholic period, the ceremony of entrance might have had a touch of solemnity. This was the case in 1556 when the eleven-year old Anne Gøye was introduced by the young princes Magnus and John in the presence of King Christian III and Queen Dorothea.[44] During the ceremony, the new nun was given her ring, called *fingerguld* (finger gold), symbolising her marriage with Christ,[45] and invested in the habit of the order. Until 1557, the habit seems to have been what had been prescribed by St Birgitta, but that year, the king sent Lady Anne Glob to Maribo with a new gown and ordered the abbess to have clothes made for the nuns according to the same pattern.[46] Concerning the veil, which had such strong symbolic value for the Brigittines, he wrote that Lady Anne would inform them how it should be in the future. She probably did so, but the nuns must have ignored her instructions, for in 1563 the superintendent, that is, the Lutheran bishop who supervised the abbey, complained that they still had their heads covered by the old veils.[47] After that, we may assume that the Brigittine veil disappeared and from then on the nuns were dressed more or less as Abbess Margrethe Urne appears on her tombstone, which can still be seen in the church at Maribo.

After the Reformation, monastic vows were no longer taken by the nuns. Nonetheless, they lived under obligation of obedience to the monastic rules and regulations. If a man of noble birth asked for their hand in marriage, they had the right to leave. This permission, a deliberate violation of St Birgitta's

---

42 Kall Rasmussen (1886), pp. 165-166.
43 At Vadstena, a deceased nun's ring was returned to the community, which often sold it to get an income in its hard-pressed financial situation, Silfverstolpe (1895-1898), passim.
44 Kall Rasmussen (1886), p. 157 note.
45 One of those rings has been found during excavation, Nørlund (1934), pp. 1-5.
46 KBB 1556-1560, p. 64.
47 Pontoppidan (1747), p. 394, § XII.

The tombstone of Abbess Margrethe Urne, died 1582. Drawing by Søren Abildgaard, 1765. Photo: The National Museum of Denmark

and all other monastic rules, had been laid down in the Church Ordinance of 1537/39 and repeated in the Charters of 1556, 1572 and 1596.[48] However, a marriage could only take place with the consent of the family. If a nun married against the wishes of her family, she was ostracised and lost her right of inheritance. Only three nuns are known to have left Maribo to get married and nearly all others thus stayed in the nunnery for the rest of their lives. After their deaths, at least five were removed for burial in their family's parish church.[49]

According to the Charter of 1556, the nuns were allowed, if a "peculiar and extraordinary situation" arose, temporarily to leave the monastery.[50] In the Charter of 1572, this permission was changed into a right to leave once a year to pay a visit to family and friends. If they lived in the island of Lolland, the nuns were permitted to stay away for eight days, if in the neighbouring island of Falster, for fourteen, and if in other parts of Denmark, for up to six weeks. The nuns were not allowed to travel alone, but must be met and returned by a respectable female relative of mature years.[51]

With the permission of the abbess, the friends and relatives of the nuns were also allowed to visit them inside the monastery and stay with them until the doors were locked for the night. In Catholic times, the friends and relatives had only been permitted to talk to the nuns through the grating in the parlour, so this was another infringement of the *Regula*.[52] From 1596, friends and relatives were even permitted to stay for one or two nights inside the monastery.[53] However, this permission only applied to men and women of the nobility. If they sent a messenger, he was still only allowed to speak to the nuns through the grating.

Entombment in parish churches, visits to the family and their return visits to Maribo indicate that even after entrance, the nuns were still regarded as members of a family and thus in no way dead in the eyes of the world. Even before the Reformation, however, St Birgitta's prescription that they should

---

48 *Kirkeordinansen 1537/39* (1989), pp. 139, 237; *Charter 1572*, p. 511, § 20; *Charter 1592*, p. 18, § 27. Banned by *Regula* VIII, § 85.
49 DAA (1896), p. 149; (1901), p. 448; (1927), p. 14.
50 Kall Rasmussen (1886), p. 159.
51 *Charter 1572*, p. 510, § 14, repeated *Charter 1592*, pp. 15-16, § 14.
52 *Charter 1572*, pp. 509-510, § 13, repeated *Charter 1596*, p. 15, § 13. Moreover, according to *Regula* VII, § 84, on Sundays and feast days the nuns were only allowed to talk to secular persons from Nones until Vesper (between four and six p.m.).
53 *Charter 1596*, p. 18, § 25, cf. p. 15, § 13.

show contempt for the world and forget their relatives,[54] had been ignored. This fact is evident from letters written and sent by the nun Elsebe Rud, later abbess at Mariager, to her family during the years 1527-36.[55]

The religious life of the nuns

The nuns' service in the choir and their prayers and meditations on the passion and death of Christ were essential to St Birgitta. This devotion was only changed to a certain degree by the Church Ordinance of 1537/39, which stipulated that a Lutheran priest should be appointed who could preach the Gospel without superstition and celebrate a Lutheran mass for the nuns.[56] But it was not easy to convert them. The first Lutheran priest was the erudite theologian Niels Palladius, a brother of the superintendent Peder Palladius in Copenhagen. He came to Maribo from Wittenberg in 1543 or 1544, but gave up after only a year and went back to Germany.[57] After him, there seems to have been no Lutheran priest at Maribo until Hans Jepsen in 1551.[58] A few months before his appointment, the king had ordered the nuns' confessor to move to Sorø Abbey because he was a hindrance to the creation of "a correct, Christian atmosphere" in the monastery.[59] But even after his removal, which was accompanied by a change of abbess, the Lutheran priest encountered problems with the nuns. In 1563, Superintendent Niels Jespersen of Odense submitted to the king a long report in Latin on the situation within the abbey. In thirty-four paragraphs, packed with Protestant indignation, he complained about the deplorable religious and social life of the nuns.[60]

Regarding religion, the superintendent mentioned that the nuns still adhered to their old faith, worship and devotions. They invoked and adored the Virgin Mary and other saints and shamelessly used the rosary, banned by the national synod at Antvorskov in 1546.[61] Their choir was decorated with pictures of saints and other idols and their books were full of fables and impious prayers. Daily, they sang their *horae canonicae*, after asking with mumbling

---

54 *Regula* X, § 101.
55 DM 6, (1752), 270-275.
56 *Kirkeordinansen 1537/39* (1989), pp. 140, 238.
57 Kornerup (1959), p. 46; Schwarz Lausten (1982), p. 124.
58 KBB 1551-1555, p. 72.
59 Rørdam (1883), pp. 305-306; KBB 1551-1555, pp. 5-6.
60 Pontoppidan (1747), pp. 393-397.
61 Cf. Rørdam (1883), p. 251.

voices for pardon for what they had done to one another. This ritual of for-giveness, prescribed by St Birgitta,[62] he regarded as pure hypocrisy. The same was the case with their service in the choir, as they would talk to each other during the singing. How this was possible he did not say, but, presumably, some sang while others chatted. Moreover, only a few of the nuns were present during the sermons of the priest, the majority pleading that they had more important things to do. Upon hearing something they disliked, they would leave the choir immediately, loudly cursing the priest. Usually, they would pay no attention to his sermons at all. Instead, they were reading old Brigittine prayer-books, *The Hours of Our Lady*, *The Hours of the Holy Spirit* and *The Seven Psalms*, which they even tried to foist on the young nuns.[63] Each day during Lent, they prayed a number of Pater Nosters and Ave Marias and in the chapter-hall they said the prayers that they did not dare to recite in public. Before their two daily meals, they did not say a decent, Christian prayer, and during meals they let one of the nuns read aloud from a book containing fables and legends, and not from the Bible.

The nuns refused to receive the Eucharist administered by the priest, and during confession, they fumbled with their rosaries. They moreover confessed in a room designed in a way so that the priest was unable to see them, and if asked, they refused to tell him their names.[64] Furthermore, they only accepted his visits to a dying nun in the dormitory if he was accompanied by two nuns. When a nun died, they lit the forbidden candles and, standing around the bier, recited *Miserere nostri Deus* (Ps. 122) and *De profundis* (Ps. 129).[65]

On Rogation Days, decreed by the king, they recited the Latin litany, but at the same time ordered their servants and employees to work, so they were unable to attend the service in the church. On the other hand, they rang the big bell on Our Lady's birthday, calling the whole town and parish together for the celebration of this feast that was supposed to have been abandoned.[66]

Upon receiving these complaints, one might believe that King Frederik II (1559-88) had to intervene, but, in fact, he did not react immediately. Only after receiving new complaints about the nuns two years later did he command them to live "a Christian and decent life" and in 1570, after further

---

62 *Regula*, IV, § 68.

63 On these prayer-books, see *Officium parvum beate Marie Virginis* (1976), cf. Nyberg, (1990), pp. 81-82.

64 Cf. *Regula* XXV, § 247: the nuns should be heard, not seen during confession.

65 Like the rosary, candles by the bier were regarded as papist superstition and thus banned by the national synod at Antvorskov in 1546, Rørdam (1883), p. 251.

66 *Kirkeordinansen 1537/39* (1989), pp. 108, 180, accepted only *Mariae Purificatio*, *Annuntiatio* and *Visitatio*, i.e. the Marian feasts with relation to Christ.

complaints, he sent the chancellor Eiler Grubbe and two other noblemen to Maribo for inspection and composition of a new charter for the monastery.[67] This charter was signed by the king on June 17, 1572.[68]

The Charter of 1572

The charter established that the nuns were not only obliged to listen carefully to the Word of God, but also that their chairs should be arranged in the choir so that they were able to hear it. Thus, they should be able to see the preacher. It would have been logical to move the nuns to the monks' old choir by the high altar, but this does not seem to have happened, for in 1596, the nuns' choir is still mentioned as being "over" the church.[69] Presumably, their chairs were just turned around, so the nuns, instead of sitting facing each other, now faced the pulpit and the high altar.

Nine times every day and night, seven for the hours and two for thanksgiving after dinner and supper, the nuns had been gathered in their choir. Now the number of hours was reduced to three – early morning, nine o'clock and three o'clock – during which the nuns were ordered to sing the psalms, pray the collect of the previous Sunday and read a chapter from the Bible.[70] Permitted psalms and hymns were *Kyrie, Benedictus, Te deum, Magnificat, Da pacem, Qui habitat in adiutorio altimissimi* (Ps. 90) and *Beati immaculati* (Ps. 118). There is no mention of the *Salve Regina*, which St Birgitta had prescribed to be sung on Saturdays.[71] In spite of their Latin titles, the psalms and hymns were to be sung in Danish because the nuns were no longer allowed to use the Latin language when reading and singing. Latin was forbidden in the choir, in the convent hall and in the nuns' cells. In addition, they were permitted only to read texts and hymns available in the Bible and in Hans Thomesen's hymn book, published in 1569. All the above-mentioned psalms and hymns were printed in a Danish translation by Thomesen.[72]

The nuns did not follow these regulations concerning psalms, hymns and language. Not until 1583 did they petition the king to be excluded from sing-

---

67 KBB 1566-1570, p. 635.
68 KBB 1571-1575, p. 145.
69 *Charter 1596*, p. 12, § 2. Only when the church became the parish church in 1596 was the monks' choir converted for the use of the nuns, *Danmarks Kirker*, Maribo Amt, pp. 29-30.
70 *Charter 1572*, pp. 506-507, § 2. In 1596, the services in the choir were further reduced to twice a day, *Charter 1596*, pp. 12-13, §§ 2-3.
71 *Regula* V, § 72.
72 Thomissøn (1968), pp. 3, 191, 254, 264, 303, 303, 304.

ing in Latin. The reason, they wrote, was that many of them were too old and weak to participate in the service and that the others, not knowing any Latin, were unable to understand what they were singing. Naturally, the king granted the request.[73] From then on, the use of Latin ceased.

With regards to the church, the Charter of 1572 decreed that there should be only one altar in the church, not fourteen as prescribed by St Birgitta, and that the nuns together with the parishioners should receive the Eucharist at that altar. St Birgitta's prescriptions for the nuns' acceptance of Holy Communion were annulled.[74] Besides, the mass should be celebrated on Sundays at a convenient time (between eight and nine in the morning), but in accordance with Lutheran practice only if someone was present in the church. An early sermon, an evensong sermon on Sundays and, as in other town-churches, a mass on Wednesdays and Fridays were permitted.[75] Thus, with the Charter of 1572, King Frederik had regulated not only the arrangement of the church and the choir, but also the number of canonical hours and their content.

Problems, described in more detail below, however, caused the king to order a rearrangement of the interior of the monastery. The charter repeated his request, presented to the abbess two years earlier, that she converts the monastery into apartments for the nuns, each consisting of a living-room, a chamber and a kitchen. They should not live alone, but in pairs, each having their own maid, and each pair their own cook and a room in the cellar for their beer. When the apartments were ready, the nuns should draw lots, not for the forming of pairs, but for the apartments. Two of the most fundamental monastic principles, the common dormitory and the common table, were thus definitively abandoned, but with the custom of having individual cells in the dormitory, one of these two principles had already been violated before the Reformation.[76] The same applies to the third principle, the ban of private ownership.[77] From the late fifteenth century onwards, the nuns seem to have had private belongings in their cells and, perhaps on a limited scale, also

73   KBB 1580-1583, pp. 633-634.
74   *Charter* 1572, p. 507, § 4. *Regula* XVII, §§ 181-182 prescribed that the nuns should receive the Eucharist on Maundy Thursday, Easter Sunday, Ascension Day, Whitsunday, Christmas Day and on all feasts, on whose vigils they fasted on water and bread.
75   *Charter* 1572, pp. 507-508, § 5.
76   As individual cells had been established at Vadstena in 1405, the nuns must have slept in cells right from the beginning at Maribo, cf. *Diarium Vadstenense* (1988), p. 142, § 128.3.
77   *Regula* II, §§ 50-51, banned private properties, and XIX, §§ 194-195, the reception of gifts from parents and friends.

private funds. We know that they often received gifts from their relatives – another indication that they were not dead in the eyes of the world.[78]

The decisions of 1570-72, an infringement of the letter and intention of the *Regula*, can thus be seen as the logical conclusion to a process that had begun already in the Late Middle Ages.

The social life of the nuns

Traditionally, one is "well dined and well wined" at an abbot's table. This, too, seems to apply to the food that was served at Maribo. In 1545, when there were still many nunneries in Denmark, the king had issued a general act concerning the maintenance of nuns. Of bread and other grain products, each nun was annually to receive about 360 kg, of meat half an ox, two pigs, two sheep, six lambs, two geese and twenty hens, and of fish 520 salted herrings, 160 smoked herrings, 150 dried whitings, 100 flatfish and 110 kg of other salted fish.[79] In his book about Mariager, Hans Dahlerup argues that this was only a codification of what had been consumed by the nuns in the Middle Ages, including those in the convents of St Birgitta.[80] But this claim cannot be correct for it would mean that the Brigittines already before the Reformation had abandoned the regulations concerning food and fasting in their *Regula*.[81] The quantity of beer was 4.37 litres a day, nearly the same as the crew on the royal vessels received in 1536.[82] This corresponds to 13 1/3 bottles of Carlsberg a day, in cubic content, not in alcoholic strength. It was light beer with 2.5 to 3 % alcohol.

Still, there must have been stronger beer available in the monastery. It emerges from the superintendent's complaint of 1563 that the nuns let young

---

78 In his will of 1505, Eskil Gøye donated 20 mark to the abbess, 10 mark to each of the nuns Anne and Birgitte Brahe, Elsebe Friis and Margrethe Walkendorff, and one mark each to the rest of the nuns and monks at Maribo. At Mariager, Erik Ottesen Rosenkrantz († 1503) gave his daughters Anne and Karen a picture of St Anne, made of silver, and a golden cross, and Elsebe Rud in the same convent received 10 mark in 1527, 30 mark in 1530 and 30 mark in 1536 from her sister and was the recipient of salted salmon and dried codfish in 1530. In her letters of thanks, she asked for herbs, pepper, saffron and wax. Heise (1882), p. 13; DM 6 (1765), pp. 272-275.

79 Rørdam (1883), p. 234. The conversion into modern measurements is based on Aakjær (1936), pp. 175-282.

80 Dahlerup (1882), p. 22.

81 *Regula* IX, §§ 88-95, contain rules for the different forms of fasting, some days on fish and dairy food, others on water and bread. In total, there were between 230 and 240 meatless days a year.

82 DM 5, (1751), pp. 12, 355. At Vadstena, the nuns consumed about three litres a day, Granlund (1976), c. 696.

noblemen into the monastery who under the influence of alcohol tore off their veils and associated with them as if they were harlots. Furthermore, the nuns themselves often got drunk, collapsed on the floor and were unable to get up by themselves.[83] Considering this information, one may wonder why, in his charter nine years later, the king doubled the ration of beer.[84] The explanation is, however, that out of the allocated rations of bread, meat, fish, vegetables, beer, etc., called *genant*, they had to provide for their maid, their shared cook and, probably, also for their guests.[85] This, too, seems a plausible reason why the abbess, who had several maids and servants and more extensive social obligations, was granted a *genant* twice as big as that of the other nuns in the convent.[86]

In his complaint of 1563, the superintendent furthermore mentions sexual excesses in the convent. Explicitly, he says that the male labourers had intercourse with the nuns' maids, who consequently became pregnant and had to leave the monastery.[87] With regards to the nuns themselves, he is more discreet and cautious. As they were members of the aristocracy, he had to watch his tongue in order not to insult them. Thus, apart from his mentioning of noblemen who drank with the nuns and treated them as harlots, he only notes that the young nuns invited their male relatives and friends into their cells, where they would talk for hours and arouse the older nuns' suspicion of sinful behaviour.[88] It was with their relatives and friends, not with their employees, he hints, that they might have affairs. Class conscious as they were, it would not be likely for the nuns to have a relationship with a man of simple, common stock.[89] And yet we know that a commoner persuaded one of them to elope with him in 1565,[90] and that Hans Jørgensen Sadolin, vicar in the nearby village of Flintinge, got the nun Anne Baad pregnant in 1575.[91] But this is all, as far as I can tell. Motherly love and mutual affection

---

83 Pontoppidan (1747), pp. 393, 395, §§ 1, 21.
84 The quantity was raised from fourteen barrels (c. 1560 litres) or three *skippund* of malt and ten *skæpper* of hops in 1545 to four *skippund* of malt and twenty-four *skæpper* of hops in 1572, cf. Kall Rasmussen (1886), p. 178.
85 The quantity of meat, fish, peas, butter and salt was also put up by 100 to 150 percent in 1572, cf. Kall Rasmussen (1886), p. 178.
86 *Charter 1572*, p. 509, § 11, repeated *Charter 1596*, p. 14, §§ 9-10.
87 Pontoppidan (1747), p. 395, § 22.
88 Pontoppidan (1747), pp. 393, § 1, 396, § 31.
89 Cf. Sophie Gyldenstierne's comment to the rumours that she supposedly have had an affair with the thief in 1568: "Even if the evil unvirtuousness (*udyd*) might have been in me, then I would have to think of the good, honest people, of whom I have sprung", MG III (1941), p. 215.
90 KBB 1561-1565, p. 611.
91 DAA (1884), p. 39: KBB 1566-1570, p. 675.

between the nuns did exist,[92] but nothing is known of potential homosexual relations. Were this the case, it certainly did not seem to have worried the king, when he ordered them to live together in pairs in 1570/72. Men were, in fact, considered more dangerous, and thus the king had decreed that a nun who consented to lie with a man should be walled in and live on water and bread in the monastic prison for the rest of her life.[93]

Imprisonment was also the penalty for those who rebelled against the abbess[94] or for those who returned late after visiting family. They were sent to the "dark chamber", as the prison was called by the nuns, on bread and water for as many days as they had been late.[95]

The lack of harmony and concord

Neither the superintendent's complaint in 1563 nor the Charter of 1572 conceal the fact that there was disagreement among the nuns and that the abbess had problems maintaining good order in the monastery. It was not easy for her, Kall Rasmussen says in his book about the monastery, "to govern such a large company of women of every age, from merry, perhaps naughty youngsters, to old, rigid spinsters".[96]

The lack of harmony, however, does not seem to have been caused by the nuns' different ages, but more by the fact that some of them had been granted privileges by the king. In 1568, as already mentioned, Johanne Falster, a cousin to Anne Gøye, obtained permission to have a chamber containing a fireplace, a maid and to wear her own clothes.[97] In 1585, Margrethe Rønnow was allowed to leave Maribo twice a year and to stay with her family for as long as she wanted.[98] In 1597, Else Huitfeldt and in 1600 Alhed Venstermand were exempted from service in the choir.[99] In addition, some of the nuns had been born into more aristocratic families and had a longer line of ancestors

---

92 Cf. Sophie Gyldenstierne's and the abbess' mutual references in their letters to Mogens Gyldenstierne, MG III (1941), pp. 214-223, 288-293.
93 Decided in 1565, KBB 1561-1565, p. 611; repeated *Charter 1572*, p. 510, § 15, *Charter 1596*, p. 16, § 15. Presumably, this was only meant as a warning, not as something which would necessarily be effectuated.
94 KBB 1561-1565, p. 612.
95 *Charter 1572*, p. 510, § 14; repeated *Charter 1596*, p. 16, § 14.
96 Kall Rasmussen (1886), p. 170.
97 KBB 1566-1570, pp. 389, 424.
98 KBB 1580-1583, p. 502.
99 KBB 1596-1602, pp. 206, 491.

with more coats-of-arms than others.[100] Family pride and sense of honour seem constantly to have sown the seeds of mutual envy and aversion. As a consequence, the nuns often quarrelled and cursed each another with the meanest and most insulting language, slandered and badgered each other, and sometimes even became engaged in brawls and fights – despite the king's repeated orders to live in harmony.

Whether a similar lack of harmony existed before the Reformation is difficult to know. On the one hand, it would clearly have contradicted everything prescribed by St Birgitta. But on the other, one ought not to romanticise medieval monasticism.[101] To think that family pride and rivalry, so common among the aristocracy in pre-modern times, did not have an impact on family members in the monasteries, would be naïve. So perhaps here, too, continuity occurred from pre- into post-Reformation eras?

Two episodes in the late 1560s may illustrate a lack of harmony. Twenty-three year old Anne Gøye and Sophie Gyldenstierne of nearly the same age both had their chests placed in the abbess' chamber. When one morning it became clear that a thief had taken something from the chests belonging to the abbess and Miss Sophie, but not from the one belonging to Miss Anne, Sophie Gyldenstierne suspected the latter of the crime. Anne Gøye called in her mother, Karen Walkendorff, who rushed to Maribo in order to clear her daughter of all charges. On arrival, Lady Karen made an inquiry and revealed as the thief one of the town's artisans, who had been working at the monastery. After having paid the civil authorities to have the man prosecuted and hanged, she left Maribo.

A year or two later, a visiting nobleman told the guests and nuns gathered in the convent hall that, before his execution, the thief had confessed that Sophie Gyldenstierne had taken a wax imprint of the abbess' keys for him to copy, so that he could break into the monastery during the night. Moreover, the rumour spread that she had alledgedly had an affair with the man. She was said to have taken him around inside the monastery, begging him to kill all the old nuns so she herself could become abbess.

---

100 On the tombstone of Anne Gøye, there were sixteen ancestral coats of arms and on the tombstones of Ermegaard Gyldenstierne, Margrethe Urne and Margrethe Norby, sixteen, eight and sixteen, respectively, *Danmarks Kirker*, Maribo Amt, pp. 72, 74.

101 As the majority of nuns all over Europe had been forced into the convents, one can see many tragic features and hear many of them deploring their fate and begging their relatives to take them out, King (1991), pp. 86-93, Laven (2002), passim. In Danish sources, we do not find similar complaints, but nonetheless we know that the nun Elsebe Rud at Mariager expressed her longing for her sister and disappointment over her brother and sister having been to Northern Jutland without visiting her at the monastery, DM 6 (1752), pp. 270-271.

Now, it was Sophie Gyldenstierne's turn to ask her father to clear her, as it was not "apples and pears", but her honour that was at stake. As she, in her letter, omits to mention names, it is impossible to identify the nobleman, but it becomes clear that one of the nuns was behind the rumours, because she told her father: "Has any of mine at any time harmed the good woman, then she had in truth avenged herself on me". There is no doubt this woman was Anne Gøye, as revealed by these words: "if I am not able with my family and my friends to defend the good and honest name of Gyldenstierne in the same way, as she the name of Gøye, then it would be a great disgrace".[102]

One can ask whether Miss Anne was taking revenge for having once been under suspicion. Or was it just two young nuns' mutual jealousy in their wish to be a favourite of the abbess and one day, perhaps, her successor?

The other episode also included Sophie Gyldenstierne as one of its main characters. One day before Christmas of 1568, she was ordered by the abbess to bring a nun, named Gese Hack, to the "dark chamber". However, on their way, she was attacked by the nun Karen Friis and seven or eight of her fellow-sisters. Miss Sophie's screams summoned the abbess, the prioress, and all the rest of the nuns. There followed a full-blown brawl, during which Karen Friis slapped Miss Sophie's ear, with the result that her hearing was impaired. Eventually, Karen Friis and her party succeeded in driving the others away and liberating Miss Gese from a disgraceful imprisonment. Triumphantly, they rushed to the convent hall, locked themselves in and, like modern hooligans, celebrated their victory by smashing up the furniture.

Again, Sophie Gyldenstierne sent a letter of complaint to her father. Naturally, the concerned 88-year old father wrote to the abbess, asking for an explanation. In her response, the abbess deplored the incident which, according to her, was caused by evil women, and reassured him that his daughter, whom she loved as her own, was innocent of all charges.[103] Karen Friis herself appealed to the king's representative Albert Oxe at the nearby Aalholm Castle and furthermore sent a complaint to the king himself. It was this episode that in 1570 forced King Frederik to order his chancellor and two other noblemen to examine the state of the convent.

The last episode bears witness to the existence of two factions within the monastery, one led by the abbess Margrethe Urne and another by the nun Karen Friis, a relative of the former chancellor Johan Friis. Based on the complaint made by the superintendent five years earlier, that the elder nuns tried to force "their superstitious and impious books" onto the younger nuns, one

---

102 MG III (1941), pp. 214-218.
103 MG III (1941), pp. 220-223.

might believe that the controversies originated in the wishes of abbess and the elder nuns to preserve the old monastic traditions and St Birgitta's prescriptions concerning devotions, silence,[104] fasting,[105] penance[106] and the worship of death.[107] But there is no proof of such a concern. We only know that Karen Friis and her supporters refused to participate in the weekly chapters. Moreover, the abbess herself seems to have had some difficulty living up to the old standards. With her loving dog and her many servants, she lived just like any other aristocratic widow in the second half of the sixteenth century.

In spite of the fact that Karen Friis had collected several of the young nuns around her in their discontent with the food, there does not seem, as postulated by Kall Rasmussen, to have been an older and a younger faction at the monastery. On the one hand, it is known that the young nuns Sophie and Ermegaard Gyldenstierne supported the abbess, and we can assume that Anne Gøye did the same, since she, too, had her chest placed in the abbess' chamber. On the other hand, when Karen Friis took the veil in the 1520s, she herself was no spring chicken.[108] According to Sophie Gyldenstierne, it was purely a matter of family honour and pride.[109] One may thus ask whether the opposition of Karen Friis could have been caused by a defeat in one of the abbatial elections held in 1547, 1551 and 1556?

As we have seen, the three noblemen who examined the complaints ordered a reorganisation of the interior of the monastery and solved the food problem by assigning individual cooks to the nuns. In other respects, they seem to have supported the abbess, as she was allowed to continue until her death on August 9, 1582.[110] After her, Sophie Gyldenstierne, her friend and protégée, was elected abbess.[111]

---

104 *Regula* VI, §§ 75-78, only allowed the nuns to talk to each other in the morning after mass until dinner, in the afternoon after the thanksgiving until Vesper and in the evening after the thanksgiving until the beginning of the spiritual reading.

105 On fasting, see note 81.

106 At the weekly chapter on Thursdays, the nuns were imposed penance, i.e. different degrees of fasting or flogging. The last was called *disciplina* and consisted of individual flogging or mutual whipping with a scourge, Nyberg (1974b), p. 80, cf. Verger (1984-1986), c. 1108-1110; Angenendt (1987-1989), c. 1177.

107 *Regula* XXVII, §§ 264-267, prescribed that there should be an open grave in the monastery around which the nuns should gather every Friday afternoon. The abbess would then sprinkle a handful of earth on the grave and the nuns sing the psalm *De profundis*, followed by a prayer.

108 Cf. DAA (1886), p. 122.

109 Cf. her remark: "With regard to family and friends, honour and esteem, my abbess with her adherents is as worthy [to govern] the abbey as the others". MG III (1941), p. 219.

110 DAA (1904), p. 492. What happened to Karen Friis is not known, but she was probably removed from Maribo. Anne Gøye died in 1576. On her epitaph, her brother ambiguously wrote that "with an honest and pious life she defeated all her enemies. God be merciful to her", Resen (1987), p. 87.

111 KBB 1580-1583, p. 568.

If the king had expected that the new abbess was able to establish harmony and good order in the monastery, he was soon disappointed. Sophie Gyldenstierne, who with her dogs and maids lived exactly as her predecessor had done, seems to have been rather high-handed in her style of management. Even worse, she had taken possession of an impoverished monastery with financial problems.[112] Consequently, she tried to cut down the monastery's spending, but only with the result that she, too, endured problems with the nuns. In the autumn of 1586, the king sent his councillors Sten Brahe, Hack Ulfstand and Arild Huitfeldt to Maribo in order to reexamine the situation. On the basis of their report, the king instructed the abbess, in a letter dated January 5, 1587, to repair the roof of the church and of the monastic buildings, to renovate the fireplace in the convent hall and to respect the rules concerning the nuns' food and pension. At the same time, he issued a ban on keeping dogs in the nunnery and reiterated the nuns' obligation to obey the abbess and to live in harmony.[113]

Alas, he wrote in vain. Later the same year, the nun Johanne Falster started a rebellion among the nuns, interpreting the privileges granted her by the king's father to exonerate her of any obligation to be obedient to the abbess. The king, however, supported the abbess and threatened the refractory nun with expulsion and loss of pension.[114] Also in the same year, the abbess reduced the pension of another privileged nun, Margrethe Rønnow. But she complained to the king, who ordered the abbess to pay her the amount to which she was entitled.[115] Some years later, in 1595, the abbess herself complained about the large amount of food she had to provide daily for the nuns and their guests and asked for permission to expel the widows Lene Gøye and Margrethe Huitfeldt, as they had their own funds and could support themselves. The king granted her the request, but following an appeal from the

---

112 In spite of several attacks on the abbey's possessions in the late 1530s, the loss was, in fact, trifling. Unlike King Gustav in Sweden, the Danish kings wanted the abbey to keep its farmland. At its dissolution in 1620, it consisted of 3 estates, 477 copy-farms, 5 mills, some deserted land and over 100 cottages, cf. the register of 1624, printed in *Archivregistranter* (1860), pp. 253-312; Kall Rasmussen (1886), p. 213. On the other hand, the money coming from the pilgrims' offerings and the nobility's endowment of masses and payments for burial in the church disappeared at the Reformation. There can be no doubt that these losses had consequences for the financial situation of the abbey. Nevertheless, the nuns at Maribo lived much more comfortably than their fellow-sisters at Vadstena and Nådendal. On the situation in those two abbeys, see Silfverstolpe (1895-1896), pp. 186-205, and Klockars (1979), pp. 174-193.

113 KBB 1584-1588, p. 637.

114 KBB 1584-1588, pp. 736-737.

115 KBB 1584-1588, p. 848.

two women, changed his mind and ordered the abbess to continue giving them lodging, food and pension in the monastery.[116]

That same year, the councillors Christoffer Walkendorff, Breide Rantzau and Arild Huitfeldt were sent to Maribo for another inspection. The result of their visit was a new charter, signed by the king on June 7, 1596.[117] This charter, in outline identical to that of 1572, tried to restore the abbey's financial order, stating that the number of nuns should be determined by the monastery's income and that the abbess was not allowed more than six maids. Furthermore, it fixed the wages of the twenty-seven servants and workers employed by the abbey[118] and repeated earlier decisions that the abbess should keep a truthful and correct account, which was to be audited annually by two noblemen.[119] Lastly, the nuns were given permission to take infant girls of noble birth as lodgers in order to teach them sewing, weaving, reading and good manners.[120]

The removal of Sophie Gyldenstierne

The visitation by the three councillors must have convinced the king that Sophie Gyldenstierne was unable to manage the abbey, for she was deposed only two months after the publication of the charter.[121] By a special grant, she was permitted to retain the double *genant* she had received as abbess. She still, however, kept her dogs, which she even brought with her to church, and continued to have her servants staying overnight in the monastery. Consequently, the new abbess Margrethe Norby was in 1597 ordered to reduce her allowance.[122] This measure seems, however, not to have had any effect because already the next year the former abbess was expelled from the monastery.[123] After thirty-three years at Maribo, Sophie Gyldenstierne moved to Jutland where she found a refuge for the rest of her life at Stjernholm Manor,

---

116 KBB 1593-1596, pp. 510, 541, 561, 597. There might have been some personal animosity behind the abbess' wish, because Lene Gøye was a sister to Anne Gøye, an old enemy of the abbess, and Margrethe Huitfeldt was an aunt of the Chancellor Arild Huitfeldt with whom the abbess had a dispute over land in 1591, DAA (1896), p. 149; DAA (1887), p. 219; KBB 1588-1592, p. 685.

117 KBB 1593-1598, pp. 596, 674.

118 *Charter 1596*, p. 17, § 23.

119 *Charter 1596*, pp. 18-19, § 28, cf. *Charter 1572*, p. 508, § 9.

120 *Charter 1596*, p. 15, § 11.

121 KBB 1593-1596, p. 720-721.

122 KBB 1596-1602, p. 15.

123 KBB 1596-1602, pp. 222, 238.

owned by her cousin Karen Gyldenstierne, a widow of Holger Rosenkrantz of Boller.[124]

During the reign of the succeeding abbesses, Margrethe Norby, Else Huitfeldt and Margrethe Hardenberg, only a few complaints were made about discord among the nuns, so the expulsion of Sophie Gyldenstierne must have dampened the problems. It is also likely that her generation of nuns had begun to die out.[125] In 1601-02, the plague carried off the abbesses Margrethe Norby and Else Huitfeldt and six other nuns.[126] The women who entered hereafter must have been born after 1580 and thus had no real knowledge of Catholicism, monastic life or St Birgitta.[127] But they, too, could find it difficult to cope with the restricted life at Maribo, as can be seen from the fact that a young nun, Anne Kaas, was expelled in 1618 after only one and half years in the monastery.[128]

The dissolution of the monastery

The many letters from the royal chancellery to the abbesses of Maribo provide us with some glimpses of life behind the walls of a nunnery, normally hidden from the eyes of a historian. On the basis of these, it can be established that Brigittine traditions continued to exist at Maribo for several decades after the Reformation. Until 1551, when the confessor was removed, there seem to have been no changes in the life of the nuns, but after that the Brigittine wine was gradually replaced by bottles with Lutheran labels. The nuns, however, preferred the old wine and only reluctantly uncorked these new bottles. As late as 1572, we still hear about the "many bad religious habits" within the nunnery. Despite the demand for immediate changes, the singing of Latin

---

124 The year of her death is unknown, but she was alive in 1607. Her sister Ermegaard died in 1590 and was buried in the abbey church, DAA (1926), pp. 24-25; Resen (1987), pp. 84-86.

125 E.g. Margrethe Rønnow died in 1591, DAA (1913), p. 48.

126 Resen (1987), pp. 83-84.

127 Isolated from Catholic Europe, the nuns must have had little, if any, knowledge of the monastic reforms introduced by the Council of Trent in 1563. The same applied to the nuns at Vadstena, so when the Italian Jesuit Antonio Possevino inspected the abbey in 1580, he was shocked to see how the nuns practiced their monastic life. He thus carried out *una mutatione della religione*, which consisted in *exercitia spiritualia*, according to Jesuit models, and the new Italian devotion, called *Quarant'ore*. Afterwards, Abbess Karin Bengtsdotter Gylta sent letters about the reform to the other Brigittine monasteries in the hope that they, too, could be revitalised in the same way. Whether Margrethe Urne and the nuns at Maribo received her letter is not known. On the reform of Vadstena, see Cnattingius (1970), pp. 48-70; Härdelin (1998), pp. 53-55.

128 The reason being that she gave rise to discord among the nuns and had failed to return in time after a visit to her family, KBB 1616-1620, pp. 429-430.

hymns was not abolished before 1583 – forty-seven years after the Reformation. From that time onwards, all the wine seems to have a Lutheran bouquet and taste. But even then problems continued, as before, due to the nuns' family pride and wilfulness.

In December 1620, King Christian IV put an end to this situation. He may not have remembered the word of Christ that one ought not to "put new wine into old bottles" (Mt. 9.17, KJV), but this was, in fact, what he, his father and grandfather had done in order to restore monastic life at Maribo.

On December 30, the king asked Palle Rosenkrantz of Aalholm Castle to make a list of the nuns in the monastery, with information about their ages and the number of years they had been living at Maribo. At the same time, he was to inform the abbess that, as a consequence of the nuns' bad habits, the king, with the consent of his council, had decided to close the monastery, leaving it to the nuns to find another place to stay.[129]

As the list is not preserved, we do not know the number of nuns in 1620/1621. From later letters, however, it emerges that the abbess, her sister Regitze and a third nun, Ingeborg Lange, with royal support found a place to live in the town of Maribo, and that Sir Palle was ordered to take care of a fourth nun, Ingeborg Norby, who "owing to her old age is forced to be in bed and has no mind and intellect". He was to find her, the king wrote, a maid and a room with "a good and honest citizen in Maribo" and pay for her until she died.[130] Furthermore, the nuns Lisbeth and Berte Skinkel, Sophie Lindenov, Anne Basse, Sara Heidenstrup and Margrethe Brand moved to other places, receiving royal endowments as compensation for their former *genant*.[131]

The abbey itself, with its many copyholders, was handed over to the newly established noble academy at Sorø.[132] The income from the abbey's possessions was thus still to be used for the benefit of the aristocracy. Their superfluous daughters were no longer to be supported, but their industrious sons were to be given a higher education. Sons who would later serve the realm.

---

129 KBB 1616-1620, p. 954.
130 KBB 1621-1623, p. 431, 46.
131 KBB 1621-1623, 47. The nuns Mette Lykke, Anne Rosenkrantz and Anne Parsberg did not get a pension as they had only been at Maribo for nine, nine and four months, cf. DAA (1903), p. 279-280; (1907), p. 357; (1985-1993), p. 789.
132 KBB 1616-1620, p. 954; 1621-1623, pp. 46, 47, 170, 431. The abbey's large collection of books, manuscripts and papers was also transferred to Sorø, where, in 1813, they vanished together with the latter's library and archive in the fire of Sorø Abbey. The monastic buildings at Maribo were demolished by royal order of September 26, 1622, KBB 1621-1623, p. 436.

Bibliography

Angenendt, A., 'Geisselung', in *Lexikon des Mittelalters*, IV (Munich, 1987-1989), c. 1177.

APD: *Acta Pontificum Danica*, vols. IV and VII, eds. A. Krarup and J. Lindbæk (Copenhagen 1910, 1943).

Archivregistranter = De ældste danske arkivregistraturer, II, ed. T.A. Becker (Copenhagen, 1860)

Charter 1572 = The Charter of 1572, in *Corpus Constitutionum Daniæ* (Forordninger, Recesser og andre kongelige Breve, Danmarks Lovgivning vedkommende, 1558-1660), 1, ed. V.A. Secher (Copenhagen, 1887-1888), pp. 506-512.

Charter 1596 = The Charter of 1596, in *Corpus Constitutionum Daniæ* (Forordninger, Recesser og andre kongelige Breve, Danmarks Lovgivning vedkommende, 1558-1660), 3, ed. V.A. Secher (Copenhagen, 1891-1894), pp. 11-21.

Cnattingius, H., 'Vadstena klosters sista tid', *Annales Academiæ Regiæ Scientiarum Upsaliensis, Kungl. Vetenskapssamhällets i Uppsala Årsbok* 13/1969 (Stockholm, 1970), pp. 46-102.

DAA = *Danmarks Adels Aarbog* 1-94, eds. H.R. Hiort-Lorenzen e.a. (Copenhagen, 1884-1996).

Dahlerup, Hans, *Mariager Kloster og Bys Historie* (Copenhagen, 1882).

Dahlerup, Troels, 'Den danske reformation i den samfundsmæssige placering', *Reformationsperspektiver*, (Acta Jutlandica LXII:3, Teologisk serie 14) (Aarhus, 1987), pp.. 65-79.

Danmarks Kirker, Maribo Amt, 8:1, eds. O. Norn and Aa. Roussell (Copenhagen. 1948).

Danske Kancelliregistranter 1535-1550, eds. Kristian Erslev and William Mollerup (Copenhagen, 1881-1882).

Diarium Vadstenense, ed. C. Gejrot, (Acta Universitatis Stockholmiensis, Studia Latina Stockholmiensis 33) (Stockholm, 1988).

DM = *Danske Magazin*, vols. 5-6 (Copenhagen, 1751-1752).

Granlund, J., 'Øl', in *Kulturhistorisk Leksikon for Nordisk Middelalder*, XX (Copenhagen, 1976), cc. 694-696.

Heise, A., *Familien Rosenkrantz's Historie*, 2 (Copenhagen, 1882).

Hsia, R.P.-C., *The World of Catholic Renewal, 1540-1770* (Cambridge, 1998),

Härdelin, A., 'Das Schicksal des Mutterklosters Vadstena im 16. Jahrhundert', in *Der Birgittenorden in der Frühen Neuzeit*, ed. W. Liebhart (Frankfurt am Main, 1998), pp. 37-62.

Kall Rasmussen, A., *Historisk-topographiske Efterretninger om Musse Herred paa Laaland*, 1: Maribo Sogn, (Laaland og Falster, typographisk beskrevne af J.H. Larsen 2:1) (Copenhagen, 1886).

KBB = *Kancelliets Brevbøger vedrørende Danmarks indre Forhold*, eds. C.F. Bricka et al., 39. vols., 1-16 (Copenhagen, 1885-1922).

King, M.L., *Women of the Renaissance* Chicago 1991).

Kirkeordinansen 1537/39, ed. Martin Schwarz Lausten (Copenhagen, 1989).

Klockars, B., *I Nådens Dal. Klosterfolk oc andre c. 1440-1590*, (Skrifter utg. av Svenska Litteratursällskapet i Finland, 486) (Helsingfors, 1979).

Kornerup, Bjørn, *Den danske kirkes historie*, 4 (Copenhagen, 1959).

Laven, M., *Virgins of Venice. Enclosed Lives and Broken Vows in the Renaissance Convent* (London, 2002).

MG = *Breve til og fra Mogens Gyldenstierne og Anne Sparre* II-III, ed. E. Marquard (Copenhagen, 1936-1941).

Nyberg, Tore, 'Den heliga Birgitta och klostertanken', in *Birgitta klostergrunderskan. Verket och dess aktualitet*, eds. E, Segelberg and P. Hansson (Kumla, 1974a), pp. 34-60.

Nyberg, Tore (ed.), *Dokumente und Untersuchungen zur inneren Geschichte der drei Birgittinenklöster Bayerns 1420-1570*, (Quellen und Erörterungen zur Bayerischen Geschichte, Neue Folge 26.2) (Munich 1974b).

Nyberg, Tore, 'Kvinder og mænd i Birgittinerordenen: en middelalderlig tolkning af opgavefordeling og æresfortrin', in *Middelalder, metode og medier. Festskrift til Niels Skyum-Nielsen på 60-årsdagen den 17. oktober 1981*, eds. K. Fledelius et al., (Copenhagen, 1981), pp. 195-222.

Nyberg, Tore, 'Texter för andaktsbruk', in *Vadstena klosters bibliotek*, (Acta bibliothecae Regiae Universitatis Upsaliensis, XXIX), eds. M. Hedlund and A. Härdelin (Stockholm, 1990), pp. 79-91.

Nyberg, Tore., *Birgittinsk festgåva*, (Uppsala, 1991).

Nørlund, Poul, 'Nye Fund paa Lolland og Falster, 1: En Nonnering fra Maribo Kloster', *Lolland-Falsters historiske Samfunds Aarbog* XXII (Nykøbing Falster, 1934), pp. 1-5.

Officium parvum beate Marie Virginis, [av] den heliga Birgitta och den heliga Petrus av Skänninge I-II, ed. T. Lundén, (Acta Universitatis Upsaliensis, Studia Historico-Ecclesiastica Upsaliensia 27-28) (Uppsala, 1976).

Petrus Olai, 'De ordine fratrum minorum', in *Scriptores historiæ Danicæ minores* II, ed. M.Cl. Gertz (Copenhagen, 1918-1920), pp. 279-324.

Pontoppidan, E., *Annales Ecclesiæ Danicæ*, 3 (Copenhagen, 1747).

Regula = Sancta Birgitta, *Opera Minora*, 1: S. Eklund (ed.), *Regula Salvatoris*, (Samlingar utg. av Svenska Fornskriftsällskapet 2. ser., Latinska skrifter VIII:1) (Lund, 1975).

Reuelaciones extrauagantes, Den heliga Birgittas. ed. L. Hollman, (Samlingar utg. av Svenska Fornskrift-sällskapet ser. 2, Latinska skrifter 5) (Uppsala, 1956).

Resen, P.H., *Atlas Danicus*, V, ed. H. Hertig (Odense, 1987).

Rübner Jørgensen, Kaare, 'Mariager klosters oprettelse og etablering (til ca 1490)', in *Birgitta, hendes værk og hendes klostre i Norden*, ed. T.Nyberg (Odense, 1991), pp. 231-279.

Rübner Jørgensen, Kaare, 'New Wine into Old Bottles. Maribo Abbey after the Reformation', in *Birgittiana* 12 (2001), pp. 121-153.

Rübner Jørgensen, Kaare, 'Ny vin på gamle flasker. Livet i Maribo Kloster efter Reformationen' *Kirkehistoriske Samlinger* (2015), pp. 31-66.

Rørdam, H.F., 'Mester Jørgen Jensen Sadolin, Fyens Stifts Reformator og første evangeliske Biskop', *Samlinger til Fyens Historie og Topographie* 4 (Odense, 1867).

Rørdam, H.F., *Danske Kirkelove*, 3 vols. (Copenhagen, 1883-1889).

Schwarz Lausten, Martin, 'Niels Palladius', in *Dansk Biografisk Leksikon,* vol. 11 (Copenhagen, 1982), pp. 124-125.

Silfverstolpe, C., 'Vadstena klosters uppbörds- och utgiftsbok 1539-1570', *Antiqvarisk Tidskrift för Sverige* 16 (Stockholm, 1895-1898), pp. 1-207.

Silfverstolpe, C., *Klosterfolket i Vadstena* (Skrifter och handlingar utgifna genom Svenska autograf sällskapet IV) (Stockholm, 1898-1899).

Skyum-Nielsen, Niels, 'Ærkekonge og ærkebiskop. Nye træk i dansk kirkehistorie 1376-1536', *Scandia* 23 (Lund, 1955-1957), pp. 1-101.

Smidt, C.M., 'Birgittinerklostret i Maribo. Søsterklostret og dets Forbindelse med Kirken', *Aarbøger for Nordisk Oldkyndighed og Historie* (Copenhagen, 1935), pp. 225-256.

Thomissøn, Hans, *Den danske Psalmebog aff Hans Thomissøn* (Copenhagen, 1569, reprinted Odense, 1968).

Vedel Simonsen, L.S., *Samlinger til den fyenske Herregaard Elvedgaards Historie*, 1 (Odense, 1845).

Verger, J., 'Disciplina', in *Lexikon des Mittelalters*, III, (Munich, 1984-1986), cc. 1108-1110.

Wiesner, M.E., 'Nuns, Wives, and Mothers: Women and the Reformation in Germany', in *Women in Reformation and Counter-Reformation Europe*, ed. Sherrin Marshall (Bloomington & Indianapolis, 1989), pp. 8-28.

Wiesner, M.E., *Women and Gender in Early Modern Europe* (Cambridge, 1993)

Aakjær, Svend, *Maal og Vægt*, (Nordisk Kultur 30) (Stockholm, Oslo, Copenhagen, 1936).

Environment: Remaining Buildings, Furniture and Books

Between King and Congregation

Monastery Churches and Parish Organization in the
Kingdom of Denmark after the Reformation

Per Seesko

Though only a few new churches were built in the kingdom of Denmark in
the century following the Danish Reformation of 1536, quite a few congregations nevertheless acquired new parish churches. This was the case in some
places where former monastery churches now became the focus of parish
life, while older parish churches were torn down or abandoned. In the process, parishioners had to come to terms with leaving those churches behind
where they had been baptized, listened to sermons, taken communion and
where their ancestors had for generations been buried. But they also had to
deal with more practical matters, such as the maintenance of buildings and
securing income and residences for priests in newly established offices, in
places where monasteries had formerly been responsible for pastoral care
in the parish. During the reign of Frederik I (1523-33), the transformation
of monastic churches often followed the forced departure of the monks or
friars of urban monasteries, but the reformation and dissolution of monasteries also played an important role in the attempts to reorganize the pastoral
care and economical foundation of rural parishes during the reign of his son,
Christian III (1534/1536-59) and grandson, Frederik II (1559-88).[1]

---

1   Of course, some monastery churches did not acquire their new status until the early seventeenth
    century. For example, the Benedictine church and cathedral of Odense was not a parish church be-
    fore 1618 when the congregation, which had moved from St Alban's to the city's Franciscan church in
    1539, was moved to the cathedral to secure its economic maintenance, *Danmarks kirker*, Odense amt,
    pp. 70, 79-80. In Maribo, where the local parish church was destroyed in a fire in 1596, the congrega-
    tion moved to the church of the former Brigittine abbey. When the convent for noble women there
    was finally closed in 1621, the church was given to the town, but without the estates of the convent,
    Boyhus (1976), p. 35. In both Odense and Maribo, there is evidence that the churches were also used

The changes in Danish parish organization before and after the Reformation of 1536 have, among others, been studied by priests such as P. Severinsen and L. Vesten in the early part of the twentieth century and later also by historians such as Troels Dahlerup and Ejvind Slottved. In his survey of the churches and parishes of the Hardsyssel region in western Jutland, Dahlerup stressed that, as a rule, Danish parish boundaries have remained relatively constant since the Late Middle Ages. But he also emphasized that for instance the special circumstances of the parishes around former monastery churches, such as that of the Cistercian abbey of Tvis, meant that exceptions to this rule were possible.[2] Such exceptions were again highlighted by Slottved in his study on the economic conditions of Danish clergy during the reign of Christian III. In response to supplications from priests complaining about insufficient means, a series of royal letters ordering the redistribution of church revenues was issued. This royal policy culminated in 1555 with a series of open letters that also made use of annexations of parishes and even the demolition of existing parish churches in an attempt to create economically self-reliant parishes and to secure sufficient revenues for resident parish clergy. In his earlier study, Severinsen had drawn attention to the special circumstances concerning the appropriated parishes of monasteries on Zealand that were still served by clergy living in the remaining monasteries as late as the 1560s and 1570s. James France did the same in his 1992 account of the Cistercians in Scandinavia.[3]

Quite a few monastery churches had, in fact, already functioned as parish churches before the Reformation. Some convents, for instance, had shared their church with a local congregation, the church being in effect divided, with a separate area for the nuns during services. And at some monasteries, those monks who were also ordained as priests had served the parish adjacent to the monastery as well as neighbouring parishes.[4] But even in such cases, provisions would often have to be made for the office, income and residence of a new parish priest. In 1541, for instance, a royal letter to the city of Odense confirmed that the Hospitaller church of St John (*Sankt Hans*) could be used as a parish church, and that the old hospital building in the churchyard could be used as a rectory.[5] Similar measures would have to be taken in

by local inhabitants even before they officially acquired the status of parish churches. In the cathedral of Odense, for example, pews were installed and sermons heard several decades before 1618, Rørdam (1883-1889), 2, p. 279; Haugner (1937), pp. 110-112; Rørdam (1860-1862), pp. 760-761.

2   Dahlerup (1960), pp. 94-96. See also Dahlerup (1956), pp. 5-87.

3   Vesten (1930-1932), pp. 1-22; Severinsen (1928), pp. 34-68; Slottved (1973), pp. 465-493. France (1992), pp. 473-474. See also Gabriel Thulin's account of the history of patronage rights in Denmark, with special attention to the development within the diocese of Lund, Thulin (1901a).

4   Krongaard Kristensen (2013), pp. 72-73, 81, 123-129, 135.

5   Rørdam (1883-1889), 1, pp. 191-193; *Danmarks kirker*, Odense amt, pp. 1231-1233. See also for Ran-

rural parishes appropriated by or under the patronage of monasteries. The Danish Church Ordinance of 1539 emphasized the importance of economically self-reliant parishes, ideally, it seems, served by resident clergy, although the difficulties for the less affluent and populous parishes in achieving these goals were acknowledged.[6] In this respect, as we shall see, the proximity of monasteries continued to shape parish organization in Lutheran Denmark well into the second half of the sixteenth century.

Our most important – and in some cases our only – source of knowledge about the changes in parish organization caused by the reformation of monasteries, are letters issued by the royal chancellery. Royal letters of confirmation seem to have been issued in most cases where monastery churches, which had not functioned as parish churches before the Reformation, acquired this new status during the Reformation era. Such letters would also be issued to confirm changes meant to secure incomes and residences for new parish clergy, or to confirm the annexation of a neighbouring parish to a newly established parish at a monastery church.

As we shall see, such royal letters were often the result of a course of events involving legislators on the one hand and local groups and individuals, such as priests, congregations, magistrates or noble patrons, who all had their specific interests, on the other. This was not least the case where the reformation of monasteries was part of the equation.

The early transformations of urban monasteries' churches

The first wave of Danish monastery churches transformed into parish churches during the Reformation century followed the often violent suppression of the Franciscan friaries and urban houses belonging to other mendicant orders during the late 1520s and early 1530s. In 1527, a Diet (*Herredag*) in Odense had allowed monks to leave their monasteries and marry. A contemporary account – the so-called "Chronicle of the Grey Friar's Expulsion" (*De Expulsione Fratrum Minorum*) – describing the attacks on the order's houses in cities throughout Denmark in the years between 1528 and 1532,[7] reveals that they were in many cases forced out in towns where the

---

ders (1542), *Danske Kancelliregistranter 1535-1550* (1881-1882), p. 225.

6   *Kirkeordinansen 1537/39* (1989), p. 192.

7   "Cronica seu breuis processus in causa expulsionis fratrum Minoritarum de suis cenobiis prouincie Danice". Danish translation: *Krøniken om Graabrødrenes fordrivelse fra deres klostre i Danmark* (1967). It also describes the suppression of the friars in Flensburg and Tønder in the duchy of Schleswig.

Reformation movement had taken hold early. The subsequent confiscation of their churches for parish use can be traced by combining the chronicle with sources from the royal chancellery. Another phase began after King Frederik I's death in 1533. Even before his final victory in the civil war that followed, Frederik's son, Christian III, granted the last abbot of the Cistercian abbey Ås in Halland, which had been destroyed in the ongoing war, the churches of Ås and Veddinge along with their rectories. He was in turn required to preach God's pure gospel to the parishioners.[8] In the years that followed Christian III's ascent to power, the remaining rural monasteries were treated as belonging to the Crown, but this was not followed by a general and immediate transformation of their churches for parish use. In the cities, however, a second wave of such transformations of mendicant and other monastic churches followed in the years after 1536.

In both of these early phases of the Danish Reformation, royal letters permitting the use of urban monastery churches as parish churches were often issued to magistrates, and the permission was generally presented as a favour to the town or congregation in question. The royal letters would commonly allow burghers and/or magistrates to take over the churches and other buildings of monastic houses "once the friars had left". This was the case in Viborg – an important centre for the early Reformation movement in western Denmark – in 1529, and during the following years, the king permitted the burghers of towns such as Trelleborg and Ystad in Scania, Nykøbing on Falster, Svendborg on Funen and Horsens in Jutland to transform Franciscan churches into parish churches and – in other towns as well – to confiscate other buildings once the friars had left.[9]

---

8 "Mester Mats Erichsen fik Brev, at efterdi Aas Kloster i Halland nu er "forvøstet", nedbrudt og forstyrret af Fjenderne, saa at der ingen Tjeneste holdes mere dér, som det var funderet og stiftet, har Kgl. Maj. forlent forskr. M. Mats, som var Abbed i Aas, efterskrevne Kirker og Gaarde, som tilforn laa til Aas Kloster: Aas Kirke og Vedig Kirke med deres Præstegaarde som Hr. Jens og Karl Engelbretsen nu ibo, med al deres Rente og Rettighedder, …, dog at han skal lære og prædike sine Sognefolk Guds klare og rene Evangelium og gjøre dem al den Tjeneste inden Kirken og uden, som de bør hae af deres rette Sognepræst og han vil ansvare for Gud og være bekjendt for os, …", *Danske Kancelliregistranter 1535-1550* (1881-1882), pp. 7-8, France (1992), pp. 474-475.

9 *Diplomatarium Vibergense* (1879), pp. 170-171. Svendborg in December 1530, 1532 and again in 1541; Ystad and Trelleborg in March 1532; Nykøbing in June 1532, *Kong Frederik den Førstes danske Registranter* (1879), pp. 272-273, 300-301, 316, 336; *Danske Kancelliregistranter 1535-1550* (1881-1882), p. 204. The magistrate of Horsens was first promised some of the city's properties now under the friary, once the friars had left, in July 1530, while the permission to use the church as a parish church was given in November 1532, ibid. pp. 258, 337-338. In the royal letter to the magistrate and burghers of Køge on Zealand of March 1 1531, there is no direct mention of the church; instead, they are simply promised the buildings "for the service of God as a hospital" ("… att the skulle forwende thett vdi Gutzs tiennistte till ith hospital…") once the friars had left, *Kong Frederik den Førstes danske Registranter* (1879), p. 277.

In several cases, royal letters allowing the confiscation of mendicant churches and other monastery churches in cities and market towns specifically mention that they are issued in *response* to a request from the magistrates of the cities in question. In February 1529, the burghers of Viborg received King Frederik I's permission to tear down their many existing parish churches and chapels, which, they claimed, were far too expensive to maintain, and instead use the city's two mendicant churches as parish churches, thus dividing the city into only two parishes.[10] In 1537, the magistrate of another diocesan town, Ribe, where there had been no early Reformation movement, obtained the king's permission to tear down several older parish churches and keep the Dominican St Catherine's as a parish church along with the cathedral. In a statement from 1542, the mayors and councilmen explain how they had obtained this permission from the king personally.[11] A visit from the king could be an opportunity for change. In Nykøbing Falster, the royal letter from 1532 allowing the magistrate and congregation to take over the Franciscan church was issued while the king was in town, as were the royal letters to the magistrates of Odense and Faaborg from 1539.[12] In Faaborg, the prior of the monastery belonging to the Order of the Holy Ghost had as late as 1528 received King Frederik's confirmation that the parish church of St Nicholas would pass to the monastery after the death of its priest. Now, in 1539, when the monastery's property had already passed to the hospital established in Odense's Franciscan friary, the town was instead given the monastery church as a parish church, while the king would take over St Nicholas' to use as a granary. He soon changed his mind, however, and the old church was given back to the city and seems to have been torn down during the 1550s. All that was left was the bell tower, which still stands today, and the church of the Holy Ghost remained as the city's only church.[13]

10 *Diplomatarium Vibergense* (1879), pp. 170-171.
11 The royal letter was issued at Gottorp, January 18 1537, Terpager (1736), pp. 374-375, 395; Kinch (1884), pp. 7-8.
12 *Kong Frederik den Førstes danske Registranter* (1879), p. 316-317; *Danske Kancelliregistranter 1535-1550* (1881-1882), pp. 89, 94. The confirmation letter of 1541 to the city of Odense about the church and rectory of St John's parish was also issued in Odense, ibid., p. 207.
13 *Kong Frederik den Førstes danske Registranter* (1879), pp. 178-179; *Danske Kancelliregistranter 1535-1550* (1881-1882), pp. 94, 459; Rørdam 1883-1889, 1, pp. 264, 298. In 1530, as a response to a petition from the burghers of Faaborg claiming that some of the priests wished to leave the monastery and suggesting that it should be given to the city, a royal letter was issued, giving the magistrate some say in matters concerning the hospital care of the monastery. Rather than leave, however, the prior and convent seem to have sought the protection of the local nobleman Jacob Hardenberg, who had in 1524 been given the city by the king. His rights to the income of the monastery's estates were since passed on to another local nobleman, Anders Emmiksen, Fasmer Blomberg (1955), pp. 64-65.

In some cases, noblemen played an important role alongside burghers or magistrates in the process of transforming the churches of urban monasteries for parish use. A driving force behind the closure of several Franciscan houses was Mogens Gøye, member of the Council of the Realm and a high ranking official at court, and for some years already openly defiant towards the established Church. In Randers in May 1530, it was he, rather than the king, who handed the Franciscan church over to the Evangelical preacher Mads Lang, since he had obtained the friary as his personal property a few months earlier, and he was also involved in the suppression of convents in several other cities.[14] In Skælskør, an active part seems to have been played by the noble Johan Urne, who, in contrast to Gøye, was part of the Catholic faction of the Council of the Realm. A few years earlier, he had been given the town as a fief by Frederik I and he also held the nearby Borreby manor. Now, in 1532, he reported to the king that the Carmelite monastery could no longer be maintained because of the poverty of the friars. A royal letter granted Urne the monastery with the exception of the church, which was given to the burghers for use as a parish church.[15]

In Copenhagen, the church belonging to the Order of the Holy Ghost, which had already been used for some years for Evangelical preaching, also became a parish church when a reorganization of the city's parishes was carried out by a commission of members of the magistrate and the king's council.[16] The city's collegiate church of Our Lady became a parish church on the same occasion, but that was not necessarily the case with other cathedrals or, indeed, monastic churches, during these early Reformation years. Odense's cathedral, the Benedictine St Canute's, was not a parish church before 1618. Instead, the old parish church of St Alban's was replaced by the impressive

---

14   *Kong Frederik den Førstes danske Registranter* (1879), p. 246; Rørdam (1869-1871b), p. 790. Gøye had received the convent in Randers, where his grandfather was buried, in exchange for the convent in Flensburg in the duchy of Schleswig, which he had obtained in 1528. He was also an active player in the suppression of the Franciscans in Næstved, Kalundborg and Horsens in 1532, *Krøniken om Graabrødrenes fordrivelse fra deres klostre i Danmark* (1967), pp. 9, 26-27, 54-56, 70-75. See in general *Dansk biografisk Lexikon*, vol. 6., pp. 78-80. He is mentioned as *relator* in the royal letters concerning Trelleborg, Ystad and Nykøbing on Falster, as well as in the case of the Carmelite house in Skælskør, see *Kong Frederik den Førstes danske Registranter* (1879), p. 300-301, 316, 322. Gøye had held the Dominican convent of Gavnø since 1523, and in 1532, he received the Benedictine convent of Ring as a crown fief, ibid., pp. 9-10, 467. His son Axel was active in the expulsion of the Franciscans from their convent in Aalborg, *Krøniken om Graabrødrenes fordrivelse fra deres klostre i Danmark* (1967), p. 53. On the other hand, other noblemen are mentioned as protectors of the Franciscans in Horsens, Halmstad and Flensburg (Schleswig), *Krøniken om Graabrødrenes fordrivelse fra deres klostre i Danmark* (1967), pp. 8-9, 28, 60-62, 73.

15   *Kong Frederik den Førstes danske Registranter* (1879), p. 322; *Dansk biografisk Lexikon*, vol. 18., pp. 96-97

16   Huitfeldt (1977), p. 229-230.

royal burial church at the Franciscan friary in 1539.[17] Furthermore, it was not always a given that a parish would actually be established around churches, which were confiscated during this early Reformation phase. In Svendborg, the royal letter issued in November 1541 stated that the Franciscan church was to be used as a parish church. But the town already had two parish churches and a third parish was never established. Instead, the friars' church became a sort of extra chapel for both of the existing parishes. In fact, at a meeting in January 1541 between the new Lutheran superintendent of Odense and the king's fief holders at Næsbyhoved and Nyborg, in the presence of mayors, councilmen and the rural dean of the district, held at the town hall in Svendborg, it had already been decided that the priests of both parishes, or their assistants, should use the church for sermons "for young people" on Sundays and on different weekdays.[18] The church also remained in use for burials, and sometime during the late sixteenth century, when the noble Helvig Hardenberg of Arreskov and Kjærstrup had bought the north wing of the friary and founded a hospital, a burial-chapel was even added north of the choir.[19] In Køge too, the Franciscan church may have functioned as a chapel for the city's main church, St Nicholas.[20]

As mentioned, it is evident from the account of the suppression of the Franciscan houses that it was often force, rather than a desire to leave, that brought about the friars' departure. The case of Ystad furthermore demonstrates that not all inhabitants of those towns, where mendicant churches became parish churches, necessarily supported the suppression of the friars.[21] All in all, though, under Frederik I, as well as under his son in the years immediately following the Reformation of 1536, even where the royal confir-

---

17 *Danske Kancelliregistranter 1535-1550* (1881-1882), p. 89. *Danmarks kirker*, Odense amt, pp. 70, 79-80. The Benedictine St Benedict's in Ringsted did not become a parish church before 1571, *Kancelliets Brevbøger*, 1571-1575, pp. 38-39. On the use of cathedrals as parish churches after the Reformation in Denmark, especially in Ribe, see Seesko (2014), pp. 97-130.

18 St Nicholas': "Oc skal han holde en predicken huer Søndag Morgen i Closter for vngt Folk, … Oc skal Sognepresten ibidem eller Capellanen, om nød er, predicke huer Fredag vdi Closteret"; Our Lady: "Oc skal Sognepresten til vor frue kirke eller hans Capellan predicke i Closter kirke huer onsdag, …, *Aktstykker*, p. 115-117.

19 Helvig Hardenberg herself, however, was probably buried with her husband Erik Rosenkrantz at Øster Hæsinge church near Arreskov, where their impressive tombstone can be seen today, *Danmarks kirker*, Svendborg amt, pp. 70, 513, 515, 559, 576-577; Krongaard Kristensen (1996), s. 22. The church was demolished as late as 1828.

20 *Danmarks kirker*, Københavns amt, p. 275. The churchyard also remained in use, as it did in Nakskov where the church of the former monastery of the order of the Holy Ghost also seems sometimes to have been used for services in the early seventeenth century, until it was finally torn down towards the end of the century, *Danmarks kirker*, Maribo amt, p. 126.

21 *Krøniken om Graabrødrenes fordrivelse fra deres klostre i Danmark* (1967), pp. 66,68. See also pp. 9, 72.

mation letters cannot be said to have been issued in response to the initiative of burghers or magistrate, or where no new parish was actually established, it is difficult to find in the sources available traces of local opposition from the urban parishes and congregations affected against the transformation of monastery churches for parish use.

The royal open letters of 1555

A few decades after the Reformation of 1536, by contrast, such transformation was sometimes met by local resistance when some congregations were ordered to abandon their old houses of worship to attend monastery churches. As mentioned, the ideal in the years following the Reformation of 1536 seems to have been that of economically self-reliant parishes each served by their own resident priest. According to the Danish Church Ordinance of 1539, each priest in a rural parish should receive one third of the tithes as well as offerings on the major offering days and the income from a residence or rectory. As this would not be sufficient in some of the smaller parishes, he could be allowed to serve two or even three parishes. No priest, however, should be responsible for the pastoral care at more churches than he could properly serve in terms of both giving sermons and administering the sacraments. Where superintendents, rural deans and the king's lay diocesan officers found it necessary, two or more churches or parishes could be joined into one parish.[22]

During the following years, Christian III received a seemingly endless stream of supplications from priests asking for supplementary provisions. In 1552, he ordered the bishops, cathedral chapters and lay diocesan officers of the three dioceses of Jutland to consider how the upkeep of priests could be secured in their poorer parishes.[23] In October 1554, superintendents and lay

---

22 The Latin version of 1537 has "Fiat ergo ex his *ecclesiis* … parochia una"; the Danish version of 1539 has "… aff flere *sogner* bliffue een Sogen…" (… of more *parishes* become one), *Kirkeordinansen 1537/39* (1989), pp. 114, 192; ibid., pp. 125, 211; see also Slottved (1973), p. 482; Dahlerup (1956), p. 67. In November of 1539, the first Evangelical superintendent of the diocese of Lund, Frans Vormordsen, had suggested to the king that commissioners be appointed in his diocese to hold a series of meetings with priests and lay representatives of all parishes and in the presence of the superintendent himself to make arrangements concerning the revenues of the clergy. Vormordsen suggested that no priest should be responsible for more than one church, and to achieve this ideal goal, some churches would have to be demolished. Alternatively, the parishioners would have to find a way of supporting a priest of their own, Rørdam (1860-1862), p. 706; Severinsen (1928), pp. 52-53.

23 Slottved (1973), pp. 465-467; Rørdam (1883-1889), 1, p. 331. The following year (October 23, 1553), a number of priests in the diocese of Aarhus received supplements to their income, Rørdam (1883-1889), 1, p. 357.

diocesan officers of all Danish dioceses received orders to travel through their respective dioceses, where they were to meet with the priests and rural deans of each district (*herred*), to enquire which offices had insufficient revenues, and judge whether complaints were justified or not. Their recommendations should be submitted to the king's chancellery as soon as possible, the intention being to secure sufficient provisions once and for all.[24] Finally, in 1555, a series of open letters ("*klemmebreve*" – so called after the official seal of the realm) were issued for each diocese based on these reports.[25]

In general, the methods employed were redistribution of tithes or other income, but also the above-mentioned possibilities presented in the Church Ordinance; the annexation or even amalgamation of parishes.[26] These changes also involved those parishes that were located in the proximity of monasteries. In a few places, monastic churches replaced former parish churches as part of the merger of two or more existing parishes whose old churches were then torn down or abandoned. In other cases, neighbouring parishes kept their own church but not their own priest, as they were annexed to the parish of a former monastic church. Finally, the open letters also addressed another problem. Where rural monasteries had been responsible for the pastoral care of neighbouring parishes, there were not always rectories or residences for the new Lutheran pastors. As we shall see, some landed monasteries – such as the larger Cistercian abbeys – still existed as Evangelical communities under the leadership of an abbot,[27] while others had been given to noblemen as crown fiefs or even as personal property. Some of these noble fief holders were now ordered to provide residences or to let the parish priests at churches formerly under the monasteries keep the full income of their offices.

In the diocese of Vendsyssel, for example, the Augustinian monastery of Vestervig, now a crown fief, had been in the hands of the noble Erik Rud since 1547.[28] In May 1555, he was instructed to provide residences for four priests of nearby parishes and to let them keep the full income of their offices. Furthermore, there was now also to be a parish priest at the monastery itself. The community around the monastery had had its own parish church, but

---

24   Rørdam (1883-1889), 1, pp. 389-390; Slottved (1973), p. 467-468.

25   See in general Slottved (1973).

26   Slottved (1973), p. 475.

27   The monks were still expected to observe their office, although its contents received a new Evangelical form by Johannes Bugenhagen, *Kirkeordinansen 1537/39* (1989), pp. 165, 236-237; *Den danske Kirkeordinants af 1539* (1936), pp. 68, 130-139; Sehling (1911), p. 344-353; see also Widding (1933), pp. 166-170.

28   *Danske Kancelliregistranter 1535-1550* (1881-1882), p. 347; he also received Halsted monastery as a fief in 1559, *Dansk biografisk Lexikon*, vol. 14, p. 397.

it had been torn down a few years earlier and its materials used for Aalborg-hus Castle. Now, it was emphasized that Vestervig parish should have its own priest – presumably at the monastery church – and that he, too, should be provided with a residence.[29] Similar steps were taken to secure residences and provisions for the parish priests serving the churches of two other Augustinian monasteries, Tvilum and Grinderslev,[30] and demands were also presented to the noble fief holders or owners of several other convents and monasteries in Jutland.[31] The owner of the former Benedictine convent of Stubber in the diocese of Ribe, a noble dignitary of the Ribe cathedral chapter, Iver Juel, who only the year before had been given permission to tear down the nearby parish church of Trandum to use its materials for the church in Sevel, was now reminded to provide a residence for the priest in Sevel.[32] In Vestervig, it seems that no residence was actually provided until 1568, and then only after the priest had complained to the king.[33]

Getting the noble fief holders to provide the necessary means for the new parish clergy could prove difficult. In the diocese of Aarhus, the Benedictine monastery of Alling had been bestowed to the noble Johan Høcken, who was now ordered to provide the priests of the nearby parishes of Grønbæk and

---

29 Slottved (1973), pp. 479, 491-492; Bolt-Jørgensen (1990), pp. 13, 16.
30 Rørdam (1883-1889), 1, pp. 449, 454. Grinderslev had already been promised a residence in 1540, see Dahlerup (1956), p. 12, 62.
31 For Vrejlev, Ø, Hundslund and Mariager, see Slottved (1973), pp. 491-492; Vesten (1930-1932), pp. 12-13, 27. For Ørslev, Rørdam (1883-1889), 1, pp. 448-449. For Gudum (1556), ibid. p. 494. Similar demands were presented to a few monasteries on Zealand and in Scania. For Æbelholt and Bäckaskog, ibid., pp. 429, 438-439; Slottved (1973), p. 478. The Cistercian nunnery in Roskilde, whose church the king had confirmed as a parish church for some of the neighbouring villages in 1539, was on the other hand promised a fee ("Pension") from the parish priest who was to serve the church in Sengeløse after the death of Jens Rosengaard, a noble canon of the cathedral chapter in Roskilde, Rørdam (1883-1889), 1, p. 437, II, p. 6.
32 Rørdam (1883-1889), 1, pp. 374, 458. Through his prelature in Ribe, Juel was also entitled to certain fees from the churches in the district of Hardsyssel. Exempted from these fees were, among others, some churches under monasteries, such as the Cistercian Tvis Abbey. In 1537, a fellow member of the cathedral chapter, Oluf Munk, who would have been bishop in Ribe had it not been for the Reformation, received Tvis as a crown fief, and eventually, in 1547, bought the abbey. In 1554, the king confirmed Munk's rights as patron of the abbey church as well as the nearby Nørre Felding situated within the monastery's *birk* (area exempted from the ordinary courts), while the monastery's rights at the churches at Aulum and Mejrup were lost. Munk was ordered to provide a rectory for the parish priest, who was to serve both Tvis and Nørre Felding. He also received the king's permission to tear down both churches and build a new one instead, but both were nevertheless left standing, as in 1558 a royal letter dictated that Sønder Felding should remain a parish church, since it was "beautiful" ("… meget skjøn…") and well situated, *Danske Kancelliregistranter 1535-1550* (1881-1882), pp. 50, 319-325; Rørdam (1883-1889), 1, pp. 370-371; *Kancelliets Brevbøger*, 1556-1560, p. 166; Dahlerup (1960), pp. 94-96.
33 Rørdam (1883-1889), 2, p. 113.

Svostrup, of Vejerslev and of Serup with rectories. One version of the royal letter reveals that Høcken was keeping the priest in Vejerslev from taking possession of his residence, and both here and in relation to Grønbæk and Svostrup, it is clearly stated that Høcken has received the king's letter to let the priests have their rectories, under threat of losing the monastery if he did not comply.[34] Nevertheless, these royal orders did not challenge the very idea that monasteries, whether they had passed to a noble fief holder or owner or not, could retain certain rights and revenues at nearby churches.

The interests of noble fief holders or owners, priests and congregations were not necessarily the same and could not always be given equal attention. This was also the case when the solution devised to secure sufficient provisions for parish clergy was to replace the churches of small adjacent parishes with that of a monastery or abbey. One example of how different interests could lead to a prolonged dispute about how to carry out the decrees of the royal open letters is related to the church of the Cistercian abbey of Holme in the diocese of Odense. In 1541, the abbey had been sold to Jacob Hardenberg of the nearby Sandholt manor, but in 1551, it was confiscated and became a crown fief again, after accusations against his widow, Sophie Lykke. In 1568, the abbey was once again sold to the noble statesman Henrik Rantzau, and changed its name to Rantzausholm (today Brahetrolleborg).[35] Holme was situated within the parish of Haagerup, which, together with the nearby churches of Krarup and Fleninge, had formerly been under the pastoral care of the monks. The royal letter of 1555 now stipulated that the churches in Fleninge and Haagerup should be torn down and the two parishes merged into one, with the abbey church functioning as parish church, as they were too small to maintain their churches properly and provide for the upkeep of a pastor in each parish. It was also decided that upon the death of the priest in Krarup – somewhat further away from the abbey than Fleninge and Haagerup (about 6 km.) – the church there should be reduced to a chapel-of-ease under the same priest as the two other parishes.[36]

---

34 Rørdam (1883-1889), 1, pp. 454-455.
35 Venge (1982), p. 40.
36 "… Fleningh, Hogerup och Krarup ere icke vden iij smaa sogne och ligge nest op till Holmcloster och then stundt ath ther vor Muncke vdi for^ne closter. Giorde the thienesten tiill for^ne kircker, och samme sogne icke ere saa formuende, athi kunde huer holde en prest eller och holde theris kircker ved magt: Tha paa thet ath vore undersatthe … mue fange theris tilbørlig gudts thieniste, haffue vij beuilgit och samtøgt, ath Holmclosters kircke skall ighen tiilflyes, och Fleninge och Haagerup kircker affbrydis, … och nar Her Jørgen er dødt och affgangen, som nu haffuer Krarup soghen, tha skall Krarup kircke vere annexe tiill Holmclosters kircke, …" Rørdam (1883-1889), 1, p. 409.

The church of Holme Abbey, today Brahetrolleborg. Photo: Per Seesko

When the priest in Krarup finally died in 1562, however, the parishioners successfully resisted this annexation. In a letter to his mother, Queen Dorothea, to whom the monastery had now passed, Frederik II informed her that the priest of the new parish in Holme, a man called Jens, had appeared before him, complaining that the parishioners of Krarup were unwilling to accept him as their new pastor, although they were unable to support a resident priest of their own. Frederik, who was reluctant to change his father's decision from 1555, supported Jens, but the parishioners had already asked Dorothea to install a new priest in Krarup.[37] As is evident from later sources, they must have been successful, and once installed, removing the new priest would mean a violation of his rights, which would have to be compensated. The new owner of the abbey, Henrik Rantzau, was aware of this situation when, in 1569 and 1570, he and his wife Christina tried to convince the bishop in Odense, Niels Jespersen, to find a living elsewhere for the priest in Krarup, Jørgen Marquorsen.[38] They would have to wait patiently, however, for in 1596, when the new bishop, Jacob Madsen, visited Krarup, Jørgen

---

37   Rørdam (1883-1889), 2, pp. 64-65.
38   Rørdam (1887), pp. 556-558.

Marquorsen was still in possession of his office.[39] Forty-one years after the decision to reduce the status of the church in Krarup to a chapel-of-ease, the parish still had its own resident priest.

Holme was not the only monastery church meant to be transformed into a parish church in 1555. The church of the Augustinian abbey of Æbelholt in Zealand, like Holme, was intended to replace two local churches. But in 1561, the decision was reversed, since, as the parishioners of Alsønderup had pointed out to the king, the abbey church was too far away and too expensive to maintain.[40] The Benedictine church at Voer in Jutland had also been intended to replace two local parish churches, but instead, the monastery church was torn down some years later.[41] Even where distance was hardly the problem, a monastic church was not always a welcome gift. In 1554, the year before the general letters to each diocese, a royal letter decreed that the church of Our Lady in the former Benedictine convent in the city of Aalborg in northern Jutland, already a parish church before the Reformation, was to be taken out of use. It had fallen into decay and its location was inconvenient in relation to the castle of Aalborghus. Instead, the church of the monastery of the Order of the Holy Ghost – now a hospital – should be used as a parish church.[42] After having sent representatives to meet the king in Odense however, the parishioners in February 1555 were allowed to keep their church, although they had to take down its tower and rebuild its vaults.[43]

Perhaps not surprisingly, local resistance to the closure of old parish churches was not limited to cases where the congregations were ordered to move to the church of a monastery. As shown by Slottved, the inhabitants of other parishes would also petition the king to keep their old churches. And many were successful. In total, of the thirty-seven churches marked out for closure in the open letters of 1555, only eight were actually demolished as a direct consequence and, as we have seen, some parishes also managed to avoid or postpone annexation.[44] The fact that they were monastic churches does not seem to have played an important role in local opposition to the replacement of older parish churches with those of monasteries. As in the earlier phase of the Danish Reformation, it could still also be the case that

---

39   *Biskop Jacob Madsens visitatsbog 1588-1604* (1995), pp. 250-251.
40   Rørdam (1883-1889), 1, p. 439; *Kancelliets brevbøger*, 1561-1565, p. 38.
41   Rørdam (1883-1889), 1, p. 454-455; *Danmarks kirker*, Århus amt, p. 3876.
42   Rørdam (1883-1889), 1, p. 387.
43   A few months later, the parishes of Sønder and Nørre Tranders near Aalborg were annexed to the city parish, Rørdam (1883-1889), 1, pp. 416, 447.
44   Slottved (1973), pp. 483-484.

parishioners saw an interest in taking over a monastery church. In 1562, representatives of the burghers of Slangerup on Zealand actively sought out the king and were given permission to use the church of the Cistercian convent, as the old parish church was too small and needed repairs.[45]

As we have seen in nearby Æbelholt, on the other hand, difficulty in meeting the costs involved in maintaining a large monastery church could be a concern. Of course, some of the old parishes had been so small that it might also have proven difficult to maintain the old parish churches. When in 1560, Herluf Trolle, admiral and member of the Council of the Realm, received the Benedictine Skovkloster (renamed Herlufsholm) near the market town of Næstved in Southern Zealand from the Crown in exchange for Hillerødsholm (Frederiksborg Castle) in North Zealand, he also gained the rights of patronage to the monastic church, which was now replacing the churches of the two small parishes of Vridsløse and Ladby. These were merged into one parish comprising of only 33 families. During the following years, more villages formerly belonging to the parishes of Næstved became part of the new parish, much to the dismay of at least one of the town's priests, who complained to the king and in 1576 received a yearly payment in grain as compensation.[46] The churches at Vridsløse and Ladby, however, were not torn down immediately following the amalgamation. Considering the fact that congregations elsewhere were unwilling to give up their local churches, it is interesting to note that the churchyards at Vridsløse and Ladby were still used for burials in the following centuries. In 1618, when the parishioners were asked to contribute to the renewal of the pews at Herlufsholm, they complained that although they already paid what they owed to the former monastery church, their churchyards were nevertheless neglected. Also the bells of both churches could not be rung without putting one's life in danger.[47]

---

45 Rørdam (1883-1889), 2, pp. 62-63. Some decades later, the abbey church was replaced by one of the few new churches built in sixteenth-century Denmark, Lorenzen (1941), p. 197.

46 *Kancelliets Brevbøger*, 1556-1560, pp. 425-426; 1561-1565, p. 66; 1566-1570, p. 493; 1576-1579, p. 113. Tolstrup (1965), pp. 20-22.

47 "Effter som welacht Morten A[nder]βen, fouget paa Herluffsholmb, paa schoel[e]herrens weigne er begierendis aff for:ne Herluffsholms sognemendt schrifftlig suar anlangendis forbygning och bekostning paa stole vdj deris sognekircke, da suaret Peder Olβen och Lauridz Nielauβen i Ladbye paa menige Ladbyemendz weigne, at de giffuer deris kirckeschyldt till Herluffsholms kircke, och deris begraffuelβestedt Ladbye kirckegaardt er fast forfalden och ligger saa godt som vnder fæfoedt, huorfore de ere gierne begierendis, att de maatte forhielpis aff huis rettighed, de haffuer giffuett till Closters kircke, att holde samme deris begraffuelβestedt wed magt medt, som det sig burde, och huis Closters kircke icke formaar att hielpe dennem, wille de hielpe der till aff deris formouge, saawijt dennem mougeligt er. Wdj ligemaade suaret Lauridz Jacobβen och Andrijs Hanβen i Wreddzløβ paa menige bymendz veigne der i byen, lige som Ladbymendt suaret haffuer… Och beklager for:ne dan-

Old allegiances did not disappear overnight. Bishop Jacob Madsen's visitation report from 1589 reveals that the aisle of the new parish church at Holme Abbey, rather than separating men from women, separated the pews of parishioners belonging to the former parishes of Fleninge and Haagerup. When the bishop visited Krarup, the parish marked out for annexation under Holme, he noted that the income was so small that the aging priest was unable to hire a chaplain to assist him, which, according to the bishop, he needed.[48] But at least, the thirty-eight tithe payers were able to keep their own priest. Generally, it seems, parishioners wanted their own church and a resident priest, if they could afford it. In the nearby parish of Vejle, for example, the local nobleman Eggert Henriksen Sandberg and sixteen tithe payers managed to persuade the king to retract his decision to have their church torn down, although they would have to share a priest with the twenty-four tithe payers of the neighbouring parish of Allested, as the parish still does today.[49]

The parishes of the remaining landed monasteries

As mentioned above, and in contrast to the situation at Holme, some of the Cistercian abbeys and other landed monasteries (*Herreklostre*) were still under the leadership of an abbot or prior at the time of the open letters of 1555. Christian III may have had good political and economic reasons not to secularize all monasteries immediately, but as Brian Patrick McGuire also mentions in his contribution to the present volume, Cistercian abbeys such as Vitskøl, Esrum and Sorø were also allowed to continue after the Reformation to provide education in Scripture and support university studies, as were other important landed monasteries, such as the Benedictine monastery in Ringsted and the Hospitaller Antvorskov in the diocese of Zealand.[50] Accord-

---

nemendt, att klockeuerkerne vdj Ladbye och Wreddzløøe kircker ere forraadnit och forderffuit, saa mandt icke kandt ringe klockerne vden liffsfare", *Herlufsholms Birks Tingbog 1616-1619* (1954), p. 53; Tolstrup (1965), pp. 22-23. In Fleninge near Holme, on the other hand, excavations in 2014 revealed that there is no reason to believe that the churchyard remained in use after the congregation moved to Holme abbey. I thank Mikael Manøe Bjerregaard, Odense City Museums, for this information.

48 *Biskop Jacob Madsens visitatsbog 1588-1604* (1995), pp. 249-250; Troels-Lund (København, 1929-1931), VI, pp. 44-46.

49 Rørdam (1883-1889), 1, pp. 397, 505-506. Vejle had for a time also been under the pastoral care of the rector of Sønder Broby, *Biskop Jacob Madsens visitatsbog 1588-1604* (1995), pp. 254, 257-258.

50 See also Bisgaard in the present volume; Jakobsen (2015), pp. 26-27. In Germany, too, Lutheran monasteries such as Maulbronn and Bebenhausen in Württemberg had been transformed into monastic schools, France (1992), pp. 465-466. As early as 1533, before his election as duke, the young Christian had been advised by Phillip of Hesse that the resources of monasteries could be used for educational

ing to the letter of foundation for the reopened University of Copenhagen from 1539, these monasteries were to become monastic schools for the education of poor young men, who, as long as they stayed in the monastery, were expected to wear a monastic habit, to be "obedient to their superiors, lead a life of chastity, honesty, prayer and study, and to sing and read in the choir in accordance with the rules laid down in the church Ordinance".[51] The abbeys and monasteries were expected to employ a learned theologian, who could be one of the monks, to teach Scripture, and they should also provide a basic education in grammar, logic and rhetoric.[52] In 1541, the king also demanded from twelve monasteries throughout the country that they support students at the University of Copenhagen.[53]

The responsibilities that some of these monasteries had been given in the educational effort of the reformed Church and state would continue to affect nearby parishes well into the second half of the sixteenth century. In 1551, Sorø, Esrum, Antvorskov, Ringsted and Skovkloster were reminded by the king of their responsibility to employ a theologian to give lectures at the monastery school. These were important land-owning monasteries and some of them held several of the nearest parishes as incorporations. Interestingly, the royal letter states that, if they were not able to pay this lecturer, they *could* let him serve as a parish priest in one of the nearby parishes "usually cared for by one of the monks".[54] Towards the end of the 1555 letter to the diocese of Zealand, it was noted that, if monasteries such as Sorø, Esrum and Antvorskov were not able to provide their affiliated parishes with "learned priests, riding out" from the monasteries to each church, they should *instead* employ resident priests within the parishes. But interestingly, this procedure is only presented as an alternative.[55] As the clergy of such parishes was allowed to continue to stay at the abbeys and monasteries rather than move to rectories in their individual parishes, royal confirmation of rights and revenues,

purposes, Seesko (2016), pp 251-252.

51 Rørdam (1883-1889), 1, p. 38-39; English translation by France (1992), pp. 467-468.

52 Rørdam (1868-1877), p. 52; Severinsen (1928), pp. 53-54; Rørdam (1881-1882), pp. 95-96.

53 Rørdam (1883-1889), 1, p. 187.

54 "Oc ther som i icke haffue nogenn besolding att wdlegge for[ne] Lessemester for hans tienniste, tha mue i lade hannem besøge enn aff the neste omliggendis sogne, som brødrerne ther wdj closterit pleige att besøge, oc bruge hannom ther til enn sogneprest, …" Rørdam (1883-1889), 1, p. 311.

55 "Epthertij ther findes, at the Kircker, som ligger tiill Anduordskouff, Soer, Esserum och andre Herre Closter her vdj Sieland, icke ere besørget mett lerde Mend tiill Sogne Prester, thij at Preste Renten vpeberes til Closterne, tha skall ther mett saa holles, at huor ther icke vdj Closterne kan holles lerde Prester, som kand ride vd tiill Sogne Kirckerne och giøre Sogne Folckett ther sammestedz theris tilbørlig Tieniste, tha skall Forestanderne for samme Clostere vere pligtig at sette boesiddendes Prester hos Kicrken og vdlegge thennom Preste Gaarde, och tillegge thennom en tilbørlig Vnderholling", Rørdam (1883-1889), 1, pp. 440-441; Severinsen (1928), p. 58.

which the monasteries held at nearby churches, was thus made part of the foundation for the educational effort of the Lutheran state, even if one senses a gradual shift in priorities.[56] Perhaps we might even speculate that some of the older students at the monastery schools could have gained part of their practical education by assisting at these churches.[57] In other words: although it was important to provide parishes with resident clergy, so was the education of future clergy and the resources to finance this education.

One of the few named individuals educated and later serving at these monastery schools of whom we know a little is the priest Christiern Nielsen Juel (1533-96). He had studied at Vitskøl Abbey in Jutland and later at Sorø. At Vitskøl, where the church seems to have replaced the parish church of Aale at some point after the Reformation, the open letter of 1555 had prescribed that the "preacher" of the abbey should serve the nearby parish of Malle, which had been under the abbey since the thirteenth century, as a chaplain ("*Capellan*"). He was to have his lodgings at the monastery, as was the chaplain of the abbey's other parish, Strandby, who also served as a schoolmaster ("*skollemester*") at the abbey.[58] In his autobiographical records, Christiern Nielsen Juel describes how he returned to Vitskøl in 1559. Here, he "obtained" (*fick*) Strandby parish in 1561 and, like the last abbot, Anders, moved outside the abbey in 1563 when the noble Henrik Gyldenstierne had been granted the abbey as a fief. In 1564, he finally obtained a rectory in Strandby chosen by the parishioners.[59]

During the early years of Frederik II's reign, a number of the smaller Cistercian abbeys, like Vitskøl, were now finally closed. At the same time, conditions of parishes near the last remaining monasteries would come to resemble those of other parishes more. In 1567, the king granted the priests

---

56 In 1546, a royal letter had confirmed the rights of the abbot and convent of Ringsted to the church and rectory of Haraldsted, allowing them to appoint a learned preacher to teach "God's pure Gospel" to the parishioners: "… Hr. Niels, Abbed I Ringsted Kloster, nu har havt for os Breve af fremfarne Konger I Danmark, lydende, at Harrestedt Kirke og Præstegaard med al sin Herlighed skal være og blive hos forskr. Ringsted Kloster, hvis Abbed og Konvent skulle dèr indsætter en sognepræst af deres Brødre, hvem de lyste. Da have vi af synderlig Gunst tilladt, at same Kirke og Præstegaard maa blive til Klostret, og at Abbeden og Konventet maa tilskikke dèr en god, lærd Prædikant, som rettelig vil og skal lære og prædike Almuen Guds rene og klare Ord og være vor Ordinans om Religionen underdanig, dog saa at den Præst, der nu er forlenet dermed, skal beholde den I sin Livstid.", *Danske Kancelliregistranter 1535-1550* (1881-1882), p. 311; Thulin (1901a), p. 37.

57 Severinsen (1928), p. 55; Nielsen (1899), pp. 408-409.

58 "Predicanterenn wdj Wiidskyld Closter skall were capellan tiill Malle sogenn oc nyde presterenthen aff samme sogenn oc ther tiill haffue kost, kledningh och woningh wdj Wiidskyld closter", Rørdam (1883-1889), 1, pp. 450-451; Dahlerup (1956), p. 32.

59 Abbot Anders had come to Vitskøl from Tvis Abbey in 1537, Rørdam (1869-1871a), pp. 351-355; Nielsen (1899), pp. 408-412.

of the parishes, which had been under the Cistercian nunnery of Roskilde the same rights to enjoy the full income of their offices as priests "under the Crown", while, in accordance with the Church Ordinance, the congregations under the nunnery would henceforth also be allowed to choose their own priests.[60] Eventually, change would also come to the remaining larger abbeys and monasteries where schools were still in operation. As we have seen above, parish organization had already been adjusted around Skovkloster in 1560, but a register of parishes in the diocese of Roskilde reveals that a number of parishes in the areas surrounding Antvorskov, Ringsted and Sorø were still without rectories as late as 1567.[61] Sorø's rights to the tithes of its churches were confirmed in 1567, and Antvorskov's patronage of three churches in 1568. But in July 1569, when Frederik II was at Sorø, new letters were issued to Ringsted, Antvorskov and Sorø and to the bishop and lay diocesan officer of Zealand, stating that they were to carry out a reorganization of the parishes under the monasteries, as the king had been made aware of the fact that some priests were still living at the monasteries rather than in their parishes. They were now to have their own rectories "*like other priests do in their parishes in Zealand*".[62] The accounts of Sorø show that the priests living there left the abbey already the following year, and in 1574, the king confirmed the division of twenty parishes belonging to the three monasteries among ten resident priests.[63] In Ringsted, for the sake of the better maintenance of the church itself and its royal burials, the Benedictine church had also replaced the old parish church of St John along with the chapel in Slanerup in 1571. The learned abbot Iver Bertelsen, who had a profound interest in Danish history, was told to make space for pews by removing some of the altars, albeit not the ones established by past kings and queens.[64]

60 *Kancelliets Brevbøger*, 1566-1570, p. 199.
61 *Sjællands Stifts Landebog 1567* (1956), pp. 83-84, 98-99, 107, 116-117, 124, 159-160; Severinsen (1928), pp. 39-40, 44. Esrum, on the other hand, seems to have had only two appropriated churches, Esbønderup and Tikøb, France (1992), p. 218.
62 "… som andre preste haffue vdj theris sogner her vdj Sieland, …", Rørdam (1860-1862), pp. 764-765; Severinsen (1928), pp. 60-61; Thulin (1901a), pp. 24-26.
63 Nørlund (1924-1931), pp. 121, 127; Rørdam (1883-1889), 2, p. 219. In the meantime, the peasants of Alsted and Slaglille had complained to the king that the building of rectories had diminished the worth of their adjoining land, Severinsen (1928), pp. 62-63, 67.
64 *Kancelliets Brevbøger*, 1571-1575, pp. 38-39, 54; Severinsen (1928), pp. 64-65.

Clearly, the situation had changed, and attempts to finally secure the rights and revenues of parishes and their clergy were made in other dioceses as well during these same years. A register of two districts on Funen from 1568 has survived, and in August 1569, King Frederik ordered that registers be made of the property of all churches and priests in the diocese of Lund. Superintendents and lay diocesan officers were ordered in May 1571 to make inquiries as to the revenues and residences of clergy in all dioceses.[65] In 1573, the right to nominate priests at those parishes in the diocese of Aarhus, which had been under the patronage of monasteries, was given to the parishioners. In 1574, the same rights were given to congregations in the diocese of Viborg, whose parishes had been under the patronage of Sebber, Vitskøl and Mariager, while the priests themselves were to enjoy the same rights as elsewhere in the diocese.[66]

Although other factors of course influenced the secularization of the remaining monasteries as well, perhaps the need to have monastery schools was not as obvious as it had been either. The importance of these monastery schools should probably be seen in light of the specific circumstances in the decades immediately following the Reformation, when university education had been a realistic possibility for only a limited number of priests. Due to increased funding, more stipends for students at the cathedral schools of each diocese and at the University of Copenhagen became available during the reign of Frederik II.[67] When the school at Øm was abandoned, as the abbey was turned into a royal hunting lodge in 1560, the king made sure to support the cathedral school in Aarhus instead, granting it one third of the

---

65 Rørdam (1883-1889), 2, pp. 151-153; *Lunds stifts landebok*, 4, pp. 1-2; ibid., 6, pp. 31-43. In the register from the diocese of Lund, it was noted that there was no rectory at Ås, and, if there had ever been one, it was now under the abbey. A later addition, however, relates that this has been remedied, and there was also a rectory in the parish of Veddinge, also under the patronage of the former abbey, ibid., 5, p. 441, 444. The rectory of Svalöv had been under Herrevad Abbey and the priest still had to live in the sexton's residence (ibid., 4, p. 148), while the parishioners at Munka Ljungby had provided some land for a monk ("… tiill en munck…"), Thulin (1901b), p. 225. The priest of Vånga parish had lost his rectory, which now belonged to the former Premonstratensian abbey of Bäckaskog, and the priest of Kiaby even lived at the manor where he was paid an annual salary for food and clothes, ibid., 5, pp. 215, 217, 219. There were also no rectories in the parishes of the Premonstratensian abbeys of Öved and Tommarp, but the pastor at Öved had a rectory in his main parish Skartofta. Tommarp became an annex of Gladsaxe in 1578, ibid., 4, p. 221 and 5, p. 239. The parish priest of the Premonstratensian Børglum in Northern Jutland lived at the monastery until 1579, Vesten (1930-1932), p. 9.
66 Rørdam (1883-1889), 2, pp. 197-198, 216-217, 245-246. See also Dahlerup (1956), pp. 31-32, 54, 71. The fief holder at Mariager, however, seems to have kept the monastery's rights within the parish of Staby in the diocese of Ribe, Dahlerup (1960), pp. 97-98
67 Grane (1990), pp. 165-168, 171-172.

tithes of ten parishes in the district of Hads for the upkeep of 24 poor school children.[68] While at least Sorø continued as a school, neither this one nor the school in operation since 1565 at Herlufsholm functioned as monastic schools in the sense that the old schools had been.[69]

Concluding remarks

Even though we can identify a royal policy seeking to secure sufficient income for parish priests, it was not a simple matter to convert a monastery church for congregational use, nor to make sure that the conditions of appropriated or newly annexed parishes corresponded with the principles of economically self-reliant parishes served by resident clergy. Royal letters confirming the use of a monastery church as a parish church or the annexation of neighbouring parishes under a former monastery church could be issued in response to supplications from congregations, priests or local nobility. But even though the final decision rested with the king, local groups and individuals could also oppose these royal letters, sometimes convincing the king to reverse a decision.

On some occasions during the early Reformation years of the 1520s and 1530s, when especially the Franciscans were forced to leave their friaries in the towns, it is evident that local initiative preceded the royal letters of confirmation. The transformation of mendicant churches and churches of other urban monasteries, which had not served as parish churches before the Reformation, would also generally be presented as a favour to the local community. When new attempts were made to create parishes out of monastic churches in the years around 1555, they were to a large extent motivated by the need to create a solid economic foundation for the upkeep of parish clergy. But in contrast to the earlier transformations, these changes were not always welcomed at the local level, because some congregations preferred to keep their old parish churches and opposed annexation or the forced move to a larger monastery church. For some parishes, their proximity to a monastery meant that they would not have a resident parish priest until several years after 1555.

The religious, institutional and political circumstances – and with them the concerns of legislators as well as local authorities and parishioners – were

---

68   *Kancelliets Brevbøger*, 1556-1560, p. 398; Rørdam (1881-1882), pp. 101-102.
69   Mackeprang (1924-1931), p. 322-340; Tolstrup (1965), pp. 211-215.

not the same in the early stages of the Danish Reformation, as later on, when the post-Refomation Church was becoming more consolidated. This was also mirrored in the process of integrating monastery churches and their affiliated parishes into regular parish organization.

Bibliography

Aktstykker = Aktstykker til Oplysning især af Danmarks indre Forhold i ældre Tid (udg. Af Fyens Stifts literaire Selskab) 1 (1841).

Biskop Jacob Madsens visitatsbog 1588-1604. Ved Jens Rasmussen og Anne Riising (Odense, 1995).

Bolt-Jørgensen, Henrik, *Vestervig Kirke* (Thyholm, 1990).

Boyhus, Else-Marie, *Maribo – historisk set* (Maribo, 1976).

Dahlerup, Troels, 'Sogn og Pastorat. Bidrag til Viborg Stifts Historie i Senmiddelalderen', *Fra Viborg Amt* (1956), pp. 5-87.

Dahlerup, Troels, 'Hardsyssels provsti i senmiddelalderen', *Hardsyssels Aarbog* 54 (1960), pp. 77-141.

Danmarks kirker, Københavns amt, 3:4 (Copenhagen, 1944).

Danmarks kirker, Maribo amt, 8:1 (Copenhagen, 1948).

Danmarks kirker, Odense amt, 9:1 (Herning, 1990).

Danmarks kirker, Odense amt, 9:3 (Herning, 1998-2001).

Danmarks Kirker, Svendborg amt, 10:2-3 (Copenhagen, 2011).

Danmarks kirker, Århus amt, 16:8 (Herning, 1992-1996)

Dansk biografisk Lexikon = C.F. Bricka (ed.), *Dansk biografisk Lexikon, tillige omfattende Norge for Tidsrummet 1537-1814*, 19 vols. (Copenhagen, 1887-1905).

Danske Kancelliregistranter 1535-1550, eds. Kristian Erslev and William Mollerup (Copenhagen, 1881-1882).

Den danske Kirkeordinants af 1539 og andre Aktstykker vedrørende den lutherske Kirkereformations Indførelse i Danmark, ed. Max W. Olsen (Copenhagen, 1936).

Diplomatarium Vibergense = Diplomatarium Vibergense. Breve og Aktstykker fra ældre viborgske Arkiver til Viborg Bys og Stifts Historie 1200-1559, ed. A. Heise (Copenhagen, 1879).

Fasmer Blomberg, Aage, *Faaborg by's historie*, 2. vols. (Faaborg, 1955), 1.

France, James, *The Cistercians in Scandinavia* (Kalamazoo, 1992).

Grane, Leif, 'Teaching the People – the Education of the Clergy and the Instruction of the People in the Danish Reformation Church', in Leif Grane and Kai Hørby (eds.): *Die dänische Reformation vor ihrem internationalen Hintergrund* (Göttingen, 1990), pp. 164-184.

Haugner, C.C., *Maribo Historie*, 1 (Maribo, 1937).

Herlufsholms Birks Tingbog 1616-1619, ed. Karen Marie Olsen (Copenhagen, 1954).

Huitfeldt, Arild: *Danmarks Riges Krønike: Frederik I's Historie 1597* (Copenhagen, 1977).

Jakobsen, Johnny Grandjean Gøgsig, 'Esrum Klosters nedlæggelse', in Jens Anker Jørgensen and Bente Thomsen (eds.): *Esrum Klosters storhed og fald* (Helsinge, 2015), pp. 11-37.

Kancelliets Brevbøger = Kancelliets Brevbøger vedrørende Danmarks indre Forhold i Uddrag, eds. C. F. Bricka et al., 39 vols. (Copenhagen, 1885-2005).

Kinch, J.F., *Ribe Bys Historie og Beskrivelse 2den Del. Fra Reformationen indtil Enevoldsmagtens Indførelse. (1536-1660)* (Odder, 1884).

Kirkeordinansen 1537/39, ed. Martin Schwarz Lausten (Copenhagen, 1989).

Kong Frederik den Førstes danske Registranter, eds. Kristian Erslev and William Mollerup (Copenhagen, 1879).

Krongaard Kristensen, Hans, 'Nedrivning af klosterkirken i Svendborg – og hvad der blev bevaret', *Årbog for Svendborg & Omegns Museum* (1996), pp. 21-38.

Krongaard Kristensen, Hans, *Klostre i det middelalderlige Danmark* (Højbjerg, 2013).

Krøniken om Graabrødrenes fordrivelse fra deres klostre i Danmark, trans. Henning Heilesen (Copenhagen, 1967).

Lorenzen, Vilh., *De danske Cistercienserklostres Bygningshistorie* (Copenhagen, 1941).

Lunds stifts landebok = Skånsk senmedeltid och Renässans, 4-6. *Lunds stifts landebok*, eds. K.G. Ljunggren and Bertil Ejder (Lund, 1950-1965).

Mackeprang, M., 'Den kgl. frie Skole i Soer 1586-1623', in *Sorø, Klostret, Skolen, Akademiet gennem Tiderne*, 2 vols. (udgivet af Soransk Samfund) (Copenhagen, 1924-1931), 1, pp. 321-373.

Nielsen, A.C., 'Vadgaard i Himmerland som Præstebolig og Bondehjem', *Samlinger til jydsk Historie og Topografi*, 3:2 (1899), pp. 401-436.

Nørlund, Poul, 'Klostret og dets Gods', in *Sorø, Klostret, Skolen, Akademiet gennem Tiderne*, 2 vols. (Copenhagen, 1924-1931), 1, pp. 53-131.

Rørdam, Holger Fr., 'Om Reformationen af Herreklostrene', *Kirkehistoriske Samlinger*, 2:2 (1860-1862), pp. 736-765.

Rørdam, Holger Fr., *Kjøbenhavns Universitets Historie*, 4 vols. (Copenhagen, 1868-1877), 1.

Rørdam, Holger Fr., 'Uddrag af Præsten Christiern Nielsen Juels Aarbog', *Kirkehistoriske Samlinger*, 2:5 (1869-1871a), pp. 342-377.

Rørdam, Holger Fr., 'Fra Reformationstiden. Kirkehistorisk Smaabidrag', *Kirkehistoriske Samlinger*, 2:5 (1869-1871b), pp. 773-822.

Rørdam, Holger Fr., 'Efterretninger om de to sidste Abbeder i Øm Kloster', *Kirkehistoriske Samlinger*, 3:3 (1881-1882), pp. 94-111.

Rørdam, Holger Fr., *Historiske Kildeskrifter og Bearbejdelser af dansk Historie især fra det 16. Aarhundrede*, 2:2 (Copenhagen, 1887).

Rørdam, Holger Fr., *Danske Kirkelove samt Udvalg af andre Bestemmelser vedrørende Kirken, Skolen og de fattiges Forsørgelse fra Reformationen indtil Christian V's danske Lov, 1536-1683*, 3. vols. (Copenhagen, 1883-1889).

Seesko, Per, 'De aldrig nedlate domkapitler – Ribe domkapitels lokale forankring, ca. 1536-1660' (unpublished Ph.D. thesis, University of Southern Denmark, 2014).

Seesko, Per, 'The cathedral chapter of Schleswig as a source of inspiration for reform in Odense', in *Schleswig Holstein – contested region(s) through history*, eds. Michael Bregnsbo and Kurt Villads Jensen (Odense, 2016) pp. 243-262.

Sehling, Emil, *Die evangelischen Kirchenordnungen des XVI. Jahrhunderts*, vol. 4 (Leipzig, 1911).

Severinsen, P., 'Sorø Amts Klostersogne og Frigørelsen i 1569', *Aarbog for Historisk Samfund for Sorø Amt* (1928), pp. 34-68.

Sjællands Stifts Landebog 1567, ed. Svend Gissel (Copenhagen, 1956).

Slottved, Eivind, 'Studier over præsternes økonomi under Christian III.', *Historisk Tidsskrift* (Denmark), 12:6 (1973), pp. 465-493.

Terpager, Peder, *Ripæ Cimbricæ seu urbis Ripensis in Cimbria sitæ descriptio ex antiqvis monumentis, bullis, diplomatibus eruta et variis iconibus æri incisis et suis locis insertis illustrata per Petrum Terpager* (Flensborg, 1736).

Thulin, Gabriel, *Utredning rörande patronatsrättigheterna i Skåne, Halland och Bohuslän* (Stockholm, 1901a)

Thulin, Gabriel, *Samling af urkunder rörande patronatsrättigheterna i Skåne, Halland och Bohuslän* (Stockholm, 1901b).

Tolstrup, Flemming, *Det ældste Herlufsholm, 1560-1788* (Copenhagen, 1965).

Troels Troels-Lund, *Dagligt Liv i Norden i det sekstende Aarhundrede*. 5th edn. (Copenhagen, 1929-1931).

Venge, Mikael, 'På sporet af Holme Kloster', *Fynske Årbøger* (1982), pp. 39-64

Vesten, L., 'Annekssogne', *Vendsysselske Aarbøger* 9 (1930-1932), pp. 1-22.

Widding, S., *Danske Messe, Tide- og Psalmesang 1528-73*, 1. vol. (Copenhagen, 1933), 1.

Stones and Bones at Large

Post-Reformation Use of Sepulchral Monuments and Remains from the Danish Monastery Churches

Rasmus Agertoft

When King Frederik II sent off the daily letters regarding the internal affairs of the State on 6 June, 1571, he had ample opportunity to send, too, his thoughts to his father and predecessor as king. It was in the early years of his reign that the Danish Lutheran Reformation had been carried through thirty-five years earlier, thus considerably increasing crown lands by confiscating former church property, and the consequences of these events were tangible for Frederik II on this summer day.

First, the letters in question were dispatched from the new castle of Frederiksborg.[1] The castle, named after the king, was built as a result of what was perhaps the most famous instance of exchange of former monastery property in Denmark, a deal which gave the king the manor of Hillerødsholm in exchange for the former monastery of Skovkloster just outside Næstved. Secondly, the four royal letters from that day dealt with the administration of church property in Odense and Ringsted, where a reorganization of the churches had been initiated and was still taking place as a result of the Reformation.

In Odense, the lion's share of the reorganization had already been completed in the decade following the Reformation year of 1536. A number of monastic institutions, particularly in Odense but also to a smaller extent in other parts of the Diocese of Funen, had been closed down and unified in the foundation of a hospital located in the city's former Greyfriars Monastery.[2]

---

1 The royal letters are summarized in *Kancelliets Brevbøger* (1898), pp. 38-39.
2 On the foundation, see Engelstoft (1861-1890), 5, pp. 1-34. The economic base for the new institution included the properties of the former Dominican monastery in Odense and the former Monastery of the Holy Ghost in Faaborg, cf. also *Danmarks Kirker*, Svendborg Amt, p. 614.

Some years later, a new chapel was established in this new almshouse[3] but, at the same time, the monastery's church was retained. As a matter of fact, its status was enhanced, since it was elevated to a parish church already in 1539, replacing the existing parish church of St Alban's, which was subsequently demolished.[4]

The maintenance of the Greyfriars Church did not come out of thin air, but was most likely caused by the fact that the church contained several royal tombs. In the decades prior to the Reformation, the devout Catholic and Franciscan supporter Queen Christina, spouse of King John, had established a mausoleum for herself and her family in the church, which had also previously been favoured by Danish royalty.[5] As late as 1559, the church was still used for a royal interment when the deposed King Christian II, son of King John and Queen Christina, was buried there next to his father.[6]

A remarkable parallel to this interment was the burial just a week previously of the deposed king's cousin, the reigning monarch, King Christian III. He had chosen as his resting place the cathedral in the same city, itself a former monastery church, named St Canute's Church after the sainted king Canute the Holy, whose tomb was also in the church. Shortly before his death on 1 January, 1559, Christian III had ordered that the building of the cathedral's tower be finished, using the building materials from the tower of the demolished St Alban's Church.[7] The decision to complete the cathedral tower, thereby making the building more imposing, has been seen in the context of the king's selection of the church for his sepulchre. As opposed both to his Catholic predecessor, the sainted king, and to the royal mausoleum closely affiliated with monasticism in the neighbouring Greyfriars Church, Christian III in St Canute's Church could be appropriately represented as the country's first Lutheran king.[8]

However, the late king did not rest in Odense. Almost twenty years later, in 1578, Christian III's remains were transferred by his son, King Frederik II, from the cathedral of Odense to that of Roskilde. Here, King Christian I, the

---

3   Engelstoft (1861-1890), 5, pp. 27-28; *Danmarks Kirker*, Odense Amt, pp. 1559-1560.

4   *Danmarks Kirker*, Odense Amt, pp. 1730-1732. The use of the name St Alban's continued, however, as shows one of the royal letters mentioned as well as the slightly younger visitation book by the Lutheran Superintendent Jacob Madsen, cf. *Biskop Jacob Madsens visitatsbog 1588-1604* (1995), e.g. p. 51 (12 March, 1591).

5   The royal mausoleum is thoroughly described and analysed in Bøggild Johannsen (2005), pp. 79-105; Bøggild Johannsen (2014a), 2, pp. 172-195; Bøggild Johannsen (2014b), 2, pp. 196-217; *Danmarks Kirker*, Odense Amt, pp. 712-742; *Danmarks Kirker*, Odense Amt, pp. 1825-1830.

6   Bøggild Johannsen (2014c), 2, p. 220.

7   *Danmarks Kirker*, Odense Amt, p. 283; *Danmarks Kirker*, Odense Amt, p. 1732.

8   This and the following is extracted from the penetrating analysis of the symbolism of Christian III's resting places in Johannsen (2014a), 2, pp. 267-295, especially pp. 267-268, p. 275 and pp. 288-290.

first member of the House of Oldenburg on the Danish throne, had already been laid to rest,[9] and the choice of Roskilde Cathedral can be seen as providing a symbolic emphasis on dynastic continuity more relevant to Frederik II than an indication of confessional rupture.

Dynastic continuity also lies behind the second two letters issued by King Frederik II on 6 June, 1571, and this time in a more explicit manner. The letters deal with the church situation in Ringsted, where there was at the time both a parish church, St John's (*Sankt Hans*) and a former monastery church (*Sankt Bendts*). As one of the most important medieval burial churches in Denmark, the former monastery church contained several royal tombs.[10] However, after the dissolution of the monastery, the church was left unused, while the parish church remained in use placing the monastery church in danger of becoming derelict.[11] Specifically giving as his reason the presence of the royal tombs, Frederik II therefore wanted to secure the former monastery church. In one of the letters, he stated that »since many of our ancestors, kings and queens who have reigned here in Denmark, are interred in Ringsted Monastery Church, then so that their sepulchres may be decently kept, to eternal memory, and that the said monastery church can be built in a better manner and can always be kept in good repair and force, we have given and permitted and now with this our patent letter give and permit that the parishioners in St John's Parish in Ringsted henceforth may and must go to Ringsted Monastery Church and consider it their own parish church, and whose tithe and privilege that was given to the above-mentioned St John's Church is henceforth to be given to Ringsted Monastery Church, and the churchwardens should collect it and direct it to the fabric and the improvement of the church«.[12]

Preoccupation with dynastic continuity did not confine itself to the ecclesiastical realignments of Odense and Ringsted. Rather, the concern for the preservation of the royal tombs in both places forms part of a royal renovation

9   Kruse (2014), 2, pp. 148-157.
10 For an overview of the monastery church as a royal funeral church, see Kryger and Engberg (2014), 1, pp. 252-271.
11 Worsaae (1858), p. 41.
12 Quoted from Worsaae (1858), p. 42 (»efftherthj ther findes mange wore Forfedre, Konninger saa oc Drottninger, som haffue regeritt her vdi Danmarck, att were begraffuit vdj *Ringsted Closters Kircke*, tha paa thett theris Leggersted maa bliffue hederlig holdett, thennom til en evig Ihukommelsse, oc same Closter Kircke saa møggit thessbedre kand bliffue byggitt, oc altid wed god Heffd oc Macht ferdig holdes, haffue wij vndt oc tilladt, oc nu mett thette wort obne Breff vnde oc tillade, att Sogne-Folckitt vdi *Sanctj Hans Sogen* vdj Ringsted her effther mue oc schulle søge til *Ringsted Closters Kircke*, oc then holde for theris rette *Sogne Kircke*, oc hves Tiinde oc Rettighet som gaffs til forskreffne Sancti Hans Kircke, skal her effther giffuis til Ringsted Closters Kircke, oc Kircke-Wergerne thet att skulle vpbere, oc forwende thil Kirckens Bygning oc Forbedring«).

campaign also including royal tombs in the churches and cathedrals of Sorø, Ribe, and Roskilde.[13] What is singular in the cases of Odense and Ringsted, however, is the circumstance that, in all probability, former monastery churches were secured from demolition because of the presence of royal tombs.

The degree to which one could affect the former monastery churches was of course greater if one was endowed with royal power, but the desire to take care of one's dead kin was by no means exclusively royal. This paper aims to describe how the Reformation and the dissolution of the monasteries influenced stones and bones, or the sepulchral monuments and remains, located in the former monastery churches. Through examples from different parts of sixteenth-century Denmark, the paper analyzes the approaches to the remains and the sepulchral monuments of royal, noble and, to a lesser extent, ecclesiastical origin, giving also an overview of the situation in the centuries following the Reformation. The focus of the paper is on late medieval (and thus pre-Reformation) monuments, but since many former monastery churches were still used for burials after the Reformation, post-Reformation monuments are considered as well. Although utilizing material previously published, the attempt to deliver a comprehensive investigation of the topic is new in a Danish context.

Kinship across death I

Although it is difficult to obtain full clarity regarding the exact number of monastery churches demolished in the Reformation century, it is certain that more churches were preserved than were not.[14] Still, an unknown number of sepulchral monuments must have been lost in the process of demolition, since monastery churches made up sought-after burial sites before the Reformation.

This popularity was based on a double interdependency. First, according to Catholic belief, interaction between the living and the dead was possible. After death, most souls were believed to go to Purgatory to be purified for an indefinite period, but different kinds of intercessory actions on the part of the living were believed to be able to shorten the torments or even re-

---

13 On this subject, see the inspiring analysis in Bøggild Johannsen (2013), pp. 254-267.

14 Based on a count of demolition years in Garner (1968). The demolition years are, however, not always given. The count includes present-day Denmark, the Duchy of Schleswig and the provinces of Scania, Halland and Blekinge, but does not include the island of Gotland.

lease the dead souls. These actions included the establishment of altars and masses in favour of oneself and one's family as well as recurrent intercessory prayers commemorating the dead, all of it termed together *memoria*. In return, a group of distinctly holy dead, the saints, were believed to be able to intercede to the benefits of the living before God.[15] In order to put into effect necessary intercession, however, clerical assistance as offered by the monasteries was required. Thus, secondly, both the wealthy and the monasteries profited by the intercession system, or as the British art historian Paul Binski has put it, »Burials of this type were beneficial to all the parties involved: the privileged dead ensured care for their souls, and the clerical and often monastic carers gained substantial financial inducements in return«.[16]

With the Reformation and the dissolution of the monasteries, both types of interdependency ceased. This meant that, in principle, the stones and bones in the monastery churches were now at large. Although the question does not seem to have been adequately investigated in a Danish context, evidence suggests that, before the Reformation, sepulchral monuments were not unusually connected with intercessory masses meant to be celebrated and prayers meant to be said at specific locations. In the former monastery church of St John (*Sankt Hans*) in Odense, for instance, no less than two sepulchral monuments were made for the fifteenth-century benefactress Elsebe Kabel, the first one being a double monument for her and her third husband and the other one being solely her own. To all appearances, both monuments were located in the same chapel built by her second husband, but they were, it has been suggested, placed close to separate altars where specific masses were being celebrated, the second monument possibly closest to the altar particularly favoured by her.[17]

The fact that ties like these, connecting the sepulchral monuments to certain locations in religious ways, were cut with the Reformation, did not mean that the monuments were suddenly dispersed. We lack information about the funeral monuments in many monastery churches, both the ones demolished during the Reformation century and the ones preserved, but judging from the known cases, the relocation activity does not seem to have been very high. Many, if not most, funeral monuments simply stayed where they were.

At any rate, the relocation activity does not seem to have been rooted in confessional differences, let alone religious rage. Thus, it is not uncommon

---

15 On the intercessory system before and after the (German) Reformation, see Koslofsky (2000), pp. 19-39. On the presence of the dead in medieval thought, see Oexle (1983), pp. 19-77.

16 Binski (1996), p. 74.

17 *Danmarks Kirker*, Odense Amt, pp. 1224-1225, pp. 1431-1432, and pp. 1481-1482.

that monuments commemorating clergymen from the pre-Reformation period remained, also in cases where noble ties of kinship cannot explain the veneration. This was the case, for instance, in Ystad, where the sepulchral monument for the guardian Jep Pedersen (died 1490) remained in the former Franciscan monastery church.[18] When the former Cistercian monastery church of Øm was demolished about 1561,[19] the fifteenth-century funeral monument for the twelfth-century Bishop Svend, cofounder of the monastery, was even relocated to the nearby parish church of Rye along with the monument for the monastery's next-to-last abbot, who died in 1554.[20]

As for the relocation of funeral monuments that did take place during the Reformation century, two basic approaches can be discerned. First, pragmatism seems to have been prevalent. Sepulchral slabs made up valuable material both for new sepulchral monuments and other practical purposes, as did bricks and woodwork from the former monastery churches, and the fact that it had previously been used in a Catholic context does not seem to have alarmed anybody. This is illustrated by the case of Ryd Monastery in the Duchy of Schleswig. Since 1564, the parishioners of Munkbrarup had utilized the former Cistercian monastery church, because their parish church had been destroyed by fire. In 1580, however, the monastery church was reportedly unfit for services because of its bad state of repair, so the parishioners applied for permission to either demolish the monastery church and rebuild the parish church using its materials or to restore the monastery church and use that instead. This latter alternative was proposed in spite of racy stories about profligacy in the monastic period, fed by the ostensible find a few years later of children's skulls behind the vaults.[21]

It is difficult to estimate the degree of reuse of sepulchral slabs from monastery churches in the Reformation century. A cautious guess, however, would be that it was not uncommon.[22] One distinct example of reuse is a sepulchral slab dating from 1435 that was originally inscribed to commemorate two priors of the monastery of Næstved, which is presumably the Benedictine Skovkloster to which the town belonged, including its two parish churches.[23]

---

18 Jensen (1951-1953), 2, p. 161 (no. 31); Lindbæk (1914), p. 291.
19 *Danmarks Kirker*, Århus Amt, p. 3780.
20 *Danmarks Kirker*, Århus Amt, p. 3778 and pp. 3758-3760; Jensen (1951-1953), 2, p. 166 (no. 79) and p. 248 (no. 556).
21 Schulze (2006), pp. 40-41. Shortly hereafter, building materials from the monastery where used to erect the castle of Glücksburg. At least some sepulchral monuments seem to have been left at the now flooded monastery ruin, cf. Glawischnig (2006), p. 32.
22 Michelsen (1983) only mentions in passing sepulchral slabs from monastery churches, yet suggests that noble sepulchral monuments were not very commonly reused in the sixteenth century (pp. 181-200, especially pp. 189-190).
23 *Danmarks Kirker*, Præstø Amt, p. 72 and p. 131.

A now lost sepulchral slab in Gunderslev Church near Næstved spans both Catholic and Lutheran times. Originally made to commemorate two monastic priors in Næstved, it was later relocated and reused by a Lutheran vicar. The Priors' black-letter inscription in Latin and the vicar's secondary inscription in Danish were both extant when the stone, at this point broken into three pieces, was drawn by the archive illustrator Søren Abildgaard in 1757. Photo: The National Museum of Denmark.

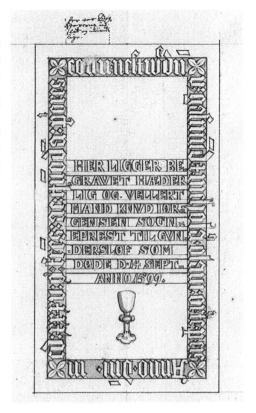

The sepulchral slab thus probably originates from the still existing monastery church of Skovkloster[24] but was later relocated to the nearby Gunderslev Church, which was also owned by the monastery.[25] In this parish church, it was reused as a funeral monument for the Lutheran vicar Knud Jørgensen (died 1599).[26]

Sepulchral monuments were also removed from Næstved's two churches of the mendicant orders, both demolished after the Reformation.[27] Presumably from the Franciscan monastery church, too, a monument was thus relocated to Gunderslev Church. The monument commemorates the noblewom-

24   *Danmarks Kirker*, Sorø Amt, p. 1189. It has been suggested that the original location was instead the Dominican monastery church in Næstved, cf. Birk Hansen (1992), p. 26.
25   *Danmarks Kirker*, Sorø Amt, p. 1011.
26   *Danmarks Kirker*, Sorø Amt, p. 1026.
27   *Danmarks Kirker*, Præstø Amt, pp. 162-163.

an Mette Bydelsbak,[28] the first wife of the influential state official and wealthy landowner Mogens Gøye. When she died in 1512, he was a whole-hearted supporter of Catholicism and was around this time picking out his final resting place in the Franciscan monastery church and bequeathing some money, his best horse and his favourite suit of armour to the monastery.[29]

By choosing the monastery church, he was probably keeping up the family tradition since, at least according to some sources, his paternal grandfather was already buried there and had also donated a chalice to the monastery.[30] A few years later, however, Mogens Gøye changed course and became a pillar of the dawning Lutheranism, receiving for instance the Eucharist in the Lutheran manner a decade before the Reformation's official adoption in Denmark.[31] As the highest ranking state official, he thus turned against the Franciscan monasteries, earning the name of »originator of all evil«, a »very ungodly heretic« and »both the Devil's servant and his warrior« in a contemporary Franciscan description of the expulsion of the Greyfriars from their monasteries.[32]

Mogens Gøye's maternal great-grandfather, too, was buried in a Franciscan monastery church, that of Randers,[33] and on a previous occasion, Mogens Gøye himself had bestowed benefactions upon this monastery.[34] It is therefore hardly a coincidence that the places where Mogens Gøye headed the expulsion included just the monasteries of Næstved and Randers.[35] Prior to the latter expulsion, Mogens Gøye, to whom the Franciscan monastery of Flensborg had previously been handed over by the king, even exchanged this gift for the monastery of Randers,[36] which indicates that, although he acted on behalf of the king, Mogens Gøye was also driven by personal interests.

---

28 Jensen (1951-1953), 2, p. 173 (no. 120); *Danmarks Kirker*, Sorø Amt, p. 1024.
29 Lindbæk (1914), p. 178.
30 According to *Krøniken om Graabrødrenes fordrivelse* (1967), Mogens Gøye's grandfather was buried in the church together with his second wife (p. 70). According to Lindbæk (1914), p. 178, the grandfather in question was either Mogens Gøye's or Mette Bydelsbak's.
31 Heise (1887-1905), 6, p. 78.
32 *Krøniken om Graabrødrenes fordrivelse* (1967), p. 53 (»ophavsmand til alt det onde«) and p. 70 (»Den meget ugudelige kætter« and »både Djævelens tjener og hans stridsmand«).
33 Heise (1887-1905), 6, p. 80, asserts erroneously that the relative buried in Randers was Mogens Gøye's maternal grandfather.
34 Runge Kristoffersen (1972), p. 5.
35 For the account of the expulsion from these monasteries (in the years 1532 and 1530 respectively) seen from a Franciscan angle, see *Krøniken om Graabrødrenes fordrivelse* (1967), pp. 70-72 and pp. 54-56.
36 Lindbæk (1914), p. 118 and p. 136.

Apparently, Mogens Gøye did not deal with the relocation of stones and bones from the monastery churches thus brought under control. It has been suggested that he transferred the remains of Mette Bydelsbak from Næstved to the parish church of Voldum in Jutland,[37] where he was later buried himself and where his sepulchral monument shows full-length portraits of him as well as of both of his wives. A report of an 1899 examination of his tomb, however, does not mention Mette Bydelsbak's remains,[38] and although there is some uncertainty, it is probable that they followed her sepulchral monument when it was relocated from Næstved to Gunderslev.[39] This must have happened before 1552, when Næstved's Franciscan monastery church was demolished.[40] Probably as part of the relocation process, the sepulchral monument was partially altered, replacing an unknown central motif with a full-length (and very posthumous) portrait of her.[41]

Kinship across death II

What happened to Mette Bydelsbak's sepulchral monument illustrates the second basic approach governing the relocations of funeral monuments in the Reformation century, that of kinship. The significance of strong family ties was by no means a new phenomenon in an ecclesiastical context. Catholic masses for dead souls usually included several members of the family, and in many cases, these members were interred in the same chapel, thus constituting a kind of family mausoleum. Contrary to traditional belief, however, the significance of kinship did not weaken at the opening of Early Modern times,[42] but it changed its character, becoming perhaps more deliberately ideological, at least for the nobility.

The relocation of Mette Bydelsbak's funeral monument to Gunderslev Church was probably ordered by her son Eskil Gøye, at that time owner of the neighbouring estate of Gunderslevholm. One reason may very well have been a wish to protect his mother's memory, which was endangered by the demolition of the monument's original setting. This does not, however, rule out other possible explanations. In terms of society, the sixteenth century was

---

37 Lindbæk (1914), p. 179.
38 Berner Schilden Holsten (1943), pp. 48-49.
39 Cf. Løffler (1888), p. 89.
40 *Danmarks Kirker*, Præstø Amt, p. 162.
41 Cf. Jensen (1951-1953), 1, pp. 63-64; Michelsen (1983), p. 182.
42 Cf. Teuscher (2011), pp. 85-87.

a period when the Danish nobility, challenged by military development, had to find new ways of maintaining its foothold. In this process of transformation, looking backwards was a prevalent means of gaining both identity and legitimacy. The argument for maintaining the nobility's traditional position was thus one of precedent, stating that the privileges pertaining to the nobles constituted a time-honoured practise rooted in the authority of certain families.[43] Consequently, the nobles plunged into a preoccupation with genealogy that expressed itself in a variety of respects, including gathering dead family members in family mausoleums.[44]

When Mette Bydelsbak's funeral monument and, possibly, her remains were relocated to Gunderslev, the church already contained the funeral monument of her son-in-law, Anders Ebbesen Galt (died 1529), whose spouse, Mogens Gøye's daughter Pernille Gøye, was supposed to rest by his side as states the inscription on the monument.[45] Later that century, another child of Mogens Gøye, Christoffer Gøye, was also interred in the church as the next owner of Gunderslevholm.[46] Simultaneously, however, members of the Gøye family were buried in two other churches. One of them was Voldum Church near another family estate, that of Clausholm, where several family members found their last resting place. The mausoleum was initiated by the interment of Mogens Gøye's son Axel Gøye, whose sepulchral monument was made six years after his death in 1537,[47] and later, his remains were joined by those of his father, who got his funeral monument in 1560, the same year as his other son Eskil Gøye.[48] All three monuments were commissioned by Mogens Gøye's daughter Birgitte Gøye or her husband, Herluf Trolle.[49] She herself, however, chose the church of Herlufsholm, the former monastery of Skovkloster, as her resting place and was joined there by her sister Pernille Gøye, who had married Herluf Trolle's brother after the death of her former husband Anders Ebbesen Galt.[50]

43   On the transformation process of the Danish nobility in the sixteenth century, see Jespersen (2001), pp. 604-607. On the significance of kinship in this process, see Agertoft (2015a), pp. 102-107; Agertoft (2015b), pp. 68-81.
44   Cf. Nyborg and Bøggild Johannsen (2009), 3, pp. 253-254; Heiberg (1999-2002), 1, p. 400; Bay (2001), p. 293.
45   Jensen (1951-1953), 2, p. 175 (no. 129); *Danmarks Kirker*, Sorø Amt, p. 1024.
46   Jensen (1951-1953), 2, p. 268 (no. 654); *Danmarks Kirker*, Sorø Amt, pp. 1022-1025.
47   Jensen (1951-1953), 2, p. 190 (no. 207); Honnens de Lichtenberg (1989), pp. 201-202 (no. A 13).
48   Jensen (1951-1953), 2, p. 226 (nos. 409-410); Honnens de Lichtenberg (1989), pp. 224-225 (nos. A 35-A 36). Mogens Gøye's daughter Helvig Gøye, too, was later buried in the church together with her husband, cf. Jensen (1951-1953), 1, p. 264, and 2, p. 249 (no. 560).
49   Jensen (1951-1953), 1, pp. 145-146 and pp. 234-237.
50   *Danmarks Kirker*, Sorø Amt, pp. 1148-1155; Honnens de Lichtenberg (1989), pp. 288-291 (no. B 2).

Jørgen Rosenkrantz, who founded the Rosenkrantz mausoleum in Hornslet Church, entertained the greatest veneration for the sepulchral monuments of his family. The veneration, however, did not extend to all sorts of ecclesiastical antiquities. When building the manor of Rosenholm, he used building materials from several churches. In the northern wing plinth, a carved stone, believed to have a past as a Romanesque tombstone or as part of a portal, has been reused. Photo: Rasmus Agertoft

The three more or less completed mausoleums of the Gøye family, perhaps more adequately referred to as kinship centres, were created, by and large, by accumulating family members, who were buried there when they died. In the case of another influential noble family, the Rosenkrantz family, relocations of long dead relatives in establishing family mausoleums were, however, almost the rule. From about the 1560s, three members of the family, two of them brothers and the third one their distant cousin, gathered stones and bones from relatives and mutual ancestors, also from former monastic churches. Each of the three endeavours being fairly well described, a comprehensive account of the complete and, admittedly, highly complex process seems to be lacking. The following outline does not claim to supply the full story but only to suggest how the genealogical preoccupation of the nobles was connected to the dissolution of the monasteries.

In the fifteenth and sixteenth centuries, the Rosenkrantz family was one of the most powerful in the country. Several family members were members of the influential Council of the Realm and three generations in a row, Otte Nielsen (died 1477), Erik Ottesen (died 1503) and Niels Eriksen (died 1516),

The assertion on Pernille Gøye's sepulchral monument that she is interred in »Torbenfeld Church« (»Torpenfelde Kirke«) (*Danmarks Kirker*, Sorø Amt, p. 1152), now known as Frydendal Church, is not confirmed by *Danmarks Kirker*, Holbæk Amt, pp. 864-865. For a comprehensive account of the Gøye funeral monuments, see Berner Schilden Holsten (1943), pp. 45-62.

held the highest ranking state office.[51] All three of them, together with their wives, strongly manifested their religious beliefs. Otte Nielsen built or rebuilt several churches, including the parish church of Tirstrup close to his estate of Bjørnholm, now known as Høgholm, on the peninsula of Djursland.[52] In addition, he was a strong supporter of monasticism. Perhaps most notably, he was considered one of the founders of the Brigittine monastery of Mariager,[53] but there were also strong family affiliations with the Franciscan movement[54] and both his wife (died 1470) and he were interred in a funeral chapel, built by himself, in the Greyfriars monastery church of Randers.[55] His son, Erik Ottesen, took the monastic affiliation even further. In addition to other monastic involvements, one of his sons became a monk in the Brigittine monastery of Maribo, at least one daugther became a nun in Mariager,[56] and he himself divided his estates in 1494 and a few years later withdrew to Mariager, where he and his wife (died 1477) were also buried in a funeral chapel founded by himself already in 1457.[57] Their son, Niels Eriksen (who succeeded to Bjørnholm) was interred in Randers, presumably in the family chapel,[58] whereas another son, Holger Eriksen (who succeeded to another family estate, that of Boller), was buried in Mariager, as was his childless son, likewise named Holger (died 1534).[59] Randers and Mariager, although in fairly close proximity, thus constituted two separate monastic kinship centres for the family.

Both the iconographic and epigraphic elements of Niels Eriksen's sepulchral monument inform us that his wife, Birgitte Thott, as well as their daughter, were supposed to rest beside him in Randers.[60] As for the wife, however, this did not come about. When she died in 1528, the situation concerning the Franciscan monastery was apparently assessed as being too un-

---

51 Porskrog Rasmussen (1991), pp. 40-44; *Danmarks Adels Aarbog* (1988), p. 644. The Rosenkrantz family name was not used until later, the earliest record being from 1524, a few years prior to Frederik I's name reform of 1526, cf. *Danmarks Adels Aarbog* (1988), p. 691; Thiset (1912), p. 225.
52 Porskrog Rasmussen (1991), p. 43; Holsting (1981), pp. 8-10 and pp. 13-15.
53 Rübner Jørgensen (1991), pp. 241-242 and pp. 248-50; cf. Dahlerup (1882), pp. 3-4.
54 Holsting (1981), pp. 15-16.
55 Lindbæk (1914), p. 133; Løffler (1889), p. 36.
56 Holsting (1981), p. 16, mentions two daugthers; Sloth Carlsen (2014), p. 11 and pp. 130-31, mentions one daughter; Rübner Jørgensen (1991), p. 250, mentions one or two daughters and one or two other girls.
57 Rübner Jørgensen (1991), p. 241 and pp. 250-252; Holsting (1981), pp. 16-17.
58 Holsting (1981), p. 18.
59 Dahlerup (1882), p. 70; Rübner Jørgensen (1991), pp. 252-253; *Danmarks Adels Aarbog* (1988), p. 692.
60 Jensen (1951-1953), 2, p. 176 (no. 132); Holsting (1981), p. 42.

stable to realize the plan, and she was buried instead in the parish church of Skjern close to another of the family estates.[61]

If the ostensible anxiety concerned the fate of the actual monastery buildings in Randers, it was unfounded. Following the Reformation, the church was converted into a parish church, and after the death of Mogens Gøye, the monastery was transformed into the royal castle of Dronningborg, inaugurated in 1551.[62] Nevertheless, shortly hereafter the relocations of the Rosenkrantz remains and funeral monuments began. Chr. Axel Jensen, the grand old man of Danish research on sixteenth-century sepulchral monuments, claims that the tombs in the Randers monastery church were no longer safe, owing to the rebuilding of the monastery.[63] He does not go into detail, however, and it seems uncertain whether or not the relocations were initiated by a specific incident, for instance a possible alteration of Otte Nielsen's funeral chapel.[64] In any case, it is known that Jørgen Rosenkrantz, grandson of Holger Eriksen, was appointed fief holder at Dronningborg in 1559,[65] and it seems probable that he used the opportunity to secure the stones and bones for himself and his relatives.

The first transfer from the former Greyfriars Church in Randers took place about 1560 and was headed, presumably, by a distant relative of Jørgen Rosenkrantz, Christoffer Rosenkrantz, who had succeeded to Bjørnholm at the death of his brother Henrik Rosenkrantz in 1537. Christoffer Rosenkrantz was the son of Niels Eriksen, and the remains and funeral monument that he relocated to Tirstrup Church were those of his father, at the same time probably relocating his mother's remains from Skjern Church.[66] It has been suggested that the relocations were done in order to unite the parents' remains.[67] At the same time, however, one cannot rule out the possibility that Christoffer Rosenkrantz, apparently an ordained Catholic priest, somehow wanted to resume the intercessory prayers abolished by the dissolution of the Randers monastery, but this interpretation lies whitin the realm of speculation.[68]

---

61   Holsting (1981), pp. 19-20.

62   Runge Kristoffersen (1972), pp. 5-6.

63   Jensen (1924), p. 143.

64   The particulars concerning Otte Nielsen's funeral chapel seem to be unknown. All that is documented is a chapel to the northern side of the monastery church, next to the chancel, which Anders Jakobsen (Bjørn) and his wife obtained the right to build in 1467, cf. *Repertorium diplomaticum* (1929), pp. 11-12 (23 April, 1467); Lebech (1952), 1, p. 70; Norn (1952), 1, p. 120. Hyldgård (1996), p. 98, suggests that this chapel is identical with one found during excavations as forming part of the church tower.

65   'Jørgen Rosenkrandses til Rosenholm Levnets Løb' (1750), p. 200.

66   It is not certain whether a funeral monument was made for the mother, Birgitte Thott, as planned by Henrik Rosenkrantz, cf. Jensen (1951-1953), 1, pp. 107-109.

67   Holsting (1981), p. 42.

68   On Christoffer Rosenkrantz's Catholic faith, cf. Holsting (1981), pp. 28-34.

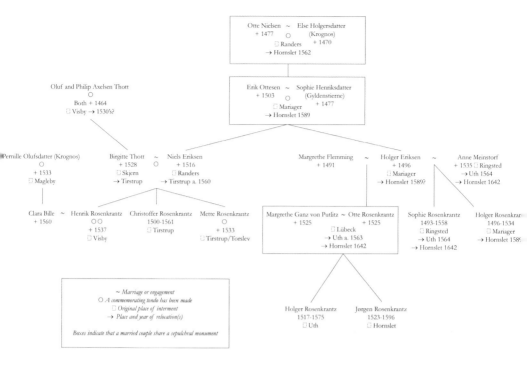

Otte Nielsen ~ Else Holgersdatter
+ 1477 O (Krognos)
☐ Randers + 1470
→ Hornslet 1562

Oluf and Philip Axelsen Thott
O
Both + 1464
☐ Visby → 1530's?

Erik Ottesen ~ Sophie Henriksdatter
+ 1503 O (Gyldenstierne)
☐ Mariager + 1477
→ Hornslet 1589

Pernille Olufsdatter (Krognos)
O
+ 1533
☐ Magleby

Birgitte Thott ~ Niels Eriksen
+ 1528 O + 1516
☐ Skjern ☐ Randers
→ Tirstrup → Tirstrup a. 1560

Margrethe Flemming ~ Holger Eriksen ~ Anne Meinstorf
+ 1491 + 1496 + 1535 ☐ Ringsted
☐ Mariager → Uth 1564
→ Hornslet 1589? → Hornslet 1642

Clara Bille ~ Henrik Rosenkrantz
+ 1560 OO
+ 1537
☐ Visby

Christoffer Rosenkrantz
1500-1561
☐ Tirstrup

Mette Rosenkrantz
O
+ 1533
☐ Tirstrup/Torslev

Margrethe Ganz von Putlitz ~ Otte Rosenkrantz
+ 1525 + 1525
☐ Lübeck
→ Uth a. 1563
→ Hornslet 1642

Sophie Rosenkrantz
1493-1558
☐ Ringsted
→ Uth 1564
→ Hornslet 1642

Holger Rosenkrantz
1496-1534
☐ Mariager
→ Hornslet 1589

Holger Rosenkrantz
1517-1575
☐ Uth

Jørgen Rosenkrantz
1523-1596
☐ Hornslet

~ Marriage or engagement
O A commemorating tondo has been made
☐ Original place of interment
→ Place and year of relocation(s)

Boxes indicate that a married couple share a sepulchral monument

Overview of selected members of the Rosenkrantz family. By Rasmus Agertoft

The idea of Tirstrup Church as a family mausoleum, if only a symbolic one, was not new. In 1535, the then owner of Bjørnholm and fief holder in Gotland, Henrik Rosenkrantz, had commissioned four tondi to be placed in a funeral chapel in Tirstrup, which was probably built at his command.[69] The tondi commemorate three generations of ancestors as well as himself and their inscriptions meticulously mentioning the locations of the ancestors' tombs.[70] One additional tondo commemorates Henrik Rosenkrantz's sister, Mette Rosenkrantz (died 1533), stating that she was buried in the church, that is of Tirstrup.[71] Furthermore, a tondo was executed for Pernille Olufsdat-

---

69 Holsting (1981), p. 39. The four tondi, now at Rosenholm and in the Museum of National History at Frederiksborg, are reproduced in Heiberg (2009), 1, pp. 62-63, although in the wrong order.

70 The presumed mention of the burial place on the tondo commemorating Erik Ottesen is, however, illegible, cf. Honnens de Lichtenberg (1989), p. 310.

71 Holsting (1981), pp. 26-27. Mette Rosenkrantz is depicted and mentioned on the funeral monument for her husband and both of his wives in Torslev Church near Sæby. The inscription on the monument states that she »is buried in Tirstrup« (»liict begrauen tho Tystrup«), cf. Jensen (1951-1953), 2, p. 201 (no. 269).

ter (Krognos) (died 1533), mother of Henrik Rosenkrantz's fiancée, and was placed in Magleby Church on the peninsula of Stevns in Zealand, where she was interred.[72] Not usually enumerated in this context, but undoubtedly to be seen as connected to the other works, are two tondi in St Mary's Church in Visby in Gotland, now the island's cathedral.[73] These two tondi, also from the 1530s, commemorate respectively Henrik Rosenkrantz and his maternal grandfather, Oluf Axelsen Thott, and his half-brother (both died 1464).[74] The religious programme of the six former tondi has been much discussed, arguing for Catholic as well as Lutheran leanings.[75] Here, however, attention should be called only to the tondi as being illustrative of a strong sense of kinship pertaining to the sixteenth-century Danish nobility. The sense of kinship is further emphasized by Henrik Rosenkrantz's supposed relocation in the 1530s of his grandfather's remains and funeral monument from a decaying parish church to St Mary's Church,[76] where Henrik Rosenkrantz was presumably also buried himself.[77]

Christoffer Rosenkrantz died in 1561 and was also interred in Tirstrup.[78] On the occasion of his death, a young Hieronymus Justesen Ranch, later to be known for his school comedies, wrote a collection of poems in Latin and Greek, commemorative of the departed and his parents and with copious puns on the word rose. The poems were published in 1562 and apparently mounted on wooden tablets to be seen in Tirstrup Church, as recorded by the vicar in 1623.[79]

---

72 The six tondi are thoroughly discussed in Honnens de Lichtenberg (1989), pp. 309-318 (nos. C 1-C 3). Cf. also Bergild and Jensen (1991), pp. 103-106; Holsting (1981), pp. 24-28. On the tondo in Magleby Church, cf. Lund (1895-1910), 9, pp. 157-158; *Danmarks Kirker*, Præstø Amt, pp. 379-381.

73 Rare mentions of the connection are made in Ambrosiani (1913), 1, pp. 82-87; Svahnström (1978), p. 51 (note 18); Svahnström (1986), p. 84. *Danmarks Adels Aarbog* (1988), p. 805, is aware of the connection, but only mentions one of the tondi still in Gotland.

74 Svahnström (1986), pp. 86-88. Drawings by Søren Abildgaard of the two tondi are reproduced in Grinder-Hansen (2010), p. 631 (nos. 791-792). According to Grinder-Hansen (2010), p. 631, both tondi are lost. However both still exist.

75 Cf. Holsting (1981), pp. 24-28 (Catholic); Honnens de Lichtenberg (1989), pp. 312-316 (Lutheran).

76 Hamner (1933), p. 48; Svahnström (1978), p. 48. On the funeral monument also commemorating the half-brother, see Hamner (1933), pp. 48-51 (no. 22); Svahnström (1986), pp. 115-116. A drawing of the monument by Søren Abildgaard, now partially destroyed, is reproduced in Grinder-Hansen (2010), p. 632 (no. 795).

77 On Henrik Rosenkrantz's funeral monument, see Hamner (1933), p. 31 (no. 1); Svahnström (1986), p. 110; Jensen (1951-1953), 2, p. 189 (no. 201).

78 Holsting (1981), p. 33. A sepulchral monument for Christoffer Rosenkrantz does not exist.

79 *Præsteindberetninger til Ole Worm* (1970-1974), 2, pp. 22-35. The Danish translation of the vicar's Latin report claims, rather confusingly, that the commemorative poems were »put up« (»opsat«) at the expense of Otte Nielsen. The right translation must be that the church was »constructed« at his expense (p. 35).

In the 1530s, Henrik Rosenkrantz, fief holder in Gotland, commissioned a number of tondi, presumably all produced in the island, to be put up in parish churches in order to commemorate dead relatives and ancestors. One tondo not usually mentioned in this context commemorates himself. It was finished after his death in 1537 and bears resemblance to the majority of the other tondi, but differs in both motif and language. The tondo was placed in St Mary's Church in Visby, where Henrik Rosenkrantz was presumably also interred. Undated drawing, probably from 1753, by Søren Abildgaard. Photo: The National Museum of Denmark

Being unmarried and childless, Bjørnholm left the family with the death of Christoffer Rosenkrantz, and therefore the family mausoleum in Tirstrup Church was not supplemented by new burials. Two other Rosenkrantz family mausoleums, however, were just getting started. About 1560, both Jørgen Rosenkrantz and his brother Holger Rosenkrantz obtained patronage over a parish church, Jørgen Rosenkrantz over Hornslet Church, close to the new family seat of Rosenholm,[80] and Holger Rosenkrantz over Uth Church, close to the old family seat of Boller.[81] Two years later, Jørgen Rosenkrantz, still a fief holder at Dronningborg, headed the relocation of the stone and bones of his great-great-grandparents, Otte Nielsen and his wife, from Randers to Hornslet[82] whereas Holger Rosenkrantz secured himself other mutual relatives for his new funeral chapel in Uth,[83] most notably their parents, who died in Lübeck in 1525 and were buried there.[84] In 1564, Holger Rosenkrantz's parents were joined in Uth by the remains of his father's half-sister, Sophie Rosenkrantz (died 1558), as well as her mother, Anne Meinstorf (died 1535), second wife of his paternal grandfather. They were both originally buried in the former monastery church of Ringsted,[85] which was at this point, as documented by Frederik II's letter from a few years later, in bad repair. Anne Meinstorf's original sepulchral monument from about 1550 was relocated from Ringsted, whereas Holger Rosenkrantz commissioned a new one for his aunt, the inscription stating that her coffin was now placed by the side of her brother and his wife.[86] The date of the relocation of Holger Rosenkrantz's parents being unknown,[87] Sophie Rosenkrantz's funeral monument thus contributes important information as to the order of the relocations.

Holger Rosenkrantz's family mausoleum in Uth was further supplemented by his own interment in 1575 and the interments of his closest family members,[88] but no new relocations took place, possibly because his wife, Karen Gyldenstierne, although rebuilding the church and adorning it with a frescoed genealogical frieze,[89] handed over the initiative to Jørgen Rosenkrantz. After the first 1562 relocation to Hornslet, Jørgen Rosenkrantz's father-in-law was buried there in 1564 and, later the remains of his mother-in-

---

80 Hansen (1909), pp. 49-50.
81 *Danmarks Kirker*, Vejle Amt, p. 1029.
82 Hansen (1909), p. 51; cf. Jensen (1951-1953), 2, pp. 165-166 (no. 74).
83 *Danmarks Kirker*, Vejle Amt, pp. 1032-1036. A daughter of Holger Rosenkrantz (died 1551) was already buried in the church, cf. p. 1074; Jensen (1951-1953), 2, p. 197 (no. 240).
84 *Danmarks Kirker*, Vejle Amt, p. 1032; Jensen (1951-1953), 2, p. 184 (no. 178). Cf. Hansen (1909), p. 38. The funeral monument is not registered in Krüger (1999).
85 According to *Danmarks Kirker*, Vejle Amt, p. 1075, Sophie Rosenkrantz's sepulchral monument states that she both died and was interred in Ringsted. The monument, however, states that she died in the monastery of Næstved and was buried in the monastery of Ringsted, where she was a fief holder, cf. Pontoppidan (1739-1741), 2, p. 144; Jensen (1924), p. 146; Jensen (1951-1953), 2, p. 249 (no. 559).
86 *Danmarks Kirker*, Vejle Amt, p. 1032 and pp. 1074-1075; Jensen (1951-1953), 2, p. 200 (no. 262) and p. 249 (no. 559).
87 The 1563 dating of the relocation in Kjær (1980), p. 89, is probable, albeit unsubstantiated.
88 *Danmarks Kirker*, Vejle Amt, pp. 1065-1072; Honnens de Lichtenberg (1989), pp. 292-294 (no. B 4); Jensen (1951-1953), 2, pp. 259-260 (no. 615).
89 *Danmarks Kirker*, Vejle Amt, pp. 1037-1038 and pp. 1050-1051; Holst (1999-2002), 4, p. 55.

law, who died in 1550 and was buried in the parish church of Fjelstrup near Haderslev, were transferred to Hornslet, too.[90] Jørgen Rosenkrantz's largest extension of the family mausoleum, however, took place in the 1580s. Probably about 1580, he built a funeral chapel for himself,[91] in 1582, his eldest son was interred in the church,[92] and in 1584, he commissioned a sizeable monument with a lengthy inscription commemorating his great-great-grandfather, Otte Nielsen, and mentioning the previous relocation of his remains.[93]

Since the remains of Jørgen Rosenkrantz's father, Otte Holgersen, and grandfather, Holger Eriksen, were at this point lying in Uth and Mariager, respectively, he commissioned an additional monument to Hornslet Church in about 1584. The monument, resembling a sepulchral slab with its full-length portraits, symbolically commemorates both the father and the grandfather in the manner of Henrik Rosenkrantz's tondi and mentions his brother's relocation of the father as well as the then locations of both tombs.[94] Five years later, however, he got the opportunity to supplement the mausoleum with original stones and bones. Following the final dissolution of the monastery of Mariager in 1588[95] and an ostensible fire resulting in the demolition of parts of the building complex,[96] he relocated the remains and the sepulchral monument of his great-grandparents, Erik Ottesen and his wife, to Hornslet, mentioning the relocation on the big epitaph next to the inscription about Otte Nielsen.[97] Possibly, he also relocated a plaque commemorating Henrik Rosenkrantz[98] as well as the remains of his grandfather Holger Eriksen on the same occasion.[99] Søren Hansen, who has contributed important information about the development of the Hornslet family mausoleum, quotes an autograph note by the man carrying out the transfer of Erik Ottesen's funeral monument from Mariager. The note states that in »1589, on the Day of St Mark the Evangelist, 2 horses bolted with me outside Skøring Grove, as I was driving from the monastery of Mariager with 2 sepulchral slabs that are lying in Hornslet Church on both sides of the altar floor«.[100] The first sepul-

---

90 Jensen (1924), pp. 146-147; cf. Jensen (1951-1953), 2, pp. 267-268 (no. 651).
91 Jensen (1924), p. 138.
92 Hansen (1909), pp. 51-52; Jensen (1924), p. 147.
93 Honnens de Lichtenberg (1989), pp. 297-298 (no. B 6).
94 Honnens de Lichtenberg (1989), pp. 253-254 (no. A 60).
95 Dahlerup (1882), p. 26; cf. Holsting (1981), pp. 32-33.
96 Hansen (1909), p. 52.
97 Honnens de Lichtenberg (1989), pp. 297-298 (no. B 6); cf. Dahlerup (1882), p. 71.
98 Jensen (1951-1953), 2, p. 189 (no. 200); cf. Jensen (1924), pp. 145-146.
99 Hansen (1909), p. 52
100 Quoted by Hansen (1909), p. 52 (note 2) (»1589 paa S. Marcuss Ewangelist[s] Dag [...], da bleff 2

Relocations of the remains of relatives from former monastery churches also took place on a smaller scale than the ones carried out by the Rosenkrantz family. When Görvel Fadersdatter Sparre, one of the wealthiest women of her time, received the former Benedictine monastery of Börringe in Scania as a crown fief in 1582, she tore down the monastery church, which contained the remains of her third husband's sister, Else Brahe, who died an infant in the early sixteenth century. Presumably rebuilding the local parish church, Görvel Fadersdatter Sparre also relocated Else Brahe's remains and commissioned a new sepulchral monument witnessing the relocation. Today, the parish church is ruined, only parts of the church tower remain. The sepulchral monument from 1587 is hardly visible. Photo: Rasmus Agertoft

chral slab being the great-grandfather's, Hansen suggests that the second one is an unknown monument commemorating the grandfather.[101] More likely, however, the second sepulchral slab is that of his father's half-brother, Holger Rosenkrantz (died 1534), who, as mentioned above, was also interred in Mariager.[102]

When Jørgen Rosenkrantz died in 1596, he, too, was buried in Hornslet as were his descendants.[103] Following the family's loss of Boller in 1621, in 1642, several Rosenkrantz monuments from Uth Church were even relocated to

---

Heste løbsk medt mig vden for Skiøring Lundt, som ieg kam agind fra Mariager Kloster medt 2 Ligstenn, som ligger y Hornslet Kircky paa beggi Sider aff Alter Gollet«). The note is also partially quoted in Jensen (1924), p. 144, where, however, the question of the second sepulchral slab is not touched upon.

101 Hansen (1909), pp. 52-53.

102 Cf. Jensen (1951-1953), 2, p. 198 (no. 242).

103 Jensen (1951-1953), 2, p. 273 (no. 685); Honnens de Lichtenberg (1989), pp. 260-261 (no. A 65); Jensen (1924), pp. 147-151.

Hornslet,[104] the church henceforth constituting the most comprehensive noble family mausoleum in Denmark.[105]

The constructions of the Rosenkrantz family mausoleums suggest that, although the religiously conditioned presence of the dead came to an end with the Reformation, the dead were present in a different manner after the change in religion. No longer forming part of an ecclesiastical, let alone monastic *memoria* culture, the dead were now placed as part of history by virtue of a secularized memory. In a complex way, thus, they were at one and the same time cut off from the living and very usable to the strengthening of their identity as well as the manifestation of their authority.[106]

The following centuries

In addition to the two basic approaches governing the relocations of stones and bones from former monastery churches in the sixteenth century, the pragmatic approach and that of kinship, a third, if somewhat more curious, approach can be mentioned. Until at least the 1770s, a partially destroyed noble funeral monument from about 1520 was extant among the ruins of the former Augustinian monastery of Æbelholt in Zealand.[107] The monument had survived the secularization of the monastery, the changing of the monastery church into a parish church, the reversal of this alteration, the subsequent decay of the buildings and the reuse of building materials since the 1560s.[108] A possible explanation is delivered in 1808, when the monument was finally lost. A vicar retells the legend of a »very large sepulchral slab – full of runic letters«, possibly identical with the funeral monument in question,[109] which was »of such a beautiful *material* – that *Christian IV* – wanted to place it in the castle building, but the spot – on the flat soil – was so sacred – or desecrated – by evil spirits that the king abandoned his intention«.[110]

---

104 *Danmarks Kirker*, Vejle Amt, p. 1032 and p. 1081 (note 16).

105 Jensen (1924), p. 143. Cf. Pontoppidan (1739-1741), 2, pp. 134-154, for a full record of the Rosenkrantz inscriptions in the church.

106 Cf. Koslofsky (2002), pp. 25-37; Agertoft (2015b), pp. 82-88. On the continuous relationship with the dead after the European Reformations, see Gordon and Marshall (2000), pp. 11-12.

107 The monument is documented by Søren Abildgaard, whose drawing of it is undated but presumably from the 1770s, cf. *Danmarks Kirker*, Frederiksborg Amt, p. 1432. The drawing is reproduced in Grinder-Hansen (2010), p. 225 (no. 1). Cf. Jensen (1951-1953), 2, pp. 179-180 (no. 143).

108 *Danmarks Kirker*, Frederiksborg Amt, pp. 1416-1418.

109 *Danmarks Kirker*, Frederiksborg Amt, p. 1360 and p. 1362 (note 43).

110 *Danske præsters indberetninger* (1998), p. 17 (»en meget stor Liigsten – fuld af Runeskrift – saa skiøn af *Materie* – at *Christ IV* – ville have den anbragt i Slottets Bygning men Stædet – paa den flade Jord

Although the legend probably tells us more about posterity than about King Christian IV, even superstition could not prevent the monastery churches from being demolished and funeral monuments from being destroyed during the following centuries. Superstitious or not, however, authorities sometimes acted in a more attentive manner.

Just prior to the first centenary of the Reformation, one of the largest churches in Denmark, the former monastery church of Antvorskov, was somewhat reduced in size. The monastery had belonged to the Knights Hospitaller, and during the late medieval period, the church had been very popular as a burial ground for several Danish noble families, not least the Bille family. By 1633, however, when it was decided to demolish its three southern chapels, the church had been part of a royal castle for five decades and the place was no longer used frequently by the king.[111]

The actual demolition of the dilapidated chapels was carried out in the following years, showing a remarkable indication of veneration for the past. In the process, it was taken into consideration to preserve the remains of the tombs the funeral monuments from the chapels. Bones and coffins were relocated to new tombs in the remaining church building and, on these tombs, the appropriate funeral monuments were carefully replaced after having been moved on rollers, purchased for the occasion. In addition, bones from 36 tombs in the church proper were dug up and reburied in newly made coffins.

A similar meticulous care does not seem to have existed, however, when the rest of the church was torn down, neither when the three northern chapels disappeared in 1720-21, nor when the remaining building was completely demolished in the late 1770s. The latter removal very thoroughly affected the sepulchral monuments of the church. Although the number of monuments had diminished since the sixteenth century, a considerable number still existed at the time, as documented by the archive illustrator Søren Abildgaard, who visited the church in 1756 and did drawings of the majority of the more than a dozen remaining monuments or monument fragments, most of them medieval.[112] When the church was completely torn down, these were scattered and made use of for practical purposes. For instance, fragments of one of the monuments, depicting the prior Eskil Thomsen (died 1538) next to a skeleton symbolizing death, were later found in the basement of the nearby manor

---

– var saa helligt – eller vanhelliget – af onde Aander at Kongen opgav sit Forsæt«).

111 *Danmarks Kirker*, Sorø Amt, pp. 609-629. On the funeral monuments, see particularly pp. 620-629.

112 Abildgaard's drawings of the funeral monuments are reproduced in Grinder-Hansen (2010), pp. 314-321 (nos. 168-183).

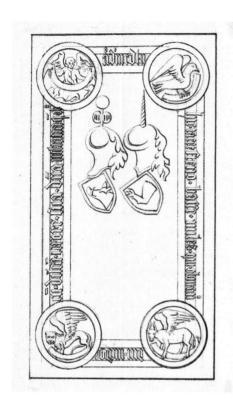

The wealthy nobleman Steen Basse (died 1448) was keen on perpetuating his family name, which was to die out with him, childless and the last man in the family as he was. He made over most of his property to his niece and her husband, ostensibly on condition that one of their sons be named after him. As it turned out, the son, Steen Basse Bille, preferred his own family name. On his funeral monument in the church of Norra Vram in Scania neither the Basse name nor the Basse coat of arms can be found. Steen Basse's own funeral monument in the former monastery church of Antvorskov, which contained both, was presumably destroyed when the church was demolished. Drawing of the latter by Søren Abildgaard, 1756. Photo: The National Museum of Denmark

house of Valbygård, where they were being used as floor tiles.[113] Similarly, a large fragment of the sepulchral slab of the nobleman Tyge Lunge (died 1460) found a new use as a doorstep in the church of Ottestrup, also in the vicinity of Antvorskov.[114]

The monastery of Antvorskov was turned into a royal castle quite late after the Reformation, and although King Frederik II died here in 1588 and lay in state in the church's chancel for more than a month,[115] the imposing church was never used for royal interment. Even if this had been the case, however, royal presence would not necessarily have saved it since not even royal tombs were a safeguard against destruction in the centuries following the Reformation.

---

113 *Danmarks Kirker*, Sorø Amt, p. 621; Jensen (1951-1953), 2, p. 186 (no. 183). The drawing of the monument is reproduced in two different versions, one of them presumably not by Abildgaard, in Grinder-Hansen (2010), pp. 315-316 (nos. 171-172).

114 *Danmarks Kirker*, Sorø Amt, p. 675; Jensen (1951-1953), 2, p. 167 (no. 82).

115 Hiort-Lorenzen (1912), p. 33; Johannsen (2014b), 2, p. 297.

In the early nineteenth century, the decision was made to close down the Greyfriars Church in Odense, which, as mentioned above, contained several royal tombs from the sixteenth century. The church had lost its own parish to St Canute's Church or Odense Cathedral in 1618 and was used only occasionally. In spite of several renovations in the intervening period, by the turn of the century, it was in such disrepair that it was considered unsafe to hold services there.[116]

The remains of the royals must have been considered the most important items to preserve since they were the first to be removed from the church. In December 1804, they were collected in a single coffin and relocated to the cathedral. The sepulchral monuments, royal and non-royal alike, remained in the church and were still there when the antiquarian Rasmus Nyerup visited it in August the following year. »When I arrived there«, he states in an account of his visit, »they were well under way taking up the church floor and taking apart the funeral monuments so it looked like the destruction of Jerusalem. Queen Christina's unequalled altarpiece had still not been touched, as was also the case with the picture in the wall depicting King John with Queen Christina and their son, Prince Francis. It was said that these treasures were to be transferred to St Canute's Church«.[117]

As for the »picture in the wall«, an expression referring to a large limestone monument from the early sixteenth century which formed an important part of the royal mausoleum, it was indeed moved to St Canute's Church, but not until ten years later.[118] A small number of other sepulchral monuments gradually joined in the transfer.[119] The majority of monuments in the former Franciscan monastery church, however, were sold at auction in 1806, and the church was finally torn down more than a decade later.[120] Since the

---

116 *Danmarks Kirker*, Odense Amt, pp. 517-520.

117 Nyerup (1803-1806), 4, p. XLI (»Da jeg kom derhen, var man ifærd med at opbrække Kirkegulvet, og omstyrte Gravmælerne, saa der saae ud som i Jerusalems Forstyrring. Endnu stod Dronning Christines mageløse Altertavle urørt, saavelsom det Billede i Muren der forestiller Kong Hans med Dronningen Christine og Sønnen Prints Frants. Det hed, at disse Kostbarheder skulde hen i St. Knuds-Kirke«).

118 *Danmarks Kirker*, Odense Amt, p. 721.

119 Both pre- and post-Reformation as well as royal, ecclesiastical and noble monuments were relocated to the cathedral, cf. *Danmarks Kirker*, Odense Amt, pp. 731-733 (Prince Francis (died 1511)) and pp. 803-805 (Superintendent Jørgen Jensen Sadolin (died 1559) and Gert Rantzau (died 1580)). The former was relocated before 1813, the latter two presumably in 1816.

120 *Danmarks Kirker*, Odense Amt, pp. 1775-1776. The sale catalogue included funeral monuments linked to the merchant Oluf Bager (died 1602). In 1839, these monuments were transferred to St John's Church in Odense (*Sankt Hans*) after having been placed at a private country house, cf. *Danmarks Kirker*, Odense Amt, pp. 1421-1423 and pp. 1451-1457. The assertion in Jensen (1951-1953), 2, p. 170 (no. 105), that the funeral monument of Anne Nielsdatter (Kabel) in St John's originates from the

Greyfriars Church, just like the monastery church of Antvorskov, had been very much in demand for centuries as a burial church, not least for the nobility, many an important monument was thus smashed by carriage wheels, cut for doorsteps, or even used to enclose a dunghill.[121]

The destruction of the national cultural heritage was not, however, uncontested. Rasmus Nyerup's visit to the Greyfriars Church formed part of a longer journey, and although the neglect he witnessed in Odense was perhaps the most extensive, it was by no means exceptional. In fact, the miserable condition of the relics of the past led Nyerup to a harsh attack on the very same Lutheranism that had been regarded as a deliverance from the popish yoke centuries before (and which, in all fairness, in many ways was preferred by Nyerup). After visiting another badly maintained church, he exclaims, »Here, one had reason to wish for the return of the Catholic cult. During Catholic religious times, our forefathers could well afford to build one house of God next to the other, which their descendants, the infidel Lutherans, are scarcely capable of – tearing down«.[122]

The contemporary historian Christian Molbech was also very critical of the lack of reverence, both when he visited the now ruined Greyfriars Church in 1813 and when, a few years earlier, he went to see the former monastery church of Herlufsholm. Among other sepulchral monuments, he sought out the tomb of a Renaissance colleague, and although the tomb in question does not date from the monastic period, both its condition and Molbech's approach to it are illustrative of the different ways in which the past was conceived of in the early nineteenth century.

»With a deep feeling of gratitude,« Molbech writes, »I came to the tomb of *Arild Huitfeldt*. I had a presentiment that I would find no magnificent mausoleum; still, I expected to see that the remains of the man to whom we owe the fact that Denmark's newer history can be written, had been treated with respect. I found a stone slab with a worn-out inscription; I found a narrow and difficult path down to an open vault with a rotten coffin, which was said to have been Huitfeldt's, and a new one, put together from pine boards, in which his bones, for a long time scandalously misused for wanton boyish games, at long last had been bundled away some years ago. I found here a

---

Greyfriars Church is not confirmed in *Danmarks Kirker*, Odense Amt, pp. 1435-1436.

121 *Danmarks Kirker*, Odense Amt, p. 1778. For an impression of the lost monuments, see Søren Abildgaard's drawings from 1760 in Grinder-Hansen (2010), pp. 386-389 (nos. 315-321).

122 Nyerup (1803-1806), 4, p. XXXI (»Her havde man Føje til at ønske sig den catholske Cultus tilbage. I de catholske religieuse Tider havde vore Fædre Raad til at bygge Guds-hus ved Guds-hus, som deres Efterkommere de vantro Lutheraner neppe have Evne til at – nedbryde«).

picture of the way in which history, too, must often let itself be treated, and left the place discontented with the state in which I saw the tomb of one of my old friends«.[123]

To be sure, critical approaches could result in official intervention. The setting up in 1807 of the Royal Commission for the Keeping of Antiquities, the predecessor of the National Museum of Denmark, was thus largely influenced by Rasmus Nyerup's ideas and critical contributions on the subject.[124] Still, the destruction of former monastery churches did not cease. In Svendborg, for instance, another former Franciscan monastery church was torn down in 1828. With no parish of its own, the church had functioned as a chapel of ease and a burial church for the town's other churches through the centuries after the Reformation. By 1825, however, its interior was considered too dilapidated to use, and in spite of a comparatively greater antiquarian interest by the national authorities at this time, the church was demolished.[125]

Part of the interest concerned the church's tombs and funeral monuments. Tradition had it that the church contained the tomb of Duke Abel, who died in Svendborg in 1279, a son of the Danish King Abel, and it was even claimed that the king himself was also interred in the church. Before the demolition, national authorities therefore demanded that the remains of the duke be relocated to another church, and as in Odense, this was given priority, although evidence was found that the remains in question could not belong to him.[126] A suggestion was also made to save the funeral monuments of the church. Nevertheless, six cartloads of unspecified sepulchral stones were carried away on the first day of the demolition, and presumably, only two medieval funeral monuments were transferred to the local Church of Our Lady.[127]

---

123 Molbech (1811), p. 322 (»Med dyb Taknemmeligheds Følelse søgte jeg *Arild Hvitfelds* Grav. Det anede mig, at jeg ikke vilde finde noget prægtigt Mausoleum; dog ventede jeg at see, at man med Ærbødighed havde behandlet den Mands Levninger, som vi skylde, at Danmarks nyere Historie kan skrives. Jeg fandt en Ligsteen, med en forslidt Indskrift; jeg fandt en snever og besværlig Nedgang til en aaben Kielder, hvor der stod en forraadnet Kiste, som man sagde havde været Hvidtfelds, og en ny, sammenslagen af Fyrrebræder, i hvilken man omsider for nogle Aar siden havde giemt hans Been, der længe forargeligen misbrugtes til kaade Drengelege. Jeg fandt her et Billede paa, hvorledes ogsaa Historien tidt maa lade sig behandle, og forlod Stedet, ilde tilfreds med den Tilstand, hvori jeg saae en af mine gamle Venners Grav«). On Huitfeldt's tomb and funeral monument, see also *Danmarks Kirker*, Sorø Amt, pp. 1154-1155.

124 Cf. Kjær (2010), pp. 99-118. Nyerup's interest in the monuments from the Greyfriars Church in Odense is also attested in Nyerup (1808), pp. 87-98 and pp. 101-109.

125 *Danmarks Kirker*, Svendborg Amt, pp. 512-519.

126 *Danmarks Kirker*, Svendborg Amt, pp. 570-571.

127 *Danmarks Kirker*, Svendborg Amt, pp. 574-576; cf. pp. 371-372. Drawings by Søren Abildgaard of the two funeral monuments are reproduced in Grinder-Hansen (2010), p. 409 (nos. 359-360).

A similar procedure took place when yet another Greyfriars church, that of Viborg, was demolished a few years after the demolition of the Greyfriars church in Svendborg.[128] In connection with later demolitions of former monastic churches, however, the most important still remaining medieval sepulchral monuments seem to have been saved. This was the case, for example, when the former Dominican monastery church of Holbæk was torn down in 1869[129] and four funeral monuments dating from the fifteenth and sixteenth centuries were kept, one of them expressly not sold off because of its relation to the town's history.[130]

Taken as a whole, it is difficult to get a detailed estimate of the number of funeral monuments from former monastery churches lost since the sixteenth century. The centuries following the Reformation, however, by no means seem to have been more lenient towards the monuments than was the Reformation century itself. During every age, stones and bones handed down to posterity have been made to serve and suit posterity's owns ends, and not always in the way one would have expected. Thus, for instance, the at times careless disposal of monuments could easily have motives not resting in confessional differences, as shown in the final case of the seventeenth-century Bishop Thomas Kingo's plans for his final resting place.

Some years after Kingo had been appointed bishop of the Diocese of Funen in 1677, he picked out a desirable spot in St Canute's Church in Odense for his future grave. Although the plans were altered later, at the time he proceeded to remove the sepulchral monument already on the spot, partly erasing the inscription on it and turning a blind eye to the destruction of it. One might suppose that the monument so zealously eradicated was commemorative of a religious opponent from the pre-Reformation era, but it was not. It commemorated no other than Jacob Madsen (1538-1606), Kingo's predecessor and one of the first Lutheran superintendents of the diocese.[131]

---

128 Garner (1968), p. 117. Presumably on this occasion, the funeral monument of the guardian Johannes Knudsen (died 1506) was relocated to the city's cathedral, cf. Jensen (1951-1953), 2, p. 171 (no. 110). A drawing by Søren Abildgaard is reproduced in Grinder-Hansen (2010), p. 467 (no. 469).

129 *Danmarks Kirker*, Holbæk Amt, p. 2820.

130 *Danmarks Kirker*, Holbæk Amt, p. 2893 and pp. 2915-2918. Drawings by Søren Abildgaard are reproduced in Grinder-Hansen (2010), pp. 262-264 (nos. 76-79).

131 Bøggild Johannsen and Johannsen (2001), p. 89.

Bibliography

Agertoft, Rasmus, 'Lad våbenerne tale: Vindinge Kirkes våbenskjolde som symbolsk kommunikation', *Nyborg – før & nu* 2014 (2015a), pp. 102-125.

Agertoft, Rasmus, 'Resten er historie: 1500-tallets adelige gravsten som biografi', *Historiske biografier: Personalhistorisk Tidsskrift* 2015 (2015b), pp. 63-91.

Ambrosiani, Sune, 'Minnessköldarna från Fogdö kyrka', in *Utställningen af äldre kyrklig konst i Strängnäs 1910*, eds. S. Curman, J. Roosval, and C. R. af Ugglas, 2 vols. (Stockholm, 1913), 1, pp. 76-92.

Augustsson, Jan Erik, 'Börringe kyrka', *Ale: Historisk tidskrift för Skåneland* 1 (1976), pp. 30-38.

Barner, Konrad and Heise, A., *Familien Rosenkrantz's Historie*, 2 vols. (Copenhagen, 1874-1882).

Bay, Ole, 'Den danske adel og kirken efter reformationen (1536-1660)', in *Riget, magten og æren: Den danske adel 1350-1660*, eds. Per Ingesman and Jens Villiam Jensen (Aarhus, 2001), pp. 286-313.

Bergild, Merete and Jensen, Jens, 'Rosenkrantzerne som kunstmæcener', in *Rosenholm*, ed. Frits Nicolaisen (Randers, 1991), pp. 103-130.

Berner Schilden Holsten, H., 'Gravmæler fra den Gøye'ske Familiekreds', in *Smaastudier tilegnet Christian Axel Jensen paa hans 65 Aars Fødselsdag* (Copenhagen, 1943), pp. 45-62.

Binski, Paul, *Medieval Death: Ritual and Representation* (Ithaca, New York, 1996).

Birk Hansen, Palle, 'Gravsten fra Sortebrødrekirken – dele af et spredt inventar', *Liv og Levn* 6 (1992), pp. 25-26.

Bisgaard, Lars, *Tjenesteideal og fromhedsideal: Studier i adelens tænkemåde i dansk senmiddelalder* (Aarhus, 1988).

Biskop Jacob Madsens visitatsbog 1588-1604, eds. Jens Rasmussen and Anne Riising (Odense, 1995).

Bricka, C. F., 'Gjørvel Fadersdatter Sparre', in *Dansk biografisk Lexikon*, ed. C. F. Bricka, 19 vols. (Copenhagen, 1887-1905), 16, pp. 197-198.

Bøggild Johannsen, Birgitte, 'Genealogical Representation in Gendered Perspective: on a Lost Royal Mausoleum from Early Sixteenth-Century Denmark', in *Care for the Here and the Hereafter: Memoria, Art and Ritual in the Middle Ages*, ed. Truus van Bueren (Turnhout, 2005), pp. 79-105.

Bøggild Johannsen, Birgitte, 'Back to the Future: Renovating Royal Funeral Monuments during the Reign of Frederik II, King of Denmark (1559-1588)', in *Monuments and Monumentality Across Medieval and Early Modern Europe*, ed. Michael Penman (Donington, 2013), pp. 254-267.

Bøggild Johannsen, Birgitte, 'Gråbrødre Klosterkirke i Odense', in *Danske Kongegrave*, ed. Karin Kryger, 3 vols. (Copenhagen, 2014a), 2, pp. 172-195.

Bøggild Johannsen, Birgitte, 'Hans og Christine', in *Danske Kongegrave*, ed. Karin Kryger, 3 vols. (Copenhagen, 2014b), 2, pp. 196-217.

Bøggild Johannsen, Birgitte, 'Christian (Christiern) 2. og Elisabeth', in *Danske Kongegrave*, ed. Karin Kryger, 3 vols. (Copenhagen, 2014c), 2, pp. 218-245.

Bøggild Johannsen, Birgitte and Johannsen, Hugo, *Sct. Knuds Kirke: Otte kapitler af Odense Domkirkes historie* (Odense, 2001).

Cinthio, Erik, 'Benediktiner, augustiner och korherrar', in *Skånska kloster*, ed. Erik Cinthio (Lund, 1989), pp. 19-45.

Dahlerup, H., *Mariager Klosters og Bys Historie* (Copenhagen, 1882).

Danmarks Adels Aarbog, 1985-1987, ed. Knud J. V. Jespersen (Copenhagen, 1988).

Danmarks Kirker, Frederiksborg Amt, 2:2 (Copenhagen, 1967).

Danmarks Kirker, Frederiksborg Amt, 2:3 (Copenhagen, 1970).

Danmarks Kirker, Holbæk Amt, 4:2 (Copenhagen, 1982).

Danmarks Kirker, Holbæk Amt, 4:4 (Herning, 1990).

Danmarks Kirker, Sorø Amt, 5:1,1 (Copenhagen, 1936).

Danmarks Kirker, Sorø Amt, 5:1,2 (Copenhagen, 1938).

Danmarks Kirker, Præstø Amt, 6:1 (Copenhagen, 1933-1935).

Danmarks Kirker, Odense Amt, 9:1 (Herning, 1990).

Danmarks Kirker, Odense Amt, 9:2 (Herning, 1990).

Danmarks Kirker, Odense Amt, 9:3 (Herning, 1998-2001).

Danmarks Kirker, Svendborg Amt, 10:1 (Copenhagen, 2010-2013).

Danmarks Kirker, Århus Amt, 16:8 (Herning, 1992-1996).

Danmarks Kirker, Århus Amt, 16:11 (Copenhagen, 2006-2008).

Danmarks Kirker, Vejle Amt, 17:3 (Copenhagen, 2010-2014).

Danske præsters indberetninger til Oldsagskommissionen af 1807: Sjælland, Samsø og Møn, eds. Christian Adamsen and Vivi Jensen (Højbjerg, 1998).

Engelstoft, C. T., 'Odense Hospitals eller Graabrødre Hospitals Historie', in *Samlinger til Fyens Historie og Topographie*, 10 vols. (Odense, 1861-1890), 5, pp. 1-62.

Garner, H. N., *Atlas over danske klostre* (Copenhagen, 1968).

Glawischnig, Rolf, 'Auf der Suche nach dem Glücksburger Rudekloster', *DenkMal!, Zeitschrift für Denkmalpflege in Schleswig-Holstein* (2006), pp. 31-33.

Gordon, Bruce and Marshall, Peter, 'Introduction: placing the dead in late medieval and early modern Europe', in *The Place of the Dead: Death and Remembrance in Late Medieval and Early Modern Europe*, eds. Bruce Gordon and Peter Marshall (Cambridge, 2000), pp. 1-16.

Grinder-Hansen, Poul, *Søren Abildgaard (1718-1791): Fortiden på tegnebrættet* (Copenhagen, 2010).

Hamner, J. W., *Visby Domkyrkas gravstenar* (Stockholm, 1933).

Hansen, S., 'Rosenholms Forhistorie og Oprindelse samt Meddelelser om Familien Rosenkrantz i ældre Tid', in *Fra Randers Amt 3, Aarbog udgivet af Randers Amts historiske Samfund* (Randers, 1909), pp. 5-78.

Heiberg, Steffen, 'Adelen og billedkunsten', in *Svøbt i mår: Dansk Folkevisekultur 1550-1700*, eds. Flemming Lundgreen-Nielsen and Hanne Ruus, 4 vols. (Copenhagen, 1999-2002), 1, pp. 391-410.

Heiberg, Steffen, 'Herskab gennem tiderne', in *Herregården: Menneske – Samfund – Landskab – Bygninger*, 2nd edn., eds. John Erichsen and Mikkel Venborg Pedersen, 4 vols. (Copenhagen, 2009), 1, pp. 37-118.

Heise, A., 'Mogens Gjøe', in *Dansk biografisk Lexikon*, ed. C. F. Bricka, 19 vols. (Copenhagen, 1887-1905), 6, pp. 75-84.

Hiort-Lorenzen, H. R., *Kong Frederik den Andens Begravelse i Roskilde Domkirke den 5. Juni 1588* (Roskilde, 1912).

Holst, Elisabeth, 'Som solen for andre små stjerner er: Karen Gyldenstjerne – en renæssancekvinde', in *Svøbt i mår: Dansk Folkevisekultur 1550-1700*, eds. Flemming Lundgreen-Nielsen and Hanne Ruus, 4 vols. (Copenhagen, 1999-2002), 4, pp. 9-114.

Holsting, Stig, *Tirstrup Kirke og Rosenkrantz'erne på Bjørnholm* (Grenaa, 1981).

Honnens de Lichtenberg, Hanne, *Tro – håb & forfængelighed: Kunstneriske udtryksformer i 1500-tallets Danmark* (Copenhagen, 1989).

Hyldgård, Inger Marie, 'De arkæologiske spor efter Gråbrødre Kloster i Randers', *hikuin* 23 (1996), pp. 95-106.

Jensen, Chr. Axel, 'Hornslet Kirke, Rosenkrantzernes Mausoleum', in *Rosenholm og Rosenkrantzerne*, ed. Palle Rosenkrantz (Copenhagen, 1924), pp. 133-152.

Jensen, Chr. Axel, *Danske adelige Gravsten fra Sengotikens og Renaissancens Tid: Studier over Værksteder og Kunstnere*, 3 vols. (Copenhagen, 1951-1953).

Jespersen, Knud J. V., 'Fra fødselsadel til rangadel: Den danske adel 1600-1800', in *Riget, magten og æren: Den danske adel 1350-1660*, eds. Per Ingesman and Jens Villiam Jensen (Aarhus, 2001), pp. 604-633.

Johannesson, Gösta, 'Från konvent till kronolän', in *Skånska kloster*, ed. Erik Cinthio (Lund, 1989), pp. 151-162.

Johannsen, Hugo: 'Christian 3. og Dorothea', in *Danske Kongegrave*, ed. Karin Kryger, 3 vols. (Copenhagen, 2014a), 2, pp. 267-295.

Johannsen, Hugo, 'Frederik 2. og Sophie', in *Danske Kongegrave*, ed. Karin Kryger, 3 vols. (Copenhagen, 2014b), 2, pp. 296-325.

'Jørgen Rosenkrandses til Rosenholm Levnets Løb, skrevet af ham selv 1590', in *Danske Magazin* 4 (1750), pp. 193-207.

Kancelliets Brevbøger vedrørende Danmarks indre Forhold, 1571-1575, ed. L. Laursen (Copenhagen, 1898).

Kjær, Henry T., *Brikker af Uth Kirke* (Uth, 1980).

Kjær, Ulla, 'Rasmus Nyerup og grundlæggelsen af det danske nationalmuseum', in *I gamle bøger, i oplukte høje: Rasmus Nyerup 1759-1829*, ed. Rasmus Agertoft (Assens, 2010), pp. 99-118.

Koslofsky, Craig M., *The Reformation of the Dead: Death and Ritual in Early Modern Germany 1450-1700* (London, 2000).

Koslofsky, Craig M., 'From Presence to Remembrance: The Transformation of Memory in the German Reformation', in *The Work of Memory: New Directions in the Study of German Society and Culture*, eds. Alon Confino and Peter Fritzsche (Urbana and Chicago, 2002), pp. 25-37.

Krongaard Kristensen, Hans, *Klostre i det middelalderlige Danmark* (Højbjerg, 2013).

Kruse, Anette, 'Helligtrekongers Kapel, Roskilde Domkirke', in *Danske Kongegrave*, ed. Karin Kryger, 3 vols. (Copenhagen, 2014), 2, pp. 148-157.

Kryger, Karin and Engberg, Nils, 'S. Bendt i Ringsted, helgengrav og kongebegravelse', in *Danske Kongegrave*, ed. Karin Kryger, 3 vols. (Copenhagen, 2014), 1, pp. 252-271.

Krüger, Klaus, *Corpus der mittelalterlichen Grabdenkmäler in Lübeck, Schleswig, Holstein und Lauenburg (1100-1600)* (Stuttgart, 1999).

Krøniken om Graabrødrenes fordrivelse fra deres klostre i Danmark, trans. Henning Heilesen (Copenhagen, 1967).

Lebech, Mogens, 'Livet i det middelalderlige Randers', in *Randers købstads historie*, ed. Povl v. Spreckelsen, 2 vols. (Randers, 1952), 1, pp. 63-108.

Lindbæk, Johs., *De danske Fraciskanerklostre* (Copenhagen, 1914).

Lund, E. F. S., *Danske malede Portræter: En beskrivende Katalog*, 10 vols. (Copenhagen, 1895-1910).

Løffler, J. B., 'Flere Gravstene over samme Person', *Aarbøger for nordisk Oldkyndighed og Historie* 2:3 (1888), pp. 87-92.

Løffler, J. B., *Danske Gravstene fra Middelalderen* (Copenhagen, 1889).

Michelsen, Vibeke, 'Genbrug af gravsten', in *Kirkens bygning og brug: Studier tilegnet Elna Møller*, ed. Hugo Johannsen (Copenhagen, 1983), pp. 181-200.

Molbech, Christian, *Ungdomsvandringer i mit Fødeland* (Copenhagen, 1811)

Mollerup, W., 'Steen Bille', in *Dansk biografisk Lexikon*, ed. C. F. Bricka, 19 vols. (Copenhagen, 1887-1905), 2, p. 242.

Norn, Otto, 'Kirker og klostre i middelalderen', in *Randers købstads historie*, ed. Povl v. Spreckelsen, 2 vols. (Randers, 1952), 1, pp. 115-131.

Nyborg, Ebbe and Bøggild Johannsen, Birgitte, 'Herregård og kirke', in *Herregården: Menneske – Samfund – Landskab – Bygninger*, 2nd edn, eds. John Erichsen and Mikkel Venborg Pedersen, 4 vols. (Copenhagen, 2009), 3, pp. 241-290.

Nyerup, Rasmus, 'Min antiqvariske Fodrejse i Fyen i August 1805', in Rasmus Nyerup, *Historisk-statistisk Skildring af Tilstanden i Danmark og Norge i ældre og nyere Tider*, 4 vols. (Copenhagen, 1803-1806), 4 (*Oversyn over Fædernelandets Mindesmærker fra Oldtiden, saaledes som de kan tænkes opstillede i et tilkommende National-Museum*), pp. XVII-LII.

Nyerup, Rasmus, *Rasmus Nyerups og Søren Abildgaards Antiqvariske Rejser i Aarhus Stift i Aarene 1771 og 1807. Med et Tillæg indeholdende en halv Snes odenseske Monumenter i Kobber. Et Anhang til 4de Del af Danmarks histor. politiske Skildring indeholdende Udsigt over danske Oldsager* (Copenhagen, 1808).

Oexle, Otto Gerhard, 'Die Gegenwart der Toten', in *Death in the Middle Ages*, eds. Herman Brae and Werner Verbeke (Leuven, 1983), pp. 19-77.

Pontoppidan, Erik, *Marmora Danica selectiora sive inscriptionum […]*, 2 vols. (Copenhagen, 1739-1741).

Porskrog Rasmussen, Carsten, 'Rosenkrantz-slægten og Rosenholm', in *Rosenholm*, ed. Frits Nicolaisen (Randers, 1991), pp. 39-70.

Præsteindberetninger til Ole Worm, ed. Frank Jørgensen, 2 vols. (Copenhagen, 1970-1974).

Repertorium diplomaticum regni danici medævalis (*Fortegnelse over Danmarks Breve fra Middelalderen*), ed. William Christensen, 2:2 (1467-1478) (Copenhagen, 1929).

Runge Kristoffersen, Hans, 'Dronningborg', *Skalk* 3 (1972), pp. 4-10.

Rübner Jørgensen, Kaare, 'Mariager klosters oprettelse og etablering (til ca. 1490)', in *Birgitta, hendes værk og hendes klostre i Norden*, ed. Tore Nyberg (Odense, 1991), pp. 231-279.

Schulze, Heiko K. L., 'Die Bauten des Rudeklosters in Glücksburg im 13. Jahrhundert: Zur Architektur der Zisterzienser in Norddeutschland', *DenkMal!, Zeitschrift für Denkmalpflege in Schleswig-Holstein* (2006), pp. 40-48.

Sloth Carlsen, Per, *Mariager Kloster: Birgittinerordenen og bygningshistorien* (Mariager, 2014).

Svahnström, Gunnar: 'Riddare med rödgul vimpel. Funderingar kring ett försvunnet konstverk', *Gotländskt arkiv: Meddelanden från Föreningen Gotlands Fornvänner* 50 (1978), pp. 43-52.

Svahnström, Gunnar and Karin, *Visby Domkyrka: Inredning*, Sveriges Kyrkor 202 (Stockholm, 1986).

Teuscher, Simon, 'Verwandtschaft in der Vormoderne: Zur politischen Karriere eines Beziehungskonzepts', in *Die Ahnenprobe in der Vormoderne: Selektion – Initiation – Repräsentation*, eds. Elizabeth Harding and Michael Hecht (Münster, 2011), pp. 85-106.

Thiset, A., 'Bidrag til Navneskikkens Historie', *Historisk Tidsskrift* 8:4 (1912), pp. 221-234.

Worsaae, I. I. A., 'Ringsted Kirke som Gravsted for den gamle danske Kongeslægt', in *Kongegravene i Ringsted Kirke, aabnede, istandsatte og dækkede med nye Mindestene ved hans Majestaet Kong Frederik den Syvende* (Copenhagen, 1858), pp. 1-48.

Reformation and the Monastery Inventory

Structures of Reuse in the Kingdom of Denmark[1]

Svend Clausen

Source material does not allow a complete comparison of all Danish monastery inventory, but patterns can be outlined with particular weight placed on inventory from monastery churches. The book series *Danmarks Kirker* (Denmark's Churches) serves as a starting point as this is the most comprehensive collection of information available.

Such a study has two weaknesses:

1. *Danmarks Kirker* is not complete yet. Monasteries primarily in northern Jutland are still not included.[2] However, these books cover roughly 70% of medieval monastery churches in present-day Denmark, including demolished ones. It should be enough to outline main structures regarding inventory from monastery churches situated in present-day Denmark. These patterns probably also reflect the remaining monastery inventories.

2. The second weakness is far worse: *Danmarks Kirker* covers only present-day Denmark. A large number of monasteries included in the Kingdom of Denmark back then have therefore been left out. Southern Schleswig (present-day Germany) had seven active monasteries at that time.[3] Scania, Halland and Blekinge had 24 and Gotland had four. Nidaros Archbishopric

---

1 Obviously, it is not enough to just identify the structures of reuse in order to attain any complete picture of the fate of the monastery inventories after the Reformation: the Reformation did bring some changes and not everything was reused. Due to limitations of space, however, the vanishing structures regarding the inventory that disappeared must be a story for some other time.
2 Holme Monastery in Funen is currently also not included.
3 I generally leave aside the minority of monasteries that were closed already during the Middle Ages.

had many active monasteries that were also associated with the Kingdom of Denmark at that time. It would perhaps also be wise to study the closing of the several monasteries in Holstein in connection or comparison with the Nordic Reformation.[4]

Both weaknesses can hopefully be compensated for to some extent by other sources of information. It is probably not wide of the mark to assume that situations would be somewhat alike in the area of the present-day kingdom and in other areas of the larger Reformation-era realm.

Ways to reuse inventory

It could be imagined that all inventory from medieval monastery churches was systematically thrown out or destroyed right away when the Reformation came. Such an assumption should be abandoned. Much inventory was actually reused in the new Lutheran churches. This shows in the sheer number of objects preserved. Reuse of inventory typically happened in four primary ways:

a) reuse of inventory within the same church.

b) reuse of inventory objects in other churches in the same city or in the same nearby region of the kingdom.

c) reuse of inventory objects in churches, castles or institutions connected to that monastery church politically, legally and personally (usually through people of noble or royal blood)

d) reuse of inventory objects at royal castles or in public buildings or institutions of city and state.

These four patterns of reuse will be outlined by examples. Categories "c" and "d" most often overlap heavily with "b": When they overlapped these three types of transfer structures typically happened within the same region of the kingdom. Such structures of transfer show a great deal of continuity regarding inventory before and after the Reformation.

---

4   Cf. e.g. Rosenplänter (2009), pp. 422-432; Schröter (2012, I), pp. 477-607.

Continuity of churches: reuse of inventory in the same church building

a) reuse of inventory within the same church.
Many monastery churches were simply converted into Lutheran churches when a monastery was closed; most often they became parish churches, but also sometimes castle or manor churches. Such reuse of the buildings meant that their medieval inventory very often simply stayed and was reused within the same church.

86 monasteries functioned within present-day Denmark at the time of the Reformation (c. 1525). 36 of the 85 monastery churches then used are still standing.[5] 24 of those 36 are included in *Danmarks Kirker*. Only 1 of 24 has no medieval inventory left today: the church of the Monastery of the Holy Ghost in Copenhagen. Its complete loss of medieval inventory was not caused by being cleared out, however, but by the city fire of 1728. The church was heavily damaged and its inventory vanished almost without a trace as accounts are preserved only from 1727 onwards. Even a glance at a few preserved monastery churches not included in *Danmarks Kirker* confirms this: medieval inventory was reused and some is still preserved.[6] The exact same picture would be seen in Copenhagen had it not been for the city fire.

However, preserved medieval inventory far from provides any true picture of the real extent of the reuse. Most often we know of lost medieval objects that definitely were reused for a while: most of these 24 churches had even more objects from former times still in use between the 1600s and the 1800s. The common standard is that Danish churches have at least a little bit of their own medieval inventory preserved, but the real extent of the reuse was undoubtedly far more widespread. Much van-

---

5   The Franciscan nunnery in Odense has been disregarded in those 85; it was very recently founded and had probably not managed to build a church yet, but simply used an existing room in founder queen-dowager Christina's manor. Nor has any inventory from this nunnery been documented: the only known object that could stem from this nunnery is a small late medieval bell. It was presumably used with the mass and later reused in a big clock in the bishop's manor in Odense, but it cannot be proven that it comes from this nunnery, cf. DK, Odense Amt, pp. 1897-1902. As for the 36 preserved monastery churches, it must be noted that two have been heavily rebuilt and are perhaps better described as medieval brickwork included in a later church building. These are the church of the Benedictine nuns in Aalborg (rebuilt 1877) and the church of the Monastery of the Holy Ghost in Copenhagen (rebuilt after the city fire of 1728). It must be noted also that 39 former monastery churches actually still stand in present-day Denmark, but that 3 have been disregarded here. The monasteries at Veng, Vejerslev and Glenstrup had been closed long before and were just parish churches when the Reformation came.

6   Cf. e.g. Ø Monastery Church: Gregersen (1974), pp. 32-45; Gadegaard (1997), p. 13; Barfoed (1891), pp. 16, 26; Mariager: Jørgensen (1981), pp. 25-30; Grinderslev: Støttrup (2001); Børglum: Krongaard (2013), pp. 80-93; Bosjö: Wåhlin (1947), pp. 238-261.

ished medieval inventory was actually not lost at the Reformation, but only gradually later on.

The wooden Christ figure from a Christ's tomb and three medieval altar-pieces still existed in Præstø Antonine Church in the early 1800s.[7] A late medieval chalice with saints' inscriptions, a lead relic capsule found inside the altar and a medieval cabinet for St Samson's relics all still existed in Halsted Benedictine Church in the 1700s. Also four medieval bells vanished between the late 1600s and the early 1900s.[8]

The choir stalls in Tvilum Augustinian Church still existed in 1773 and the medieval altar was probably not pulled down until around 1858. Not only a lion-shaped aquamanile (later used as font ewer) was thrown out during the 1800s, but also a wooden monstrance cabinet with saints pictures from the 1400s.[9]

A late medieval lead box with 16 relic capsules could still be found in Sorø Monastery Church in 1756. A side altar was not removed until 1640, while the likely medieval altar for the high altar was renewed in 1654.[10] The box with relics had been retranslated as late as 1584 and it must have been attached to the side altar that was removed late.[11] This also means that the relic box was kept even long after the side altar had been pulled down. A medieval chalice and a bell from 1510 were still here in the late 1600s despite the fact that both had saints' inscriptions. An animal shaped copper object, probably either an aspersorium or an aquamanile, had just been moved to the library by the early 1800s.[12] A medieval side altarpiece with pictures of St Canute the Holy (*St Canutus Rex*) and other saints was still here in 1756.[13] Even one or two other medieval altarpieces beside this one were perhaps preserved also.[14]

Scrapped from Skovkloster Benedictine Church (present day Herlufsholm Boarding School) between the middle of the 1600s and the early 1800s were e.g. a late medieval altarpiece with two pictures of the Danish kings Christian II and Frederik I, six chairs from the still preserved late medieval choir stalls, a lion-shaped aquamanile that had been placed in the bailiff's chamber, and the late medieval pulpitum with 20 carved wooden figures of

---

7   Cf. DK, Præstø Amt, pp. 34-36 and notes.
8   Cf. DK, Maribo Amt, pp. 600-611 and notes.
9   Cf. DK, Århus Amt, pp. 3412-3429 and notes.
10   Cf. DK, Sorø Amt, p. 61-64 and notes.
11   Cf. DK, Sorø Amt, p. 64.
12   Cf. DK, Sorø Amt, p. 66, 78, 97 and notes (esp. no. 44 p. 107).
13   Cf. DK, Sorø Amt, p. 61-64 and notes.
14   Cf. DK, Sorø Amt, p. 107, note 40.

saints (though some of these saints figures were reused again after the pulpitum had been taken down).[15]

Much monastery inventory from the Church of the Odense Hospitallers was not scrapped until between 1600 and the 1800s: at least the late medieval high altarpiece, seven wooden figures of saints and probably also a portion of other remnants from medieval side altarpieces, a blue chasuble of possible medieval origin, the late medieval pulpitum, one perhaps late medieval pulpit, an unknown number of late medieval chairs and windows with noble coats of arms, one perhaps late medieval bier, a medieval clock and two bells from the 1400s.[16]

This pattern can be clearly recognized also in monastery churches not currently included in *Danmarks Kirker* even without any thorough investigation. At least a gilt silver chalice from the 1400s and a medieval monstrance still existed in Børglum around 1769.[17] At least the choir stalls still existed in the Church of the Holy Ghost in Randers in the 1600s.[18] At least a wooden Mary with child was apparantly not lost from Mariager until after 1750.[19] A bell from 1518 in the church of the Benedictine nuns in Aalborg was recast only in 1861 and a bell from 1493 in Hundslund not until 1906.[20] A brass clock on the altar in Holme featuring a silver figure of Christ with a banner of victory also seems possibly medieval; before being sold later during the same century, it was described in 1825 as very old.[21] Some Virgin Mary motifs as well as a picture of the decapitation of St John could be seen in the great hall in the preserved medieval west wing of Vitskøl Monastery in 1669.[22] A good guess might be that both were leftover pieces of medieval inventory which had been transferred from the recently demolished monastery church to be reused as wall decorations.

This tendency can be witnessed also in demolished churches like the one in Vitskøl. Medieval objects are preserved from the Odense Greyfriars, the Svendborg Greyfriars and the Antvorskov Knights Hospitallers. In all three cases, however, quite a bit more existed in 1600. [23] Odense Greyfriars Church (demolished 1817) did not scrap many monastery objects until between 1600

---

15 Cf. DK, Sorø Amt, pp. 1130-1173 and notes (esp. note 45).
16 Cf. DK, Odense Amt, pp. 1338-1483.
17 Cf. Krongaard Kristensen (2013), pp. 88-89 and notes.
18 Kirk (2003), p. 29.
19 Dahlerup (1882), pp. 78-79.
20 Wulff (1867-1868); Stenholm (1904), pp. 68-71; Torp Andersen (2006), p. 17.
21 Søkilde (1870), p. 186.
22 Cf. Støttrup (2014), pp. 59-60.
23 Cf. DK.

and the early 1800s: an almost undoubtedly medieval altar, a lead relic capsule covered with rock crystal found inside the still preserved chancel arch crucifix, a late medieval pulpitum scrapped and reused in a now lost chancel screen, a presumably late medieval pulpit apparently auctioned off in 1806 and maybe reused for hoarding, 36 late medieval choir stalls with ancestral coats of arms for King John and Queen Christina, a very likely medieval memorial tablet commemorating the royal founding of the friary, an also very likely medieval memorial tablet commemorating the building of the church, two late medieval royal epitaphs over Queen Christina and Prince Francis, a late medieval noble memorial plaque over plague victims and brothers Hans and Erik Huitfeldt and a presumably medieval altarpiece of the Virgin Mary that perhaps also originated from this church.[24] A presumably medieval chair had been sold already in 1576.[25]

These Odense monasteries may have had unsually rich medieval inventories because that city was the centre of the cult of king and saint Canute the Holy (*Canutus Rex*) and thereby connected to the royal family, but the same tendency is seen in general in reused Danish medieval churches. Why would it have been different in all the vanished monastery churches, except if these were all just demolished immediately after the Reformation? The real extent of this kind of reuse can therefore not be determined separately from the fate of the actual church buildings.

It depends primarily on how quickly these vanished churches were demolished or removed from ecclesiastic use. Many vanished monastery churches were not demolished quickly or even just during the 1500s, however. The main part of the 85 monastery churches actually still stood by the year 1600.[26] This very same reuse should also be expected in all vanished monastery churches that really were reused ecclesiastically for a time, but where we simply do not possess the source material that could tell us about the inventory. The medieval altar for the high altar in Vitskøl Monastery Church was probably reused until the church was abandoned. Much of it was still

---

24 The latter altarpiece was actually not used in the Greyfriar's church, but in the hospital church that was established in the eastern wing of the Greyfriar's convent. Obviously, it must have been transferred from somewhere else, however, since that hospital was only established after the Reformation. Having identified these structures of transfer, one of the monastery churches in Odense seems a reasonable guess and the Greyfriars' church would seem a likely possibility. Another possibility could be the monastery church in Faaborg within the same region as they apparently delivered some side altarpieces to this hospital, cf. DK (cf. below), Odense Amt, pp. 1563, 1806-1841.

25 DK, Odense Amt, p. 1812.

26 Due to limitations of space I will not go deeply into that analysis here.

preserved when the church ruins were uncovered in the late 1800s.[27] Most monastery churches that were demolished late were actually reused ecclesiastically for a while before they vanished.[28]

The only big exception from this reuse pattern is probably churches that were never reused ecclesiastically after the Reformation. This goes for monastery churches that were demolished immediately or already within the first few years after the Reformation. That happened with quite a few mendicant churches, but it did not happen for religious or ideological reasons to do with the mendicant orders. It happened because mendicants placed themselves in urban areas. Early demolitions of present-day Danish monastery churches (before 1550) really only happened in cities: especially in quite big cities like Ribe, Aarhus, Odense and Copenhagen. Such cities now simply had too many churches and fewer were needed due to the reorganization of city parishes. Such surplus churches were demolished quickly. It is therefore rarely possible to trace their inventory in great detail, but it should probably be expected that usable parts were just transferred elsewhere and reused there instead. However, the scrapping of medieval objects that were now deemed inappropriate or no longer useful should probably be expected to have happened much quicker and much more thoroughly in churches that were demolished early: not due to any systematic cleansing as such, but objects no longer actually deemed useful were probably rarely among those that anyone bothered transferring elsewhere.

This type of reuse must therefore have been far more extensive than what is visible today in the form of preserved inventory. Not even the amount of lost but traceable medieval inventory provides any true picture of the full extent of this type of reuse. Many of those lost objects that were described as "old" or "very old" as early as the first century after the Reformation were probably also medieval.[29] Very often it is just not possible to prove either their age or origin from preserved sources. It should also be expected that many medieval objects were actually reused for a while, but that they quietly disappeared at some point without any preserved sources making it possible to prove even their existence. Given that much medieval inventory did not disappear until between the 1600s and the 1800s, it should be expected that even more was preserved throughout most of the 1500s.

The change of inventory after the Reformation seems to have been a highly gradual process. An extremely detailed inventory list from Kølstrup parish

---

27 Hjermind and Støttrup (2016), p. 54.
28 Due to limitations of space I will not go deeply into that analysis here.
29 Cf. DK for numerous examples.

church on Funen shows that it still possessed its pretty much complete Catholic inventory around 1550, roughly 15 years after the Reformation. This included side altars as well as the medieval liturgical manuscripts.[30] A detailed list of treasures in Øm Abbey's church in 1554 also seems to echo Catholicism: the order of the vestments mentioned seems to reflect their connection with the different altars.[31]

This might reflect that often surprisingly few inventory changes should be expected in general in Danish churches that were reused whether these were urban churches, village churches or monastery churches, at least for around the first decade or two after the Reformation, maybe even three decades. The new era did not show itself clearly in church interiors in Gotland until the end of the 1500s.[32] It was a highly gradual process in Norway and seemingly also in Iceland.[33] The city church in Assens was not "modernized in accordance with the Lutheran ideals" until "the last decades of the 1500s".[34] In village churches in Zealand it slowly became visible in the second half of the 1500s.[35] A study of churches in southwestern Jutland has shown that the first phase of inventory change after the Reformation came roughly between 1570 and 1590.[36] This seems to be a pattern. A contributory reason for this slow change could be that the economy of local parish churches had often worsened rather than improved after the Reformation and they therefore hesitated in throwing away the often quite rich and still usable late-medieval inventory.[37]

The main exceptions are the valuable parts of the medieval inventory: much of that disappeared quickly.[38] Most other medieval objects that were scrapped after the Reformation probably were not thrown away either suddenly, quickly or violently, but gradually over the years, decades and even centuries thereafter when they were simply deemed obsolete, too worn out or no longer useful. Much was not scrapped until the 1600s onwards, as seen above. By then it was probably not caused so much by the religious change. Most Danish churches received a lot of new inventory in the 1600s and this

---

30   Jensen (1921), p. 170-171. Jensen dates this inventory to shortly before 1551.
31   Cf. DK, Århus Amt, p. 3789.
32   Svahnström (1961), p. 60.
33   Regarding Norway cf. e.g. Blindheim (2004), p. 47; Bugge (1991), p. 85. Regarding the change of medieval inventory on Iceland cf. e.g. Hugason (1991), pp. 130-132.
34   DK, Odense Amt, p. 2612 .
35   Jørgensen (2009), pp. 14-16.
36   Nyborg (1991), pp. 228-241.
37   Bach-Nielsen (2000), p. 22.
38   Cf. below.

made the medieval things seem old and no longer of interest. Locals wanted them replaced by something new and more fashionable.

Danish Lutheran bishops such as Jacob Madsen in Odense had tried to get rid of some of the most inappropriate parts of the medieval inventory already throughout the second half of the 1500s. The late removal of the side altar in Sorø could therefore seem surprising given that the removal only of extra altars was one of the things that bishops were quite attentive of. However, Sorø is not the only example. The altar for a side altar near one of the pillars in the church of the Cistercian nuns in Roskilde was removed only in 1618 to make more room for new pews.[39] The bishops of Jacob Madsen's era only succeeded to a certain extent. Their efforts have been described as an uneven struggle because priests and churchwardens, despite orders, often deemed this old inventory good enough and let it stay anyway or perhaps just set it aside in the attic for a while instead of actually removing it.[40] Several examples of this are found in Denmark during this period.

The preservation of medieval objects as well as this very gradual change of inventory sometimes does reflect an actual disobedience in the removal of highly Catholic inventory. That happened perhaps surprisingly often. Preserved inventory such as the Christ's tomb from Kerteminde city church or the Christ's tomb's figure from Frørup village church really should have been completely lost in the 1580s if the locals had actually obeyed the direct orders of bishop Jacob Madsen when he visitated, but they clearly did not.[41] Disobedience is not the only reason, however. It also reflects an often quite pragmatic way of thinking about inventory.

Medieval objects that were highly Catholic in style could often be woven into a Lutheran context and use. Quite a lot of medieval altarpieces are still preserved in Denmark.[42] It did not necessarily matter that much if a reused altarpiece was filled to the brim with medieval Catholic saints. As long as it could still be admired as a pretty altarpiece. Sometime around 1650 the abbot on the altarpiece from Esrum Monastery Church was simply changed into a Lutheran priest, but apart from that, the main part of this highly Catholic altarpiece remained as it was.[43] It did not necessarily matter that some relics were still placed within the altar if the table itself was still useful. Many reused medieval objects had saints' inscriptions or even saints' pictures, but

---

39   DK, Københavns Amt, p. 83 and notes.
40   Bach-Nielsen (2000), p. 21.
41   JM pp. 82, 131-132; DK, Odense Amt, pp. 1960-1964; Jensen (1921), pp. 186-191.
42   Cf. e.g. Plathe (2010).
43   Jensen (1921), pp. 182-183; Cf. Plathe (1997), pp. 151-161.

that did not necessarily constitute a problem as long as it was a fine and use-ful object that could serve some kind of purpose in the church. Side altarpiec-es and figures of saints could also still be used as decorations and ornaments on the walls, as Peder Palladius had suggested.[44]

Even medieval objects that were quite specifically Catholic in function could still be useful if they could be made to serve some kind of purpose in the Lutheran church. Monstrance cabinets could sometimes be reused or even rebuilt for something else. The large oaken monstrance cabinet in Ø Monestary Church has not only stayed in the church to this day, but has even kept its top.[45] Even the medieval liturgical use of an altarpiece could sometimes be translated into a new Lutheran context. During a visitation in 1588 bishop Jacob Madsen ordered that the medieval altarpiece in Faaborg's former monastery church had to always remain open.[46] It had been opened and closed liturgically in the Middle Ages. Nonetheless, it continued to be opened and closed following a yearly cycle right until 1850.[47] Medieval thu-ribles could be used with the candles. They were therefore often kept and are preserved in quite large numbers in Denmark: they became buckets for the embers with which candles were lighted. A contributory reason here might be that Luther actually allowed thuribles.[48] The Danish reformer and bishop Peder Palladius was well aware, already in 1541, that removal of the side altars would neither be an easy task nor quickly finished. His pragmatic solution made even side altars somewhat useful in Lutheran churches and also their continued presence excusable, at least for a transitional period: until they were finally removed, they were to inspire reflection about the great delusion that we had all been liberated from.[49]

Certain types of medieval objects could quite easily be translated lastingly into a Lutheran context despite the religious change. It explains why a huge amount of medieval crucifixes, baptismal fonts and also many medieval bells are still preserved in Denmark.[50]

Other types of medieval inventory are preserved only rarely or in far fewer numbers, but the reasons were not necessarily that they were Catholic. Only

---

44   PP, p. 37; cf. Jørgensen (2009), pp. 14-16; Achen (1991), pp. 20-21.
45   The actions of bishop Jacob Madsen in Bellinge parish church show that it could be an acceptable solution to just remove the top of a monstrance cabinet, cf. JM p. 36. Even Jacob Madsen's attitude towards monstrance equipment does not seem entirely unambiguous, cf. JM p. 36, 42, 72, 92.
46   JM, p. 230.
47   DK, Odense Amt, pp. 692-693.
48   Jensen (1921), p. 168.
49   PP, p. 38.
50   Cf. below, regarding crucifixes cf. e.g. Blindheim (2004), p. 47.

a quite low percentage of the medieval chalices are probably preserved, but this is because many valuables quickly disappeared in general for obvious reasons. Textile object such as chasubles were used a lot and therefore worn out and renewed at some point. Some of these were actually also quite valuable and therefore confiscated early on with other church treasures. Monstrances seem very rarely preserved, but maybe most of them disappeared already early on as they were often of value. More chalices than monstrances are preserved as chalices were still needed in Lutheran churches and could be reused. Monstrances or reliquaries did not have that advantage.

Some types of medieval inventory seem to have been rarely preserved because of the religious change. Monstrances, reliquaries, liturgical manuscripts and side altars are examples. Such types of inventory were quite specifically Catholic in both style *and* function: It was medieval (i.e. "old"), clearly Catholic, perhaps even valuable and it could not be reused to serve any purpose in the Lutheran church. However, the rare preservation of such objects should probably not be seen just in the narrow light of cleansing of the churches. Presumably, it was caused at least as much simply by the natural consequences of the change to Lutheranism rather than just by strict religious inventory ideology. Monstrances and reliquaries were not only Catholic in style and function, but they were often valuable, too. Treasury did not disappear because of religious ideology as such, but because of its value combined with the fact that the Lutheran way made much of it surplus anyway. Fewer chalices were needed locally as only one altar was used and neither monstrances nor reliquaries were needed at all. Liturgical manuscripts and side altars did not disappear for monetary reasons, but it was probably not only because of ideology either. Presumably, it had much to do also with the fact that such objects were simply removed or thrown out at some point as there simply was not enough local interest in keeping them. Medieval liturgical manuscripts were completely useless and could be reused only for binding. The altar tables for the side altars were not only inappropriate and ideologically dangerous, but they could not serve a purpose any longer. Now they just took up space completely unnecessarily in the church room.

It should be seen as a clear reflection of the extent of reuse that even such a category of rarely preserved objects is not without exceptions. The National Museum of Denmark does in fact own a collection of medieval monstrances from Danish churches. Not just one, but two medieval chasubles from the Aarhus Dominicans from the 1300s and 1400s survive.[51]

---

51 DK, Århus pp. 1146-1154.

Considerations of whether a certain type of object is rarely preserved should also in some cases be seen in light of the presumed number that existed in medieval Denmark. The Christ's tomb from Mariager Monastery Church might seem to represent an extremely rarely preserved type of object. However, it could be argued whether certain types of objects within this rarer category were necessarily that common in Denmark even in the Middle Ages: clear evidence exists of only nine such Christ's tombs in present-day Danish churches from the Middle Ages.[52] There must have been more than those few, but not necessarily any huge amount. It could be questioned whether Christ's tombs were actually standard inventory in Danish churches during the Middle Ages. It does not seem so. Such man-sized Christ's tombs seem to be known first and foremost from Germany.[53] They were used in the symbolic burial of Christ on Good Friday, but it was apparently often just a crucifix or similar that was buried in an improvised or provisional grave.[54] Such solutions likely explain why actual Christ's tombs were perhaps a somewhat rare piece of church inventory in Denmark even in the Middle Ages. Actually, four fully or partially preserved ones from Kerteminde, Mariager, Tornby and Frørup may seem a surprisingly high number in light of this.

Considerable parts of the monastery inventories were actually just reused within the same churches after the Reformation despite the fact that they were Catholic objects. Perhaps even most of the medieval church inventory was not lost quickly at the Reformation, but retained until the inventories were gradually renewed. Many Catholic objects could be acceptable enough and useful also in the new Lutheran context. An interesting example is found in Henne parish church in Jutland where the core of the inventory nowadays is the "almost completely preserved medieval furnishings" including two side altars.[55] The only significant change to those two side altars was that one of the two side altarpieces was reused as decoration elsewhere in the church when the altar it belonged to was reused to place the pulpit on.[56]

Certain types of inventory very specifically Catholic in style and function could eventually become ousted as the inventory was gradually changed to a more clear, new Lutheran look. This process took time, however, and should probably not be seen only in the narrow light of a religious clearing out of inventory no longer acceptable. Presumably, the loss of such medieval inven-

---

52 Plathe (2010), p. 1378; cf. also Grinder-Hansen (2004), p. 237-240.
53 Grinder-Hansen (2004), p. 235.
54 Grinder-Hansen (2004), p. 233-234.
55 DK, Ribe Amt, p. 1245. Quotation translated from Danish by the author.
56 Cf. also Plathe (2015), p. 55.

tory was also due to the fact that locals in the long run simply lost interest in keeping it.

Valuables are the main exception that disappeared quickly, but the loss of medieval inventory in most other cases should probably not be seen as a huge change that took place over a few years around the Reformation. It was part of a long and highly gradual process of renewal of inventory that was far from completed long after the Reformation itself. Many such reused objects were only scrapped much later when they were deemed too old, worn-out or simply replaced by newer things or a new style. The common tendency was to throw out the oldest and most battered parts of the inventory.[57] They could then be auctioned off to private people, sold to other churches, simply thrown out or even partially reused in some way. In the end, this change of inventory was never really carried out one hundred percent because most Danish churches incorporated some medieval and thereby Catholic objects into Lutheran use on a permanent basis.

Continuity and change: reuse of moved inventory

Inventory from monastery churches was often moved to other churches after the Reformation and reused there. Such reuse could involve many different types of objects. It could happen immediately with the actual Reformation, but also long after. Very often inventory was reused within the same monastery church for a while, but then transferred, e.g. when that church was abandoned and demolished. However, it could happen also for reasons other than demolition. Such object transfers did not just happen randomly, however, but according to certain general patterns.

b) reuse of inventory objects in other churches in the same city or in the same nearby region of the kingdom
Antvorskov Monastery provides an interesting example. The prior was ordered by the king in 1568 to keep only the necessary chasubles and sell the rest to surrounding village churches; the prior thus had to choose among the poorest ones and hand them over for free if some churches could not afford to pay for them.[58] This monastery must have had huge parts of its medieval inventory intact at that point: in 1596, 28 years after the mentioned royal

57   Nyborg (1991), p. 248, note 6.
58   KBB, vol. 1566-1570 (21.3.1568); DK, Sorø Amt, p. 617.

order, Antvorskov still owned 26 chasubles and most chasubles had been described as "old" seven years before that. The monastery had been rebuilt by then to become a royal castle in the 1580s.[59] After 1603, 21 chasubles were removed from the inventory. Bailiff Ebbe Munk had been ordered by the king to distribute some church textiles to nearby village churches.[60]

When Esrum Monastery Church in northern Zealand was abandoned and demolished around 1560, the citizens of Elsinore and Copenhagen were given permission to provide their churches with leftover furniture. The timber from Esrum's pulpitum was reused in the main church of Copenhagen.[61] Much inventory ended up in St Olai Church in Elsinore. Officially, it may be just Esrum's high altarpiece from 1496 that was donated to Elsinore,[62] but it was not the only piece of inventory moved here. Also the following items (at least) were: the abbot's chair from the late 1400s, all choir stalls, the chancel screen, the organ and the organ loft, a red chasuble in cloth of gold and a green velvet cope.[63]

The foot of a gilt chalice from the late 1400s in Gjerrild parish church must originate from the church of the Monastery of the Holy Ghost in Randers. The chalice must have been moved to Gjerrild from the still preserved monastery church sometime after the Reformation.[64]

The clipeus from a late 1400s choir cope picturing the crowning of the Virgin Mary probably originates from the secluded island convent of the Greyfriars at the pilgrimage site on Torkø off the coast of Blekinge.[65] It must have been moved to Listerby church where it was placed during the 1600s. The transfer site was far from random as Torkø was placed within that parish.[66] It probably happened after the dissolution of the friary while Blekinge was still Danish.

A pew-end from the first half of the 1400s showing St Gertrud's picture entered a museum in Aarhus through Ludvig Hertel in the 1880s. This pew-end stemmed from a choir stall and in 1649 it had been reused as part of a chair for the parish clerk. As Hertel was parish priest in Sdr. Vissing and Voerladegård village churches, it had most likely been transferred to one of

---

59   DK, Sorø Amt, p. 609-613.
60   KBB, vol. 1603-1608 (16.7.1603); DK, Sorø Amt, pp. 617-18.
61   DK, København By, p. 44 and notes; DK, Frederiksborg Amt, p. 1060 and notes.
62   The decree regarding the high altarpiece is the only one we know of, KBB, vol. 1556-1560, (24.11.1559).
63   DK, Frederiksborg Amt, p. 117-202 1052-60 and notes; Jensen (1921), p. 177-84. I have chosen "cloth of gold" as translation of the old Danish word "gyldenstykke".
64   Bilde (1922), p. 55; Norn (1952), pp. 128-131; Kirk (1994), p. 95; Hyldgaard (2002), p. 31; MS Copenhagen, National Museum of Denmark, Antikvarisk-Topografisk Arkiv: Gjerrild.
65   Anderson (1932), pp. 225, 242-243, 362.
66   Cf. Anderson (1932), p. 242; Håkansson (1997), p. 23.

these two parish churches from Voer Monastery or from the monastery of the Benedictine nuns in Vissing. The latter monastery, also situated nearby, had been dissolved already in the 1400s.[67]

A late medieval pulpit in Furreby parish church may have been made out of random parts of reused wood from a late medieval pulpitum from the Børglum Premonstratensians.[68] Preserved parts of some choir stalls from Mariager Monastery had been transferred to Visborg parish church in 1592.[69] A late medieval altarpiece likely came from the Carmelite friars in Skælskør: after the Reformation it was reused in Boeslunde parish church on Zealand.[70]

The costly medieval bells were often transferred. A bell from 1324 in Avnede parish church must originate from the Halsted Benedictines.[71] It must have been transferred before 1667. This year it was clearly present in Avnede.[72] The two largest bells were moved from the Augustinian church in Vestervig to Viborg Cathedral in 1567.[73] A bell from the Benedictine nunnery at Ring was handed over to the citizens of Horsens in 1564 in exchange for sending the king an equivalent amount of copper.[74] Then it was most likely reused in a parish church in this city.[75] By 1632 Dueholm Hospitaller Church was no longer used ecclesiastically, but Resen parish church only had a small bell and could not afford a new one.[76] A bell from the early 1400s from Dueholm was therefore moved to Resen. In Voerladegård parish church a bell from 1430 had an inscription about Abbot Peter of nearby Voer Monastery. The monastery owned this church and a home-farm here in the Middle Ages. Therefore it may be uncertain whether the bell was cast for the parish church or the monastery itself, but having identified these structures of transfer it may likely be the latter. This bell is not mentioned in the parish church until 1615.[77] Two late medievals bells from the Tvis Cistercians were transferred to Vejrum and Hjerm parish churches respectively.[78] In Hjerm, it was donated by a local noblewoman around 1673 and in Vejrum it is mentioned in 1665.[79]

---

67   DK, Århus Amt, pp. 3830-3831.
68   Krongaard Kristensen (2013), pp. 85-86.
69   Cf. Plathe (2010).
70   DK, Sorø Amt, pp. 759-60.
71   DK, Maribo Amt, pp. 447, 611.
72   Haugner (1924), p. 100.
73   KBB, vol. 1566-1570 (28.6.1567); cf. DK, Thisted Amt, p. 643.
74   Cf. below.
75   Cf. KBB, vol. 1561-1565 (8.12.1564); DK, Århus Amt, pp. 4667-4670 and notes.
76   KBB, vol. 1630-1632 (9.6.1632); cf. DK, Thisted Amt, p. 88.
77   Cf. DK, Århus Amt, pp. 3868-3869 and notes.
78   DK, Ringkøbing Amt, pp. 2065, 2200, 2245-2246.
79   DK, Ringkøbing Amt, pp. 2065, 2245.

As Tvis Monastery Church was demolished in 1698, it may have happened at a time when that church was no longer used very much.

Such transfers often happened by royal decree or permission or through connections, but objects could also be transferred by sale. Odense Greyfriars Church sold a gilt paten and chalice to Særslev parish church within the same district in 1576.[80] Although this particular set was of uncertain age, the mechanism of sale also applies to clearly medieval objects. A high altarpiece from the year 1500 was moved from the Monastery of the Holy Ghost in Randers to Hald parish church in 1765. It was bought on auction by Ditlev Kirketerp who owned the church in Hald.[81]

Sometimes objects were not moved very far at all. Whenever an urban monastery church was demolished or going out of ecclesiastic use, the inventory could often simply be reused in other remaining churches in the same city. Inventory from the Cistercian nuns in Slangerup was handed over to that city's parish church. It probably includes at least the gothic lectern, but maybe also some of the other medieval objects in this parish church.[82] The largest bell from Dueholm monastery just outside the medieval city of Nykøbing Mors was transferred to that city's parish church in 1573, because the monastery church was seldomly used by then.[83] That same city church also received the choir stalls from Dueholm at some point.[84]

Two bells from the Nysted Franciscans were handed over to that city's parish church before the Greyfriars' church was torn down in the 1550s.[85] A bell from the demolished church of the Benedictine nuns in Ribe must have been transferred to the Blackfriars' church in the same city. This one was kept as a parish church, but no preserved source mentions the transfer. However, as this bell from the 1470s is still used here, its transfer is revealed by an inscription that states the name of its original church.[86] Reuse at institutions also sometimes happened within the same city.

Monastery inventory in cities could be logically reused by other remaining ecclesiastical institutions within the same city or even by rural parish churches in the surrounding region. Inventory from rural monasteries could

---

80 DK, Odense Amt, p. 1807 and notes.
81 Brunoe (1924), p. 158; Hansen (1978), pp. 21-28.
82 As e.g. the altarpiece, Plathe (1997), p. 156; cf. DK, Frederiksborg Amt, pp. 2046, 2059, 2132.
83 KBB, vol. 1571-1575 (4.2.1573); DK, Thisted Amt, pp. 76-77, 88.
84 Other chairs were likely removed in the 1800s, cf. DK, Thisted Amt, pp. 74, 88.
85 Exactly which two bells is not obvious, however, as three out of four preserved bells in Nysted are medieval. Two are from the 1400s and one from the early 1300s, but none of the inscriptions reveal it with certainty, cf. DK, Maribo Amt, pp. 195-196, 205 and notes.
86 Cf. *Lunde Domkapitels Gavebøger*, p. 298, DK, Ribe Amt, pp. 772, 840, 843.

likewise be reused by rural or urban churches within the same area. Reuse within the same city or region proves that the simple logic of geography was a primary factor. Why bother transferring inventory at all if the same church could still use it? The answer to this question seems to illustrate why the main part of the inventory was probably just reused within the same churches also after the Reformation. Why spend money and time transfering inventory to some far away part of the kingdom, if some other church nearby had need for it? Reuse within the same area, city or region was probably the most widespread tendency by far, second only to the actual main tendency that most inventory simply stayed in the same church. It also seems to show that the main part of the reused inventory from monastery churches was reused in the same overall function it had had before the Reformation: as church inventory. The fact that it was Catholic inventory from closed monasteries was not really important as long it was still practically useful.

c) reuse of inventory objects in churches, castles or institutions connected to the monastery church politically, legally and personally (usually through people of noble or royal blood)
Even reuse through connections usually happened within the same area. The Hospitaller Church in Odense handed over an alb to Højby after the Reformation as this church was its new parish-of-ease.[87] The aforementioned bell from Halsted did not end up in Avnede just randomly, but probably because Avnede was Halsted's parish-of-ease.[88]

An altarpiece from Voer Benedictine Church was handed over to the vassal at Silkeborg Castle, Erik Axelsen Rosenkrantz, in 1560, so that he could give it to his own parish church at Ejsing.[89] Another late medieval altarpiece came to Engestofte parish church because it was bought by Barbara Wittrup who owned Engestofte Manor at that time.[90] This altarpiece probably stood in the nuns' choir in Maribo's Brigittine monastery before the Reformation.[91]

Some of the medieval inventory from Ring monastery ended up in two parish churches within that region through noble connections. The high altarpiece from 1480 came to Østbirk in 1582 when it was handed over to the nobleman who owned the manor in Østbirk parish.[92] A paten and chalice

---

87 Cf. DK, Odense Amt, note 216 pp. 1517-1518.
88 DK, Maribo Amt, p. 441; DSK 21.9.1591.
89 KBB, vol. 1556-1560 (22.2.1560); cf. DK, Århus Amt, p. 3879.
90 Friis (1872), pp. 63-64.
91 DK, Maribo Amt, pp. 58, 939-942.
92 KBB, vol. 1580-1583 (6.1.1582), DK, Århus Amt, p. 4456, 4666.

from 1519 ended up in Stilling parish church in 1593. This set was probably on loan from the bailiff of Skanderborg Castle as replacement for a paten and chalice that had been stolen from Stilling a while before. The loan only lasted until the parishoners requested to keep them as they could not afford buying new ones.[93] The king must have granted this as Stilling still uses that set. It may have been transferred from Ring to the castle around 1560 as the monastery and its inventory had been assigned to the castle after the Reformation.[94]

Inventory from the Monastery of the Holy Ghost in Faaborg was handed over to the newly established hospital in Odense. All monastery buildings in Faaborg, except for the church, had been assigned to that hospital in 1540.[95] The transfer included the chest with all the monastery's documents and maybe also an unknown number of side altarpieces.[96] Faaborg had actually been ordered to deliver all altarpieces, but eventually got to keep its own high altarpiece.[97]

Such regional transfers by connection often happened through the interaction between king and local nobility. It could also be caused by legal connections, e.g. between churches in the area or because churches were connected through the same local nobleman.

However, more seldomly reuse could also happen across significant distances within the kingdom. The wooden crucifix from Holme Monastery on Funen was not moved to Fjenneslev on Zealand until 1873, however.[98] Even that late it seems unusual. Usually, such cases had a quite specific explanation when it did happen earlier on.

A bell from c. 1490 stems from Øm Monastery in Jutland, but is now used in Hesselager parish church on eastern Funen.[99] That could seem a random place of reuse, but it is no coincidence. Øm Monastery had been dissolved in 1560. It became a royal castle for a short while before its demolition around

---

93 KBB, vol. 1593-1596 (30.12.1593); DK, Århus Amt, pp. 2959-2963, 4666.
94 DK, Århus Amt, p. 2962 and notes.
95 DK, Svendborg Amt, p. 607-608.
96 DK, Svendborg Amt, p. 720 and notes esp. 26, 317. Wooden figures from side altarpieces have been preserved in this church, but it seems unclear whether these stem from altarpieces that were kept in this monastery church or whether these side altarpieces could have been transferred e.g. from Faaborg's old parish church, which was demolished after the Reformation. On the one hand it seems that the monastery church was probably permitted to keep the altarpieces from the parish chuch. On the other hand, as they eventually managed to keep their own high altarpiece, it is not impossible that they could have ended up keeping their own side altarpieces as well, DK, Svendborg Amt, pp. 680, 698-700, 775.
97 DK, Svendborg Amt, p. 680-700 and notes.
98 DK, Sorø Amt, p. 334; Bobé (1909), p. 6.
99 DK, Århus Amt, p. 3789.

The church of the former monastery of the Order of the Holy Ghost in Faaborg. Photo: Per Seesko

1561. At the time Hesselager parish church had been very recently rebuilt by Johan Friis, the owner of nearby Hesselagergård Manor.[100] Johan Friis was none other than the royal chancellor. As the bell was now inventory belonging to a royal inventory, the king had probably given it to Friis when Øm was demolished so that Friis could use it in his new church.[101]

A late medieval gilt chalice in Varberg, Halland, was made by the Antvorskov Hospitallers for their house in Nyborg on Funen. It was probably transferred in the 1560s. At this time, the king needed to finance his ongoing war with Sweden. The king had ordered an inventory to be made in that monastery when the prior of Antvorskov died. He had probably concluded then that such a clearly wealthy monastery had something to spare.[102] Soon after, he seized a chest with gold and silver from Antvorskov.[103] He did take pity on them and sent some items back for their own use including two gilt patens and chalices. He probably also took pity on Varberg, however. Danish troops reconquered Varberg Castle from the Swedish enemy the following year, in

---

100 JM, p. 178.
101 Cf. Garner (1969), pp. 36, 48-51, 53.
102 Cf. below.
103 Cf. KBB, vol. 1566-1570 (31.12.1567, 28.2.1568, 21.3.1568).

1569. Halland was probably the Danish region most heavily marked by the war.[104] It seems that the king chose to donate this chalice from his recently acquired Antvorskov treasure to Varberg. He may have given it to the new bailiff of Varberg Castle, Anders Bing, who is remembered for his donations to that city's church.[105]

Connections that explained such reuse across great distances could be war, noblemen, the king or it could be the simple fact that the kingdom only had one university. Reuse at a state institution situated in the capital necessitated that those objects were transferred to Copenhagen. In general, however, this seemingly included only very specific types of objects. Books and manuscripts had to be shipped to Copenhagen to be further examined for inclusion in the university library. Otherwise, objects were mostly sent to the capital in connection with the royal confiscations of valuables that happened especially during the early part of the Reformation period. Such things were reused, too, but very rarely for anything but their material value, which means that they were remelted. Treasures were not normally sent back as in the case of Antvorskov. Some of the confiscated bells were sent back, however, either because churches swopped in order to get better bells or simply because the amount of ore collected during the first bell tax ended up exceeding the capacity of the foundry and some local churches were therefore allowed to buy them back.[106] In this respect, the bell tax indicates that these too should be seen simply as valuables at least at the time of that tax.

Most often, however, inventory tended to disappear altogether whenever it was not reused locally or regionally. This, too, should probably be seen as a question of geography. Why bother spending money and time transfering an object to a completely different part of the kingdom, if that particular object was not deemed sufficiently useful to be reused by any locals? It is probably with very good reason that so few examples of reuse across great distances can be found. The Varberg chalice and the Hesselager bell both represent the exception rather than any general tendency. Objects did not usually end up in a completely different part of the kingdom. They were reused locally or regionally until they were scrapped, destroyed in some other way, e.g. as part of a confiscation, or eventually became of so little local interest that they were simply sold off or given away, after which they most often disappear from our view entirely.

It is also worth noticing that the transfers of the Varberg chalice and the Hesselager bell both happened only because of royal interference. This un-

---

104 Cf. KBB vol. 1561-1565 (27.11.1563, 20.10.1565); vol. 1566-1570 (29.11.1570).
105 Cf. Bennett (1979), pp. 81-83; Grandt-Nielsen (1983), pp. 20-22; cf. also DK, Svendborg Amt, p. 828.
106 Grinder-Hansen (1986), pp. 213-220.

derlines how those two transfers across distances must be seen as result of special circumstances. It seems that reuse across great distances must have happened only very rarely and primarily in special cases through royal involvement. Since he represented the whole kingdom, the king was the one mediating factor who could make the long road short, practical and realistic between transfer sites far away from one another. There may be a great distance between Øm and Hesselager, but the personal and political bond between King Frederik II and chancellor Johan Friis was very close and therefore made the long road short.

War transfers might be a possible hidden factor. The extent of this is very hard to trace, however, but it does not appear to be a clear or dominant tendency. However, the best example of war transfer of monastery inventory in Denmark should be mentioned here, even though it concerns books and not church inventory as such. No other Danish example is as illustrative regarding monastery war transfers: two books from the Greyfriars' convent in Nya Lödöse, Sweden, suddenly ended up close by on the other side of the border with the Carmelite friars in Varberg, Denmark, after Danish troops had plundered Nya Lödöse during the war in 1507.[107] They were probably taken as booty and given to the local friars instead. It should not be forgotten that the chalice in Varberg was a kind of war transfer, too, just not as actual booty, but as royal property in the form of confiscated valuables. However, it was still a transfer to a faraway site that probably only happened because of the special circumstances of war.

d) reuse of inventory objects at royal castles or at public buildings or institutions of city and state

Monastery objects could also be transferred to public institutions. It was seemingly often official urban buildings that received some inventory from closed monasteries in the same city, e.g. as charity to the local hospital for use in the hospital chapel. A royal decree from 1570 commanded that a lot of inventory from the Hospitallers in Horsens had to be delivered to the new hospital in the same city: as it was old and much of it quite spoiled the king had donated it to the poor.[108] A late medieval bell was probably reused in the chapel of Aarhus Hospital. That hospital was established in 1541 in the wings of the Blackfriars' convent.[109] Obviously, the bell must have originated from somewhere else. Likely candidates could be the demolished Carmelite church or the still preserved Blackfriars' church in the same city.

---

107 Montell (1969), pp. 131-134; Bennett (1979), pp. 31-32.
108 KBB, vol. 1566-1570 (9.4.1570); DK, Århus Amt, p. 6063, 6139.
109 Cf. DK, Århus Amt, pp. 1188, 1308-1311, p. 1352.

When the king ordered the Franciscans to leave their friary in Elsinore in 1538, they were to keep only their clothes and provisions, but leave all inventory behind. It may be because the king had plans of his own regarding the site which was to become royal property and later the site of a castle. Sadly, the friars did not respect that order. When the widow of one of the city's aldermen died, 33 years later, six gilt patens and chalices were found in her estate along with some books. The Greyfriars had hidden it with her. She also had another paten and chalice that had formerly belonged to either the Dominicans or the Carmelites of the city. The king donated all patens and chalices to the hospital that had been established in the former Carmelite monastery and allowed them to be sold so that the proceedings could be used to cover that hospital's needs. One of those sets from the Greyfriars was bought by St Olai Church in the same city.[110]

It could also be hospitals in the same region as with the inventory that was transferred from Faaborg to the hospital in Odense.[111] A gilt chalice from around 1400 was used in the church room in Hillerød Hospital in northern Zealand after the Reformation.[112] Its origin is unknown, but it must have been transferred from somewhere else. It may have come from a closed monastery within the same region as Hillerød had no monastery. The Cistercian nunnery in Slangerup seems a likely guess. Other objects from this monastery church did end up in Hillerød.[113]

Especially bells could sometimes also be reused at the town hall of the same city.

A bell from 1522 in Køge's town hall must have been transferred from the demolished Greyfriars' convent as its picture and inscription represent St Francis.[114] That may have happened in 1575 when the king gave that city a bell if the citizens compensated for it by paying its weight in copper.[115] Another bell was not even moved to the town hall in Vejle until 1780: the eastern wing of the former Blackfriars' convent had simply been kept and functioned as town hall along with the church tower and a bell from the 1400s. When these old buildings were demolished in 1780, new town halls were built twice and the bell was simply moved into the new building both times.[116]

---

110 DK, Frederiksborg Amt, p. 144, 537 and notes.
111 Cf. above.
112 DK, Frederiksborg Amt, pp. 644-649.
113 Cf. below.
114 DK, Københavns Amt, pp. 275-276; Hermansen (1932), p. 232.
115 KBB, vol. 1571-1575 (9.11.1575); Solvang (2011), p. 29.
116 DK, Vejle Amt, pp. 263-265.

Inventory could also be transferred to educational institutions. Those books that had been hidden with the widow in Elsinore were given to the church and the school.[117] The University of Copenhagen also acquired something as a state institution: mostly a lot of books and manuscripts, but once in a while also something else. A preserved register from c. 1536 describes the vestments of the Præstø Antonites including four chasubles. Accounts from the University of Copenhagen in 1554-55 enter expenses because a man had been sent to Præstø regarding some chasubles that the king had donated to them.[118] The university may have needed these chasubles for churches that were under the patronage of the university.[119] Perhaps the university received some inventory also from the Copenhagen Greyfriars after the convent closed, since that whole friary was given to the university for a period of two years for use as a study.[120] Other useful objects from the inventory list of the Greyfriars in 1530 may have been reused in other Copenhagen churches, while most valuables mentioned probably ended their days in royal pockets.

Some monastery inventory was reused at royal castles. Typically, this was inventory of a certain quality. When the prior of Antvorskov received his royal orders in 1568, that same decree also commanded that four or six of the most beautiful chasubles be sent to Frederiksborg Castle in northern Zealand.[121] Two bells in that castle had probably been transferred from the Cistercian church in Slangerup.[122]

The former Franciscan friary in Randers had now become Dronningborg Castle and an altarpiece from the Voer Benedictines was sent here in 1560.[123] Why did the king specify that it must be *not one of the most beautiful ones in the church*, when the Voer altarpiece was chosen earlier the same year for his above-mentioned vassal Erik Axelsen Rosenkrantz?[124] It was probably because the king wanted the best altarpiece from Voer for the queen mother's castle in Randers.

A gilt paten and chalice from 1533 were reused in the royal castle chapel in Copenhagen. This set was seemingly transferred from Antvorskov Monas-

117 DK, Frederiksborg Amt, p. 144, 537 and notes.
118 It must refer to the monastery church as Præstø had no other churches, cf. DK; Madsen (1899-1902), p. 455; Rørdam (1860), p. 255.
119 DK, Præstø Amt, p. 36
120 Cf. DK, København By, p. 20-22 and notes; Norvin (1929), p. 124; Villadsen (1980), p. 130.
121 KBB, vol. 1566-1570 (21.3.1568); DK, Sorø Amt, p. 617.
122 DK, Sorø Amt, p. 617, DK, Fredriksborg Amt, pp. 1686-1687, 1904 note 61, 2134 note 39.
123 KBB, vol. 1556-1560 (5.4.1560); cf. DK, Århus Amt, p. 3879.
124 KBB, vol. 1556-1560 (22.2.1560, 5.4.1560).

tery before 1624.[125] In the end the set was probably just moved from one royal castle to another as Antvorskov itself had become a royal castle in the 1580s.

Reuse at castles or at public buildings or institutions was still very much determined by the logic of geography. Such reuse happened primarily within the same city or nearby region of the kingdom. Sometimes it did not even necessitate any actual transfer of inventory as a few monasteries were simply reused as royal castles. Objects transferred to royal castles could be chosen by quality criteria because the king, as is to be expected, often wanted the best things whenever he needed some inventory. The second-hand inventory could also be used, however, e.g. to show off his generosity in the form of hospital chapel donations. Such things did not necessarily need to be quite as good as the items the king kept for himself. Old unlawfullness could also be redeemed by donating the proceeds from rediscovered valuables to hospital charity. Even public institutions that did not necessarily have their own chapels could make use of inventory from monastery churches. In these cases it would probably often be rather specific types of objects, however. Town halls in cities needed bells and a bell from a closed monastery within the very same city could be a logical solution. Even the University of Copenhagen could make use of old monastery inventory and not just of objects such as books and manuscripts.

The main structures

Some rather clear main structures can be outlined regarding the reuse of medieval monastery inventory in Denmark.

The main structures that can be indetified regarding the change of medieval inventory and regarding reuse within the same church are recognizable and seem to have been common, in Denmark, whether it was former monastery churches or other types of churches. A few differences between what happened in relation to former monastery churches and other types of churches should probably also be expected, however:

1) A potential difference in reuse concerns those three types of transfer structures named "b", "c" and "d". It might be suspected that these three types of transfer structures were a lot more widespread and conspicuous in monastery churches compared to most other types of churches. This is

---

125 Cf. DK, København By, Christiansborg Slotskirke, p. 36; DK, Sorø Amt, pp. 616-617.

because the fate of the inventory cannot be looked upon independently of the fate of the church buildings themselves: the monasteries were closed and thereby underwent a dramatic institutional change. While most other churches simply continued as Lutheran church buildings with much of their same old inventory, a far bigger percentage of the monastery churches went out of ecclesiastic use in the shorter and longer run. The result was that a much bigger percentage of monastery churches were torn down at some point, especially within the big cities. This did not happen for ideological reasons, but for practical ones as they now represented surplus ecclesiastical capacity and the stones and building sites could be better used for something else. When this happened, the useful parts of the inventory would often be transferred to somewhere else. A group of churches which could be similar to the monastery churches in this regard is the extra urban parish churches within the big cities. Such extra urban churches often disappeared just as quickly as many urban monastery churches. Therefore it is often impossible to trace their inventory in great detail. However, examples from Odense and Aarhus show that it should probably be expected that useful parts of the inventory from such extra urban churches were often simply transferred elsewhere in ways similar to the inventory from demolished monastery churches.[126]

2) Another potential difference of inventory reuse also has to do with the demolition of churches. The scrapping of medieval inventory that was no longer acceptable or useful in style and function might very well have been a much quicker and more thorough process in many monastery churches compared to churches that just continued as Lutheran buildings. This goes primarily for all those monastery churches that were torn down rather quickly. While useful objects were transferred elsewhere, objects that were no longer actually deemed useful were probably rarely among those that anyone bothered transferring. Especially quickly demolished urban churches are probably comparable in this regard, whether these were former monastery churches or just medieval urban parish churches.

In the end, much monastery inventory was actually reused. At times objects were transferred to other churches, at times to castles, public buildings or public institutions. The transfer sites were most often situated rather close by, within the same city or nearby region of the kingdom. Objects could also, more seldomly, be transferred to other churches, castles or institutions far-

126 DK, Odense Amt, pp. 1730-1741, 1808, 1824; DK, Århus Amt, 624-625, 1336.

ther away within the kingdom, but transfer sites in those special cases were not random. They can usually be explained through some specific connection.

However, perhaps even the main part of the inventory from the monastery churches was simply reused within the same church in cases where they just continued as Lutheran churches. Danish church inventory in general was not cleared out quickly by the Reformation, but only gradually changed during the many decades and even centuries thereafter. The process could be longlasting. It has actually never been fully concluded as even clearly Catholic objects could be lastingly reused in a Lutheran context.

Manuscript source

MS Copenhagen, National Museum of Denmark, Antikvarisk-Topografisk Arkiv.

Bibliography

Achen, Henrik v., 'Helgenikonografi og moralteologi. Kirkekunstens teologiske funksjoner i senmiddelalderen – en ikonologisk skisse', in *Tro og bilde i Norden i Reformasjonens århundre*, eds. Martin Blindheim, Eva Hohler and Louise Lillie (Oslo, 1991), pp. 9-29.

Anderson, William, *Sveriges Kyrkor. Blekinge*, I (Stockholm, 1932).

Bach-Nielsen, Carsten, 'Kors, krucifix og krumspring. Lidt om 1500-tallets varsomhed med billeder', *Den Iconographiske Post* 3 (2000), pp. 20-30.

Barfoed, Andreas, *Bidrag til Øklosters og Oxholms Historie* (Copenhagen, 1891).

Bennett, Richard and Forsström, Margit, *Sveriges Kyrkor. Kyrkorna i Varberg* (Stockholm, 1979).

Bilde, J., *Gjerrild Sogns Historie* (Herning, 1922).

Blindheim, Martin, 'The Cult of Medieval Wooden Sculptures in Post-Reformation Norway', in *Images of Cult and Devotion. Function and Reception of Christian Images in Medieval and Post-Medieval Europe*, ed. Søren Kaspersen (Copenhagen, 2004), pp. 47-59.

Bobé, Louis, *Brahe-Trolleborg* (Odense, 1909).

Brunoe, Aage, with Ødum, Hilmar, Andersen, R.C. and von Spreckelsen, Povl, *Randers. Historisk-Topografisk Beskrivelse med Biografier* (Copenhagen, 1924).

Bugge, Ragne: 'Ikonoklasmen i Norge og de norske katekisme altertavlene', in *Tro og bilde i Norden i Reformasjonens århundre*, eds. Martin Blindheim, Eva Hohler and Louise Lillie (Oslo, 1991), pp. 85-91 .

Dahlerup, H., *Mariager Klosters og Bys Historie* (Copenhagen, 1882).

DK = *Danmarks Kirker* [various authors, the following series]: Frederiksborg Amt, København By, Københavns Amt, Maribo Amt, Odense Amt, Præstø Amt, Ribe Amt, Ringkøbing Amt, Sorø Amt, Svendborg Amt, Thisted Amt, Tønder Amt, Vejle Amt, Århus Amt (Copenhagen, 1933-).

Dirsztay, Patrick, *Church Furnishings. A NADFAS Guide* (London and Henley, 1978).

DSK = *Frederik II's Enke Dronning Sophies Kopibøger 1588-1617*, published by Svend Thomsen (Copenhagen, 1937).

Friis, F.R., *Laaland og Falster. Topographisk beskrevne af Dr. J.H. Larsen*, vol. 2 (Copenhagen, 1872).

Gadegaard, Niels Hemming, *Nyt og gammelt om Oxholm. Særtryk af Han Herred Bogen* (1997).

Garner Nielsen, Holger, 'Øm Kloster, Cara insula, gennem fire århundreder', *Århus Stifts Årbøger* 62. (1969), pp. 7-65.

Grandt-Nielsen, Finn, *Fynsk Kirkesølv* (Odense, 1983).

Gregersen, Jens Møller, *Oxholm. Tidligere Ø Kloster* (Brovst, 1974).

Grinder-Hansen, Poul, 'Danske Klokkekonfiskationer i 16. og 17. århundrede', *Arv og Eje*, vol. 1983/84 (1986), pp. 213-228.

Grinder-Hansen, Poul, 'Public Devotional Pictures in Late Medieval Denmark', in *Images of Cult and Devotion. Function and Reception of Christian Images in Medieval and Post-Medieval Europe*, ed. Søren Kaspersen (Copenhagen, 2004), pp. 229-243

Hansen, K. Robert, *Hald Kirke* (Hald, 1978).

Haugner, C.C., *Sønder Herreds Historie, Topografi og Statistik*, (Nakskov, 1924).

Hermansen, Victor and Engelstoft, Povl, *Køge Bys Historie* (Copenhagen, 1932).

Hjermind, Jesper and Støttrup Jensen, Hugo, *Vitskøl Kloster. Den middelalderlige bygningshistorie* (Aarhus, 2016).

Hugason, Hjalti, 'Reformationens påverkan på bildframställningar i isländska kyrkor. Presentation av ett planerat forskningsprojekt', in *Tro og bilde i Norden i Reformasjonens århundre*, eds. Martin Blindheim, Eva Hohler and Louise Lillie (Oslo, 1991), pp. 127-134.

Hyldgaard, Inger Marie, Knudsen Jensen, Tina, Schaumburg Sørensen, Hanne, Schmidt-Jensen, Jørgen, Kirk, Palle, *Randers. Fra Handelsplads til Storkommune 1000-1975* (Randers, 2002).

Håkansson, Ninni and Svensson, Susanne, *Torkö. I gråbrödernas spår* (Rönneby, 1997).

Jensen, Christian Axel, 'Katolsk Kirkeinventars skæbne efter Reformationen. Studier og Exempler', *Aarbøger for Nordisk Oldkyndighed og Historie* (1921), pp. 167-204.

Jørgensen, Bjarne, 'Mariager kirkes Inventar', in Anna Holmgaard, Per Sloth Carlsen, Vagn Andreasen and Bjarne Jørgensen, *Mariager kirke og kloster 1481-1981* (Mariager, 1981), pp. 24-31.

Jørgensen, Marie-Louise, *Kirkerummets forvandling. Sjællandske landsbykirkers indretning fra reformationen til slutningen af 1800-tallet* (Copenhagen, 2009)

KBB = *Kancelliets Brevbøger vedrørende Danmarks indre Forhold i Uddrag*, ed. C. F. Bricka et al., 39 vols. (Copenhagen, 1885-2005).

Kirk, Lene, Wessel Hansen, Heino, and Berg Nielsen, Allan, *Randers i Middelalderen. En historiebog* (Randers, 1994).

Kirk, Palle, 'Helligåndshuset i Randers', *Historisk Aarbog fra Randers Amt* (2003), pp. 27-42.

Krongaard Kristensen, Hans, *Børglum Domkirke og Kloster i middelalderen* (Hjørring, 2013).

Lunde Domkapitels Gavebøger. Libri Memoriales Capituli Lundensis, published by C. Weeke 1884-89, (reprint, Copenhagen, 1973).

Madsen, Emil, 'Bidrag til Præstøs Historie', *Fra Arkiv og Museum* 1 (1899-1902), pp. 446-475.

JM = *Mester Jacob Madsens Visitatsbog*, part 1-4, published by A.R. Idum (Odense, 1929).

Montell, E., 'Två Varbergsinkunabler', *Varbergs Museum Årsbok* (1969), pp. 119-138.

Norn, Otto, 'Kirker og klostre i middelalderen', in *Randers købstads historie*, ed. Povl v. Spreckelsen, 2 vols. (Randers, 1952), 1, pp. 115-131.

Norvin, William, *Københavns Universitet i Middelalderen* (Copenhagen, 1929).

Nyborg, Ebbe, 'Lektorieprædikestole og katekismusaltertavler. Om inventarfornyelse i de sydvestjyske kirker i reformationsårhundredet', in *Tro og bilde i Norden i Reformasjonens århundre*, eds. Martin Blindheim, Eva Hohler and Louise Lillie (Oslo, 1991), pp. 223-252.

PP = *Peder Palladius Visitatsbog*, published by Helge Haar (Copenhagen, 1940).

Plathe, Sissel F., 'Altertavlen i Esrum klosterkirke', in *Bogen om Esrum Kloster*, eds. Søren Frandsen, Jens Anker Jørgensen and Chr. Gorm Tortzen (Frederiksborg Amt, 1997), pp. 150-167.

Plathe, Sissel F. and Bruun, Jens, *Danmarks Middelalderlige Altertavler*, vol. 1-2 (Odense, 2010).

Plathe, Sissel F., 'Altrene i Esrum Klosters kirke', in *Esrums Storhed og Fald*, eds. Jens Anker Jørgensen and Bente Thomsen (Esrum, 2015), pp. 55-73.

Rosenplänter, Johannes, *Kloster Preetz und seine Grundherrschaft: Sozialgefüge, Wirtschaftsbeziehungen und religiöser Alltag eines holsteinischen Frauenklosters um 1210-1550*. Quellen und Forschungen zur Geschichte Schleswig-Holsteins, 114 (Neumünster, 2009).

Rørdam, Holger Fr., 'Uddrag af Universitetets Regnskaber for Aarene 1552-57 og 1588-60', *Danske Magazin* 3:6 (1860), pp. 237-276.

Schröter, Martin J., *Kloster Reinfeld. Eine geistliche Institution im Umfeld der Hansestadt Lübeck (1186/90-1582)*, I-II, (Nemünster, 2012).

Solvang, Gunnar, 'Gråbrødremunkene og deres kirkeklokke i Køge', *Årbog for Køge Museum* (2011), pp. 19-38.

Stenholm, J.P., *Aalborg Klosterhistorie. Bidrag til Aalborg Bys Historie i Middelalderen* (Aalborg, 1904).

Støttrup Jensen, Hugo, 'Grinderslev kirke', in Hugo Støttrup Jensen, Poul Brøgger and Maja Lisa Engelhardt, *Grinderslev Kirke* (Gylling/Års, 2001)

Støttrup Jensen, Hugo, 'Vitskøls Klosters vestfløj efter Reformationen', *Årbog for Vesthimmerlands Museum* (2014), pp. 49-78.

Svahnström, Gunnar, 'Reformationstidens kyrkoinventarier. En bildsvit', in *Från Gotlands Dansktid*, eds. Lennart Bohman, Gunnar Fritzell and Gunnar Svahnström (Visby, 1961), pp. 60-70.

Søkilde, Niels Rasmussen, *Gamle og nye Minder om Brahetrolleborg og Omegn* (Copenhagen, 1870).

Torp Andersen, Ole, Dissing, Hans Kristen, Kristensen, Leif and Thomsen, Ove (eds.), *Dronninglund slot. Kongelige, Adelige og Borgerlige* (Dronninglund, 2006).

Villadsen, Villads, 'Universitetets Bygninger. Det Middelalderlige Universitet (1479-1537)' in *Københavns Universitet 1479-1979*, vol. IV (Gods – Bygninger – Biblioteker), eds. Svend Ellehøj and Leif Grane (Copenhagen, 1980), pp. 127-130.

Wulff, D.H., 'Indskrift paa den ældste Klokke fra Frue Kirke i Aalborg', *Kirkehistoriske Samlinger* 2:4 (1867-1868), pp. 740-742.

Wåhlin, Theodor, *Studier i Bosjöklosters kyrkas Historia* (Lund, 1947)

Monastic Books in Sixteenth-Century Denmark

Birgitte Langkilde

Introduction

Books have always been an essential part of monastic life. It is possible to find iconographic evidence for them in medieval Denmark for instance in illuminated medieval manuscripts, or from frescoes and altarpieces in monastic churches.

An example is to be found in the illuminated Næstved Calendar from the thirteenth century (MS Copenhagen, Royal Library, E don var 52 2°) (p. 358). In this illustration from the Næstved Calendar, one finds an almost iconographic expression of the connection between monasticism and written culture. Nearly all the monks carry a closed book in one of their hands. Moreover, some of the monks make a gesture with the other hand as if they are arguing.

The link between monks and books was repeated in the early sixteenth century – about 1510 - on frescos in the church belonging to the monastery of Sæby in Northern Jutland. The fresco painter expressed the link even more distinctly. In the corner of some of the vaulting, there are illustrations of monks with an inscription on a ribbon. All the texts are statements about important and learned Carmelite monks. Some of the monks even hold a book in their hands (p. 359). In the frescoes, the monks carry open books and draw attention to them by pointing to a page. Kaare Rübner Jørgensen has done us the service of identifying the monks and the texts and also showing them as Carmelite authors.[1]

---

1   Rübner Jørgensen (1978); Rübner Jørgensen (2007).

The Næstved Calendar (Næstved 1228-1250) (MS Copenhagen, Royal Library, E don var 52 2°), 5 verso

In discussion of medieval monasteries, there is often reference to their beautiful libraries, fine manuscripts or great quantities of books. From Sweden we have the large monastic library in Vadstena. In 1543, Gustav Vasa removed a great number of books. We do not know how many, but today more than 20,000 texts in 400 volumes from Vadstena have been catalogued and are kept in the University Library of Uppsala.[2] From the Holstein monastery of Cismar, many volumes – 110 manuscripts and 149 incunables – have been transferred to the Royal Library in Copenhagen in 1712. But we do not have such a monastic library from medieval Denmark. What is the reason for the difference between Denmark and Sweden or Holstein, remembering that Holstein was subject to the Danish king? To answer that question, this article will deal with the store of Danish monastic books from a bird's eye view and with focus on the Reformation period and after. What do we know about these books, what remains and what has been lost? In this context, it is im-

---

2   Hedlund (1990), p. 15.

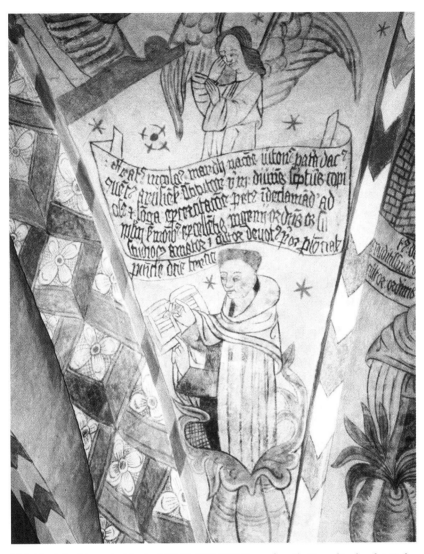

Niels Mord, Danish provincial prior 1462-72; 1486-1503. Fresco from the Carmelite church in Sæby. Photo: www.kalkmalerier.dk

portant to see what happened to the monasteries and their books in the century of the Reformation. Did awareness of the importance of monastic books change during the Reformation and the following years?

The monastic book

Before digging deeper into the subject, it is necessary to make clear how the term monastic book is to be understood in the following and what has been included in the review of them. The point of departure is the physical form: a codex or a fragment from a codex produced as a manuscript or as an incunabulum. In order to be included in the list, some connection to a Danish monastery or convent must be made probable. References to books or titles in other types of source materials will also be included, but often with the comment "lost".

The book in monastic culture

It is one matter to find illustrations which show the close relationship between monks (nuns) and books. Another issue is to understand why the book is so important. A way to characterize the book is in terms of its *form*, as an artefact. Even more important is the fact that the book also carries *content*; it is a subject for *use* for daily reference. Add to this that the book may be said to have a certain *reputation*. However, it is also necessary to understand the connection between books and monastic life in terms of *space or place* for the books in the monasteries. In this context, you should consider place and space as physical as well as a mental phenomena. Below, you will find a brief outline of the interaction between books, monastic buildings and rooms as well as the monastic life and the purpose of the outline is to provide some idea of the use and importance of the different types of books within monastic culture. The various forms of book use correspond with the different categories of books.

The place of books in a monastic environment – The *Sitz im Leben* of the books

Different types of books and different genres of literacy are connected to various places in the monastery. To clarify this very close connection between monastic life and the book, I will provide a review of what might be common knowledge concerning important rooms of the monastery and the particular type of books used in these rooms. This review will consider the most important areas within a prototype of a monastic foundation.

In *the church* – the most important room of a monastic foundation – you would find books on the altar. They may be liturgical books and biblical texts.

In the chancel, oversized liturgical books may be found on the choir lectern for the purpose of the monks' singing. When the books were not in use for mass or other proceedings in the church, they were stored in the room next to the church, *the sacristy*. However, not only liturgical books and different sorts of biblical texts were found there. You could also find different types of calendars in which the benefactors of the monasteries were mentioned. The monks needed always to know the appropriate dates and what special masses and anniversaries were to be celebrated and benefactors to be commemorated.

From the sacristy, one proceeds into the eastern wing of the monastic complex. The room next to the sacristy is the *armarium* or *library*. This is the place for the collection of monastic books, and from here, the monks received books for reading, an activity to which they were obliged. The Rule of Benedict gives some idea of what kind of books were to be found in a monastic library (Reg. Ben. C. 73, 2-5). The Rule also tells us when and where the monks were obliged to read (Reg. Ben. 48, 10ff).

From the library, one can continue to the next room, which might be the *chapter house*. After prime, this room serves for the daily meeting of the monastic community with the abbot or abbess, the monks or nuns and the young novices. At this meeting, a "chapter" from *the Rule* was read as well as the chapter for the day from the *martyrology*. Persons to be commemorated this day were mentioned from the *necrology*. On Sundays, reading of a *sermon* or a *gospel text* may have been added.

This was the religious part of the meeting. After these proceedings, practical issues could be discussed. This might be with reference to the administration of the landed estate of the monastery or other matters of business. For this purpose, the monastery made collections of letters of donations of land. During the late centuries of the Middle Ages these letters and documents could have been transcribed into a *register of real estate / land register*. The chapter house moreover served as the reception room of the monastery and for that reason you might in this room also witness e.g. the signing of agreements. Some documents state that they were drawn up in the chapter house of the monastery in question.

In the southern wing of the monastery, the *refectory* is to be found. It was the dining room for the members of the monastic community. The monks were to take their meals in absolute silence. Simultaneously, "there should always be reading at the common meals" (Reg. Ben. 38.1). A person from the community would act as reader or lector for the whole week. The books used could be Scripture or saints' lives.

All these texts and books were used in common. However, part of the reading in the monasteries was private reading, called *lectio divina*. This may have taken place in the library, if this were possible, or in one of the other rooms within the monastery. Not all private reading, however, was devotional. The monks also had to study. Both the Franciscans and the Dominicans had study programmes. In Lund, they had institutions for education and further studies for the entire province of Dacia.

Until now, focus has been the *use* of the book for many different purposes. But books were not only used. They were also written or composed in some of the Danish monasteries. Usually, this took place in the *scriptoriums* in the big monasteries all over Europe. There is no exact information, however, about special rooms or departments for this purpose in Danish monasteries. Perhaps the monks used a room such as the library or the chapter house for this purpose. There may have been one such special room in the Cistercian monastery of Sorø, since manuscripts were composed in this monastery. Some of these were books copied from other books while the monks themselves wrote others. For instance, different biblical texts have been copied and some of the still existing medieval annals were written there. The Øm Abbey Chronicle tells us that books were also written in this abbey.[3]

All the books and documents can be divided into two categories. One category consists of all texts with a normative character, such as liturgical books, the Rule, biblical texts and the devotional literature like the Church Fathers. The other category is characterized by considerations about the life lived in the monastic community. The subject matter might include a land register, accounts and cartularies. To this category, annals and other types of historical writing might be added.

I have now shown a connection between physical monasteries and written texts. But another connection would entail the identification of monks' or nuns' activities during the day, and in this only observe the situations in which there was a need for books or written materials.

A third way of categorizing the book is to make a hierarchy of the different elements of the monk's everyday life: mass, prayer, work, reading and community life, which might then tell us something about the religious value of the books and how the different categories were considered. What the priority of the tasks of the day should be was laid down in the Rule of St Benedict. In Reg. Ben. 43.3, the following clause is to be read: "Nothing comes before the Divine Office" (*Ergo nihil Operi Dei praeponatur!*). Alternatively,

---

3   *Øm Klosters Krønike*, p. 25.

as it is expressed in the bon mot about the Order of Saint Benedict: *Ora et Labora* / Pray and work.

It is important to bear in mind these areas of monastic life and their appropriate written materials in order to understand what happened to the books belonging to the monasteries during the Reformation and after.

What is known about specific books from Danish monasteries?

A status of the corpus of Danish monastic books has been made in the preliminary register: *Danske middelalderklostres bøger – en foreløbig registrant.*[4] This is not a complete register. It has to be supplemented with information concerning incunabula from the "Provenance Database" found in Wolfgang Undorf's dissertation.[5]

When working with the monastic book and seeking a total overview of the presence of books with some relation to a Danish monastery, distinctions must be made. One must distinguish as follows: Books which are known to have been in the monasteries during the Middle Ages (some may have been lost or only kept in segments), books known to have been in the monasteries when these were closed down during the Reformation, and books still extant and in the possession of libraries or other institutions today. Finally and equally important is the identification of which books have been lost and which are still extant.

A great number of books were lost over time. This fact might be significant for understanding the literary cultural heritage and influence from the medieval monastic culture on posterity.

What information is obtained if it is known that some books were in a monastery before 1537, but were at a later point lost? What does it mean if a book is still "alive" and is kept in for instance The Royal Library in Copenhagen?

It is well known that the "book" went through a transition during the medieval centuries, from the handwritten codex on parchment to the codex on paper. In the mid-fifteenth century, Gutenberg introduced the printed book on paper. From the Danish monasteries, there are examples of the different stages of the book as codex. In case you consider the Church Ordinance

---

4   Langkilde (2005).
5   Undorf (2011).

(*Kirkeordinansen*) from 1537/39 as the more or less terminal date of medieval monastic life in Denmark and thus turning point of the monastic book's life, we may ask what happened to monastic books in the years following 1537/39. The Church Ordinance expressed strong opinions about the monasteries and about the books necessary for the parish pastors.[6] One possibility is that this concern may have influenced what was saved and what was lost in Denmark.

Monastic books viewed from a quantitative perspective

What specific information may be obtained about the monastic books? In the registration of medieval books connected to Danish medieval monasteries, the number of units is between 500 and 600. Some of these have been lost and others have only survived in fragmentary form. It must be added that, in 1536, 150 volumes were found in the library of Børglum without a single mention of the titles.[7] At the same time, Børglum was the seat of the bishop of the diocese of Børglum and a monastic community for members of the Premonstratensian Order. 500-600 might seem quite a substantial number, but it should also be taken into consideration that there were about 140 monasteries during the entire Middle Ages. At the beginning of the Reformation in Denmark, about 116 monasteries were still active and some of these were quite young. Twenty-five of these houses were nunneries. Monastic life and monasticism were still important elements in Danish religious and ecclesiastical life during the early years of the Reformation. However, compared to holdings from Cismar in Holstein and Vadstena in Sweden, not much has been preserved.

It must be admitted that the figures are not accurate and it is difficult to count the books. One may count according to numbers of volumes known today or one may count numbers of titles. These two procedures result in different figures. On the one hand, some titles may consist of more than one volume,[8] and on the other hand, a volume may consist of several titles.[9] It is a problem still encountered in the library world. In light of these preliminary remarks, the following figures should be read as rough estimates.

Again, it must be emphasised that these figures are not absolute and definitive. It would not be surprising if the numbers will at some point have to be amended. There may still be manuscripts hidden away in libraries, archives

---

6   *Kirkeordinansen 1537/39.*

7   Kall Rasmussen (1855), p. 35 note 5.

8   E.g. Petrus Lombardus (1493), Pars I, Pars II, Pars IV, Pars V, (Flensburg, Die St.-Nikolai-Bibliothek, Kraack (1984), B 342, B343, B 344, B 345) [OFM, Tønder].

9   E.g. MS Uppsala, Uppsala University Library, C 353, *Sermones varii* [O.Cist., Løgum].

Manuscripts (total numbers)	Incunabula (total numbers)	Total
138	426	564

or other institutions that could eventually allow identification of the provenance of the books.

Based upon this first enumeration, it is clear that printed books or incunabula form a significant proportion of the total number in terms of books. This is nonetheless somewhat surprising, as medieval monastic books are usually understood as manuscript books.

In Table 2, the books have been listed according to the different monastic orders existing in the sixteenth century.

Table 2. Monastic orders in Denmark in the sixteenth century and books from monasteries

Religious order	Number of houses	Number of books	Rating as to number of houses / as to number of books
Order of St Anthony/ Antonines (O.Ant.)	2	1	11 / 11
Order of St Augustine/ Augustinians (O.S.A.)	6	9	6 / 6
Order of St Benedict/ Benedictines (O.S.B.)	22	22	2 / 3
Brigittine Order (Order of the Most Holy Saviour (O.S.Birg.)	2	9	10 / 7
Cistercian Order (O.Cist.) *List from the Abbey of Øm*	12	50 *325 in 378 vol.*	4 / 1
Dominican Order (O.P.)	17	11	3 / 5
Order of Friars Minor/ Franciscans (O.F.M.)	29	50	1 / 2
Order of the Holy Ghost (O.S.Sp.)	6	4	8 / 8
Knights Hospitaller/ Order of St John (O.Mel.)	7	3	7 / 9
Carmelite Order (O.Carm.) Paulus Helie	8	14 9	5 / 4
Premonstratensians (O.Praem.)*	5	2	9 / 10
Total	116	175 + Øm	

* The 150 unknown books from Børglum are not included.

Looking at Table 2, it can be noted that the large monastic orders with the greatest number of houses in Denmark supply us with the greatest numbers of books.

The top three in terms of monastic orders are: The Cistercians (50 + 325 titles in 378 volumes) – The Franciscans (50) – The Benedictines (22). Nevertheless, what might be surprising, is number four on the list when it comes to the number of books: The Carmelite Order (14). Poul Helgesen (*Paulus Helie*) from the Carmelite Order is responsible for nine titles. The Dominican Order is surprisingly only number five. This was an order with more houses than the Cistercians and well known for the obligation to study. But on the average we have less than one book per community!

The material can now be considered in detail. Table 3 may give some clue as to how many books are kept still and whether some of them come from nunneries.

Table 3: Number of books from Danish monasteries

Religious order	Total number of houses in Denmark in the sixteenth century (Total number/monks/nuns)	Number of religious houses testified via books	Number of houses for monks/nuns/double monasteries testified via books (m/n/d)	Books still preserved	Books lost	Total number of books
Order of St Anthony/Antonines (O.Ant.)	2 m	1	1 m	1		1
Order of St Augustine/Augustinians (O.S.A.)	6 (5 m/1 n)	3	3 m	7	2	9
Order of St Benedict/Benedictines (O.S.B.)	22 (8 m/14 n)	7	4 m; 3 n	20	2	22
Brigittine Order (Order of the Most Holy Saviour (O.S.Birg.)	2 d	3*	3 d	9		9
Cistercian Order (O.Cist.) (The List of books from Øm not included)	12 (11 m/1 n)	10	10 m	47	3	50
Monastery of Øm (O.Cist)				325 in 378 vol.		325 in 378 vol.
Abbot Peder				120 in 137 vol.		
The monks' books kept by abbot Peder				20 manu. in 19 vol.		
The monks' library				180 in 171 vol. + 7 manu.		
Antiphonaries and other liturgical books				5 in 44 vol.		
Dominican Order (O.P.)	17 (15 m/2 n)	6	4m; 2 n	10	1	11
Order of Friars Minor/Franciscans (O.F.M.)	29 (26 m/3 n)	12	11 m; 1 n	42	8	50
Order of the Holy Ghost ((O.S.Sp.)	6	2	2 m.	7		7
Knights Hospitaller/Order of St. John (O.Mel)	7 m	1	1 m.	2	1	3
Camelite order (O. Carm.)	8 m	3	3 m.	10	4	14
Premonstratensians (O.Praem.)	5 (4m/1n)	2	2 m.	2		2
Total (List of books from Øm Excluded)		50	41 m / 6 n/ 3 d	157	21	178
Total (List of books from Øm Included)		50	41 m / 6 n /3 d	157	346 in 399 vol.	503 in 556 vol.

*From the monastery in Vadstena in Sweden, three manuscripts are related to the Dominican house in Ribe. Their author was the Dominican lector Matthias Ripensis.

Table 4 provides a survey of how the numbers of books from the different orders are divided among named monasteries:

Table 4: Single monasteries' possession of books

Religious order	Total number of houses in Denmark during the Middle Ages (Total number/monks/nuns)	Houses with books known	Known manu-scripts	Known incu-nabula	List from Flensborg[10] (incunabula)	List from Church of Our Lady, Copenhagen[11]	Total
O.Ant.	2 m	Præstø	1				1
O.Carm.	8 m	Elsinore				2	2
		Landskrona				1	1
		Skælskør				1	1
		Sæby		1			1
		Poul Helgesen	9				9
O.Cist	18 (16 m/2 n)	Kolbaz*	1				1
		Esrum	5	1			6
		Guldholm	1				1
		Herrevad	4				4
		Løgum	7				7
		Ryd	1		1 manu. + 4 inc.		6
		Sorø	15		1		16
		Vitskøl	4				4
		Øm	5				5
O.F.M.	29 (26 m/3 n)	Elsinore		1		6	7
		Horsens			3		3
		Lund	1			1	2
		Nysted	2				2
		Næstved	1				1
		Odense	1				1
		Randers	1				1
		Ribe		1	16		17
		Roskilde	1			1	2
		Schleswig			1		1
		Tønder			11		11
O.Mel.	8 m	Dueholm	1			1	2
O.P.	20 (18 m/2n)	Stockholm	1				1
		Gavnø		1			1
		Haderslev	1				1
		Helsingborg	1	1		1	3
		Ribe	2				2
		Roskilde	1				1
O.Praem.	7 (6 m/1 n)	Bäckaskog	1				1
		Børglum	1				1

10   Kraack (1984)
11   Magnæi (1834), pp. 357-358.

Order	Count	Place				Total
O.S.A.	9 (7m/2n)	Dalby	1			1
		Grinderslev	1			1
		Æbelholt	3	2	2	7
O.S.B	24 (17 m/17 n)	Bosjö	1			1
		Essenbæk	1			1
		Lund	1			1
		Næstved	7	8		15
		Odense	4			4
		Ringsted	3		2	5
		Ørslev	1			1
O.S.Birg.	2 d	Mariager	2			2
		Maribo	4			4
		[Vadstena]**	3			[3]
O.S.Sp.	6	Randers	2	1		3
		Aalborg		7		7

*A manuscript was originally started somewhere in the diocese of Lund and later moved to the Cistercian monastery of Kolbaz in Pomerania. (MS Berlin, Staatsbibliothek zu Berlin – Preußischer Kulturbesitz., theol. lat. fol. 149, Annales Colbazenses. [Provenance: St Lawrence, Lund and O.Cist. Colbaz, Pomerania]).

**The Monastery of Vadstena owned three manuscripts originally composed by Matthias Ripensis, lector at St Catherine's Monastery in Ribe (MS Uppsala, Uppsala University Library, C 342, C 343 and C 356).

Based on the tables, it is clear that the majority of books come from Øm Abbey. However, some information is given about the collection of Sorø Abbey. Fifteen manuscript items are found from this abbey. From Skovkloster near Næstved, seven manuscripts and eight incunabula are extant. When it comes to printed books, the most significant collections originate from the Franciscans and especially from the houses in Ribe (16) and Tønder (11). Since the mid-sixteenth century, these collections have been brought to and preserved in Flensburg.[12] Finally, there is the unique Danish authorship of Poul Helgesen.[13]

The next step is to take a closer look at the materials related to Øm Abbey. This information is very important for the full picture of what a monastic library could be like. If you combine information from the Øm Abbey Inventory[14] with the extant books from the Øm Abbey, you have more than half of the total number of books that we know of from the Danish medieval monastic world. Again, most of them have been lost. Unfortunately!

The background for the Øm Abbey Inventory is that, in the year 1554, King Christian III ordered the inventory to be made.[15] Several researchers

---

12 Kraack (1984).
13 Helgesen (1932-1948).
14 'Øm Klosters Inventarium 1554'; Gregersen (2003a).
15 MS Copenhagen, Rigsarkivet, De ældste arkivregistraturer 1454-1657, Pk. 5 (Arkivnummer 717), Øm

have analyzed this inventory. Holger Fr. Rørdam in 1881[16], Brian Patrick Mc-Guire in his book *Conflict and Continuity at Øm Abbey* from 1976[17] and recently Wolfgang Undorf has done further research on the same inventory in his dissertation from 2011 and later on in the reworked and published dissertation from 2014.[18] He focuses especially on printed books and the identification of printed books. In this connection, the results of McGuire's analysis are shown in the table below:

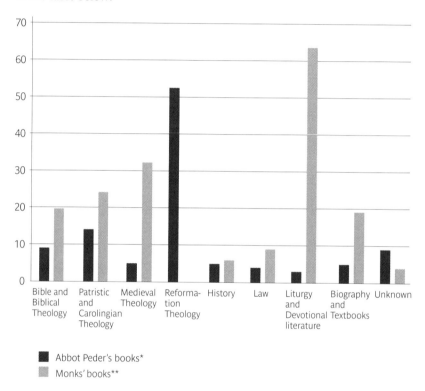

Abbot Peder's books*

Monks' books**

Subject division of the books from Øm 1554.
: Books of Abbot Peder, based on Catalogus librorum domini Petri Abbatis Senioris.
**: Books of the monks based on Libri communes in communi bibliotheca custoditi. Source: McGuire (1976) p. 134.[19]*

Klosters *Inventarium af 1554.*
16   Rørdam (1881-1882).
17   McGuire (1976).
18   Undorf (2014), pp.144-149; Undorf (2011).
19   See also: Undorf (2014), especially chapter 3; Undorf (2011), pp. 287-321.

As mentioned, the inventory was made in 1554. Moreover, it is very important to state this fact when going through the different elements of the bar chart. The next point to mention is the difference between the books from Abbot Peder's collection and the books of the monks. Almost half of the abbot's books reflect the situation post-1537 with many books about Reformation theology. Still, one also finds many liturgical and devotional books, books about medieval theology, patristic theology, Bibles and biblical theology in the monks' library collections. You could say that the abbot's library tells us about the transition into a new era and reflects the Statute of the University of Copenhagen of 10 June, 1539 (*Fundatio et Ordinatio universalis Scholæ Hafniensis*).[20] In compliance with this statute, the old monasteries in the rural areas were to be transformed into places of study intended for new evangelical pastors.[21] For instance Sorø, Esrum, Herrevad, Vitskøl and Øm were transformed into such study centres.[22]

As to the books in the monks' library, they form a sort of group portrait or picture of what you might expect to find in the most outstanding Danish monasteries in the Middle Ages.

The next step is to compare the information from the list of the monks' library with the books extant from Øm Abbey. Wolfgang Undorf has done an excellent job of identifying and dating the books on the list.[23] In all, he found 325 titles in 378 volumes. He distinguishes between undated, pre-Reformation, and post-Reformation and within each group, he distinguishes between manuscripts and printed books. He finds a group of undated manuscripts and printed books which are probably from the pre-Reformation period (27 manuscripts in 26 volumes and 23 printed books in 62 volumes). In the group

---

20 Rørdam (1868-1869) pp. 75-115.
21 McGuire (1976), p. 132; Rørdam (1868-1869), 1, p. 52: "Fremdeles forordne vi til de studerendes og boglige Kunsters Tarv, at i ethvert Munkekloster i Danmark, som kaldes med det underlige Navn verdsligt eller Herrekloster, skal være en Skole for fattige unge Mennesker, og ingen maa antages der, uden de, som ere bekvemme til Bogen. Der skal være en Theolog, enten en Klostermand eller en anden i saakaldt verdslig Dragt, en Mand af Lærdom, som kan holde Forelæsninger over den hellige Skrift og prædike. Af Klosteret skal ogsaa udvælges eller andenstedsfra hidkaldes Mænd, der kunne undervise i Grammatik, Dialektik og Rhetorik, og tyde nogle Autores. Men saalænge de studere der, bør de være deres foresatte lydige, leve i Kydskhed, Ærbarhed, Bøn og Studering, og hver Dag synge og læse i Koret efter den i Kirkeordinansen foreskrevne Skik, samt bære Munkedragt." "Men naar de forlade Klostrene, enten det er Læsemestere eller Disciple, og forlange at gifte sig efter Guds Anordning, maa der gives dem Bestillinger ved andre Kirker og Skoler, efter deres Fortjenester i Lærdom og Levned" [Translated from: Krag (1737), pp. 125-126].
22 *Academia Sorana* (1962), p. 14.
23 Undorf (2011), pp. 287-321.

containing the pre-Reformation titles, he finds 183 titles, in 192 volumes. However, Undorf estimates that 92 titles in 98 volumes are post-Reformation books, which is less than one third of the total number.[24] In the former groups with undated printed books, almost all books are liturgical. When it comes to pre-Reformation books, he observes quite an international collection of books. Most of them are in Latin and only two in Danish (Saxo and the New Testament).[25]

The monastic books according to age

It is also possible to subdivide the written materials according to centuries of origin. The manuscripts date back to all centuries during the Middle Ages.

Table 5: Extant written material distributed across periods of origin

Period of origin	Manuscripts	Incunabula and early print
Before 1200	16	
1200-1350	36	
1350-1536	56	426
Undated	30	

The above table, however, is not the whole story. It is likewise important to stress clearly that, at the end of the monastic life in Denmark, books from the thirteenth century were still owned and kept by some monastic houses and some of them were still in use. This can be illustrated by means of the Næstved Calendar (MS Copenhagen, Royal Library, E don. var. 52 2°). The first notice was written in the thirteenth century and the most recent is from the sixteenth century. As to the Dalby Gospels (MS Copenhagen, Royal Library, GKS 1324 4°), they date back to the eleventh century, but notes were inserted in the fourteenth and fifteenth centuries. Another indication of use over a long period of time is discovered by focusing on the Vitskøl theological compendium (MS Copenhagen, Royal Library, NKS 13 8°).[26] This manuscript

---

24 Undorf (2011), pp.288-289.
25 Undorf (2011), pp. 313-317.
26 MS Copenhagen, Royal Library, NKS 13 8°, *Compendium theologicæ veritatis* (See: 'Middelalderen', at *Danske bogbind i Det Kongelige Bibliotek*, http://wayback-01.kb.dk/wayback/20100902130418/http://www2.kb.dk/elib/bhs/bogbind/index.htm – Accessed 7 July 2015.)

dates back to the late fourteenth century when it was copied. Later on, in the beginning of the sixteenth century, Abbot Henrik repaired it with a fine and strong binding including a book clasp. This might be an indication that the manuscript was considered important also in the sixteenth century.

Subject categories of the monastic books

The book materials may also be considered from a genre perspective. A broad classification of the material has been made with reference to some of the categories used by McGuire. However, the works of Michael T. Clanchy and Arnvid Nedkvitne are also taken into consideration. In their studies of the whole of the medieval written culture, they use categories such as *Bureaucratic Literacy, Learned Literacy, Vernacular Literacy and Sacred Literacy*.[27]

Attention should be paid to a distinct lack of solely liturgical material despite the fact that many of the books may be considered theological works. This fact should help to illuminate the part of monastic life which, in a Benedictine context, is regarded as something *which precedes everything else* (*Ergo nihil Operi praeponantur*)[28] – but liturgical books are completely missing. However, such material may have been present, for instance at Øm Abbey. The last part of the Inventory refers to: "…. Liber chorales, Responsoria, Legenda, Antiphonaria, Missalia, Psalteria – Sunt quadraginta" as part of the monks' book collection.[29]

Regarding daily life in church and chapter house, monks also had to consult a sort of calendar. Different examples or fragments exist from Lund, Nysted, Løgum, Ribe, Skovkloster and perhaps a fragment from Mariager. All these were in manuscript form.

Various types of biblical texts can also be found at Danish monasteries. Some are in manuscripts (from Haderslev, Dalby, Bosjö and Mariager) and others are printed (from Ryd and from OFM in Horsens, Ribe and Tønder). Frands Vormodsen, the former Carmelite monk, translated the Psalms into Danish and published them in Rostock in 1528.

The category consisting of different sorts of theological literature is the biggest one and it is difficult to get an overview of it. The material registered in this category has yet to be studied carefully.

Monks cultivated a tradition of recording historical events as part of their

---

27 Clanchy (1983); Nedkvitne (2004).
28 Reg. Ben. 43,3.
29 Gregersen (2003a), p. 229.

interests. Within this category, about twenty chronicles have been found.

Only a few secular studies of science and medicine have been found in connection with Danish monasteries.

Finally, a group of schoolbooks needs to be mentioned. From Skovkloster near Næstved, we have six printed books. They were meant to be used for learning Latin. We have, however, such books from only one single monastic school.

Within the category of "bureaucratic literacy", there are some Danish legal texts in manuscripts (from Herrevad, Sorø, Antvorskov, Ørslev, and Skovkloster) and printed canon law books (from OFM in Lund, Ribe and Tønder). Another section within bureaucratic literature contains all sorts of administrative materials, such as cartularies, land registers and accounts. Within this group, there are examples from the following monasteries: Esrum, Løgum, Sorø, Vitskøl, Øm, Dueholm and St Agnes in Roskilde, Dalby, Æbelholt, Skovkloster, Ringsted and Bosjö. From the years just after the Reformation, there are inventories from Præstø, Øm, Dalby and St Peter in Lund. This is not very many if one bears in mind how many monasteries were in operation in Denmark at the time of the Reformation.

The lack of liturgical material is very striking. When the different genres of literature in the monasteries are examined, based upon those preserved, it is also necessary to consider the statements in Christiern Pedersen's *Om børn at holde till Scole och Studium Och ath skicke gode Scolemestere till dem [Jesus som Tolvaars-Barn i Templet]* from 1531.[30] The Church Ordinance (*Kirkeordinansen*) from 1537/39[31] and The Deed of Foundation for The University of Copenhagen (1537-39)[32] are other important documents that help us to understand the situation in those years. Together, they give an idea of what the post-monastic community found useful and necessary for the education of clergymen in the new parishes. These documents also show what they considered required in order to carry out the position as clergy in accordance with the evangelical demands. In his pamphlet mentioned above, Christiern Pedersen reworked and translated Luther's pamphlet: *An die Ratsherren aller Städte deutschen landis, dass sie christlicher Schulen aufrichten und halten sollen* (1524).[33] In this connection, emphasis is placed on establishing good libraries. Both Luther's and Christiern Pedersen's pamphlets also give advice regarding the types of books these libraries should contain. Among others, the

---

30 Pedersen (1531).
31 *Kirkeordinansen 1537/39.*
32 Rørdam (1868-1869), p. 52.
33 Luther (1962).

following have been mentioned: the Holy Scripture in Latin, Greek, Hebrew and German; commentaries – the best and most ancient in Greek, Hebrew and Latin; books for learning languages such as poets and orators; grammars; books on liberal arts and other arts; law; medicine; chronicles and histories in whatever language they are to be had. In Christiern Pedersen's version, chronicles in Danish, Norwegian and Swedish are mentioned.[34] In most of these categories, it is possible to find one or more examples from former Danish monasteries.

It could be claimed that the above-mentioned documents were normative statements and therefore to be regarded as laws about what a library or book collection should be like and what categories of books were necessary. From a more positive point of view, they served as guidelines for a new age.

The monastic book-collections in post-Reformation times

The years from the 1520s and onwards were very important and decisive for monastic book collections and libraries. The first communities to register the impact of the new evangelical movement were the houses of the Franciscan Order. In just a few years, the monks had been driven out of their houses one by one.[35] Afterwards, the decisions were made in Copenhagen, with the Copenhagen Recess (Recessen) of 30 October 1536, according to which the activities of the mendicant orders were forbidden, the old rural orders were to be reformed in a Protestant way and the Crown appropriated their landed holdings. In 1537 and 1539, the Church was reorganized by the Church Ordinance (Kirkeordinansen). With these laws and decisions, traditional monastic life in Denmark more or less came to an end. Monks and nuns were now free to leave their monasteries, but they could stay on and continue some kind of monastic life based upon reformed teachings. Thus, in the first years after the Reformation and the enactment of the Church Ordinance, monks and nuns were still present in many monasteries and able to protect their book collections. When they disappeared, there was a loss of tradition and changed circumstances.

King Christian III was much committed to the Reformation and involved himself in detail. At the same time, he needed to consolidate his power in

---

34   Pedersen (1531), pp. 50-53 / Pedersen (1854), pp. 515-516; Luther (1962), pp. 375-377.
35   *Krøniken om Graabrødrenes fordrivelse fra deres klostre i Danmark.*

the kingdom and was permanently in need of money. All these elements should be seen as creating a dim future for monastic libraries. In this context, a number of challenges should also be borne in mind: there was a need for education on many levels, such as common schools for children, preparatory education for the university in Latin schools, education of clergy and re-establishing the University of Copenhagen. For these educational programmes, there was a need for literature and books. It was, however, not only a question of books but also of the right books. A basic list for the common schools can be found in Christiern Pedersen's book *Om børn at holde till Scole och Studium*[36], and for the rural clergy in the Church Ordinance.[37] In addition, the king and the leading reformers in Denmark were very keen to establish a uniform Church. Heads of monasteries are admonished that they should practice good management and observe the instructions of the Church Ordinance.[38] Here are found the first steps towards organized censorship.[39] The intention was to protect against bad and questionable books. The University was authorized to say yes or no regarding publication of new titles. Overall, the king wanted to regulate the book market. The aim of this regulation was not only a matter of censorship. It was also protection of the publishers' rights. Publishers applied to the king for exclusive rights to publish a given title. The king gave the permission and the right meant exclusive rights for four or five years.[40] All these measures were intended for the age of the Reformation and the future to come.

Similarly, attention must be paid to the following question: Did the regulation just mentioned also affect existing book collections in the monasteries? Different sources exist to clarify this matter. As part of the appropriation of the monastic estates, the king ordered their new leaders to register the properties. One example is the Øm Abbey Inventory. Normally, however, only the landed holdings were registered. Another initiative was to send royal officials to many of the monasteries in Denmark in order to collect good and useful books for a new royal library in Copenhagen, for the University or for other purposes.[41] On 8 September, 1537, the king issued a letter in which he ordered books to be sent to the new library in Copenhagen. Magister Jørgen Tormand went from one monastery to the other to select books useful

---

36 Pedersen (1531).
37 *Kirkeordinansen 1537/39*, pp. 136; 230-232.
38 *Danske Kancelliregistranter 1535-1550,* pp. 68, 79, 311.
39 *Kirkeordinansen 1537/39*, p. 231; Lausten (1987), pp. 207-213.
40 *Danske Kancelliregistranter 1535-1550*, pp. 265-266; *Kancelliets Brevbøger*, 1551-1555, pp. 65, 196, 197, 201, 378, 388, 396-397, 412.
41 *Kancelliets Brevbøger*, 1551-1555, pp. 320, 411.

for the University.[42] Some of these sources give the impression that parts of the book collections were old and severely damaged and that they had been maintained under bad conditions.[43] In addition, the records leave the impression that parts of the book collections in those years were moved about the country to be used for various and new purposes. On 19 December 1555, Hans Svaning, the royal historiographer, received a letter in which he was asked to deliver all the books he himself had collected from various places, including the monasteries, for his writing of a national history. He was to hand them over to the king in the beginning of February in Copenhagen. [44]

It might be argued that censorship existed for the publishing of new books, but it is difficult to find definite information about censorship exercised on the medieval book collection. But it could be done indirectly. Good and useful books were collected and sent to Copenhagen. The ones considered useless or harmful according to Protestant thought were lost or were in 1641 delivered to the royal arsenal.[45] However, there were other destructive factors in the long history of monastic books. The Copenhagen fire of October 1728 is such an example. From the University of Copenhagen, a large number of books was lost in the fire and among them were probably many books from former monasteries.

Øm Abbey – the best known Danish monastic library

What happened at Øm Abbey? As far as Holger Fr. Rørdam has shown in an article from 1881-82, we have to suppose that there was a bond between Abbot Peder Sørensen of Øm Abbey and King Christian III. Peder Sørensen seems to have supported the king in terms of acceptance of the new religion.[46] It may have been a pragmatic relationship. Peder Sørensen was abbot from 1527-54. He took part in the meeting in Ry in 1534 where the Jutlandic nobility elected Christian king. We do not know what role he played, but some years later he was called "our beloved Abbot Peder in Øm Abbey".[47] A sort of monastic way of life seems to have continued in Øm after 1536. Peder Sørensen was still the abbot, but at the same time he was very much a part

42   Kall Rasmussen (1855), p. 37; Brandt (1853-1856), p. 422; Birket Smith (1882 / 1982), p. 13.
43   Kall Rasmussen (1855), p. 35-36.
44   *Kancelliets Brevbøger* 1 (1551-1555), pp. 411; Rørdam (1867), p. 72.
45   Kall Rasmussen (1855), p. 36; 'Adskillige Optegnelser af Etatsraad Langebeks Papirer' (1793), p. 187.
46   Rørdam (1881-1882). Gregersen (2003b).
47   *Danske Kancelliregistranter 1535-1550*, p. 79, January 22nd 1559: "os elsk. Regelbunden Mand Hr. Peder, Abbed i Emkloster".

of the royal administration. In 1554, the inventory was made together with the registration of the books in the monastery. In that year, the books were still to be found in the monastery. After the death in 1559 of Christian III, his son became king, Frederik II. He visited Øm Abbey often and used it for hunting and as his residence in Jutland. In 1560, the last abbot, Jens Simensen, was forced to leave and Øm Abbey ceased to exist as a monastery. Shortly afterwards, king Frederik II gave the order to tear down the buildings in Øm or Emborg, as he now called it. The bricks were to be sent to Skanderborg for the reconstruction of the castle. During that process, something must have happened to the books. The king called the monastic buildings useless and perhaps had the same attitude to the books. Alice Madsen says in her article: *Bøger, bogspænder og bogbeslag fra Øm Kloster* that some forty pieces of metallic book equipment, such as book clasps and book fittings, have been found as archaeological remains all over the monastic area.[48] These book remains can be dated back to the period from the thirteenth to the sixteenth centuries. Alice Madsen has identified some of the book clasps as unique for Øm Abbey and probably made in Øm. These were found all over the abbey ruins and the unique Øm book clasps were found in the demolition strata. These finds raise the question of the extent to which some of the books were badly and disrespectfully handled or, even worse, were destroyed when the buildings were demolished.

Conclusion: Interpretation of the situation for monastic books in the sixteenth century

The results of this study of medieval monastic books can be summarized as follows. First, it can once again be positively established that the Øm Abbey Inventory gives the most comprehensive information for a single monastic library. The information includes size, the allocation between the abbot and the monks' library, and genre. The Inventory from Øm Abbey also shows what kind of liturgical materials could be found in a monastery by the late Middle Ages. Abbot Peder's books tell us about the transformation from medieval monastery to evangelical school for the education of clergymen.

The Flensburg collection indicates an effort to maintain the past and shows hope of making a comeback. Moreover, this collection shows how eagerly the Franciscan Order used the new printed material and reveals an international orientation. The collection seems to be the result of the efforts of

---

48   Madsen (2003).

a single man, the former Franciscan brother Lütke Namens. However, he did not succeed in his efforts. The book collection survived because it was turned into a school library in Flensburg.

Finally and importantly, Poul Helgesen in his authorship is an example of a monastic scholar with a list of publications. He can be characterized as a member of the theological elite in Denmark.

It can also be concluded that printed books were very important in monasteries during the last decades of their lifetime. The majority of the known titles consists of printed books. Some of the manuscripts that have been preserved concern the administration and registration of the monasteries as estates.

Second, we also have to conclude on the loss of monastic books. How can this be understood and explained? A single and simple answer cannot be given. There may be numerous explanations.

We know that king Christian III was very active when it came to church institutions, whether it concerned their transformation into evangelical institutions or the closing down of the monasteries, as was seen in the Copenhagen Recess (1536), Church Ordinance (1537/39) and the Deed of Foundation of the University of Copenhagen (1537/39). In this connection, he initiated campaigns to collect the books from the monasteries suitable for the new library in Copenhagen. Perhaps these evangelical ideas about what a library should contain may have influenced what is extant today and what has been lost.

It is also worth noticing that materials important for the daily life of the monasteries as manors are still extant. These materials come from the group labelled administrative books. Contrary to these sources, materials important for the daily religious life in the monasteries, such as liturgical books, are almost absent. This situation may be a result of the new church order, the dissolution of the monasteries and the confiscation of monastic estates.

Some of the losses are due to lack of interest, but they can also have been determined by new conditions. From research in the Danish archives, we know that parchment from old liturgical books was reused as binding for accounts from different land holdings. Some of these bindings have been identified as coming from monasteries. In this category, we might still expect to find more material. The reuse of liturgical manuscript pages as bindings was another sort of secularization and destruction of the medieval liturgical tradition.

The loss of monastic books was an ongoing process with different decisive moments. With the extinction of the monastic population, there was no more use for these books in accordance with their primary purpose. Use had been the best way to protect books. In the same way, there was no longer any incentive to take care of the books, and some of the book collections fell into disrepair. This process took place especially in the last part of the sixteenth century. Another monastic policy can be seen under the kings after Christian III. Again, Øm Abbey and King Frederik II can serve as an example. The monasteries were no longer centres of learning. They were given new functions and new owners or were transformed into a part of the manorial system. This change meant that the new inhabitants were lay persons. Later on, as the loss of tradition was complete, the old "monks' books" (*munkebøger*) were delivered to the Royal Arsenal and in some cases used for fireworks. Last of all, we know that books were lost during the Copenhagen Fire of 1728.

In spite of the large number of houses, we are very poorly informed about the Dominicans and the fate of their books. We know that they had an obligation to study, but very few books are left. However, every time you walk into Our Lady's Church in Aarhus and stand in front of the high altar, you can recall the attitude of the Dominicans concerning books and reading. The altarpiece of this former Dominican church is a triptych with several references to books. In this context, only details from the predella in its open position are shown (see p. 381). This triptych of the high altar is thought to have been made in Claus Berg's workshop in Odense during the first quarter of the sixteenth century, not that many years before the Reformation. Here, we are still reminded of the importance of books and the study of books in a monastic environment.

Our Lady's Church in Aarhus, the predella to the north. To the left, St Vincent Ferrer points at a picture of Christ as Judge on Judgement Day in an open book. To the right, St Catherine of Siena with her attributes, holding a heart in her left hand and wearing a crown of thorns. Furthermore, she has a nail and a wound in her right side (stigmata). Photo: Jens Bruun, www.altertavler.dk

Our Lady's Church in Aarhus, the predella to the south. St Thomas Aquinas and St Dominicus discuss theological matters with reference to a book. Photo: Jens Bruun, www.altertavler.dk

Manuscript sources

The Næstved Calendar = MS Copenhagen, Royal Library, E don. var. 52 2⁰, *Calendarium Monasterii B. Petri Nestvedensis, Necrologium Nestvedense.* Online edition: http://www.kb.dk/ permalink/2006/manus/18/eng/ (Visited July 4th 2017)

MS Berlin, Staatsbibliothek zu Berlin – Preußischer Kulturbesitz., theol. lat. fol. 149, *Annales Colbazenses.*

MS Copenhagen, Royal Library, GKS 1324 4⁰.

MS Copenhagen, Royal Library, NKS 13 8⁰, *Compendium theologicæ veritatis.*

MS Copenhagen, Rigsarkivet, De ældste arkivregistraturer 1454-1657, Pk. 5 (Arkivnummer 717), Øm Klosters *Inventarium af 1554.*

MS Uppsala, Uppsala University Library, C 342, *Sermones varii*, 125v-135v, *[Matthias Ripensis Dacus: Sermones de tempore]*

MS Uppsala, Uppsala University Library, C 343, *Matthias Ripensis. Sermones (Acho Johannis)*

MS Uppsala, Uppsala University Library, C 353, *Sermones varii.*

MS Uppsala, Uppsala University Library, C 356, *Matthias Ripensis. Sermones (Acho Johannis). Sermones de tempore.*

Bibliography

Academia Sorana: Kloster – Akademi – Skole, udgivet af Soransk Samfund i anledning af dets 100 års dag (Copenhagen, 1962).

'Adskillige Optegnelser af Etatsraad Langebeks Papirer', in *Nye samlinger til den danske Historie*, vol. 2, ed. P. F. Suhm (Copenhagen, 1793), pp. 183-192.

Benedikts Regel, udgivet med dansk oversættelse og kommentar af Brian Møller Jensen (Copenhagen, 1998).

Birket Smith, S., *Om Kjøbenhavns Universitetsbibliothek før 1728 især dets Håndskriftsamlinger*, (Copenhagen, 1982 (1882)).

Brandt, C.J., 'Et lille Bidrag til det store kongelige Bibliotheks Historie', *Kirkehistoriske Samlinger*, 2 (1853-1856), pp. 421-422.

Brügger, Niels, 'Bogen som Medie', *Passage* 48 (2003), pp. 77-95.

Clanchy, M.T. 'Looking back from the Invention of Printing', in *Literacy in Historical Perspective*, ed. D.P. Resnick (Washington D.C., 1983), pp. 7-22.

Danske bogbind i Det Kongelige Bibliotek, website: http://wayback-01.kb.dk/wayback/ 20100902130418/http://www2.kb.dk/elib/bhs/bogbind/index.htm (accesed July 7th 2015)

Danske Kancelliregistranter 1535-1550, eds. Kristian Erslev and W. Mollerup (Copenhagen 1881-1882).

Gregersen, Bo, 'Appendiks: Øm Klosters Inventarium af 1554', in *Øm Kloster: kapitler af et middelalderligt cistercienserabbedis historie*, eds. Bo Gregersen and Carsten Selch Jensen (Odense, 2003a), pp. 217-234.

Gregersen, Bo, 'Storheden før faldet – Øm Kloster på reformationstiden', in *Øm Kloster: kapitler af et middelalderligt cistercienserabbedis historie*, eds. Bo Gregersen and Carsten Selch Jensen (Odense, 2003b), pp. 191-204.

Hedlund, Monica, 'Ny katalog – ny väg in i biblioteket', in *Vadstena klosters bibliotek. Ny katalog och nya forskningsmöjligheter*, eds. Monica Hedlund and Alf Härdelin (Stockholm, 1990), pp. 11-21.

Helgesen, Poul, *Skrifter af Paulus Helie*, udgivet af Det danske Sprog- og Litteraturselskab, 7 vols. (Copenhagen, 1932-1948).

Kall Rasmussen, M.N.C.: 'Om to nylig fundne Fragmenter af en Codex af Saxo', *Aarsberetninger fra Det Kongelige Geheimearchiv, indeholdende Bidrag til Dansk Historie af utrykte Kilder* 1 (1855) Tillæg, pp. 23-37.

Kancelliets Brevbøger vedrørende Danmarks indre Forhold i Uddrag, ed. C. F. Bricka et al., 39 vols. (1885-2005), 1 (1551-1555).

Kirkeordinansen 1537/39, ed. Martin Schwarz Lausten (Copenhagen, 1989).

Kraack, Gerhard: *Die St.-Nikolai-Bibliothek zu Flensburg. Eine Büchersammlung aus dem Jahrhundert der Reformation*. Beschreibung und Katalog von Gerhard Kraack unter Mitarbeit von Nis Lorenzen (Flensburg, 1984).

Krag, Niels, *Nicolai Cragii Annalium libri VI, quibus res Danicæ ab excessu regis Friderici I ac deinde a gloriosissimo rege Christiano III gestæ ad annum usque MDL enarrantur : His additi Stephani Jo. Stephanii Historiæ Danicæ libri duo quibus reliqua laudatissimi regis acta descibuntur*, (Copenhagen, 1737).

Krøniken om Graabrødrenes fordrivelse fra deres klostre i Danmark, trans. Henning Heilesen (Copenhagen, 1967).

Langkilde, Birgitte, *Libri monasteriorum Danicorum mediae aetatis – index ad tempus compositus / Danske middelalderklostres bøger – en foreløbig registrant*, (Aarhus, 2005). Available online: https://www.statsbiblioteket.dk/au/?locale=da#/search?query=recordID:"sb_2979621" (Accessed March 26 2017)

Lausten, Martin Schwarz, *Christian d. 3. og kirken (1537-1559)*. Studier i den danske reformationskirke 1 (Copenhagen, 1987).

Luther, Martin, *An die Ratsherren aller Städte deutschen landis, dass sie christlicher Schulen aufrichten und halten sollen* (1524). English translation: *To the Councilmen of all cities in Germany that they establish and maintain Christian schools. 1524,* Translated by Albert T.W. Steinhaeuser. Revised by Walther I. Brandt, in Martin Luther: *Luther's works*. American edition, 55 vols. (Saint Louis, MO; Philadelphia 1955-), vol. 45: The Christian in society II / ed. by Walther I. Brandt (Philadelphia, 1962) pp. 339-378.

Madsen, Alice, 'Bøger, bogspænder og bogbeslag fra Øm Kloster', in: *Øm Kloster: kapiter af et middelalderligt cistercienserabbedis historie*, eds. Bo Gregersen and Carsten Selch Jensen (Odense, 2003), pp. 121-134.

Magnæi, A., 'Notata in fronte variorum librorum in bibliotheca deperdita Ecclesiæ b. Virginis Hafniæ', in *Scriptores rerum Danicarum medii ævi*, ed. J. Langebek, 9. vols. (Copenhagen, 1772-1878), 8 (Copenhagen, 1834), pp. 357-358.

McGuire, Brian Patrick, *Conflict and Continuity at Øm Abbey: a Cistercian Experience in Medieval Denmark* (Copenhagen, 1976).

Nedkvitne, Arnved, *The Social Consequences of Literacy in Medieval Scandinavia* (Tournhout, 2004).

Pedersen, Christiern, *Om børn at holde till Scole och Studium Och ath skicke gode Scolemestere till dem [Jesus som Tolvaars-Barn i Templet]* (Antwerp, 1531).

Pedersen, Christiern, *Christiern Pedersens Danske Skrifter*, eds. C. J. Brandt and R. Th. Fenger, 5. vols. (Copenhagen, 1850-1855), 4 (Smaaskrifter 1531-33) ed. C.J. Brandt, (Copenhagen, 1854), pp. 467-518.

Petrus Lombardus: *Liber Sententiarum, cum quaestionibus S. Bonaventurae et tabula Johannis Beckenhaub*, Pars I, II, IV, V. (Freiburg (Breisgau), 1493). [Flensburg, Die St.-Nikolai-Bibliothek, Kraack (1984), B 342, B343, B 344, B 345].

Reg. Ben. (*Regula Benedicti*) = *The Rule of Benedict / Benedikts Regel*.

The Rule of St. Benedict, translated with introduction and notes by Anthony C. Meisel and M. L. del Mastro (New York, 1975).

Rübner Jørgensen, Kaare, 'Karmeliterne i Sæby Kirke', *Kirkehistoriske Samlinger* (1978), pp. 7-36.

Rübner Jørgensen, Kaare, 'Munke og Nonner på danske kirkevægge. Nogle refleksioner over karmelitermunkene i Sæby Kirke', *Hikuin* 34 (2007), pp. 101-110; pp. 162-163.

Rørdam, Holger Fr., *Historieskrivningen og Historieskriverne i Danmark og Norge siden Reformationen. 1. Tidsrummet fra Reformationen indtil Anders Vedel* (Copenhagen, 1867).

Rørdam, Holger Fr., *Kjøbenhavns Universitets Historie fra 1537 til 1621*. 4 vols. (Copenhagen, 1868-1877), 1 (I Kong Christian den Tredies Tid: 1537-1558) (1868-1869).

Rørdam, Holger Fr., 'Efterretninger om de to sidste abbeder i Øm Kloster', *Kirkehistoriske Samlinger* 3:3 (1881-1882), pp. 94-111.

Trithemius, Johannes, *Tractatus de Ortu et progressu ordinis V.M. de Carmelo* (Cologne, 1643). Available online: http://reader.digitale-sammlungen.de/de/fs1/object/display/bsb10744237_00067.html?contextType=scan (Accessed March 26 2017)

Undorf, Wolfgang, *From Gutenberg to Luther – Transnational print Cultures in Scandinavia 1450-1525* (Diss.) (Berlin, 2011). Available online: http://edoc.hu-berlin.de/dissertationen/undorf-wolfgang-2012-01-05/PDF/undorf.pdf (Accessed March 26 2017)

Undorf, Wolfgang, *From Gutenberg to Luther: Transnational Print Cultures in Scandinavia 1450-1525* (Leiden, 2014)

'Øm Klosters Inventarium 1554', in *Nye samlinger til den danske Historie*, vol. 3, ed. P. F. Suhm (Copenhagen, 1794), pp. 302-335.

Øm Klosters Krønike, trans. Jørgen Olrik, (Aarhus, 1968).

Contributors

Agertoft, Rasmus	Historical Consultant, The Round Tower, Copenhagen.
Auge, Oliver	Professor, Dr. phil., Historisches Seminar, Christian-Albrechts-Universität zu Kiel.
Berntson, Martin	Professor, University of Gothenburg.
Bisgaard, Lars	Associate Professor, University of Southern Denmark.
Cameron, Euan	Professor, Columbia University/Union Theological Seminary.
Clausen, Svend	Historian, Copenhagen.
Ekroll, Øystein	Researcher, Nidaros Cathedral Restoration Workshop, Trondheim.
Jacobsen, Grethe	Head of Dept. (retd.), The Royal Library, Copenhagen.
Jakobsen, Johnny Grandjean Gøgsig	Associate Professor, University of Copenhagen.
Jensen, Janus Møller	Director, Museum of Koldinghus.
Jørgensen, Kaare Rübner	Emeritus Lecturer, Dr. phil.
Langkilde, Birgitte	Research Librarian, The Royal Library, Aarhus.
Larsen, Morten	Curator, Head of Archaeology, Vendsyssel Historical Museum.
Kallestrup, Louise Nyholm	Associate Professor, University of Southern Denmark.
McGuire, Brian Patrick	Professor Emeritus, University of Roskilde.
Seesko, Per	Curator, The Museum of National History, Frederiksborg Castle.

Reinskloster Manor to the west of Trondheim in Trøndelag, ink-and-wash by J.F.L. Dreier c. 1800. The size of the ruined abbey church is exaggerated and the architectural details are not correct. The red wooden building to the left of the ruin with a passage through it was built in the early seventeenth century and is still preserved. Other buildings are found inside the church ruin. Photo courtesy of Mr. Hans Henrik Hornemann, Reinskloster Manor

ished after the Reformation. The general tendency was that the rural monasteries were converted into manor houses while the surviving urban houses became episcopal residences, schools, town halls or hospitals.

Reinskloster Abbey

Lady Ingjerd Ottesdatter and her family took over the nunnery of Reinskloster near Trondheim in 1531 and she kept it until her death in 1555.[20] From then until 1660, the estate was a royal fief, the income of which was given to various royal servants and officials until the king pledged it to the Dutch merchant brothers Marselius as security for a cash loan in 1648. After the introduction of absolutism in 1660, the cash-strapped king gave the abbey and its estate to the Marselius brothers *in lieu* of the debt. In 1704, the Hornemann family came into possession of the abbey and its lands. In 1888, the family donated the ruin of the abbey church to the "Society for the Preservation of Ancient Norwegian Monuments", which looks after it today.

The ruins of the abbey are situated on a windy hilltop on the north side of the Trondheim Fjord, close to the mouth of the fjord. Parts of the church

20   Lange (1856), p. 189.